W9-BRH-728

The Do-It-Yourself Investor

by James Burgauer

Probus Publishing

Chicago, Illinois

© Probus Publishing Co., 1987

ALL RIGHTS RESERVED. No part of this publication may be reproduced, stored in a retrieval system, or transmitted, in any form or by any means, electronic, mechanical, photocopying, recording, or otherwise, without the prior written permission of the publisher and the copyright holder.

This publication is designed to provide accurate and authoritative information in regard to the subject matter covered. It is sold with the understanding that the publisher is not engaged in rendering legal, accounting or other professional service. If legal advice or other expert assistance is required, the services of a competent professional person should be sought.

FROM A DECLARATION OF PRINCIPLES JOINTLY ADOPTED BY A COMMITTEE OF THE AMERICAN BAR ASSOCIATION AND A COMMITTEE OF PUBLISHERS.

Library of Congress Cataloging in Publication Data

Burgauer, James.
   The do-it-yourself investor.

   Bibliography: p.
   Includes index.
   1. Investments—Handbooks, manuals, etc. I. Title.
HG4527.B689   1987   332.6′78   87-7006

ISBN 0-917253-68-X

Library of Congress Catalog Card No. 87-7006

Printed in the United States of America

1 2 3 4 5 6 7 8 9 0

Dedicated to my wife, Twila, without whose support this project would not have been possible. "Hon, I'll be with you in just five minutes—just let me. . . ."

PREFACE

The Do-It-Yourself Investor is designed to be a reference book. Though many will want to read it from cover to cover, some will use the book as a source of information that can be referred to as needs arise. The format and presentation of the material lends itself well to both uses.

The book is organized into two sections: "Analytical Techniques" and "Doing It Yourself." The first section provides readers with sufficient background material to understand not only the "Doing It Yourself" section, but also the concepts and phraseology used throughout the investment industry. "Doing It Yourself" then builds on this knowledge, detailing where investors can acquire the information and services that they need to make their own informed investment decisions.

The book is written for individuals who have had some investment experience. However, many novice investors will find the book extremely helpful in getting started, and many experienced investors and investment professionals will uncover sources of information that they never dreamed existed.

The book contains detailed information on the subjects of life cycle analysis, fundamental analysis, technical analysis, discount brokerage, databases, investment publications, and other reference books. For your convenience, a detailed Glossary and Index have also been included so information can be readily found. The book also contains a number of illustrations and exhibits to graphically explain complex subject matter. Finally, much of the book is organized into two page spreads, to accommodate:

- readers who are extremely busy professionals and need to find information quickly;
- readers who wish to compare one source of information against another;
- readers who have only a limited amount of time to devote to reading each day; and,
- readers who prefer to concentrate on a limited amount of subject matter at one time.

ACKNOWLEDGMENTS

Though it is impossible to properly recognize everyone who has contributed to the successful completion of this project, thanks must be given to all of the respondents who contributed their time and effort in filling out my lengthy questionnaires and answering the numerous phone calls I made to clarify their responses. And most of all, a special thanks must be given to Lucille Frazier for her dedication in the preparation of this manuscript.

CONTENTS

SECTION II—DOING-IT-YOURSELF

Contents

INTRODUCTION

Over the years, thousands of books have been written on the subject of investing. Some have been written to dispel certain myths about Wall Street. Others have been written to explain the particulars of an investment system. Still others have been written to explain everything you ever wanted to know about investment analysis or financial planning. Yet of all these thousands of books, very few can be considered to be of reference quality. And fewer still tell you where you can go to get the information that you want in order to make your own informed investment decisions.

The Do-It-Yourself Investor is designed to do just that. In fact, the book is organized in two sections just to facilitate this. The first section of the book, entitled "Analytical Techniques," is designed to provide you with sufficient background to understand both the concepts and phraseology used in the rest of the book and by the investment professionals you may come in contact with. The second section of the book, entitled "Doing It Yourself," is designed to expand upon this knowledge, detailing where you can find the information and services that you'll need to do-it-yourself.

With the exception of the first topic, "Life Cycle Analysis," which should be read from beginning to end, the entire book is written so that you can concentrate your reading in those areas of greatest interest to you. Each topic begins with a brief introduction designed to provide you with the additional background you will need to fully understand the subject area. Following that, each topic presents an in-depth explanation of several subtopic areas, organized and printed in a set of one- or two-page "spreads" that completely cover the available subject matter. Each spread can be read by itself with no loss of understanding, and where applicable, it can be compared to other such spreads in the topic.

The first section of the book, devoted to "Analytical Techniques," contains three topics: "Life Cycle Analysis," "Fundamental Analysis," and "Technical Analysis."

The first topic in this section, "Life Cycle Analysis," provides an overview of how companies change as they mature. The topic begins with a discussion on the uses of investment capital, highlighting both how and why companies raise money. The topic then proceeds with a discussion on the changes that a company will undergo as it grows from a private company to a industry force, and concludes with a set of corollaries that investors should keep in mind as they evaluate various investment opportunities.

1

The next topic, "Fundamental Analysis," begins with an introduction explaining where the data used in fundamental analysis actually comes from. It ends with a set of equations describing many of the most frequently used fundamental analysis formulas. Each term used in each equation is conveniently defined right on the same page, and each equation is explained and interpreted.

The last topic of this section, "Technical Analysis," also begins with a short introduction describing the source of technical data. It ends with a "short course" on technical analysis, covering subjects ranging from charts and trends to gaps, from reversal patterns to market and sentiment theories. For your convenience, this topic contains illustrations of the concepts.

The next section of the book, entitled "Doing It Yourself," contains four topics: Discount Brokerage, Databases, Investment Publications, and Reference Books.

The first topic, "Discount Brokerage," begins with an explanation of how the industry came into being, how it transacts business, and how brokerage firms clear trades. In the process, various order processing procedures are examined, replete with the appropriate terminology. The remainder of the topic is devoted to reviewing the products and services available from some of the nation's best known, most widely respected, discount brokerage firms.

Next is the "Databases" topic, which begins with an explanation of the types of databases, the methods by which data is stored, and the methods by which data is delivered to subscribers. Having set the stage, the topic provides an in-depth review of the informational products and services available from the nation's largest and most prestigious database vendors.

The third topic in this section, "Investment Publications," describes the seven topical categories of investment publications available today. Then the topic highlights some of the most popular ones, presenting survey data and sample pages of each.

The final topic, "Reference Books," provides an annotated bibliography for more than thirty recently released or revised books of reference quality. Sufficent data is provided to enable you to determine whether or not a specific book will meet your needs and how to locate it in your local library or bookstore.

All in all, an enormous amount of work has gone into compiling the information in this book. Most of the data that you will find in "Doing It Yourself" exists nowhere else—it is the product of primary research. Dozens upon dozens of questionnaires were sent out to collect this information. Numerous follow-up mailings and phone calls were also made. After months and months of prodding, nearly 100 responses were finally received. Each was then checked for accuracy, paraphrased to remove bias, and formatted to be consistent with other responses so that you can easily identify and assess the information of primary importance to you. Although every effort has been made to ensure that the information provided herein has been obtained from sources believed to be reliable, its accuracy is not guaranteed by either the publisher or the author.

Finally, you will notice that no effort has been made to generalize data across respondents. On the contrary, the purpose of this research was to highlight the *differences* between the products and services that each of the responding companies has to offer. Only in this way can you assess which companies you would prefer to supply the products and services that you need to make your own informed investment decisions.

SECTION I
ANALYTICAL TECHNIQUES

LIFE CYCLE ANALYSIS

Throughout the entire life cycle of an organization, a business needs capital. In fact, as an organization grows, more and more capital is needed to support its infrastructure. More capital is needed for property, plants, and equipment. More is needed for inventory. More is needed for working capital. Simply stated, as a business grows and becomes more mature, its capital needs grow, and its overall funding requirements change. And as they change, so do the risks associated with the capital and the sources from which this capital can be obtained.

All too often we forget that the money we are investing actually is this capital. Over the years the financial markets have become so electronically sophisticated, matching buyers and sellers in nanoseconds, that sometimes we forget that the "paper" we hold actually represents bricks and mortar in some town, somewhere, where employees come to work, produce goods and services, and collect their paychecks. We merely think of this paper as shares of stock, bonds, or for that matter certificates of deposit. But in actuality, this paper is really capital being used to create more capital. That is what our system of capitalism is all about.

A basic tenet of this system is that investment capital needs to be rewarded by the payment of some rate of return. As a corollary to this concept, rationality suggests that the higher the risk an investment represents, the higher the rate of return necessary to attract capital into the investment. Or, more simply stated, there exists a trade-off between risk and reward that dictates "added risk requires added reward."

To ease the burden of analysis, let us simplify the financial world of today by ignoring the newfangled capital instruments that have come to fruition over the last several decades. In this simplified world, the capital market can be broken down into two broad classifications — debt and equity.

From a legalistic point of view, debt takes precedence over equity in the event of a liquidation, and interest payments must be made before excess capital can be distributed to equityholders in the form of dividends. For these reasons, we typically think of debt securities as being safer than equities. And, given the greater assurances debtholders have that they will receive their original capital back at some stated point in the future, they generally require lower rates of returns on their investment than do the equityholders.

Equity securities, generally thought of as common stock, carry virtually no assurances about the rate of return the investor will receive, nor for that matter any assurance about repayment of principal. From the investor's viewpoint, the risks associated with equities are generally thought to be much higher than those associated with debt, and therefore the rate of return required on equity capital is higher than that of debt.

We should note at this juncture that the rate of return on debt, like that of equity, is construed to be the total return generated from both cash flow and appreciation. Cash flow, in the case of debt, is determined by market forces at the time the company wishes to raise capital. It is set at a fixed rate, and it is called *interest*. Furthermore, debt securities mature at par, meaning that they return a stated amount of capital. Thus, regardless of the price the investor pays for the debt security, the total return on the investment is calculable. And assuming the issuer doesn't default on the debt, it offers no potential for either more or less return than this calculated rate.

On the other hand, cash flow of equities (that is, *dividends*) is determined by the Board of Directors of the company, and it is subject to change without notice. Appreciation, if indeed there is any, is determined by the profit generated when the investment is sold. In a perfect world, appreciation is a function of the earnings of the company. It is incalculable at the time the investment is made, though analysts and investors alike attempt to estimate the potential for it in order to evaluate an equity's rate of return. And, in the event that this rate of return is never achieved, investors merely dismiss it as one of the "risks of investing." The relationship of the risk level and required rate of return is shown in Figure 1.

Figure 1

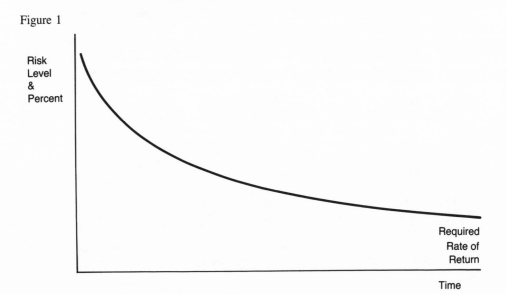

THE BUSINESS LIFE CYCLE

Equity securities generally can be categorized based on the point where a business is in its life cycle when the capital is required. The "younger" the firm, the riskier its associated security is assumed to be, and the higher the rate of return required to attract investment capital. The more mature the firm, the less risk associated with it, and the lower the required rate of return required to attract investment capital.

Combining this knowledge with the fact that it is management's express responsibility to maximize shareholder wealth, we can presume that if the firm can reinvest money at a rate of return higher than its shareholders can, then it is in the best interest of the shareholders for the firm to retain this excess cash and invest it accordingly. Younger firms with exceptional growth prospects tend to do this, reinvesting their excess funds rather than paying them out. Older firms with less exceptional prospects for growth or with too much cash flow to reinvest, typically pay the funds out as dividends. The decline in growth rate as dividends increase is shown in Figure 2. In essence, this is the basis for the inverse relationship between a company's growth prospects and its dividend yield; companies with higher prospects for growth typically have lower dividend yields because they must retain cash to fund the higher growth rates.

As a firm continues to grow and mature, management eventually runs out of investment opportunities within the confines of the company to earn rates of return higher than its shareholders can earn elsewhere. Obliged to properly manage this excess cash flow, firms often buy back their own shares, buy the shares of other more aggressive companies, or pay increasingly larger cash distributions to shareholders.

Examining equities across the backdrop of the business life cycle curve reveals that they fall into five broad categories. These categories, which basically describe both the maturity of the company and the risk level associated with its shares, are generally called: *start-up* or *seed money, venture capital, aggressive growth, growth,* and *total return* oriented securities. The point in the business life cycle in which each category is most common is shown in Figure 3.

Figure 2

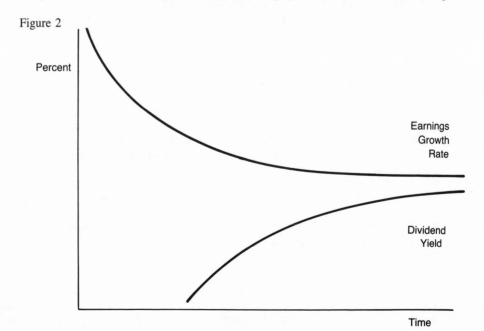

Percent

Earnings
Growth
Rate

Dividend
Yield

Time

Figure 3

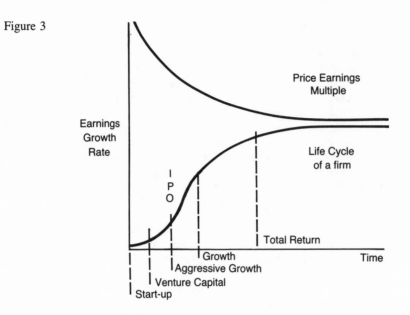

Start-up Phase

Start-up or seed money is needed at the time a new company is formed. It is generally thought to be the riskiest of all types of equity investments, because 90 percent of all start-up companies fail soon after inception. Though the rewards for finding that one company in ten that thrives can be astronomical, investing in such new companies should be left to those individuals who have the sophistication to make extremely mature investment decisions, who can afford the risk, and who have both the patience and fortitude to wait the many years it will take before any return on investment could ever come to pass.

Venture Capital Phase

The next stage in the business life cycle usually forces a firm to seek venture capital. Though sometimes these crucial funds can be generated internally, often they must be obtained through a private placement, from an "angel" or wealthy individual, a local financier, or a venture capitalist. Today, there are dozens of firms billing themselves as venture capitalists that will not only finance a small concern but will also lend professional expertise to the existing organization. Generally, they require a large percentage of the company in return for their investment, not to mention representation on the board of directors and positions as officers of the company.

   Many of these so-called venture capitalist organizations are sponsored by corporate giants; some are built around the fortunes of private individuals or closely held brokerage concerns; and still others are organized as publicly registered investment companies or mutual funds. In all cases there exists significant risk for capital invested in this fashion, and the average person predisposed to making these types of investments is advised that the "safest" way to do so is through the conduit of the mutual fund.

Initial Public Offering Phase

Once a company has generated some degree of stability, the next phase of growth is financed by an initial public offering (IPO). In an IPO, a brokerage firm evaluates the company vis-à-vis its potential sales success to its clientele and determines if it has the ability to the raise the capital the firm requires. Basically, only two groups of brokerage firms sponsor IPOs. The first type is major brokerage houses represented by national or large regional firms. The second is the "penny stock" houses that are usually small, one- or two-office firms with a high concentration of brokers in states having relatively "loose" security laws, such as Colorado (Denver) and Utah (Salt Lake City).

In general, IPOs come in only two varieties: best-efforts offerings and underwritings. In a *best-efforts offering,* the brokerage firm makes no guarantee to sell any of the shares offered by the firm wishing to go public, committing only to making its best effort in soliciting sales of the shares. In an *underwriting,* the brokerage firm guarantees that all shares will be sold, in essence, buying the entire offering for its own account and in turn reselling the shares to its clients. Generally, the better known a company, the better the chance it has to command an underwriting. The less well-known a company, the greater the chance it will have to settle for a best-efforts offering.

Typically, the large national or regional brokerage firms tend to raise capital in the capacity of underwriters. In so doing, they consider raising money for only the most prestigious, well-established businesses wishing to go public. The primary reason is the large firms refuse to accept the market risks of being "stuck" holding any unsold shares. That is, it takes the market recognition of a large, well-established firm to ensure a complete sell through. Further, the high costs of due diligence and national promotion limit the major brokerage firms to only the largest public offerings that will generate sufficient underwriting fees to cover their costs. Unfortunately, this forces the smaller, less well-known firms—or firms not wishing to raise enormous amounts of capital—to migrate toward the penny stock brokers who represent the only other reasonable alternative for raising capital publicly.

Despite the common misconception that firms that go public through penny stock brokers are somehow a greater risk, are of lower quality, or have less integrity than firms going public through a major brokerage house, to judge them on this basis alone would be grossly unfair. Furthermore, to suggest that just because a security is brought to market by a major brokerage house it represents a good value at a fair price would also be a gross misjudgment. To be very pragmatic, firms wishing to go public are out to raise the most money possible by giving up the fewest shares. By the same token, the brokerage firm taking them public is out to maximize its profit on the transaction as well, and the investors are the people who pay for it. Good values and bad values arise through both types of financings—and the best advice to investors is to use good judgment and beware of the risks.

Aggressive Growth Phase

The phase following a successful IPO is typically regarded as the aggressive growth phase for a company. Now the firm employs the new capital raised from the IPO in various ways in order to rapidly expand its scope of operations. If the firm is successful in these endeavors, earnings will expand rapidly.

Investors, noting this, will most likely bid up the price of the shares, expanding the company's price-earnings multiple. Further increases in earnings will translate into still higher prices for the stock, and as long as the growth rate continues, so presumably will the stock's price appreciation. The scenario continues until such time as the company's growth rate eventually begins to slow. This, then, causes a moderate decline in the price-earnings multiple investors are willing to apply to the shares, and the company's stock price may begin to stagnate or even decline. More aggressive investors, noting this, may liquidate their holdings, putting further downward pressure on the price of the stock. As the saying goes, what goes up does come down.

Despite this adage, aggressive growth stocks bought and sold in a timely fashion can translate into enormous gains for an aggressive growth oriented investor. But we should be aware that investing in this fashion may require a strong stomach and very active portfolio management.

Growth Phase

Having passed the aggressive growth phase, a young company begins to settle into a slightly more predictable pattern—the growth phase of its life cycle. Frequently, the firm devotes significantly more resources to research and development, with the specific intention of staying one step ahead of its competition.

With any luck, this strategy pays off, generating some new product or process that once again places the company in a phase of aggressive growth. If it doesn't, management may try to acquire a younger, more aggressive firm to rekindle the company's former, more aggressive posture, or it may settle back, choosing to run the company in a less-aggressive fashion.

In the latter case, the company typically releases several new or related products in an effort to expand its client base while solidifying ties with its existing accounts. Earnings growth will continue to slow, and investors will begin to stabilize the price-earnings multiple that they apply to the company's earnings, typically assigning lower multiples than they did during the company's aggressive growth phase. During this phase the company often begins to pay modest dividends as management attempts to ingratiate itself with the investment community. Though the firm may have several years of excellent growth left, these actions typically signal the beginning of the transition into the next phase of a company's life cycle— replete with still lower earnings growth rates and still lower price-earnings multiples.

All in all, given proper timing, investing in companies at this point in their life cycles can be very profitable as well. But the savvy investor also knows that the transition from aggressive growth to growth, and from growth to total return, can create a very rocky road for the price of a company's stoc. One should certainly consider the risks inherent with poorly timed investments of this nature before blindly jumping in.

Total Return Phase

In the total return phase of its life cycle, as the company matures further, its products will become even more established in the marketplace. Oftentimes aging products are replaced by reworked ones sporting minor improvements and billed as "new and improved," rather than by entirely new products developed through updated technology. Sales continue to generate excess cash flow, which is used partly to develop new markets, partly to streamline internal operations, and partly to fund higher dividend payouts. Earnings growth may slow further, though in cardinal numbers earnings will most likely be at record levels for the firm.

Perceiving this higher degree of stability, investors come to look on the shares as total return situations, with a reasonable degree of earnings growth predictability and a reasonable level of dividend yield. Very often management perceives this shift in investor emphasis and may even attempt to substantiate this perception by adopting a philosophy of moderate dividend increases when supported by earnings advances. Sporting both higher stability and higher yield, investing in the shares of this type of company can also be profitable, though at time, somewhat boring.

Having "made it," management may choose to embark on one of many routes to further enhance the company's future. For instance, if the industry has become either oligopolistic or highly regulated, management is likely to settle back and attempt to manipulate the marketplace to achieve some long-term profit targets without upsetting too many apple carts. Or, if the industry is still relatively competitive, management may attempt to increase market share through the acquisition of other companies within the industry—in essence, buying growth. If the industry is still extremely competitive or if the market potential for the company's product lines is expected to decline, management may choose to diversify the company's interests by acquiring firms in unrelated industries, molding the company into a conglomerate.

LIFE CYCLES AND INVESTMENT STRATEGIES

All in all, as investors we need to be aware of the overriding influences on the company and its industry in order to properly evaluate both the risk and the timing of the investment decisions we are making. We need to be cognizant of the major effects that occur when the perception of a company changes from one investment category to another, because the price-earnings multiple and future value of shares can be greatly altered by such transition. And, if we intend to make our investment into something more than a mere crapshoot, we need to understand the effects on our investments of changing interest and inflation rates, overall economic growth, and a myriad of other factors that affect security prices in general. This understanding is best achieved when the information is placed in the perspective of the firm's life cycle.

Interestingly enough, in the presence of all of this information, we can begin to discern overall patterns in the action of stock prices. We shall begin our analysis by examining the effects on the price of a company's stock as the company moves through its life cycle. Table 1 depicts a sample company. Please note, in this example, like all examples found in this chapter, the numbers are not what is important. The concepts behind the numbers, the thought process used to develop them, and the conclusions that can be drawn from them are the focal points.

Table 1. Financial History of Life-Cycle, Inc.

Year	Earnings	Earnings Growth Rate	P-E Multiple	Stock Price	Dividend Yield
1975	$(.02)	NMF	NMF	$ 3.00	0%
1976	.15	NMF	30	4.50	0%
1977	.30	100.0	24	7.20	0%
1978	.58	93.3	25	14.50	0%
1979	1.00	72.4	23	23.00	0%
1980	1.44	44.0	15	21.60	0%
1981	2.02	40.2	16	32.32	1%
1982	2.72	34.6	14	38.08	1%
1983	3.10	13.9	10	31.00	3%
1984	3.49	12.5	8	27.92	4%
1985	3.88	11.1	9	34.92	4%
1986	4.24	9.2	9	38.16	5%

On first glance, we see that our company, Life-Cycle, Inc., has had earnings increases each and every year. We also note that, despite these yearly increases, the growth rate of earnings has declined as the company has matured. Further, as we might expect, the price-earnings multiple of the company has generally declined over the years, while the dividend yield has generally increased. In essence, we have a textbook case upon which to perform a textbook analysis.

Given the table's data, we might naturally assume that since the company's earnings increased each and every year, its stock price should also have increased on a yearly basis. This assumption, predicated on the basis that stock price is fundamentally a function of earnings, seems reasonably sound on the surface. Unfortunately, it lacks the depth of understanding that we have gained by examining a company in relation to its life cycle stage.

Remember, throughout the life cycle of a company, investors constantly reevaluate the company's future earnings growth-rate potential. Young, highly concentrated companies typically have the highest future earnings growth-rate potential, whereas older, more diversified companies have lower ones. Additionally, companies with higher growth prospects command higher price-earnings multiples, while companies with lower growth prospects command lower ones. And, as companies move through the various phases of their life cycles, their future earnings growth-rate potentials decline, and the price-earnings multiples that investors are willing to pay for their shares decline as well.

Given these facts, we could conclude that Life-Cycle, Inc. would have been considered an aggressive growth stock during the period of 1975 through 1979, a growth stock from 1979 through 1983, and a total return stock from 1983 through 1986. Despite continued earnings advances, the growth rate of earnings was highest during the aggressive growth period, declined as the firm moved into its growth phase, and declined again as the firm moved into its total return phase. By the same token, the price-earnings multiple generally declined throughout the firm's history, with the most dramatic changes occurring during the transitions from one phase to another. And, interestingly enough, the combination of these factors caused share price declines during both transition phases, despite eleven years of uninterrupted earnings growth for the company and considerable earnings growth in the transition years.

In essence, what we have done in this example, is applied the set of rational analysis techniques described earlier, to the information we know about a firm, its industry, and the expectations of our fellow investors. In so doing, we have arrived at a reasonable explanation of a commonly seen stock price action. Specifically, we have developed a rational basis to explain why an individual stock's price can decline despite vibrant earnings growth in the underlying company.

We have also developed a qualitative thought process which can be used in conjunction with other analytic techniques, lending a degree of realism to otherwise raw statistical conclusions.

Let us now examine the effects on the stock prices of several companies within the same industry given an expansion of the overall economic base of that industry. In such a scenario, earnings typically tend to increase for all firms within the industry in some relation to the earnings that each firm derives from that industry. Examining three companies, one assumed to be in the aggressive growth phase of its life cycle (AG, Inc.), the second assumed to be in the growth phase of its life cycle (GR, Inc.), and the third assumed to be in the total return phase of its life cycle (TR, Inc.), reason would dictate that the share price of the aggressive growth firm is likely to appreciate more than either of the others. Why? Well, let's consider Table 2's information, constructed from basic information we know about a company just from its stage in its life cycle. Again, all of the numbers in the table have been ''created'' using only the basic knowledge we have of what happens to the average firm as it matures.

Table 2.

Company Name	Current Earnings	Earn. from Industry	P-E Multiple	Current Price	Dividend Yield	6 Mo. T-bill Rate
AG, Inc.	$ .50	100%	20	$10.00	0%	6%
GR, Inc.	1.00	80%	12	12.00	1%	6%
TR, Inc.	4.00	50%	8	32.00	5%	6%

Let's say that our three companies, AG, GR, and TR, generate earnings per share of $0.50, $1, and $4, respectively. Now, given the phase of the life cycle that each firm is in, it might be reasonable to presume that 100 percent of AG's, 80 percent of GR's, and only 50 percent of TR's earnings would be derived from within the industry in question. Furthermore, since investors price each stock in comparison with alternative investments in the same risk category, assigning price-earnings multiples based on some overall market perception of earnings growth and risk, AG would sport the highest, GR the next, and TR the lowest price-earnings multiple. The example assumes a P-E of 20, 12, and 8, respectively, numbers typical of today's stock market.

Finally, also based on a firm's stage in its life cycle, we could presume that TR would have the highest, GR the next, and AG the lowest dividend yield. The example assumes 5 percent, 1 percent, and 0 percent, respectively—again numbers typical of today's stock market.

If overall expansion occurs in the industry, the earnings base of each firm should expand according to the percentage of earnings that the company derives from the industry. In this example, let's assume the industry base doubles and so do earnings derived from within the industry. Table 3 illustrates the adjusted earnings level for each firm and the new price of each company's stock given a constant price-earnings multiple.

Table 3.

Company Name	Adjusted Earnings	Earn. from Industry	P-E Multiple	Adjusted Price	Dividend Yield	6 Mo. T-bill Rate
AG, Inc.	$1.00	100%	20	$20.00	0%	6%
GR, Inc.	1.80	80%	12	21.60	1%	6%
TR, Inc.	6.00	50%	8	48.00	5%	6%

Overlaying this adjusted information onto Table 2, it becomes apparent that the more aggressive the firm, the more concentrated its earnings base is in the expanding industry, the better off the firm will fare given such as expansion. Table 4 shows the results.

Table 4.

Company Name	Current Earnings	Current P-E Multiple	Adjusted Earnings	Adjusted P-E Multiple	Current Price	Adjusted Price
AG, Inc.	$ .50	20	1.00	20	$10.00	$20.00
GR, Inc.	1.00	12	1.80	12	12.00	21.60
TR, Inc.	4.00	8	6.00	8	32.00	48.00

Of course, it is also quite likely that during an industry expansion such as this, investors may assign higher price-earnings multiples to companies throughout the industry, thereby causing share prices to appreciate that much further. Assuming that we see an across the board expansion in these price-earnings multiples of 20 percent, our data is adjusted as shown in Table 5.

Table 5.

Company Name	Current Earnings	Current P-E Multiple	Adjusted Earnings	Adjusted P-E Multiple	Current Price	Adjusted Price
AG, Inc.	$ .50	20	$1.00	24.0	$10.00	$24.00
GR, Inc.	1.00	12	1.80	14.4	12.00	25.92
TR, Inc.	4.00	8	6.00	9.6	32.00	57.60

Generalizing the effects of an industry expansion, then, it is quite likely that the share prices of all companies within the industry will move higher as a result of improved earnings. Furthermore, the stock prices of the most aggressive firms in the industry will appreciate most, with the prices for total return phase firms appreciating the least.

Once again, by applying a set of rational techniques to the information we know regarding the firm, its industry, and the investment expectations of our fellow investors, we can easily explain another commonly seen stock price action. In this case, we have developed a rational basis to explain why the price appreciation potential on a percentage basis is higher for more aggressive firms given an expanding industry. By the same token, reversing our analysis shows why the opposite is also true. And, by extrapolating the same thought process onto the market in general, we see why the whole market moves up when the economy expands, and why more aggressive firms boast higher percentage gains during these upswings.

SUMMARY

As we analyze various market trends or combinations of trends in an effort to best manage our money, we should apply analytical techniques to help us intuitively understand what effects various market occurrences might have on our portfolio. For one thing, these techniques force us to consider how the broad picture affects a specific company or industry. Furthermore, they bring to light several factors we otherwise might overlook. Specifically, the thought process developed in this discussion and its corollaries can be summarized as follows:

1. All companies, regardless of industry, tend to sport the same general characteristics at equivalent stages in their life cycles. From an earnings perspective, it is often of little consequence what industry a company actually belongs to—as long as management knows how to manage, the company will do well.
2. Earnings growth rates, including their history, their future, and investors' changing perception of them, are key determinants in predicting the price-earnings multiples that will be applied to a company's future earnings. Slowing of these growth rates generally foreshadows declines in a company's price-earnings multiple, which in turn leads to a decline in the company's stock price. Thus, we must learn to look beyond the level of a company's

earnings when attempting to evaluate the underlying value of a stock in relation to its current market price.

3. Industry expansion generally benefits aggressive firms in the industry the most, and the stock prices of these companies are likely to boast the highest percentage appreciation. Thus, if we expect an industry expansion, we should seek to find the more aggressive companies in the industry. On the other hand, if we expect an industry contraction, we should seek out the shares of total return oriented securities.

4. When the economy starts to slow, we should weight our portfolios more towards total return securities because they offter better price protection. Conversely, when the economy begins to heat up, we should weight our portfolios more towards aggressive companies because they offer more growth potential. By following this procedure, we end up lowering the risk in our portfolio by selling off aggressive equities during the market upswing, replacing them with total return shares in preparation for the upcoming market downturn. Then, when the market declines, we reverse this procedure. In so doing we end up being less aggressive at market tops and more aggressive at market bottoms, positioned just the way we want to be.

5. We should not weight our portfolio too heavily in any one industry, regardless of life-cycle category diversification, or in any one category, regardless of industry diversification. Following this rule, we will adequately protect ourselves on the downside and participate wholeheartedly on the upside when the market makes a general move.

Unfortunately, these generalizations are no substitute for other techniques of good empirical analysis. They fall short of telling us which industries to look at, what percentage of our money should be invested in equities at any given moment in time, or for that matter what other information we should be using to help manage our portfolio. However, they do serve a useful purpose because they represent a rational process through which to focus our thinking while we conduct fundamental and technical analyses.

FUNDAMENTAL ANALYSIS

Fundamental analysis is the process of evaluating the worthiness of a security by analyzing the financial strength of the company underlying it. It focuses on *quantitative* factors like book value, earnings per share, price-earnings ratios, and dividend yield.

There are literally thousands of different methods used by fundamentalists to analyze companies. Some are asset-based, some are earnings-based, some are cash flow-based, and some use entirely different methodology. Although each may be different in terms of its application of data, they all do have one thing in common—the source of the data itself.

The primary source for the data used in fundamental analysis is the company's own financial statements—that is, its balance sheet and its net income statement. Audited versions of these statements are furnished to shareholders each year in the company's annual report, and unaudited versions are furnished quarterly, along with other corporate information. Other good sources for this data include several of the electronic databases and investment publications highlighted later in this book.

The job of fundamental analysis is to run a set of financial calculations on this data to evaluate and determine a company's current position. Then, with the current position in mind, the fundamentalist looks to the company's past to see what this position was, compares it to the company's present position, factors in any new or changing circumstances, and attempts to predict what the company's future position will be. Having completed this, the company's presumed future position is used to determine what the future price of the company's securities will be, and a final judgment is made about the investment worthiness of these securities.

To analyze a security properly, fundamentalists concentrate on four key areas they believe affect the price of a security in the open market. These areas are:
- *Management*—the style, professionalism, and track record of the company's corporate management team.
- *Financial position*—the company's current financial position, as related to the type of business the company is in, the industry in which it operates, the business climate it faces, and the financial position of its competition.
- *Earnings*—the amount of money the company is making which is ultimately available to shareholders.

  • *Market multipliers*—the value placed on the earnings of the company as determined by the price investors are willing to pay to "own" those earnings.

Unequivocally, the methodology used to interpolate the data derived from each of these four areas of concentration is different for every fundamental analyst. That notwithstanding, generally the more information that can be factored into the analysis, the more accurate the analysis becomes.

Management

Probably the most esoteric of all fundamental analysis procedures is the analysis of management and management style. In a sense, the average investor is not capable of doing this empirically. Furthermore, it is not something that someone outside a company can do with relative ease or timeliness, and in a more global sense, it may have less value than the cost of the effort needed to acquire the information. That notwithstanding, several avenues are open for investors or potential investors to get a "feel" for the type of management policies and procedures that permeate the company.

If you are fortunate enough to know or have a close acquaintance who knows a member of the top management team, the feelings you get regarding this individual and the type of business person he or she is are probably well founded. From this you can extrapolate what kind of a person this individual must be to work for or with and thereby build an image of the kind of people that most likely make up the rest of the company's top management.

If you are not so fortunate to know someone, another good source for determining management style is an in-depth report on the company written by a Wall Street analyst. Generally, the better known analysts have developed contacts within the companies they analyze. From these individuals they often get and report "tidbits" of information that shed light on both the company and what the management team is thinking and doing. Additionally, extremely in-depth reports, such as those prepared for institutional money managers, often include a discussion on exactly this subject and can be an invaluable source of information.

Another source for this information is the President's letter contained in the annual report. Typically, this letter reveals the type of individual who is running the company on a day-to-day basis, what he expects of himself and what he expects from the people that work for him.

Other sources that shed light on what management is thinking or doing are insider buying and selling patterns—information which, by law, is publicly available and is followed and reported by several databases and investment publications.

Financial Position

The two primary financial statements issued by a company are the income statement and balance sheet. They are distinctly different in their creation and purpose, and they each tell an entirely different story about the company.

When interested in the financial position of a company, we need only to turn to the company's statement of assets and liabilities, better known as the company's balance sheet.

The *balance sheet* is designed to state the position of a company at a specific moment in time. That is to say, a balance sheet provides a snapshot of a company—its assets, its liabilities, and its shareholders' equity. Typically, the balance sheet is calculated and reported on both a quarterly and annual basis.

By definition, a company's assets must be exactly equal to the sum of its liabilities and shareholders' equity—that is, from an accounting perspective, this statement must be always be in "balance."

Intuitively, this statement tells us that every dollar invested in assets owned by the company must have originated from either a liability incurred by the company or, in one form or another, from the shareholders. In essence, then, the balance sheet represents nothing more than a list of all of the assets balanced against a list of all the liabilities and shareholder claims.

In an effort to agglomerate the many individual asset, liability, and shareholders' equity items held by a company, the balance sheet combines similar assets into categories, reporting only category totals as opposed to individual items. Though any specific balance sheet may include more or less categories than the example in Figure 1, they all tend to include categories similar to the ones described.

Figure 1

Balance Sheet	

Assets
  current
  fixed
  miscellaneous
  intangible
	Liabilities
	  current
	  fixed
	  miscellaneous
	
	Shareholders' equity
	  preferred stock
	  common stock
	  paid-in capital
	  retained earnings

Assets = Liabilities + Equity	

Though by no means are the following definitions intended to offer complete accounting explanations for the terminology used in a balance sheet, suffice it to say that they do represent good working definitions for concepts which will be discussed in the remainder of this chapter.

- *Current* refers to items which will be affected in the current year, such as inventory, receivables, and payable.
- *Fixed* to items which will not be affected in the current year, such as property, and long-term debt.
- *Miscellaneous* (sometimes referred to as *sundry*) refers to physical items which are being held for an indefinite period of time and are not involved in the company's day-to-day business, such as unimproved land.
- *Intangible* refers to items which have value which is difficult to determine, such as trademarks and goodwill.
- *Preferred stock* refers to the par value of stock with a preferential claim on income and assets.
- *Common stock* refers to the par value of stock with no preferential claims on income and assets, sometimes referred to as the claims held by the ''true'' owners of the company.
- *Paid-in capital* (sometimes referred to as *capital surplus*) refers to the difference between the price actually received by the company for the common stock and its par value.
- *Retained earnings* (sometimes referred to as *earned surplus*) refers to undistributed corporate profits.

From the balance sheet alone, a variety of measures can be calculated in order to determine and evaluate a company's:

- *Capital structure*—the capital makeup of the company, as determined by the bond, common, and preferred stock ratios.

- *Collateral*—the relative worth behind the securities that the company has outstanding, as determined by the book value, net assets per bond, and net assets per preferred share ratios.
- *Leverage*—the amount of nonequity capital that the company is using in its capital structure, as determined by the debt-to-asset and debt-to-equity ratios.
- *Liquidity*—the company's ability to raise cash, as determined by the cash, current, and quick asset ratios.

These measures are then compared against other measures for the same company, compared against themselves over time and compared against other companies within the same industry to determine the worthiness of the company's securities.

Earnings

The earnings of a company are calculated and presented in the form of the statement of operations, better known as an income statement.

The *income statement* is designed to review the activities of a company over a specified period of time. It, too, is calculated and reported on both a quarterly and annual basis, the former reviewing the results of operations for the quarter and the latter reviewing the results of operations for the full year.

Basically, the income statement tells us three things: how much income has been earned for the period, how much expense has been incurred to earn the income, and how much profit or net income is left over.

As related to the balance sheet, the income statement provides a breakdown of what changes occurred to retained earnings during the period. That is to say, if one were to compare a balance sheet created immediately before and after the period in question, the income statement would show how the change in retained earnings came about.

As with the balance sheet, the income statement agglomerates the myriad of transactions that occurred during the period into a few categories, reporting only the category totals (as opposed to individual items). Though any specific income statement may include more or fewer categories than Figure 2, they all tend to include categories similar to the ones described.

Though the following definitions are not intended to offer complete accounting definitions for the income statement terminology used in Figure 2, suffice it to say that:

- *Gross sales* refer to the total operating revenue for the period, whatever product or service the company may be selling.
- *Returns* refers to the gross dollars of refunds given for sales which were returned or refused.
- *Net sales* refer to the net operating revenue for the period, after returns have been paid back.
- *General and administrative expenses* refers to all direct costs incurred in generating the revenue, such as wages and cost of goods sold.
- *Depreciation* refers to the expenses attributed to the use of the company's fixed assets as apportioned over the accounting life of those assets.
- *Operating income* refers to the net operating income for the period after all expenses have been paid except for interest and taxes.
- *Other income* refers to the other net income earned by the company from all sources other than normal operations, such as investment income.
- *Earnings before interest and taxes (EBIT)* refers to the net income for the period after all expenses have been paid except for interest and taxes.
- *Interest* refers to all charges that must be paid on the company's fixed liabilities.
- *Earnings before taxes (EBT)* (sometimes referred to as *income before taxes*) refers to the net income for the period after all expenses have been paid except for taxes.

- *Taxes* refer to the government's charges which are paid on the company's earnings.
- *Net income* refers to the net earnings of the company for the period after all expenses have been paid.

Figure 2

Income Statement
Gross Sales
− Returns
= Net sales
− Cost of sales
− Selling expenses
− Administrative expenses
− Depreciation
= Operating income
+ Other income
= Earnings before Interest and Taxes (EBIT)
+ Interest
= Earnings or Income before Taxes (EBT)
− Taxes
− Net income

From the income statement alone, a variety of measures can be calculated in order to determine and evaluate a company's:

- *Coverage*—the extent to which the company's earnings cover its anticipated cash outlays, as determined by the fixed charge, interest, are preferred dividend coverages, as well as the payout ratio.

Using data from both the balance sheet and the income statement, a number of additional measures can be calculated in order to determine and evaluate a company's:

- *Activity*—the amount of revenue the company is generating relative to the amount of assets it has deployed, as determined by the average collection period, fixed asset turnover, inventory turnover, receivables turnover, and total asset turnover ratios.
- *Earnings*—the amount of profit generated by the company that is ultimately available to shareholders, as determined by earnings per share, fully diluted earnings per share, and primary earnings per share.
- *Profitability*—the amount of profit generated by the company relative to its activity and assets deployed, as determined by the operating costs, profit margin, return on assets, return on equity, and return on invested capital ratios.

These measures are then compared against other measures for the same company, compared against themselves over time, and compared against other companies within the same industry in order to determine the worthiness of the company's securities.

Be aware that sometimes in the normal course of business, extraordinary events occur that may have dramatic effects on the income statement for the period. For example, suppose a company bought a piece of property in downtown Manhattan during the early part of twentieth century with the intention to eventually build its headquarters there. Then, after 80 years of holding the property, the company finally determines that it no longer wants to build in New York, so it decides to sell the property. The gain on this asset, which is sure to be significant, and is most unequivocally an *extraordinary* event, could have a dramatic effect on the income statement if it were simply included as "other income." Thus, in order to avoid the confusion that might otherwise result in the eyes of shareholders and the investing public, and to "remove" the event from the books so as to maintain consistency in presentation, such transactions are segregated and treated as extraordinary or nonrecurring items.

A myriad of circumstances can result in an extraordinary gain or loss for a company. Some of the more typical transactions that are classified as extraordinary, and are therefore segregated, include:

- any material gains or losses on the sale of assets;
- the write-down or write-off of goodwill;
- the condemnation or expropriation of assets;
- any major changes in the valuation of foreign currencies; and
- the sale of any significant portion of the business.

Market Multipliers

Of all the facets of fundamental analysis, evaluating market multipliers deals the most with factors external to the company. In many ways, evaluating market multipliers approaches technical analysis in that it is based on estimating how the changing perceptions of the investing public will translate into the public's willingness to pay more or less for a specific security or groups of securities.

As previously discussed in the chapter on life-cycle analysis, market multipliers are a measure of investors' willingness to buy the future stream of income that is part and parcel to the ownership of a company. As changes in the economy, the industry, and the company occur, investors' willingness to own these streams of income also change. As changes in investors' *perceptions* of the economy, the industry, and the company occur, so too will their valuation of a company's securities.

Methodology used to evaluate changes in market multipliers ranges from the simplistic approach of ignoring any changes and just using last year's numbers to much more sophisticated approaches that employ trend analysis and growth rate models of the economy and the company. Suffice it to say, many of these techniques are proprietary, and most require significant computing power and databases from which to draw information.

However, using data from the balance sheet, the income statement, and the stock transaction pages of your local newspaper, two universally recognized measures can be calculated to determine and evaluate a company's:

- *Market valuation*—the multipliers that investors are willing to apply to the company's earnings and dividends to arrive at the price they are willing to pay for the securities in the open market, as determined by the dividend yield and price-earnings ratios.

These measures are then compared against other measures for the same company, compared against themselves over time, and compared against other companies within the same industry in order to determine the worthiness of the company's securities.

Fundamental Analysis Formulas

AVERAGE COLLECTION PERIOD   **Activity measure**

$$\text{Average Collection Period} = \frac{\text{Net accounts receivable} \times 365 \text{ days}}{\text{Net sales}}$$

Where:

1. *net accounts receivable* means money due from customers within the current year less any provisions for returns, trade discounts for early payments, and bad debts.
2. *net sales* means gross sales less any discounts, returns, and refunds.

This ratio, composed of items from both the balance sheet and the income statement, tests the efficiency of the company's use of its assets. Stated differently, the average collection period is a measure of the speed in which the company turns sales into cash. Generally, the lower the number, the more efficiently the company is operating.

A low average collection period can signal highly efficient collections and efficient asset utilization. Or, it can signal that the company has too stringent of a collection policy and therefore may be losing potential sales.

A high average collection period can signal poor sales or slow collections. Or, it can signal that the collection policy of the company is too lenient, and that sales are being made but not being paid for. By comparing the average collection period to the stated collection policy of the company, a judgment can be made about whether sales are being lost because the policy is too stringent, or revenue is being lost because the receivables are not being adequately collected.

An increasing average collection period can signal either slowing sales or slowing payments, both of which foretell of potential problems for the company. A declining average collection period could signal increasing sales, more efficient asset utilization, or tighter management controls.

This ratio should be examined in the context of the company's other ratios, in comparison to other companies within the same industry, and in comparison to itself over time.

Note: This ratio is the contrapositive of the receivable turnover ratio.

BOND RATIO

Capital structure measure

$$\text{Bond Ratio} = \frac{\text{Funded debt}}{\text{Total capitalization}}$$

Where:

1. *funded debt* means all long-term obligations of the company that will mature in five years or more.
2. *total capitalization* means all fixed liabilities and shareholders' equity—in essence representing the total long-term investment in the company from all sources.

This ratio, composed entirely of balance sheet items, measures the percentage of the company's funds that are provided by debtholders. In essence, it represents the leverage effect on shareholder money. Generally, the higher this ratio, the higher leverage that shareholders have working for them, the higher the company's cost of capital, and the more risk the company's securities have.

A low bond ratio can be a signal that management may not be using a sufficient amount of leverage and therefore may not be maximizing the rate of return for shareholders. If, for instance, the amount of debt being used is insufficient in total, then the company is not maximizing shareholder wealth. On the other hand, if short-term debt or bank financing is being used in place of funded debt, the company may be injudiciously financing long-term assets with short-term liabilities, potentially threatening the company's capital structure or subjecting the company to an inordinate amount of interest rate risk.

An unreasonably high bond ratio can be a signal that the company may be using too much borrowed capital in its financial structure, thereby taking on an inordinate amount of risk and saddling the company with excessive interest obligations. Additionally, an especially high bond ratio may make it difficult for the company to raise additional capital in the marketplace, especially with debt financing.

A declining bond ratio is generally a good sign, usually indicating that the company's overall cost of capital, its interest expenses, and its breakeven point will be lowered. Conversely, an increasing bond ratio is generally not a good sign, though it is important to know what the company's capital structure is and what is the cause of the change.

This ratio should be examined in the context of the company's other ratios, in comparison to other companies within the same industry, and in comparison to itself over time.

BOOK VALUE   **Collateral measure**

Two commonly used methods:

$$\text{Book Value Per Share of Common Stock} = \frac{\text{Total assets} - \text{Intangibles} - \text{Total debt} - \text{Preferred stock}}{\text{Number of shares of common stock outstanding}}$$

$$\text{Book Value Per Share of Common Stock} = \frac{\text{Common stock} - \text{Intangibles}}{\text{Number of shares of common stock outstanding}}$$

Where:

1. *total assets* means all assets owned by the company, whether they are currently being used or not, including current, fixed, sundry, and intangible assets.
2. *intangibles* means all assets whose actual value is difficult or impossible to determine, such as goodwill, copyrights, patents, trademarks, or leasehold improvements.
3. *total debt* means all obligations of the company, including current, fixed, and miscellaneous liabilities.
4. *preferred stock* means the par value of all stock that has preferential claims to income and assets over those claims held by common stock.
5. *number of shares of common stock outstanding* means the sum of all common stock issues that are in the hands of shareholders.
6. *common stock* means all stock that has no preferential claims to income or assets.

This ratio, composed entirely of items from the balance sheet, is a measure of the relative worth of each share of common stock issued by the company. In essence, it represents the amount of assets backing up each common share, and it therefore gives some indication as to the safety of the shares and the accounting value that each represents. Generally, the higher this ratio, the better off common shareholders would be in the event of liquidation, though the liquidating value of a company may be vastly different from its book value.

A low book value per share of common stock can be a signal that the company has an insufficient amount of real assets standing behind its shares to fully repay common shareholders if the company must be liquidated. However, a low book value could also indicate that the company has adopted extremely conservative accounting policies or has invested quite heavily in intangible assets such as research and development. Too low of a book value per share of common stock could make it difficult for the company to raise additional capital in the marketplace through debt or equity financing.

BOOK VALUE (continued)

An unreasonably high book value per share of common stock may suggest that the accounting policies adopted by the company are extremely aggressive or that the company is running in a very efficient, profitable manner.

An increasing book value per share of common stock is generally a good sign in that the company is accumulating assets faster than it is accumulating debt or preferential stockholder obligations. On the other hand, a declining book value per share of common stock is generally not a good sign, though it may not necessarily be bad. That is to say, if the reason that the ratio is declining is because the company has just issued shares or is heavily engaged in successful research and development, then the decline may be entirely justifiable. However, if this is not the case, the company may be losing money from operations or may be writing down certain assets.

Note that liquidating value and book value are not necessarily the same. Book value is often presumed to approximate liquidating value, though the accounting policies adopted by the company and the price that a company may get for its assets during a "distress sale" accompanying liquidation may indeed be vastly different.

This ratio should be examined in the context of the company's other ratios, in comparison to other companies within the same industry, and in comparison to itself over time.

CASH RATIO   **Liquidity measure**

$$\text{Cash Ratio} = \frac{\text{Cash on hand in bank } + \text{ Marketable securities}}{\text{Current liabilities}}$$

Where:
1. *cash* means currency and currency equivalents.
2. *marketable securities* means U.S. government securities, banker's acceptances, commercial paper, and corporate securities, valued at market rather than at cost.
3. *current liabilities* means items that must be paid within the current year, such as accounts payable, accrued expenses, accrued and withheld taxes, unearned revenues, notes payable, dividends payable, and the current maturities of long-term debts.

This ratio, composed entirely of balance sheet items, tests the company's ability to raise cash quickly. The higher this ratio, the easier it will be for the company to meet its short-term financial obligations.

This ratio, though less frequently used than the current ratio or quick asset ratio, gives a more critical analysis of the company's cash position. The cash ratio is especially well suited for evaluating companies in cash-intensive industries.

Since cash is a crucial resource in the operation of a company, a company with too low a cash ratio may be in danger of running out of the funds necessary to keep going. That is to say, the company could run out of cash during an economic downturn; fall behind on payments for raw materials and be forced to halt production; or have to delay an advertising campaign, which could disrupt its marketing efforts. All in all, too low a cash ratio does not bode well for a company and can make it difficult to raise additional capital just when it is most critically needed.

An unreasonably high cash ratio should be analyzed in conjunction with the company's other measures. Too high of a ratio could suggest anything from an overly conservative management stance to a company that is seeking a takeover or is a takeover target itself.

A declining cash ratio is generally not a good sign, though quite often companies in seasonal industries will accumulate cash during certain times and spend cash during other times.

This ratio should be examined in the context of the company's other ratios, in comparison to other companies within the same industry, and in comparison to itself over time.

COMMON STOCK RATIO

Capital structure measure

$$\text{Common Stock Ratio} = \frac{\text{Common stock}}{\text{Total capitalization}}$$

Where:
1. *common stock* means all stock that has no preferential claims to income or assets.
2. *total capitalization* means all fixed liabilities and shareholders' equity—in essence representing the total long-term investment in the company from all sources.

This ratio, composed entirely of balance sheet items, measures the percentage of the company's funds that are provided by common shareholders. In essence, it represents the leverage effect on shareholder money. Generally, the lower this ratio, the higher leverage that shareholders have working for them, the higher the company's cost of capital, and the more risk the company's securities have.

A low common stock ratio can be a signal that management may be using too much leverage and therefore subjecting common shareholders to too much risk while at the same time saddling the company with too many fixed obligations. For instance, if the amount of funded debt and preferred stock being used is excessive, the company may be spending too much money to compensate the debt and preferred shareholders, increasing the company's cost of capital, and there not maximizing common shareholder wealth.

An unreasonably high common stock ratio can be a signal that the company may be using too little borrowed capital in its financial structure, thereby losing the leverage effect that fixed payment obligations have for common shareholders.

Whether it is a good or bad sign if the common stock ratio is declining or increasing is entirely dependent on what other concurrent changes are being made in the company's capital structure.

This ratio should be examined in the context of the company's other ratios, in comparison to other companies within the same industry, and in comparison to itself over time.

CURRENT or WORKING CAPITAL RATIO   Liquidity measure

$$\text{Current Ratio} = \frac{\text{Current assets}}{\text{Current liabilities}}$$

Where:
1. *current assets* means those items that either represent cash or will be or could be converted into cash in a relatively short period of time, such as cash, marketable securities (valued at cost), accounts receivable, notes receivable, inventory, and prepaid expenses.
2. *current liabilities* means items that must be paid within the current year, such as accounts payable, accrued expenses, accrued and withheld taxes, unearned revenues, notes payable, dividends payable, and the current maturities of long-term debts.

This ratio, composed entirely of balance sheet items, tests the company's ability to raise cash to meet its current liabilities. The higher this ratio, the easier it will be for the company to meet its short-term financial obligations. Generally, this ratio should be 2.0 or above.

The current ratio should be examined in conjunction with the company's other measures. The level of this ratio is often dependent on the kind of business the company is in, because the items that compose this ratio are typically dependent on industry factors. That is to say, the numerator of the equation includes both inventory and accounts receivable (the inventory may be perishable, subject to obsolescence, or otherwise not readily salable, and the accounts receivable may be aging and potentially uncollectible).

A low current ratio can be a signal that the company may be in danger of running out of funds or at the very least, may be having financial difficulties. That is, if the current ratio of a company gets too low, the company may be having trouble paying its bills. The reasons for this are simple: the timely payment of current liabilities is dependent upon the company's cash reserves, its timely receipt of cash from receivables, and its ability to convert other current assets into cash.

An unreasonably high current ratio should be analyzed in conjunction with the company's other measures. Too high a ratio could suggest anything from an overly conservative management stance to a company that is seeking a takeover or is a takeover target itself.

A declining current ratio is generally not a good sign, though quite often companies in seasonal industries will accumulate cash during certain times and spend cash during other times.

This ratio should be examined in the context of the company's other ratios, in comparison to other companies within the same industry, and in comparison to itself over time.

DEBT TO ASSET

Leverage measure

$$\text{Debt to Total Assets} = \frac{\text{Total debt}}{\text{Total assets}}$$

Where:
1. *total debt* means all obligations of the company, including current, fixed, and miscellaneous liabilities.
2. *total assets* means all assets owned by the company, whether they are currently being used or not, including current, fixed, sundry, and intangible assets.

This ratio, composed entirely of balance sheet items, measures the percentage of the company's funds provided by creditors. In essence, it measures the amount of leverage the company is using. Generally, companies with debt-to-asset percentages lower than 50 percent are considered to be well balanced in terms of leverage and risk, whereas ratios around 50 percent are typically thought to be too high.

From an earnings perspective, the more debt a company has, the higher its interest costs will be. In turn, the greater the amount of money a company spends on interest, the less earnings will be available for shareholders. Of course, if a company can earn returns higher than its cost of interest on the borrowed funds, then the leverage effect of the debt will be beneficial. If it can't, the leverage effect will be detrimental. In essence, the leverage effect of debt tends to magnify the returns that a company makes on its invested assets.

Typically, the lower this ratio, the more stable a company's earnings, the less risk the shares carry, and the lower the expected rate of return for shareholders. Creditors, debtholders, and preferred shareholders all prefer companies with low debt-to-asset ratios.

Typically, high leverage translates into more volatile earnings. The higher the debt-to-asset ratio, the higher the company's risk and the greater the potential rate of return is for shareholders.

A declining ratio can indicate anything from the company becoming more stable to insufficient use of leverage by management.

This ratio should be examined in the context of the company's other ratios, in comparison to other companies within the same industry, and in comparison to itself over time.

DEBT TO EQUITY   Leverage measure

$$\text{Debt to Equity Ratio} = \frac{\text{Funded debt}}{\text{Shareholders' equity}}$$

Where:
1. *funded debt* means all long-term obligations of the company that will mature in five years or more.
2. *shareholders' equity* means the total equity investment in the company, including preferred stock, common stock, paid-in capital, and retained earnings.

This ratio, composed entirely of balance sheet items, measures the percentage of the company's funds provided by creditors. In essence, it measures the effects of leverage on shareholder money.

From an earnings perspective, high debt translates into high interest charges. This means that a greater amount of company revenues will be used to pay interest on creditor's funds, and therefore, less revenue will be available for shareholders. Of course, if the company can earn returns higher than its costs of funds, then the leverage effect will be beneficial. If it can't, the leverage effect will be detrimental. In essence, leverage magnifies the returns earned on shareholder assets.

Typically, high leverage translates into more volatile earnings. The higher the debt-to-equity ratio, the higher the company's risk and the greater the potential rate of return is for shareholders. Usually, 100 percent or more is construed to be a high debt-to-equity ratio.

The lower this ratio, the more stable a company's earnings will be, the less risk the shares carry, and the lower the expected rate of return for shareholders. Creditors, debtholders, and preferred shareholders all prefer companies with low debt-to-equity ratios.

A declining ratio can indicate anything from the company becoming more stable to insufficient use of leverage on the part of management.

This ratio should be examined in the context of the company's other ratios, in comparison to other companies within the same industry, and in comparison to itself over time.

DIVIDEND YIELD
Market valuation measure

$$\text{Dividend Yield} = \frac{\text{Annual per share dividend}}{\text{Price per share}}$$

Where:

1. *annual per share dividend* means the amount of dividend to be paid on each share of the company's stock.
2. *price per share* means the current market price of each share as determined by buyers and sellers in the marketplace.

This ratio, composed of items from the balance sheet, the income statement, and the market, is a measure of the cash yield that an investor earns for investing in the shares of the company. In essence, it represents the percentage cash return that a stockholder receives. Typically, the higher the yield, the safer the investment, and the less growth-oriented the stock.

A low dividend yield can be a signal that the company has better uses for its excess earnings than to pay them to shareholders, and therefore retains earnings as a source of investable funds. On the other hand, a low dividend yield can also be a signal that the company is earning an insufficient return on the assets it has invested, and therefore cannot afford to pay out any money to shareholders in the form of dividends. A dividend yield that is low primarily because the stock price has risen dramatically may be a sign that the dividend rate, which is set by the board of directors, is about to be increased. Or, it could be a sign that the shares are overpriced in the market.

An unreasonably high dividend yield can be a signal that the company has nothing better to do with its excess earnings than to pay them to shareholders, thereby suggesting that the company is unable to identify any suitable investment opportunities. On one hand, this can mean that management sees little future for the company and its industry, and on the other hand it could mean that the company is so profitable that it wants to heavily reward its shareholders for making their investments. A dividend yield that is high primarily because the stock price has fallen dramatically may be a sign that the dividend rate will be cut or that the shares are underpriced in the market.

An increasing dividend yield caused by an increasing annual dividend rate (the numerator) is generally a good sign, because it shows that the board of directors feels comfortable enough with the company's future to more heavily reward its shareholders. Conversely, a declining dividend yield caused by a declining numerator does not bode well at all, as it suggests that the future prospects of the company may be so bad that the board of directors is willing to risk the scorn of shareholders by lowering the dividend rate.

This ratio should be examined in the context of the company's other ratios, in comparison to other companies within the same industry, and in comparison to itself over time.

EARNINGS PER SHARE   **Earnings measure**

$$\text{Earnings Per Share} = \frac{\text{Net income} - \text{Preferred dividends}}{\text{Number of shares of common stock outstanding}}$$

Where:

1. *net income* means net profit, the excess of all revenues less all expenses.
2. *preferred dividends* means the total amount of money required to be paid to holders of the company's preferred shares.
3. *number of shares of common stock outstanding* means the sum of all common stock issues that are in the hands of shareholders.

This ratio, composed of items from both the balance sheet and the income statement, is a measure of the company's overall performance as it relates to common shareholders. In essence, it represents the amount of money that each share of common stock is ultimately entitled to, whether it is paid out in the form of dividends or reinvested in the company's future in the form of retained earnings.

A low earnings per share figure basically says that the company is not making very much money. It can be a signal of many things: the company may be inefficiently run, may have too many fixed obligations which need be paid, or may be too heavily investing in research and development, while using overly conservative accounting policies. Negative earnings per share indicate a company is actually losing money—that is, shareholder equity is being used to keep the company operational. Negative or low earnings per share can make it difficult for a company to raise additional capital in the marketplace, whether it be through debt or equity financing.

On the other hand, an unreasonably high earnings per share could indicate that the company may not be properly investing for the future. Specifically, it could mean that very little money is being spent on such items as research and development, advertising, marketing, or infrastructure, and that eventually the company may face serious problems due to competition or technological changes that may not have been anticipated or prepared for.

A declining earnings per share can signal anything from a decline in profitability to an increase in the number of shares outstanding. It could signal that the company is having hard times, or conversely, may be preparing for hard times by investing heavily in technology that has not yet begun to contribute to operating profits.

This ratio should be examined in the context of the company's other ratios, in comparison to other companies within the same industry, and in comparison to itself over time.

FIXED ASSET TURNOVER

Activity measure

$$\text{Fixed Asset Turnover} = \frac{\text{Net sales}}{\text{Fixed assets}}$$

Where:

1. *net sales* means gross sales less any discounts, returns, and refunds.
2. *fixed assets* means physical assets that are used by the company in its current operations and are not expected to be converted into cash within the current year, such as property, plant, and equipment.

This ratio, composed of items from both the balance sheet and the income statement, tests the efficiency of the company's use of its assets. Stated differently, the fixed asset turnover ratio is a measure of the speed in which the company turns over the money it has invested in fixed assets. Generally, the higher the fixed asset turnover ratio, the more efficiently the company is operating.

A low fixed asset turnover ratio can signal poor sales relative to the amount of money invested in property, plant, and equipment, signaling, among other things, inefficient production procedures, poor production controls, or bad purchase decisions.

A high fixed asset turnover ratio can indicate highly efficient production procedures on one hand and inadequate investment in fixed assets on the other hand. The former can be exceptionally advantageous for the company, and the latter can have a severely stifling influence on the company's long-term prospects.

A declining ratio can signal anything from slowing sales, declining efficiency, and aging equipment, to the company becoming more capital intensive in its production procedures. An increasing ratio can signal increasing sales, improving efficiency, or better asset utilization.

This ratio should be examined in the context of the company's other ratios, in comparison to other companies within the same industry, and in comparison to itself over time.

FIXED CHARGE COVERAGE   **Coverage measure**

$$\text{Fixed Charge Coverage} = \frac{\text{Income before fixed charges and taxes}}{\text{Fixed charges}}$$

Where:

1. *income before fixed charges and taxes* means income from all sources less all the expenses associated with generating this income with the exception of interest charges, lease obligations, taxes, and extraordinary items.

2. *fixed charges* means the interest payable on all of the company's fixed liabilities plus all payments on leaseholds.

This ratio, composed entirely of items from the income statement, measures the extent to which income covers the company's fixed charges. In essence, it measures how much of a revenue cushion the company has in order to meet its financial obligations to both debtholders and leaseholders. Generally, the higher this ratio, the more protected the creditors and leaseholders are, and the stabler the shareholders' position.

Despite its similarity to the interest charge coverage ratio, the fixed charge coverage ratio provides a more complete analysis since it includes virtually all the fixed charges a company is obligated to pay, not just the interest portion of these charges.

A low fixed charge coverage can signal a very aggressive management posture using potentially excessive amounts of leverage. Or, it can signal that the company is not earning an adequate return on the capital it has borrowed or the lease obligations it has outstanding.

A high fixed charge coverage can signal that the company may not be adequately using the leverage effect of debt, and therefore shareholders may not be earning the rate of return that they could be earning. The higher the ratio, the easier it should be for the company to raise capital through borrowing.

A declining fixed charge coverage can signal anything from a decline in sales and profitability, to an increase in the company's debtload, cost of debt, or lease obligations. Note that the interest rate a company pays on its debt can dramatically affect this ratio, insomuch as an increase in interest rates will cause a decline in fixed charge coverage.

This ratio should be examined in the context of the company's other ratios, in comparison to other companies within the same industry, and in comparison to itself over time.

FULLY DILUTED EARNINGS PER SHARE

Earnings measure

$$\frac{\text{Primary}}{\text{Earnings}} = \frac{\text{Net income} + \text{Convertible preferred dividends} + \text{Convertible bond interest} - \text{Interest tax adjustment}}{\text{Number of shares of common outstanding assuming conversion}}$$

Where:

1. *net income* means net profit, the excess of all revenues less all expenses.
2. *convertible preferred dividends* means the total amount of money required to be paid to the holders of the company's preferred shares which could be converted to common shares.
3. *convertible bond interest* means the interest payable on all of the company's fixed liabilities which could be converted to common shares.
4. *interest tax adjustment* means any additional taxes which would result if the above specified bond issues were converted and therefore the interest could no longer be deducted for tax purposes.
5. *number of shares of common stock outstanding assuming conversion* means the sum of all common stock issues that would be in the hands of shareholders assuming that all of the company's convertible securities were converted to common shares.

This ratio, composed of items from both the balance sheet and the income statement, is a measure of the company's overall performance as it relates to common shareholders and potential common shareholders. In essence, it represents the amount of money that each share of common stock is ultimately entitled to, whether it is paid out in the form of dividends or reinvested in the company's future in the form of retained earnings.

A low fully diluted earnings per share figure basically says that the company is not making very much money. It can be a signal of many problems: the company may be inefficiently run, may have too many fixed obligations that need to be paid, or may be too heavily investing in research and development while using overly conservative accounting policies. Negative fully diluted earnings per share indicate the company is actually losing money—that is, shareholder equity is being used to keep the company operational. Negative or low fully diluted earnings per share can make it difficult for a company to raise additional capital in the marketplace, whether it be through debt or equity financing.

Unreasonably high fully diluted earnings per share can indicate that the company may not be properly investing for the future. Specifically, it could mean that very little money is being spent on such items as research and development, advertising, marketing, or infrastructure, and that eventually the company may face serious problems due to competition or technological changes that may not have been anticipated or prepared for.

Declining fully diluted earnings per share can signal anything from a decline in profitability to an increase in the number of shares outstanding. It could signal that the company may be having hard times, or conversely, may be preparing for hard times by investing heavily in new technology that has not yet begun to contribute to operating profits.

This ratio should be examined in the context of the company's other ratios, in comparison to other companies within the same industry, and in comparison to itself over time.

INTEREST COVERAGE   Coverage measure

$$\text{Times Interest Earned} = \frac{\text{Income before interest and taxes}}{\text{Interest}}$$

Where:
1. *income before interest and taxes* means income from all sources less all the expenses associated with generating this income with the exception of interest charges, taxes, and extraordinary items.
2. *interest charges* means the interest payable on all of the company's fixed liabilities.

This ratio, composed entirely of items from the income statement, measures the extent to which income covers the company's interest requirements. In essence, it measures how much of a revenue cushion the company has in order to meet its financial obligations to debtholders. Generally, the higher this ratio, the more protected the creditors are and the more stable the shareholders' position.

Though less complete than the fixed charge coverage, this ratio represents a reasonable method by which to judge how well the company is able to cover its costs of borrowing. Unfortunately, since many income statements do not break down fixed charges in a fashion sufficient enough for a fixed charge coverage calculation to be made, the interest coverage ratio must often suffice.

A low interest coverage can signal a very aggressive management posture using potentially excessive amounts of leverage. Or, it can signal that the company is not earning an adequate return on the capital it has borrowed.

An unreasonably high interest coverage can signal that the company may not be adequately using the leverage effects of debt, and therefore shareholders may not be earning the rate of return that they could be earning. The higher this ratio, the easier it should be for the company to raise capital through borrowing.

A declining interest coverage can signal anything from a decline in sales and profitability to an increase in the company's debtload or cost of debt. Note that the interest rate a company pays on its debt can dramatically affect this ratio, insomuch as an increase in interest rates will cause a decline in the interest coverage ratio.

This ratio should be examined in the context of the company's other ratios, in comparison to other companies within the same industry, and in comparison to itself over time.

INVENTORY TURNOVER RATIO   Activity measure

Three commonly used methods:

$$\text{Inventory Turnover Ratio} = \frac{\text{Net sales}}{\text{Year-end inventory}}$$

$$\text{Inventory Turnover Ratio} = \frac{\text{Cost of goods sold}}{\text{Average inventory}}$$

$$\text{Inventory Turnover Ratio} = \frac{\text{Cost of goods sold}}{\text{Year-end inventory}}$$

Where:
1. *net sales* means gross sales less any discounts, returns, and refunds.
2. *inventory* means raw materials, work in progress, and finished merchandise waiting for sale, valued at the lower of cost or market value.
3. *cost of goods sold* means the cost of the inventory sold during the period.

This ratio, composed of items from both the balance sheet and the income statement, tests the efficiency of the company's use of its assets. Stated differently, the inventory turnover ratio is a measure of the speed at which the company sells its inventory. Generally, the higher the inventory turnover ratio, the more efficiently the company is operating.

A low inventory turnover ratio can be a signal of poor sales or excessively high inventory levels. In essence, a low inventory turnover ratio indicates that too much money is tied up in inventory relative to the sales level of the company, and the costs associated with carrying that inventory are thus higher than they should be.

A high inventory turnover ratio can signal anything from highly efficient inventory control procedures to insufficient inventory levels to adequately cover sales and shipping. Be aware that a high inventory turnover ratio is generally good, but if it is caused by insufficient inventory levels, then it may result in the sales staff having to turn away orders or back order too many items, neither of which is good for the company's image or financial picture.

A declining ratio can signal slowing sales or inefficient use of the company's assets, whereas an increasing ratio can signal a pickup in sales or tighter management controls. On the other hand, a declining ratio could also signal bulging inventories, whereas an increasing ratio could be a warning of a future inability to fill customer orders.

This ratio should be examined in the context of the company's other ratios, in comparison to other companies within the same industry, and in comparison to itself over time.

NET ASSETS PER BOND   **Collateral measure**

$$\begin{matrix} \text{Net Asset} \\ \text{Value} \\ \text{Per Bond} \end{matrix} = \frac{\text{Total assets} - \text{Intangibles} - \text{All liabilities preceding bonds}}{\text{Number of bonds outstanding}}$$

Where:

1. *total assets* means all assets owned by the company, whether they are currently being used or not, including current, fixed, sundry, and intangible assets.
2. *intangibles* means all assets whose actual value is difficult or impossible to determine, such as goodwill, copyrights, patents, trademarks, or leasehold improvements.
3. *all liabilities preceding bonds* means all obligations of the company, such as taxes, that must be paid before debtholders receive any return of their investment in the event of the company's liquidation.
4. *number of bonds outstanding* means the sum of all bond issues that are in the hands of bondholders.

This ratio, composed entirely of items from the balance sheet, is a measure of the amount of collateral standing behind the bonds issued by the company. In essence, it represents the number of dollars of assets backing up each bond, and therefore gives some indication as to the bonds' safety. Generally, the higher this ratio, the safer the bond is, and the higher the likelihood that the company will have sufficient assets to return bondholders' principle in the event of liquidation.

A low net asset per bond can be a signal that the company does not have sufficient capital to repay bondholders in the event it were to terminate operations and begin dissolution. Furthermore, a low net asset per bond could make it difficult for the company to borrow additional capital in the marketplace. That is, if a company with too low of a net asset value per bond needed cash, it might not be able to raise it, or might have to pay significantly higher interest rates to get it.

On the contrary, an unreasonably high net asset per bond ratio can be a signal that the company is not using enough debt in its capital structure and therefore has too little leverage to maximize shareholder net worth.

NET ASSETS PER BOND (continued)

An increasing net asset value per bond ratio is generally a good sign, in that the company is accumulating assets faster than it is accumulating debt. On the other hand, a declining net asset value per bond ratio is not a good sign, although it may not necessarily be bad. That is to say, if the reason that the ratio is declining is because the company has just issued debt, then the reason may be entirely justifiable. However, if this is not the case, then the company may be taking on debt faster than it is accumulating assets, possibly because it is losing money from operations or is being forced to write down certain assets.

This ratio should be examined in the context of the company's other ratios, in comparison to other companies within the same industry, and in comparison to itself over time.

NET ASSETS PER PREFERRED SHARE   Collateral measure

$$\text{Net Asset Per Share of Preferred Stock} = \frac{\text{Total assets} - \text{Intangibles} - \text{Total debt}}{\text{Number of shares of preferred stock outstanding}}$$

Where:

1. *total assets* means all assets owned by the company, whether they are currently being used or not, including current, fixed, sundry, and intangible assets.
2. *intangibles* means all assets whose actual value is difficult or impossible to determine, such as goodwill, copyrights, patents, trademarks, or leasehold improvements.
3. *total debt* means all obligations of the company, including current, fixed, and miscellaneous liabilities.
4. *number of shares of preferred stock outstanding* means the sum of all preferred stock issues that are in the hands of shareholders.

This ratio, composed entirely of items from the balance sheet, is a measure of the amount of collateral standing behind the preferred shares issued by the company. In essence, it represents the number of dollars of assets backing up each preferred share, and therefore gives some indication about the safety of the preferred shares. Generally, the higher this ratio, the safer each preferred share is, and the higher the likelihood that the company will have sufficient assets to return preferred shareholders' money in the event of liquidation.

A low net asset per share of preferred stock ratio can be a signal that the company does not have sufficient capital to repay preferred shareholders in the event it were to terminate operations and begin dissolution. Furthermore, a low net asset per share of preferred stock could make it difficult or more costly for the company to raise additional capital in the marketplace, especially through the sale of additional preferred shares. This in turn might prevent the company from choosing this route for additional financing, forcing the company to raise additional capital, either through borrowing or through diluting common stock.

On the contrary, an unreasonably high net asset per share of preferred stock ratio can be a signal that the company is not using enough preferred in its capital structure and therefore has too little leverage to maximize shareholder net worth.

An increasing net asset per share of preferred stock ratio is generally a good sign in that the company is accumulating assets faster than it is accumulating preferred equity. On the other hand, a declining net asset per share of preferred stock ratio is not a good sign—although it may not necessarily be bad. That is, if the reason that the ratio is declining is because the company has just issued preferred shares, then the reason may be entirely justifiable. However, if this is not the case, then the company may be losing money from operations or may be writing down certain assets.

This ratio should be examined in the context of the company's other ratios, in comparison to other companies within the same industry, and in comparison to itself over time.

OPERATING or EXPENSE RATIO   Profitability measure

$$\text{Operating Ratio} = \frac{\text{Cost of goods sold} + \text{Operating expenses}}{\text{Net sales}}$$

Where:
1. *cost of goods sold* means the cost of the inventory sold during the period.
2. *operating expenses* means all of the other expenses associated with operating the company, including selling and administrative expenses, and depreciation.
3. *net sales* means gross sales less any discounts, returns, and refunds.

This ratio, composed entirely of items from the income statement, is a measure of the company's operating efficiency. Stated differently, the operating ratio is a comparison of the total expenses associated with sales to the revenue generated by those sales. The lower the operating ratio, the more efficiently the firm is operating.

A low operating ratio can be a signal of a highly efficient operation or exceptionally effective management. On the other hand, it can be a signal that the company may be using overly conservative accounting policies or spending insufficient money on research and development.

A high operating ratio can be a signal of general inefficiency or ineffective management. Or, such a situation can result in a company that uses extremely aggressive accounting policies, is spending too much on research and development, or does not have enough sales to justify its infrastructure.

An increasing operating ratio can signal aging property, plant, and equipment, declining sales volume, declining overall efficiency, or inappropriate management policy making.

This ratio should be examined in the context of the company's other ratios, in comparison to other companies within the same industry, and in comparison to itself over time.

Note: This ratio is the complement of the profit margin ratio—that is, this ratio plus the profit margin ratio will always total to 100 percent.

PAYOUT RATIO   Coverage measure

$$\text{Dividend Payout Ratio} = \frac{\text{Common stock dividends paid}}{\text{Income available for common stock dividends}}$$

Where:
1. *common stock dividends paid* means the total amount of money paid to common shareholders.
2. *income available for common stock dividends* means the total amount of money that could be paid to common shareholders, calculated by subtracting preferred dividends from net income.

This ratio, composed entirely of income statement items, measures the percentage of distributable earnings that are actually distributed to common shareholders. In essence, it represents the percentage of money that the board of directors *is able to* distribute to common shareholders that is *actually* distributed to them. The board determines the payout ratio, and it is typically based on their analysis of the working capital requirements of the company, its future prospects, the needs of the shareholders, and the board's own desire for consistency.

A low payout ratio that occurs frequently can be a sign that the company has better uses for its investable funds than paying them out to shareholders. Specifically, companies that need additional money for working capital because of losses or marginal profitability, and companies that are using all of their excess cash to fund a program of rapid expansion, often have a low payout ratio. On the other hand, some companies, despite their youth and growth orientation, adopt low payout ratios just because investors prefer some dividends to none at all. This gives the company an opportunity to satisfy its need to retain capital and makes it easier for the board to maintain a constant dollar dividend payout despite the volatility in earnings so typical of younger, more growth-oriented companies.

An unreasonably high payout ratio that occurs on a frequent basis, can be a sign that the company has little else to do with excess cash flow than to pay it to shareholders. Though shareholders may be happy to receive the cash, the effect on the company's growth rate is detrimental. On the other hand, if an unreasonably high payout ratio occurs infrequently, it may just be a sign that the company has had an exceptionally bad year but wants to maintain a consistent dollar dividend payout.

An increasing dividend payout ratio can be a sign that the company is maturing and has less need for expansion or working capital. By the same token, an increasing dividend payout rate is also a sign that the growth rate of the company may be slowing. It is quite typical for the board of directors to adopt a higher payout ratio as a company matures for these reasons: to ingratiate themselves with shareholders, to more directly compensate shareholders for the use of their money, and to change the character of investors who own the company by making it more attractive to conservative individuals and institutions.

This ratio should be examined in the context of the company's other ratios, in comparison to other companies within the same industry, and in comparison to itself over time.

PREFERRED DIVIDEND COVERAGE

Coverage measure

$$\text{Preferred Dividend Coverage} = \frac{\text{Net income}}{\text{Preferred dividends}}$$

Where:
1. *net income* means net profit, the excess of all revenues less all expenses.
2. *preferred dividends* means the total amount of money required to be paid to holders of the company's preferred shares.

This ratio, composed entirely of items from the income statement, measures the extent to which income covers the company's preferred dividend requirements. In essence, it measures how much of a revenue cushion the company has in order to meet its financial obligations to preferred shareholders. Generally, the higher this ratio, the more protected preferred shareholders are, and the more stable their position. That is to say, since the protection afforded preferred shareholders lies principally in the company's ability to earn and pay the dividends to which they are entitled, this ratio gives a good indication of the company's ability to accomplish this task.

A low preferred dividend coverage can signal a very aggressive management posture or that the company may be too highly leveraged. Or, it could signal that the company is not earning an adequate return on the capital it has borrowed or the preferred equity it has raised.

A high preferred dividend coverage can signal that the company may not be adequately using the leverage effect of debt and preferred equity, and common shareholders may not be earning the rate of return that they could be earning. The higher the ratio, the easier it should be for the company to raise capital through borrowing.

A declining preferred dividend coverage can signal anything from a decline in sales and profitability, to an increase in the company's preferred dividend requirements. Specifically, the dividend rate a company pays on its preferred stock can dramatically affect this ratio, insomuch as an increase in the amount of preferred dividends to be paid will cause a decline in preferred dividend coverage.

This ratio should be examined in the context of the company's other ratios, in comparison to other companies within the same industry, and in comparison to itself over time.

PREFERRED STOCK RATIO   Capital structure measure

$$\text{Preferred Stock Ratio} = \frac{\text{Preferred stock}}{\text{Total capitalization}}$$

Where:

1. *preferred stock* means the par value of all stock that has preferential claims to income and assets over those claims held by common stock.

2. *total capitalization* means all fixed liabilities and shareholders' equity, in essence representing the total long term investment in the company from all sources.

This ratio, composed entirely of balance sheet items, measures the percentage of the company's funds that are provided by preferred shareholders. In essence, it represents the leverage effect on common shareholder money. Generally, the higher this ratio, the higher the leverage that common shareholders have working for them, the higher the company's cost of capital, and the more risk the company's securities have.

A low preferred stock ratio can be a signal that management is not using a sufficient amount of leverage and therefore may not be maximizing the rate of return for common shareholders. If, for instance, the amount of preferred stock being used is insufficient in total, then the company may be using too much equity or debt in its capital structure and thereby not maximizing shareholder wealth. On the other hand, if short-term debt or bank financing is being used in place of preferred stock, the company may be saddled with an inordinate amount of interest obligations.

An unreasonably high preferred stock ratio can be a signal that the company may be using too much "borrowed" equity in its financial structure, thereby losing the tax benefits inherent to interest expenses, but still saddling the company with excessive fixed payment obligations.

Whether it is a good or bad sign if the preferred stock ratio is declining or increasing is entirely dependent on what other concurrent changes are being made in the company's capital structure.

This ratio should be examined in the context of the company's other ratios, in comparison to other companies within the same industry, and in comparison to itself over time.

PRICE-EARNINGS RATIO   Market valuation measure

$$\text{Price-Earnings Ratio} = \frac{\text{Price per share}}{\text{Earnings per share}}$$

Where:
1. *price per share* means the current market price of each share as determined by buyers and sellers in the marketplace.
2. *earnings per share* means the amount of money each share is ultimately entitled to, whether it is paid out or retained.

This ratio, composed of items from the balance sheet, the income statement, and the market, is a measure of the value that investors place on the company's earnings. In essence, it represents the amount of money investors are willing to pay today for the future stream of benefits that they expect to get from an investment in the company's shares, including dividends, their "portion" of retained earnings, and share price appreciation. Typically, the higher the price-earnings ratio, the riskier, more volatile the investment is presumed to be.

A low price-earnings ratio can be a signal that investors: regard the company as a conservative, safety oriented investment; expect the company's earnings to drop or its growth rate of earnings to slow; have little confidence in the company's reported earnings or earnings trend; or expect the industry or economy as a whole to do poorly. Typically, older, safer, more mature companies have lower price-earnings ratios than faster growing, riskier companies.

An unreasonably high price-earnings ratio or one that is "not meaningful" is a sign that investors perceive the company to be extremely risky, expect the company to experience a turnaround or explosive growth in earnings, or, for one reason or another, have become enamored with the stock. Please note, "not meaningful" price earnings ratios result when a company does not have any earnings or is losing money. In these situations, even though a price-earnings ratio may be mathematically calculable, it is not meaningful because the divisor of the equation is a negative number.

An increasing price-earnings ratio is generally a good sign, though the reason behind the increase is extremely important. By the same token, a declining price-earnings ratio is generally not a good sign, though the reason behind the decline is of equal importance.

Note that contrary to what might otherwise be expected, some investment strategies concentrate on buying the shares of those companies with low price-earnings ratios and short-selling those with ratios that are unreasonably high.

This ratio should be examined in the context of the company's other ratios, in comparison to other companies within the same industry, and in comparison to itself over time.

PRIMARY EARNINGS PER SHARE   **Earnings measure**

$$\text{Primary Earnings Per Share} = \frac{\text{Net income} + \substack{\text{Convertible} \\ \text{(to common)} \\ \text{preferred} \\ \text{dividends}} + \substack{\text{Convertible} \\ \text{(to common)} \\ \text{bond} \\ \text{interest}} - \substack{\text{Interest} \\ \text{tax adjustment}}}{\text{Number of shares of common outstanding assuming conversion}}$$

Where:

1. *net income* means net profit, the excess of all revenues less all expenses.

2. *convertible (to common) preferred dividends* means the total amount of money required to be paid to the holders of the company's preferred shares that:
   - could be converted to common shares;
   - carry a dividend rate of two-thirds or less than the concurrent bank prime interest rate; and,
   - would dilute ordinary earnings calculations by 3 percent or more if converted.

3. *convertible (to common) bond interest* means the interest payable on all of the company's fix liabilities that:
   - could be converted to common shares;
   - carry an interest rate of two-thirds or less than the concurrent bank prime interest rate; and,
   - would dilute ordinary earnings calculations by 3 percent or more if converted.

4. *interest tax adjustment* means any additional taxes that would result if the above-specified bond issues were converted and therefore the interest could no longer be deducted for tax purpose.

5. *number of shares of common stock outstanding assuming conversion* means the sum of all common stock issues that would be in the hands of shareholders assuming that all of the company's convertible securities were converted to common shares.

This ratio, composed of items from both the balance sheet and the income statement, is a measure of the company's overall performance as it relates to common shareholders and potential common shareholders. In essence, it represents the amount of money that each share of common stock is ultimately entitled to, whether it is paid out in the form of dividends or reinvested in the company's future in the form of retained earnings.

PRIMARY EARNINGS PER SHARE (continued)

A low primary earnings per share figure basically says that the company is not making very much money. It can be a signal of many things: the company may be inefficiently run, may have too many fixed obligations that need be paid, or may be too heavily investing in research and development while using overly conservative accounting policies. Negative primary earnings per share indicate the company is actually losing money—that is, shareholder equity is being used to keep the company operational. Negative or low primary earnings per share can make it difficult for a company to raise additional capital in the marketplace, whether it be through debt or equity financing.

Unreasonably high primary earnings per share can indicate that the company may not be properly investing for the future. Specifically, it could mean that very little money is being spent on such items as research and development, advertising, marketing, or infrastructure, and that eventually the company may face serious problems due to competition or technological changes that may not have been anticipated or prepared for.

Declining primary earnings per share can signal anything from a decline in profitability to an increase in the number of shares outstanding. It could signal that the company may be having hard times, or conversely, may be preparing for hard times by investing heavily in new technology that has not yet begun to contribute to operating profits.

This ratio should be examined in the context of the company's other ratios, in comparison to other companies within the same industry, and in comparison to itself over time.

PROFIT MARGIN RATIO   Profitability measure

$$\text{Profit Margin} = \frac{\text{Operating income}}{\text{Net sales}}$$

Where:
 1. *operating income* means gross sales less any discounts, returns, and refunds, less the cost of these sales, all selling and administrative expenses, and depreciation.
 2. *net sales* means gross sales less any discounts, returns, and refunds.

This ratio, composed entirely of items from the income statement, is a measure of the company's operating efficiency. Stated differently, the profit margin ratio is a measure of the percentage contribution to operating income that each dollar of sales generates. The higher the profit margin, the more efficiently the firm is operating.

A low profit margin ratio can be a signal of general inefficiency or ineffective management. Such a situation can also result if a company is using extremely aggressive accounting policies, is spending too much on research and development, or does not have enough sales to justify its infrastructure.

An unreasonably high profit margin ratio can be a signal of a highly efficient operation or exceptionally effective management. Or, on the other hand, it could be a signal that the company is using overly conservative accounting policies, or spending insufficient money on research and development.

A declining profit margin can signal aging property, plant, and equipment, declining sales volume, declining overall efficiency, or inappropriate management policy making.

This ratio should be examined in the context of the company's other ratios, in comparison to other companies within the same industry, and in comparison to itself over time.

Note: This ratio is the complement of the operating ratio—that is, this ratio plus the operating ratio will always total to 100 percent.

QUICK ASSET or ACID TEST RATIO   **Liquidity measure**

$$\text{Quick Asset Ratio} = \frac{\text{Current assets} - \text{Inventory} - \text{Prepaid expenses}}{\text{Current liabilities}}$$

Where:

1. *current assets* means those items that either represent cash or will be or could be converted into cash in a relatively short period of time, such as cash, marketable securities (valued at cost), accounts receivable, notes receivable, inventory, and prepaid expenses.
2. *inventory* means raw materials, work in progress, and finished merchandise waiting for sale, valued at the lower of cost or market value.
3. *prepaid expenses* means payments or deposits made in anticipation of the receipt of goods or services which will be used at some future point in time.
4. *current liabilities* means items that must be paid within the current year, such as accounts payable, accrued expenses, accrued and withheld taxes, unearned revenues, notes payable, dividends payable, and the current maturities of long-term debts.

This ratio, composed entirely of balance sheet items, tests the company's ability to raise cash in a temporary financial crisis. The higher this ratio, the easier it will be for the company to raise cash in an emergency.

The quick asset ratio should be examined in conjunction with other asset, liability, and activity measures. The level of the ratio is often dependent on the kind of business the company is in and the general economic condition of the industry.

A low quick asset ratio can be a signal that the company may be in danger of running out of funds or at the very least, may be having financial difficulties. That is, if the quick asset ratio of a company gets too low, the company may be having trouble paying its bills. The reasons behind this are simple: the timely payment of current liabilities is dependent upon the company's cash reserves, its timely receipt of cash from its receivables, and its ability to convert other current assets into cash.

An unreasonably high quick ratio should be analyzed in conjunction with the company's other measures. Too high a ratio can suggest anything from an overly conservative management stance to a company seeking a takeover or becoming a takeover target itself.

A declining quick ratio is generally not a good sign, though quite often companies in seasonal industries will accumulate cash during certain times and spend cash during other times.

This ratio should be examined in the context of the company's other ratios, in comparison to other companies within the same industry, and in comparison to itself over time.

RECEIVABLES TURNOVER   Activity measure

$$\text{Receivables Turnover} = \frac{\text{Net sales}}{\text{Net account receivables}}$$

Where:
1. *net sales* means gross sales less any discounts, returns, and refunds.
2. *net account receivables* means money due from customers within the current year, less any provisions for returns, trade discounts for early payments, and bad debts.

This ratio, composed of items from both the balance sheet and the income statement, tests the efficiency of the company's use of its assets. Stated differently, the receivables turnover ratio is a measure of the speed in which the company turns sales into cash. Generally, the higher the receivables turnover ratio, the more efficiently the company is operating.

A low receivables turnover ratio can signal poor sales or slow collections. Or, it can signal the collection policy of the company is too lenient, and that sales are being made but not being paid for.

A high receivables turnover ratio can signal highly efficient collections and efficient asset utilization. On the other hand, it could also signal that the company has too stringent of a collection policy and therefore may be losing potential sales.

A declining ratio can signal slowing sales or slowing payments, both of which foretell of potential problems for the company. An increasing ratio may signal higher sales levels, more efficient asset utilization, or tighter management controls.

This ratio should be examined in the context of the company's other ratios, in comparison to other companies within the same industry, and in comparison to itself over time.

Note: This ratio is the contrapositive of the average collection period.

RETURN ON ASSETS   Profitability measure

Two commonly used methods:

$$\text{Return on Assets} = \frac{\text{Net income}}{\text{Total assets}}$$

$$\text{Return on Assets} = \frac{\text{Net income}}{\text{Net Sales}} \times \frac{\text{Net Sales}}{\text{Total assets}}$$

Where:
1. *net income* means net profit, the excess of all revenues less all expenses.
2. *total assets* means all assets owned by the company, whether they are currently being used or not, including current, fixed, sundry, and intangible assets.
3. *net income/net sales* means net income divided by sales.
4. *net sales/total assets* means sales divided by total assets (total asset turnover).

This ratio, composed of items from both the balance sheet and the income statement, tests the efficiency of the company's use of its assets. Stated differently, the return on assets ratio is a measure of the company's ability to earn profits on its asset base. Generally, the higher the return on assets ratio, the more efficiently the company is operating.

This ratio, similar in nature to the return on invested capital and the return on equity ratios, measures efficiency in use of the company's assets. By its very nature, a high return on assets translates into a still higher return on equity, because the numerator of both equations is the same and the denominator of the former has to be equal to or greater than the latter.

A low return on assets ratio can signal a company with inefficient operations or ineffective management. On the other hand, such a situation could result from extremely aggressive accounting policies, significant expenditures on research and development, or insufficient sales to justify the company's infrastructure.

A high return on assets can be a signal of a highly efficient operation or exceptionally effective management. Or, it could be a signal that the company is using overly conservative accounting policies, or spending insufficient money on research and development.

A declining return on assets can signal a weakening company, declining sales volume, declining overall efficiency, or inappropriate management policy making.

This ratio should be examined in the context of the company's other ratios, in comparison to other companies within the same industry, and in comparison to itself over time.

RETURN ON EQUITY   **Profitability measure**

Two commonly used methods:

$$\text{Return on Equity} = \frac{\text{Net income}}{\text{Shareholders' equity}}$$

$$\text{Return on Equity} = \frac{\text{Return on assets (investments)}}{(1 - \text{Debt/Assets})}$$

Where:
1. *net income* means net profit, the excess of all revenues less all expenses.
2. *shareholders' equity* means the total equity investment in the company, including preferred stock, common stock, paid-in capital, and retained earnings.
3. return on assets means net income divided by total assets.
4. *debts/assets* means total debt divided by total assets.

This ratio, composed of items from both the balance sheet and the income statement, tests the efficiency of the company's use of its equity capital. Stated differently, the return on equity ratio is a measure of the company's ability to earn profits on shareholder equity. Generally, the higher the return on equity ratio, the more efficiently the company is operating, and the better the return available to shareholders.

This ratio, similar in nature to the return on invested capital and the return on assets ratios, measures efficiency in use of the shareholder capital. In general, this ratio is the cornerstone of the financial analysis process, because it is management's express responsibility to maximize this ratio.

A low return on equity ratio can signal a company with inefficient operations or ineffective management. On the other hand, such a situation could result from extremely aggressive accounting policies, significant expenditures on research and development, insufficient sales to justify the company's infrastructure, or a preponderance of debt in a company's capital structure.

An unreasonably high return on equity can be a signal of a highly efficient operation or exceptionally effective management. Or, it could be a signal that the company is using overly conservative accounting policies, or spending insufficient money on research and development.

A declining return on equity can signal a weakening company, declining sales volume, declining overall efficiency, or inappropriate management policy making.

This ratio should be examined in the context of the company's other ratios, in comparison to other companies within the same industry, and in comparison to itself over time.

RETURN ON INVESTED CAPITAL

Profitability measure

$$\text{Return on Invested Capital} = \frac{\text{Net income} + \text{Interest on funded debt}}{\text{Total capitalization}}$$

Where:

1. *net income* means net profit, the excess of all revenues less all expenses.
2. *interest on funded debt* means the interest payable on all of the company's fixed liabilities.
3. *total capitalization* means all fixed liabilities and shareholders' equity, in essence representing the total long-term investment in the company from all sources.

This ratio, composed of items from both the balance sheet and the income statement, tests the efficiency of the capital employed by the company. In essence, this ratio tests the productivity of the company's long-term invested capital. The higher this ratio, the better the company is managing its operations and the more profitably it is employing capital.

This ratio, similar in nature to the return on assets and the return on equity ratios, measures efficiency in the use of capital. Unfortunately, a high return on invested capital does not necessarily translate into a high return on assets or a high return on equity, since this ratio excludes the effects of interest. Thus, a company could have a high return on invested capital yet have a low (or negative) return on equity or assets.

A low return on invested capital can signal a company with inefficient operations or ineffective management. On the other hand, such a situation could result from extremely aggressive accounting policies, significant expenditures on research and development, or insufficient sales to justify the company's infrastructure.

An unreasonably high return on invested capital can be a signal of a highly efficient operation or exceptionally effective management. Or, it could be a signal that the company is using overly conservative accounting policies or spending insufficient money on research and development.

A declining return on invested capital can signal a weakening company, declining sales volume, declining overall efficiency, or inappropriate management policy making.

This ratio should be examined in the context of the company's other ratios, in comparison to other companies within the same industry, and in comparison to itself over time.

TOTAL ASSET TURNOVER   Activity measure

$$\text{Total Asset Turnover} = \frac{\text{Net sales}}{\text{Total assets}}$$

Where:
1. *net sales* means gross sales less any discounts, returns, and refunds.
2. *total assets* means all assets owned by the company, whether they are currently being used or not, including current, fixed, sundry, and intangible assets.

This ratio, composed of items from both the balance sheet and the income statement, tests the efficiency of the company's use of its assets. Stated differently, the total asset turnover ratio is a measure of the revenue generated by the company's invested assets. Generally, the higher the total asset turnover ratio the more efficiently the company is operating.

A low total asset turnover ratio can signal poor sales or general inefficiency. It can also signal that the company has assets deployed in an inefficient fashion—that is, the company is not generating sufficient sales to justify the assets it has deployed.

An unreasonably high total asset turnover ratio can signal highly efficient use of company's assets, indicating that the company is generating a lot of sales per dollar of invested capital. On the other hand, it could be a sign that the company lacks sufficient infrastructure or is in need of more capital with which to operate.

A declining ratio can signal anything from slowing sales, declining efficiency, and aging equipment, to a company generating excess cash that is being poorly used. On the other hand, an increasing ratio can signal increasing sales and better asset utilization.

This ratio should be examined in the context of the company's other ratios, in comparison to other companies within the same industry, and in comparison to itself over time.

TECHNICAL ANALYSIS

Technical analysis, whether applied to a specific security or to the market as a whole, focuses on the *qualitative* factors of trading. Technicians concentrate on studying chart patterns, price trends, market theories, sentiment indicators, and price action of the market averages and indices to determine what the future holds. In short, technical analysis lets past and present price and trading patterns predict what future price and trading patterns will be.

For years controversy has raged between fundamental and technical analysts regarding the technician's place on Wall Street. Strict fundamentalists cite the Random-Walk theory as the basis for their case. In a nutshell, the theory says that each successive change in price is statistically independent of the last—that is, neither the size nor the direction of the last step or set of steps is of any predictive value in determining the size and direction of the next step as "a drunk wanders in the woods." Technical analysts counter this argument in two ways. First, they say "don't fight the tape" and show how their charts have helped them to accurately predict price actions in the past, and then they point to the number of technical analysts on the "Street" collecting large paychecks.

As far as this author is concerned, both technical and fundamental analysts have earned their place on Wall Street—that is, both techniques have their own use. And, as long as a sufficient number of investors follow them, then the techniques themselves will have the characteristics of "self-fulfilling" prophecies.

SOURCE OF DATA

The primary source of the data used in technical analysis is the ticker tape. Originally, the words *ticker tape* referred to the data tape that was printed by the old NYSE ticker machines. These machines "reported" transactions as they occurred, including ticker symbols, volume, and other specialty characteristics as noted, running at speeds up to 900 characters per minute. However, with the onset of the age of electronics and the expansion of trading volume, the term has come to refer to the new, faster electronic display boards that have replaced the old ticker machines.

Along the same lines, in 1974, a new computerized system was implemented to report securities transactions occurring in the various marketplaces on a single ticker tape system known as the *consolidated tape*. Under this system, all NYSE-listed securities are reported on the NYSE ticker tape (Network A), and all AMEX-listed and regionally traded securities are reported on the AMEX ticker tape (Network B).

Identification of the particular exchange on which each transaction occurs is noted by a letter character following an ampersand (&), which in turn follows the normal ticker symbol. The lettering system is simple: B stands for Boston, C stands for Cincinnati, M stands for the Midwest, O stands for Instinet (an institutional trading system), P stands for Pacific, T stands for the Third market (OTC trading of listed securities), and X stands for Philadelphia. Thus, the tape now contains more data than it ever did, and it is organized in an easier-to-use fashion.

This new technology notwithstanding, the source of the data used in technical analysis is still the same—it comes from the tape. By ''reading'' the tape, technicians are able to discern a number of things about the market: what is being traded, how heavily it is being traded, how fast the market is moving, what direction it is moving in, and how widespread the movement is. Then, by applying a set of time-tested techniques to analyze this data, the technician can ''listen'' to what the market is saying, and invest accordingly.

The three key pieces of data that technical analysis employs are *price, volume,* and the *time* of occurrence. Though used in a variety of ways, several general rules apply to the usage of this information:

1. Trends continue until such time as they are broken, at which point they reverse.
2. Price data, sequentially organized, is used to determine what trends are currently in force.
3. Volume data, when studied in relation to price, is used to confirm or deny the conclusions drawn about trends. Strong volume is generally supportive; weak volume is generally neutral or unsupportive.
4. Momentum, which is defined as the rate of change in price and volume movements, are used to confirm changes in trends. Increasing momentum is supportive, decreasing momentum is unsupportive.

In addition to using the raw data provided by the tape, technical analysis also employs a number of data manipulation techniques to get as much information out of this data as possible.

One such technique is to examine the momentum of the data. *Momentum* is calculated by taking the difference between pieces of data separated by a fixed interval of time. For instance, to calculate a five-day momentum value for price, each day's price is subtracted from the price that occurred five days before. Then, this new set of data, which represents the rate of change in price over a five-day period, is analyzed for its trend. From this then, conclusions can be drawn whether a price trend is strengthening or weakening, which in turn will help determine whether the trend is likely to continue or reverse.

Another frequently used technique examines moving averages of the data. *Moving averages* are used in technical analysis to help smooth out the random day-to-day variations that occur in data, so that legitimate trends can be more accurately identified. To calculate moving averages, rolling daily data is summed and divided by the number of days in the average. For instance, a simple three-day moving average is constructed by taking a rolling three days' worth of data, summing it, and dividing the resulting number by three. In this fashion, the effects of any random occurrence, which would otherwise significantly distort the data, is reduced. But, by the same token, the effects of any legitimate occurrence is also reduced. Thus, one should be aware that as the number of days in a moving average increases, the indicator becomes less responsive to short-term fluctuations and is slower to identify changes in trends.

Aside from the number of days used to construct a moving average, a number of other variations have also been developed. One such variation, known as the *simple moving average,* treats all data equally, thereby ignoring the data's timing and pattern of occurrence. In contrast, *weighted moving averages* apply weighting factors to some of the data, typically giving the most recent data the heaviest weighting in order to give it added importance.

Some technical systems even go so far as to ignore current data in favor of moving average data, and some study the relationship between current data and moving average data or between sets of moving average data. In general, however, all technical systems that employ moving averages follow the same set of rules: they buy when prices move above the moving average and sell when prices move below the moving average.

Along the same lines, a number of other proprietary techniques have been developed using data manipulated in a variety of fashions. Just about every well-known technician has developed some methodology that he or she uses to draw conclusions about the market. And, since each of these technical gurus use slightly different methodology, it should be no surprise to find them making public pronouncements at different times with different objectives in mind, all from reading the same tape.

AVERAGES AND INDICES

Averages and indices describe the general tone and direction of the market. Additionally, they are used as a basis for comparison.

The primary difference between an index and an average is the number of securities that each is based on:

- An *average* is based on a small number of securities.
- An *index* is based on a large number of securities.

Two primary methods used in calculating averages are:

- summing the market value of the selected stocks and dividing by the number of issues; and
- summing the market value of the selected stocks and dividing by some divisor that takes into consideration an allowance for stock splits or other changes in capitalization.

Following is a list of, and brief description for, several of the more typically referred to averages and indices.

The Dow Jones Averages

There are four separate Dow Jones Averages, each based on a different subset of NYSE listed securities—the *Industrial Average,* based 30 large industrial companies; the *Transportation Average,* based on 20 large transportation companies; the *Utility Average,* based on 15 large utility companies; and the *Composite Average,* based on all 65 stocks that comprise the other three averages.

The divisor for each average is adjusted, although only downward, for stock splits and stock dividends that would affect the average by five or more points.

All four averages are expressed in points, not dollars and cents.

Standard & Poor's Index

There are five separate Standard & Poor's Indices, each based on a different subset of securities, most of which are traded on the NYSE. The S & P *400 Industrial Index* is based on 400 large industrial companies; the *20 Transportation Index* is based on 20 large transportation companies; the *40 Utility Index* is based on 40 large utility companies; the *40 Financial Index* is based on 40 large financial service companies; and the *500 Index* is based on all 500 stocks that comprise the other four indices.

Each index is weighted—in making the calculation, the price of each stock is multiplied by its number of listed shares. Thus, companies with larger market capitalization reflect more heavily in the indices than do companies with smaller market capitalization.

All five indices are expressed in points, not dollars and cents.

The New York Stock Exchange Indices

The New York Stock Exchange Indices are actually five separate indices, each based on a different subset of NYSE securities. Every stock on the exchange is classified into one of four industry groups: the *industrials, transportations, utilities,* and *financials.* The *composite* comprises all the stocks making up the other four groups, thereby representing the "market."

The indices are calculated and printed on the tape every half-hour, and reflect the combined market-value change in their component issues. Each index is weighted—in making the calculation, the price of each stock is multiplied by its number of listed shares.

The composite index is quoted in dollars and cents, and the other four indices are shown only in terms of point movements. All five indices were originally set to a value of 50.00 as of the close of the market on December 31, 1965.

The American Stock Exchange Price Change Index

The American Stock Exchange is based on all common stocks and warrants traded on the ASE. The index is computed without weighting and is based on the net change in price for all issues from their previous close. Since the index is not weighted, each issue traded on the exchange is given equal consideration in the calculation. The divisor is adjusted for all new listings and delistings on the exchange.

The index is expressed in dollars and cents, and is reported on the tape every half hour.

The NASDAQ-OTC Price Indices

The NASDAQ-OTC Price Indices are actually seven separate indices, each based on a different subset of NASDAQ securities. All domestic common stocks traded on NASDAQ are classified into one of six industry groups: the *industrials, banks, insurance, transportation, utilities,* and *other financials*. The *composite* comprises the stocks that make up the other six groups. Each index is adjusted for all changes in capitalization, as well as for any domestic additions or deletions to NASDAQ.

Each index is expressed in points, not dollars and cents. All seven indices were originally set to a value of 100.00 as of the close of the market on February 5, 1971.

The Value Line Average

The Value Line Average is comprised of 1700 stocks listed on various exchanges that are regularly reviewed by the Value Line Investment Survey. The average is a geometric average computed without weighting, expressed in the form of an index. The index is adjusted for changes in capitalization, as well as for any additions and deletions to the list of stocks that is regularly reviewed.

The index is expressed in points, not dollars and cents. It was originally set to a value of 100.00 as of the close of the market on June 30, 1961.

CHARTS AND TRENDS

Charts

Charts are used by market technicians to describe and evaluate the price actions occurring in the market. Charts are helpful in identifying trends, spotting changes in trends known as *reversals,* underscoring significant trading developments, and predicting the timing and strength of future developments.

Several different charting methods are used, but the two most predominant are:

- *Point and figure charts*—these plot price movements without regard to the timing of such movements, using a series of X's to represent price rises and a series of O's to represent price declines.
- *Vertical line charts*—These plot price movements through a series of vertical lines, with distance along the vertical axis representing price and distance along the horizontal axis representing time. Several variations exist on this theme, including: *close only; high, low charts; open, high, low charts; open, close, high, low charts;* and the like. For example, an open, high, low, close chart, uses vertical lines to represent the extent of the price move, with the ends of each line representing the high and low price, and the horizontal bars on the left and right side of each line representing the opening and closing prices, respectively.

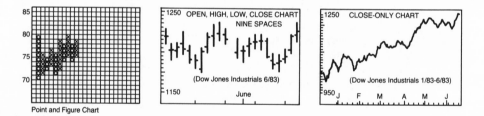

Trends

Trendlines are helpful in determining the trends currently in force. Trends that are very brief are called *minor trends;* those lasting a few weeks are known as *intermediate trends;* and those lasting for a period of months are *major trends.*

In an up market, the trendline is drawn by connecting each successively higher "bottom." As long as the market remains on or above the line, the uptrend remains in force.

In a down market, the trendline is drawn by connecting each successively lower "top." As long as the market remains on or below this line, the downtrend remains in force.

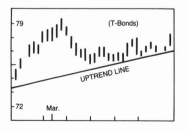

The theory behind trendlines is that when a trendline is penetrated, the trend that was previously in force is reversed. Thus, if an uptrend line is penetrated, a downtrend is put in force. Conversely, if a downtrend line is penetrated, an uptrend is put in force. Obviously, when an uptrend line is penetrated it is time to sell, and when a downtrend line is penetrated it is time to buy.

The slope of a trendline is also very important. The steeper the trendline, the more easily it can be broken—even a brief sideways move can do it. Thus, extremely steep trendlines are not considered very authoritative, whereas gentler sloping trendlines are.

Other factors to consider in evaluating trendlines are: the number of tops or bottoms that have formed to support the trendline; the duration of the trendline; and the slope of the trendline.

As trendlines are penetrated, new trendlines must be drawn. As this occurs, a pattern of *fan lines* will be created. Though trendline theory suggests that a reversal occurs whenever a trendline is penetrated, one must examine the penetration to determine its relative validity. This is done by examining what the volume was at the time of occurrence and what the closing price of the security was for the day. The typical rule of thumb is that when the third fan line is broken, the trend has been reversed.

Be aware that once a trendline has been legitimately penetrated, a *pullback* often will occur. That is to say, when an uptrend is broken, a security will sell off for a few days and then rally back before it begins to finally trend lower.

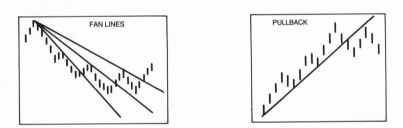

During the normal course of trading, price levels will also, from time to time, be reached that temporarily halt a downward movement in price. Such levels are called *support levels*. By the same token, from time to time, price levels will be reached that temporarily halt an upward movement in price. Such points are called *resistance levels*.

Support and resistance levels occur for many reasons, among them congestion areas, former tops, and former bottoms. In the case of a downtrend, a former bottom, once penetrated, becomes a resistance level. In the case of an uptrend, a former top, once surpassed, becomes a support level. A congestion area, once broken out of, becomes either a support or a resistance level, depending on the direction of the trend.

Note that once a support or resistance level has been tested, it is weakened. Tested again, it may still hold. But tested a third time, it will usually give way.

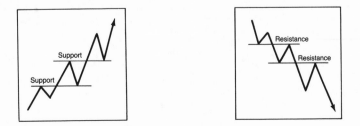

REVERSAL PATTERNS

Reversal patterns predict future price movements by identifying trend changes as they occur. Though price action itself is the primary means used to identify these trend changes, more often than not, timing and volume validation is required to confirm such conclusions.

To reverse intermediate or major trends requires significant price action to occur. Typically, these patterns will take on one of the following forms.

Head and Shoulders Tops—these signify an upcoming decline. In this pattern, which is known as one of the most reliable of all reversal patterns, the left shoulder is usually formed at the end of an extensive, high volume advance. Then the head forms on heavy upside volume and lighter downside volume, and the right shoulder forms on a rally having less volume than either of the two previous rallies have had. Penetration of the neckline (the line formed by the bottoms of the two shoulders), provides final confirmation of the reversal and completes the pattern. Be aware, most head and shoulder patterns are not perfectly symmetrical.

Head and Shoulders Bottoms—these signify an upcoming rally. Though the chart pattern appears to be an upside-down image of the head and shoulders top, the volume pattern is different—it increases as the price rallies from the bottom of the head and increases even more dramatically on the rally from the right shoulder. If this is not the case, the head and shoulders bottom may be false, and the decline most likely will continue.

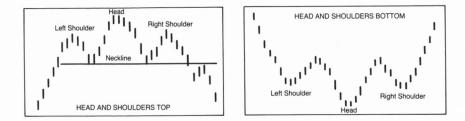

Double Top Formations—these signify an upcoming decline. Probably one of the trickiest patterns to identify, a double top forms after a significant rally. True double tops are differentiated from "consolidation" patterns through validation of volume, time, and extent of decline from the highs. For a true double top to occur, the first sell-off should be deep and long, the right top should occur on lighter volume than the left top, and the lows created that separate the left and right tops should be easily broken by the sell-off from the right top.

Double Bottoms—these signify an upcoming rally. Though the chart pattern appears to be an upside-down image of the double top, the volume pattern is different—it shows a marked increase on the rally from the second bottom.

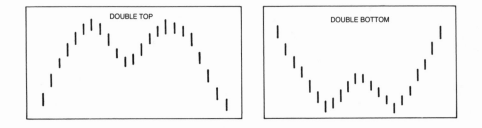

Triple Tops—these signify an upcoming decline. The triple top typically forms after a long advance, and is comprised of a sell-off, a light volume rally, another sell-off, a still lighter volume rally, and another sell-off, the last one penetrating both valleys.

Triple Bottoms—these signify an upcoming rally. Though the chart pattern appears to be an upside-down image of the triple top, the volume pattern is different—it shows a marked increase in the rallies, especially on the rally from the third bottom.

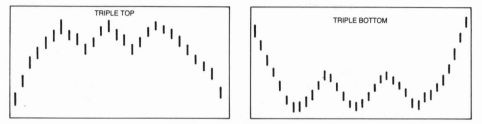

Some price action, though not strong enough to reverse intermediate or major trends, is strong enough to reverse minor trends. Typically, these patterns will take on one of the following forms.

Rising Wedges—these signify an upcoming decline. Denoted by the upper boundary line, constructed from successive tops, slanting up at an angle shallower than the lower boundary line, constructed from successive bottoms, this rising wedge-shaped pattern suggests a price decline will occur as soon as the lower boundary line is penetrated. Be aware that rising wedges are only applicable in bear markets—otherwise they represent "flags" or "pennants."

Falling Wedges—these signify an upcoming rally. Though the chart pattern appears to be an upside-down image of the rising wedge, price action moving out of a falling wedge is quite different. Typically, the price is apt to drift sidewise and "saucer-out" before it begins to rise.

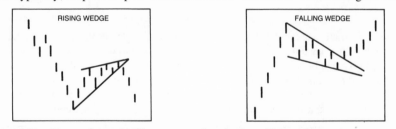

Reversal Day Tops—these signify an upcoming decline. This trading pattern occurs when prices move higher throughout the day, but then close near the lows of the day. Typically, the close is below both the opening and the midpoint of the day's range.

Reversal Day Bottoms—these signify an upcoming rally. This trading pattern occurs when prices move lower throughout the day, but then close near the highs of the day. Typically, the close is above both the opening and the midpoint of the day's range.

CONSOLIDATION PATTERNS

Markets do not always move either up or down—sometimes they move sideways. These sideway movements can be extremely brief, or they may take a considerable amount of time to occur. In fact, sometimes these sideway movements will even penetrate the trend before the market resumes its previous course. Therefore, it is imperative to be able to recognize these sideway movements for what they are, so as to not confuse such "consolidation" patterns with true reversals.

Triangles

Triangles describe a sideways movement in price action resulting from indecisiveness by both buyers and sellers. In essence, they represent a period of consolidation from which prices will almost always continue in the direction of the original trend. Typically, they are characterized by a narrowing in the range of trading highs and lows accompanied by *decreasing* volume. Then, when break-out does occur, it is usually accompanied by a sharp *increase* in volume.

The Symmetrical Triangle—this is formed by a succession of narrowing price fluctuations, resulting in a chart pattern bounded by both a downslanting line and an upslanting line. Each symmetrical triangle, by definition, must have at least four reversal points.

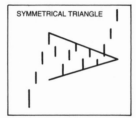

Normally, break-out from a symmetrical triangle results in a continuation of the trend, although from time to time, reversals have been known to occur. Be aware that if volume is light when a break-out occurs in the same direction as the trend, it may be a false move called an *end run,* and the trend may soon be penetrated. On the other hand, if volume is heavy and the break-out occurs in the direction opposite to the trend, then it may be a false move called a *shakeout* and the trend may well continue along its original course.

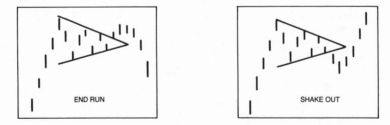

Ascending Right Angles—these are formed by a succession of narrowing price fluctuations, resulting in a chart pattern bounded by an upsloping line and a horizontal line. As the triangle lengthens, volume tends to diminish. Typically, when prices finally do break, they will break out on the upside.

This formation occurs when there is a large amount of supply overhanging the market at a fixed price.

Descending Right Angles—these are formed by a succession of narrowing price fluctuations, resulting in a chart pattern bounded by a downsloping line and a horizontal line. As the triangle lengthens, volume tends to diminish. Typically, when prices finally do break, they will break out on the downside.

This formation occurs when there is a large amount of demand overhanging the market at a fixed price.

Rectangles

Rectangles—these are formed as a result of a battle between two groups overhanging the market at different fixed prices. They appear on the chart as a sideways movement bounded by a horizontal line on both the top and the bottom. As the rectangle lengthens, volume tends to diminish.

Unfortunately, rectangles are of little predictive value in determining whether the trend will continue. In addition, break-outs, when they finally do occur, are quite likely to be followed by a pullback.

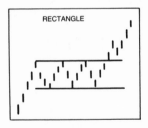

Flags and Pennants

Flags and Pennants—are formed after a dynamic, nearly straight move up or down that occurs on heavy volume. On the chart, a pennant looks very similar to a flag, except that it is bounded by converging rather than parallel lines. Both flags and pennants are quite reliable indicators that the trend will continue, though they must conform to three rules in order to be valid: First, they should occur after a very sharp move up or down. Second, volume should decline as the pattern lengthens. And third, prices must break out of the pattern within a few weeks.

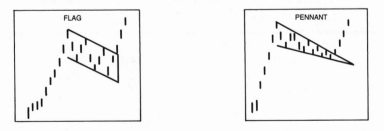

GAPS

When a market is rapidly trading, sometimes *gaps,* or holes, occur in the trading pattern. Basically, a gap is formed in an up market when the highest price one day is lower than the lowest price the following day. Conversely, a gap is formed in a down market when the lowest price one day is higher than the highest price the following day.

Most gaps mark the beginning or end of a trend, although some are found in the middle. Thus, it is important to be able to determine which type of gap has occurred in order to avoid getting on the wrong side of a market.

Common Gaps—these are formed when order imbalances occur during sideways trading ranges known as "congestion areas." In this kind of trading pattern, once a gap has occurred, prices move up and down through the trading range until they eventually return to the price level of the gap. Then they trade normally through the gap area, thereby acting to "fill the gap."

Common gaps, which are a relatively frequent occurrence in consolidation patterns, are a signal that a break-out is going to occur, and that the break-out will be in the same direction as the preceding trend. Be aware, common gaps also called by a number of other names, including: "congestion gaps," "temporary gaps," "pattern gaps," and "area gaps."

Breakaway Gaps—these occur as prices break away from areas of congestion, especially from those patterns known as *ascending* or *descending right angles*. The significance of breakaway gaps is that they demonstrate the strength behind the "change in sentiment" that caused the gap in the first place.

If a breakaway gap occurs on extremely heavy volume, the market most likely will not "fill the gap." In this event, prices will continue to move in the direction of the trend. On the other hand, if volume is relatively light on a breakaway gap, then there is a good chance that the gap will be filled before prices resume their trend.

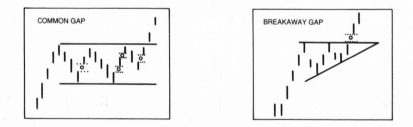

Measuring Gaps—these are formed during rapid, straightline advances or declines, usually somewhere around the midpoint of a move. Since they only occur around the halfway point, they are enormously helpful for approximating the move's ultimate price objective. To do this, merely double the distance between the beginning point and the measuring gap.

Exhaustion Gaps—these occur at the end of a large, rapid, move and signal that the end of the move is near. This notwithstanding, the major problem with exhaustion gaps is that they can easily be mistaken for measuring gaps. Obviously, a mistake of this nature could be very costly. Thus, it is imperative to confirm that a gap is an exhaustion gap before drawing any conclusions. To do this, one should examine other factors.

Typically, exhaustion gaps are accompanied by particularly heavy volume. Also, they have been known to occur in conjunction with reversal day patterns.

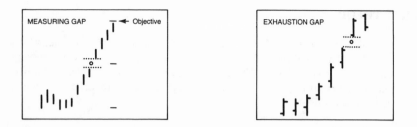

Island Gaps or Island Reversals—these are formed when an exhaustion gap is followed very closely by another gap, at or around the same price point but occurring in the opposite direction of the previous trend. In essence, this kind of price action isolates the trading that occurs between the two gaps, creating an "island of activity" that is separated from the rest of the trading pattern.

Though occurring relatively rarely, island gaps are an extremely good indicator of a trend reversal, graphically demonstrating the strength behind the "change in sentiment."

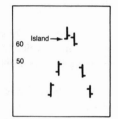

MARKET THEORIES

Over the years, many technical analysis theories have come and gone, working well for brief periods of time and then failing miserably when some unforeseen market event causes the theory to go awry. This notwithstanding, several theories have lasted for periods of time long enough to have become well respected throughout the entire technical community, and deserve mention accordingly.

The Dow Theory

Dow Theory is based on the writings of Charles Dow, an editor of *The Wall Street Journal* in the early twentieth century. His theory proposes that market averages rise or fall in advance of similar changes in business activity. Therefore, by properly reading the averages, one can predict possible future market trends.

According to Dow Theory, there are three basic market movements.

Primary Movement (Major Trend)—is a long-term trend lasting from one to five years, typically known as a bull or bear market.

Secondary Movements (Intermediate Trends)—are a reverse of the primary movement and last for a short period of time, typically in the range of one to three months. Many such shifts will occur during a bull or bear market before there is a reversal in the primary trend.

Secondary movements do two things: they provide information for medium-term trading decisions, and they help identify the life expectancy of the primary movement. In this regard, the theory states that a major trend is reversed only when it is penetrated by a secondary movement.

Day-to-Day Movements (Minor Trends)—these fluctuations usually last for less than six days and are of little importance.

The Advance-Decline Theory

Advance-Decline Theory is based on the Breadth-of-the-Market Index. This index is computed by taking the net advance-decline figure and dividing it by the total number of issues traded that day, thus giving an indication of whether the market as a whole is gaining or losing strength.

If the advance-decline net balance is cumulatively positive, the market may well have enough strength to reach for higher ground. Conversely, if net declines continually surpass net advances, the market may be facing a ''sell-off.''

The Short Interest ''Cushion'' Theory

The Short Interest ''Cushion'' Theory states that short sellers will become buyers of stock at some future point to cover their positions, and the trading cushion of these potential buyers will support a declining market or accelerate a rising one. Short interest is calculated by dividing the total number of short sales outstanding on the NYSE by the average daily trading volume on the exchange for the month. It is published monthly in *Barron's*.

Short interest exceeding one day's average trading volume is a bullish sign, and short interest above one-and-a-half times daily volume indicates a ''buy'' signal.

The Confidence Theory

The Confidence Theory states that price movements are based on increases and decreases in the amount confidence that investors hold regarding the future trends of the market. In other words, the feelings that investors have regarding what the *future* holds are more important than the feelings they hold about the *present*.

Barron's calculates and publishes a confidence index that uses bond yields to measure investor's willingness to assume risk. This index is based on the following presumption: if the yield differential between high-grade bonds and low-grade bonds contracts, this suggests that investors have greater confidence, are willing to assume more risk, and thus expect the market to rise. By the same reasoning, when the yield differential expands, the market is expected to fall.

Dow Jones Utility Average Theory

The Dow Jones Utility Average Theory states that the Dow Jones Utility Average is a leading indicator of changing trends in the stock market. The basis for this assumption is simple: since utility stocks are so interest sensitive, they tend to react more quickly to changes in the expectation for interest rates. Thus, if the Dow Jones Utility Average is moving up, expectations are that interest rates will fall. Lower interest rates, of course, mean that the cost of doing business will be lowered, that corporate profitability will rise, and that the market is sure to follow.

Over time, it has been found that if the current reading for the Dow Jones Utility Average plots *above* its own 15-week moving average, then the market as a whole can be considered in an uptrend. By the same token, when the current reading drops *below* its 15-week moving average, the market as a whole can be considered in a downtrend.

Retracement Theory

Over the years technicians have noted that markets never seem to move steadily in one direction or the other, but rather seem to "see-saw" their way toward their eventually price objective. With this in mind, retracement theory suggests that each movement in the primary direction of the trend is followed by some reaction or retracement in the opposite direction, and that the amount of retracement is some mathematical function of the primary move.

Though typical retracements recapture from one-third to two-thirds of the primary move, most technicians agree that 50 percent of the move is the single most likely amount of retracement to expect. Proprietary work has been done in this area by several noted technicians, but suffice it to say that Gann, Fibonnaci, and Elliott Wave Theories are all based on the general concept of retracement theory.

SENTIMENT THEORIES

Over the years, many theories have been developed that measure the "mood" of the market in order to determine its future direction. To characterize the "mood," these so-called market sentiment theories concentrate on the market's three main groups of participants: the small investor or customer; the floor specialist; and the exchange member.

Odd-Lot Purchases and Short Sales Theory

Based on the work by George A. Drew, who noted that the "odd-lot" customer is frequently wrong, this theory suggests that a trend toward increased odd-lot selling is bullish, whereas a trend toward decreased odd-lot selling is bearish.

The odd-lot short sale ratio is calculated by dividing the odd-lot short sales on the NYSE by the weekly total short sales of all NYSE participants. The odd-lot purchase ratio is calculated by dividing total odd-lot purchases on the NYSE by the weekly total purchases of all NYSE participants. Both sets of figures can be found in *Barron's* and *The Wall Street Journal,* although there is a two-week lag.

The higher the odd-lot short sale ratio is, and the lower the odd-lot purchase ratio is, the more bearish the small investor—thus, the more bullish the market.

Specialist Short Sales Theory

Specialist Short Sales Theory is based on the principle that the "smart money" knows what is about to happen in the market. Thus, the theory suggests that heavy specialist short selling is bearish, and light specialist short selling is bullish.

The specialist short sale ratio is computed by dividing the weekly total of shares sold short by the NYSE specialists by the weekly total of shares sold short by all NYSE participants. These figures are available in *Barron's* and *The Wall Street Journal,* although there is a two-week lag in the publication of this data.

A "buy" signal is generated whenever a one-week reading falls below 33 percent, or the average of the past four weekly readings is below 35 percent. A "sell" signal is generated whenever a one-week reading exceeds 58 percent, or the average of the past four weekly readings exceeds 55 percent.

Member Short Sales Theory

Similar to the Specialist Short Sale Theory, the Member Short Sale Theory suggests that heavy short selling on the part of the members is bearish, and light short selling on the part of members is bullish.

The member short-sale ratio is calculated by dividing the total of shares sold short by members of the NYSE by the weekly total number of shares sold short by all NYSE participants. This data is available in *Barron's* and *The Wall Street Journal,* although there is a two-week lag in the publication of this data.

Member short sale ratio readings of under 65 percent suggests that members are extremely bullish, often times indicating that a major or intermediate market uptrend may be at hand.

Member Trading Theory

The Member Trading Theory suggests that net buying by members is a bullish sign, whereas net selling by members is a bearish sign. Net buying or selling is calculated by subtracting the number of shares sold by NYSE members from the number of shares bought by NYSE members. This data is available in *Barron's* and *The Wall Street Journal,* although there is a two-week lag in the publication of this data.

Please note that some technicians feel that an exponential moving average of member net buying generates one of the best indicators of changes in intermediate and major trends.

Advisory Sentiment Theory

Advisory Sentiment Theory looks, from a contrarian perspective, at the opinions held by the segment of investment professionals who act as investment advisors. As a group they are slow to recognize the beginning of a bull market, though they typically turn bullish very quickly after market prices have started up. By the same token, they are very poor in picking the top of a bull market, which is the start of a bear market. However, whenever this group turns overly pessimistic, with 60 percent or more expressing negative sentiments, this should be construed as a strong "buy" signal—the bear market has just bottomed out.

An excellent source to get a reading on advisory sentiment is the "Sentiment Index" maintained by *Investor's Intelligence,* a publication highlighted in the newsletter section of this book.

Customer's Margin Debt Theory

Customer's Margin Debt Theory suggests that the buying patterns of margin investors are a good indicator of the future trend of the market. That is to say, when these sophisticated investors are borrowing money heavily to buy into the market, the future market trend will be up. By the same token, when these individuals are liquidating stocks and reducing their margin debt, it is a good indicator that the market will be moving lower.

On the last trading day of each month, the NYSE calculates the total amount of debt owed to member firms by their customers, although the information is not released for two to three weeks. Then, at that time, it is available directly from the NYSE and published in *Barron's.*

In analyzing a plot of customer margin debt against its own 12-month moving average, "buy" signals are generated whenever the current figure moves above the moving average line, and "sell" signals are generated whenever the figure moves below it.

Free Credit Balance Theory

Free Credit Balance Theory is based on the fact that only small, less-sophisticated investors allow money to sit idly by in a free credit balance state with a brokerage firm. Thus, the theory suggests that when this free credit balance increases, it is a sign that the small, less-sophisticated investors have decided to raise cash, which in turn is a sign that the market will be moving higher. On the other hand, when this balance falls, it is a sign that the market will be moving lower.

The total free credit balance held by member firms is calculated monthly by the NYSE and is available directly from the exchange. It is also published in *Barron's.*

BREADTH-OF-MARKET AND SHORT-TERM TRADING INDICATORS

Breadth-of-market indicators are used to measure how widespread the trading patterns seen in the market are. Aside from acting as a barometer of the market's general condition, they also help determine what phase of the trend the market is in and the length of time left in the phase.

Short-term trading indicators also measure the market's condition, looking at internal activity on a moment to moment basis.

The Advance-Decline Line

The advance-decline line is the most commonly used indicator for measuring the condition of the market. It is calculated by taking the difference between the number of advancing and the number of declining issues on a daily basis, and adding or subtracting the resulting number to a running total. The running total is then plotted over time, and the resulting chart is used to draw conclusions about the internal strength or weakness of the market.

In general, when the advance-decline line is rising, the market is gathering internal strength, and higher prices are in store. On the other hand, when the advance-decline line is falling, the market is losing strength and lower prices will follow. At market tops and bottoms, the advance-decline line diverges from the trend of the market averages, showing weakness before the market hits the top and strength before the market hits the bottom. This notwithstanding, practical experience has shown that the advance-decline line is better at picking tops than it is at picking bottoms.

Many proprietary indicators and indices have been developed that use the advance-decline line as a basis for their analysis. Some employ moving averages of the advance-decline line. Others analyze the relationship of the advance-decline line to its moving average. Still others apply weights to the advance-decline line based on time or trading volume.

The Unchanged Issues Index

The Unchanged Issues Index represents a commonly used indicator for measuring the condition of the market. It is calculated by dividing the number of issues which are unchanged in price each day by the total number of stocks traded during the day.

In general, this index ranges from 5 percent to 25 percent— readings close to 5 percent are considered bullish whereas readings close to 25 percent are considered bearish.

Relative Strength

Relative strength is a measure of an industry group's market performance in comparison to the market's overall performance. It is calculated by individually comparing the performance of each industry group against the performance of the New York Stock Exchange Composite Index, and then rank ordering each industry group in terms of its relative strength to all the other groups.

In general, it is better to buy issues in strong industry groups than in weak ones, since the strong industry groups, by their very definition, are leading the market.

The Most Active Issues

The Most Active Issues represent those stocks that are trading the most volume each day. A list of the 15 most active issues is published daily and can be found in *The Wall Street Journal*.

The Most Active Issues list is used in two ways: to determine what "class" of stocks is leading the market and what direction the market will move in the near term. To determine the "class" of leadership, each issue on the list is cross-referenced against its price. Then, the percentage of issues priced at or above the arbitrary price of $40 per share is calculated. When this percentage is more than 50 percent, the market is said to be led by *quality* issues. When this percentage is below 50 percent, the market is said to be led by *speculative* issues. Quality markets show internal strength, and speculative markets show internal weakness.

When used for determining the near-term direction of the market, each issue on the list is examined to see if it shows a gain for the day. Then, a "percentage gainer" figure is calculated and worked into a 10-day moving average from which a chart is constructed. Then, the chart is analyzed according to the following rules: A chart showing the indicator moving into the 60-70 percent region and turning down predicts a short-term correction, whereas a chart showing the indicator moving into the 60-70 percent region and continuing up predicts a powerful near-term rally. A chart showing the indicator moving into the 30-35 percent region and turning up predicts a short-term rally, whereas a chart showing the indicator moving into the 30-35 percent region and continuing down predicts a further near-term decline.

New Highs and Lows List

The New Highs and Lows List represents stocks that are at new highs or new lows for the past 52-week period. On a daily basis, this list is available in *The Wall Street Journal*.

Generally speaking, when the number of new highs is expanding, it is a bullish sign for the market, especially if the number of new lows is contracting. Conversely, if the number of new highs is contracting while the number of new lows is expanding, it is a bearish sign for the market. This notwithstanding, it is also imperative to consider what phase the market is in and what types of diverges are occurring between these indicators and the market before any intelligent conclusions can be drawn.

Short-Term Trading (TRIN) or Arms Index

TRIN evaluates buying and selling pressure in the market by measuring the amount of volume going into advancing issues versus the amount of volume going into declining issues. It is calculated as follows:

$$\text{TRIN} = \frac{(\text{\# of advancing issues}/\text{\# of declining issues})}{(\text{upside volume}/\text{downside volume})}$$

TRIN readings below .65 are very bullish, between .65 and .90 are bullish, between .90 and 1.10 are neutral, and above 1.10 are bearish. TRIN is continuously being calculated throughout the trading day, and its readings reflect extremely short-term market sentiment.

Cumulative Tick

Cumulative tick is the single most sensitive of all market indicators. It is calculated by subtracting the total number of stocks that have traded down in price from their previous trade (known as "downticks") from the total number of stocks which have traded up in price from their previous trade (known as "upticks"). All readings above +100 are considered bullish; all readings from −100 to +100 are considered neutral; and all readings below −100 are considered bearish.

SECTION II
DOING IT YOURSELF

DISCOUNT BROKERAGE

On May 1, 1975, the New York and American Stock Exchanges changed the course of Wall Street history forever. It was on that fateful "May Day" that the exchanges agreed to abandon the minimum commission schedule they imposed on their members, thus ushering in the age of negotiated commissions. To be sure, many firms treated the change with scorn and contempt, and some ignored it entirely. But the initial reaction aside, this change ultimately led to the creation of the discount brokerage industry of today.

In almost every issue of *The Wall Street Journal, Barrons,* or any major metropolitan newspaper like the *New York Times* or the *Chicago Tribune,* you can find five to ten advertisements from firms claiming to offer the biggest commission savings coupled with the best execution. Some offer to execute transactions on a cents-per-share basis. Some boast that they will give even small investors up to 70 percent off the pre-1975 standard commission charges. Some even offer a wide range of financial planning services, coupled with a discount commission schedule.

Unfortunately, though these advertisements are indeed eye catching, the fine print associated with each is at best confusing. On one page you find a comparison made by Firm A showing how part of its commission schedule boasts significant savings over that of Firm B's, and on the next page you find an example showing just the reverse. Interestingly enough, both advertisements are right—they just show different subsections of each firm's commission schedule.

It was for these reasons, then, that I conducted an in-depth analysis of the firms calling themselves discount brokers. In each case I asked the firm to complete a standardized questionnaire, asking exactly the same questions in exactly the same manner. Then, in an effort to simplify your job of comparing and contrasting the responses, I made every effort to standardize both the phraseology and the format of their answers. The results of this survey compose the bulk of this chapter.

But before turning our attention to the specific results of the survey, it seems reasonable to provide a little background about the industry in general. In this way you should get a deeper understanding of why specific questions were asked and what the answers purport to tell us. In so doing, you should also gain an enhanced understanding of the process by which the brokerage business transacts the business of buying and selling securities.

BROKERAGE MEMBERSHIP AND WATCHDOG ORGANIZATIONS

The National Association of Securities Dealers

The National Association of Securities Dealers, Inc., or NASD, is a nonstock-issuing, nonprofit organization. It was incorporated under the laws of Delaware in 1936, and registered with the Securities and Exchange Commission (SEC) in 1939. Basically, its primary purpose is to promote high standards of commercial honor in the observance of federal and state securities laws, to adopt and enforce rules of fair practice within the securities industry, to promote equitable treatment of investors, and to investigate grievances between members and the public sector, disciplining members as need be. In essence, it is the self-regulating body of the securities industry which oversees that the industry is acting in a fair and equitable fashion in treating the investing public.

Every firm engaged in the buying or selling of securities for customer accounts must be a member and therefore is under the scrutiny of the NASD.

Securities Investor Protection Corporation

Additionally, every firm engaged in the holding of customer securities must be a member of the Securities Investor Protection Corporation (SIPC). SIPC was established in 1970 as a government-sponsored private corporation designed to ensure the protection of customer accounts.

In the event that a firm holding customer securities gets into financial trouble, SIPC steps in to see that customer accounts are protected up to the full extent of the firm's coverage. Under current rules, SIPC insures and guarantees the repayment of customer accounts up to the value of $500,000, with as much as $100,000 of this insurance available for the repayment of credit or cash balances.

Stock Exchanges and Clearing Corporations

Additionally, many firms at their own option may also maintain membership in one or more of the nation's stock exchanges and/or clearing corporations. Though these memberships are not required, they can be helpful in executing or processing securities transactions. Specifically, an exchange membership allows a firm to execute and clear a transaction on the exchange by "giving up" or specifying its own name as the security buyer or seller. In the event that a firm does not have a "seat" on the exchange, that is, is not a member of the exchange, it must transact business on that exchange through a correspondent firm that does hold a membership. In so doing, the firm is forced to pay for the services of the correspondent through slightly higher transaction charges. Virtually all large firms are members of at least one exchange, with the very largest firms holding memberships in many stock exchanges.

Some firms may also choose to become a clearing member of an exchange but not maintain a seat on that exchange. The benefit of this decision is that the firm has access to the formalized clearing process provided by the clearing corporation, but is not obliged to expend the resources necessary to maintain and staff a seat on the exchange. Under this alternative, the firm maintains both security and bank accounts under the control of the clearing corporation.

Then, when the firm or one of its customers buys a security, the firm's security account is credited for the appropriate security, and the firm's bank account is debited for the appropriate cash. Conversely, when the company or one of its customers sells a security, the reverse occurs. In this way, the settlement of a security transaction, which by decree must occur within five business days from the date on which the transaction actually occurs, is reduced from an otherwise cumbersome physical paper transaction to a computer entry transaction. With less paper to be shuffled, the clearing corporation member benefits from increased back office efficiency and lower overall paper processing costs.

This factor, combined with greater transaction accuracy and the preferential execution rates available to clearing members (higher than those for exchange members but lower than those for nonexchange, nonclearing firms) makes this alternative a very advantageous one for relatively small brokerage firms.

As a further option, some firms may choose to be entirely self-clearing, meaning that they settle all security transactions with physical delivery of certificates. In some sense, this type of processing is at best outdated, but it may represent the most financially advantageous choice for firms doing very small amounts of exchange-related business. Firms that process transactions in this fashion typically act just like an intermediary between the client and the discount window at a correspondent firm.

In effect, the self-clearing firm pays its correspondent firm to process a trade just as you or I would, except the trade is done on a deep commission discount. The correspondent firm in turn processes the trade in its normal fashion through its floor brokers and clearing corporation membership, thus allowing it to amortize its fixed cost over a greater volume of transactions and generating an incremental revenue stream.

Over the years, two different types of self-clearing/correspondent arrangements have come into being: omnibus and fully disclosed. Under an *omnibus* arrangement, the self-clearing firm buys all securities in its own name and does not disclose the name of its client to the correspondent or the name of its correspondent to the client. The self-clearing firm prints all confirmations, receives all money, and corresponds directly with the client with no reference to the firm through which it processes its trades. The self-clearing firm maintains an account on the correspondent's books and settles up with the correspondent accordingly. Meanwhile, the customer maintains an account at the self-clearing firm and settles up with the self-clearing firm accordingly.

Since both transactions settle at the same time, the self-clearing firm's position always remains flat—except for the difference in money caused by the differing commission charges. Specifically, the same security comes in and goes out of the account at the same time, thus leaving the account unchanged. Additionally, money flows into and out of the account in the reverse direction, with the difference in the respective commission charges remaining as compensation for the services rendered by the self-clearing firm.

A significant benefit to this type of arrangement is that the self-clearing firm maintains its independence, both in the eyes of its customers and in its ability to transact business with more than one correspondent. In fact, under this arrangement, a self-clearing firm may have several correspondent relationships going at any one time, and the client will be totally oblivious to them all. Additionally, the self-clearing firm takes on much of the paperwork burden itself, handling customer receipts and deposits, comparing and clearing security trades, mailing out proxies, preparing 1099 forms, sending out monthly statements, and so on. Since this arrangement lifts this burden off of the correspondent, the self-clearing firm can negotiate a larger commission discount and earn a bigger slice of the commission pie.

Under a *fully disclosed* arrangement, the self-clearing firm processes all trades through just one correspondent, and all accounts are held on the books of that correspondent in a fully disclosed fashion. All deliveries of securities and money are made to and from the correspondent, and all documentation will bear the name of the correspondent. In fact, for all intents and purposes, the self-clearing firm will be transparent to the client, except that the correspondent may refer to the self-clearing firm in its paperwork in a "through the courtesy of" fashion.

Under this arrangement, the self-clearing firm pays higher commission rates for these services since the correspondent takes on significantly more paperwork and responsibility, and loses the potential benefit of being completely independent.

THE CAGE

Of course, whether a firm is a member of an exchange, a clearing corporation, or is completely self-clearing, some physical paper processing will be required. In fact, every trade, regardless of size, eventually has to be handled in physical form, if only to get the position onto or off of the firm's and the clearing corporation's computer. A brokerage firm's back office (or "cage") staff is the group responsible to see that it happens correctly. The cage, then, is responsible for confirming the trade to both the client and the contrabroker, receiving and disbursing security certificates and monies, maintaining the status of every cash and security position held by the firm at any given time, maintaining all of the required regulatory papers for each account, researching dividend and interest problems, adjusting securities for splits and name changes, complying with a myriad of rules and regulations imposed by the SEC and NASD and completing the corresponding paperwork, distributing proxy materials, collecting and reporting 1099 information, and a host of ofther jobs too numerous to mention.

In a typical firm, the cage may employ one individual for every two or three brokers. Obviously, the staffing of such a group is a costly process, with some of the largest firms employing several thousand individuals in this capacity alone. But, regardless of the firm's size, it has to maintain a back office—it's just a cost of doing business.

TYPES OF ORDERS

Bearing in mind the paperwork process which occurs behind the scenes, it is important to note that for a trade to occur, there also needs to be someone who desires to execute the same transaction in reverse. That is to say, for every seller there must be a buyer, and vice versa. It is the job of the brokerage industry to match these two individuals, wherever they may physically be, and transact the business.

In the case of an exchange-listed security, this matching process actually occurs on the floor of one of the nation's stock exchanges. Though it may take several correspondent firms to get there, each earning a small slice of the commission pie, it does eventually get to the floor. Once an order has been received on the floor of an exchange, it is transacted in accordance with the qualifications placed on that order by the original customer. Various types of orders exist, but basically three types are used in great frequency: the market order, the limit order, and the stop order.

Market Order (MKT)

A *market order* can best be defined as an order that is to be executed immediately upon reaching the floor of the appropriate exchange—regardless of the price at the time it reaches the exchange. Since it typically takes only a few minutes for an order to be transmitted from the customer to an exchange, the price typically is at or near the price quoted to the client at the time the order was placed.

But that point notwithstanding, if some earth-shaking event takes place during those few minutes of transmission, the order will be executed promptly upon reaching the exchange at whatever price the security may be trading at at the time, even if it differs significantly from what the price was at the time the order was entered.

Limit Order (LMT)

A *limit order,* on the other hand, obviates this problem by requiring that a transaction occur at the specified price or better. If the price is unavailable at the time the order reaches the exchange, then the order will pend until such time as the price qualification is met or the time limit placed on the order elapses. Thus, if a customer desires to sell 100 shares of XYZ, Inc. at 42, and by the time it gets to the floor of the exchange the stock is trading at 41, the order will be held in abeyance until such time as it can be executed or is no longer valid.

By the same token, if the stock is trading at 43 at the time the order gets to the exchange, the customer will be entitled to a fill at 43.

Stop Order (STP)

A *stop order* can best be described as a market order that occurs only at such time as a specified price barrier has been broken. For instance, if a customer places an order to sell 100 shares of XYZ, Inc. at 42 stop, the order will pend until such time as some other order transacts at a price of 42 or less. At this time then, the order will become a market order and immediately execute on the next trade.

This type of order is used by many individuals to "lock up" the paper profits they may have made in their portfolio by setting a so-called "floor" at which to get out. As long as the stock keeps moving up, they may move the floor up with it. But, the second the stock trades at or through their floor price, the sell transaction occurs and the individuals have locked up the approximate price they wanted out of the security.

Orders on the exchange remain in effect until the time frame specified by the customer has elapsed. The exchange provides for two such time frames: day orders (DAY) and good-until-canceled (GTC) orders. By definition, *day orders* are good only for the day they are entered. *Good-until-canceled orders* remain in effect until they are canceled. To alleviate the paperwork that would otherwise come to bear on each floor broker who receives an order that cannot be executed immediately, the exchange appoints brokers called "specialists" to maintain a book of all orders that cannot be immediately transacted.

Other Types of Orders

In addition to the three type of orders just described, there are several other, lesser-used types of orders available through brokers. Among them are the:

- *Stop-Limit (STP-LMT)* order, a stop order that becomes a limit order when the barrier is broken;
- *Do not reduce (DNR)* order, which does not have its price adjusted when dividend payments are made;
- *Participate but do not initiate (PNI)* order, in which customers do not want the floor broker to act in an aggressive manner to transact a large order that might upset an orderly market;
- *Not held (NH)* order, which allows the broker to use his or her personal judgment to

determine the best time to execute the order, relieving the floor broker of any responsibility for error in judgment;

- *All or none (AON)* order, which stipulates that all shares of a multiple hundred share order must execute at the same time or none should be executed;
- *Fill or kill (FOK)* order, which is like the AON but must happen immediately or it must be canceled; and,
- *Immediate or cancel (IOC)* order, which stipulates any portion of a multiple hundred share order must execute immediately and the remainder should be canceled.

The specialist assists in the transaction of many of these orders, though most orders do not have any standing in the specialist's book. Additionally, the specialist is also responsible for maintaining an orderly market in the security or securities for which the specialist has been appointed. Specifically, this means that the specialist is obliged to act as a buyer when no one else is available to buy, and as a seller when no one else is available to sell, risking his or her own capital to do so. In this way, the specialist serves the public by maintaining liquidity in securities that might otherwise become "instantaneously illiquid" for whatever reason, while earning floor brokerage fees and eighths (an eighth of a point or twelve and a half cents per share) for doing so.

ELECTRONIC MARKET LINKS

To further facilitate this job of maintaining orderly markets, the exchanges, which at one time were run on a totally independent basis, are today linked electronically. Thus, securities that trade on more than one exchange (known as *dually listed securities*), and securities whose prices are dependent on the prices of other securities (such as options, warrants, and convertible stocks and bonds) tend to have, at any given time, less price discrepancy between exchanges than they used to have in the past.

To further this same cause, floor brokers on the various exchanges are under obligation to execute transactions for their clients at the best possible execution price, regardless of the exchange to which the order is routed. Thus, even if a broker only maintains a seat on the Midwest Stock Exchange, he or she may actually execute a transaction on the New York Stock Exchange if the price quoted there is better. To accommodate this, most floor brokers have made arrangements with firms on the other exchanges, and they gladly trade business back and forth as needed.

The net effect of these accommodations is as follows: customers always get the best possible execution, regardless of the memberships maintained by the brokers they deal with; and the price discrepancy between exchanges is minimized since floor brokers throughout the system compete for the same trades.

Of course, not all securities are traded on one of the nation's many stock exchanges, and most securities are not traded on more than one exchange. But, with the introduction of the National Market Exchange (NME), which is an electronic link designed to accomplish a similar job in the over-the-counter (OTC) market as the links between the various stock exchanges, great strides have been made to ensure that price discrepancies are minimized. Add to that the electron linking of the nation's several clearing corporations, allowing trades to settle between a broker at one clearing corporation and a broker on another clearing corporation, and you end up with a system that allows firms of vastly different sizes and locations to have equal access to the various exchange-related services.

In this way, all clients of all firms have equal access to the nation's various securities exchanges, get the same quality executions, and benefit from the same clearing facilities. And, by reducing price and access discrepancies, these policies help to ensure a fair and equitable treatment for all clients, regardless of the firm with which they choose to deal. Thus, contrary to what a full-service broker might like customers to think, clients are not placed in a disadvantageous position because they don't deal with a major Wall Street firm or because they choose to deal with a discount brokerage house. Rather, the only difference between such firms may be the products that the firms choose to handle, the speed and efficiency of the firm's back office, and the cost to transact the business—in essence, the accoutrements. And, who is to say that it's not the discount firms that shine on these points.

EXECUTION COSTS

To put it in perspective, then, the cost for a firm to execute a security transaction for one its clients can be broken down into three separate categories:
1. the cost of executing the trade on the appropriate exchange;
2. The out-of-pocket cost to clear it through the exchange's clearing corporation; and,
3. the cost to process the paperwork in the firm's own back office.

Obviously, under some of the arrangements described earlier, some of these costs are borne by the correspondent and passed along to the firm indirectly, but in any case, they still exist.

The typical cost to execute a transaction on the floor of an exchange ranges anywhere from 1 to 4 cents per share, with 3 cents being quite typical. The out-of-pocket cost to clear a transaction through the clearing corporation ranges anywhere from about $3 to $12 per trade, with $8 representing a reasonable estimate. And, the cost to internally process the trade through the firm's own back office is likely to approximate $12 per trade, though there are no reliable public figures to support this estimate.

So, when a discount broker tells you that it costs roughly $25 to process a minimal trade, there exists good justification for this estimate. But when a full-service broker tells you it costs $1850 to sell 2500 shares of a $100 stock, it seems that there might be some room for error in the estimate, because the trade is probably being executed at one to two cents per share plus about $20 for processing.

BROKERAGE QUESTIONNAIRES—BACKGROUND

With this brief overview on transaction processing complete, it's time to turn to a more direct review of the responses received in answer to the brokerage questionnaires. The information that follows has been obtained from a survey of more than thirty so-called discount brokerage firms. Unfortunately, despite repeated attempts to cajole some firms to respond, only those listed herein felt they had sufficient need to publicize their services to the consuming public. One must therefore presume that the others are not encouraged to expand their clientele.

In an effort to present an unbiased reporting of the results of these surveys, several conventions have been adopted. Each respondent has been asked exactly the same questions in exactly the same fashion. Every attempt has been made to report all responses consistently; exactly the same terminology was used across respondents so that comparisons can be made and conclusions drawn. Additionally, the information is presented in a consistent fashion page by page, so that you can easily flip through the pages comparing response with response. This, of course, simplifies your task in choosing the firm that best suits your specific needs.

Exchange Information

As discussed earlier, all firms must be members of the NASD. Additionally, at their option, some firms may choose to become members of one of the country's many principal security exchanges. These are: the New York (NYSE), the American (ASE), the Midwest (MSE), the Pacific (PSE), the Philadelphia (PhSE), and the Chicago Board of Options (CBOE).

Related to each of the exchanges are their respective clearing corporations and depositories. Related to the NYSE is the National Securities Clearing Corporation (NSCC) and the Depository Trust Company (DTC). Related to the MSE is the Midwest Clearing Corporation (MCC) and the Midwest Securities Trust Company (MSTC). Related to the PSE is the Pacific Clearing Corporation (PCC) and the Pacific Securities Depository Trust Company (PSDTC); and related to the PhSE and the CBOE is the Options Clearing Corporation.

Transaction Capabilities

Depending on each brokerage firm's licensing and clearing arrangements, its back office capabilities, and its desired target market, transactions can be accommodated in a variety of different financial service product areas. Some firms may choose to offer only the basic services, such as transacting agency stock and bond business; other firms may choose to offer a wide array of products to their clientele. Some firms may offer investment advice, whereas others may offer none. Some firms may have a research staff, while others may use only general research, and still others may offer no research at all.

These decisions are entirely left up to the principals of the firm, and I would strongly recommend that you consider what types of transactions each firm can accommodate as you search for an acceptable firm to process your business.

In reporting the types of business, types of accounts, and types of trades a firm handles, I have adopted the following conventions. In the section entitled "Can accommodate transactions of:" in the parentheses following stocks and corporate and government bonds:

- An *a* means that the firm transacts this type of business only on an "agency" basis. This means that the firm acts as a broker or middleman when buying or selling the security for its customers' accounts. All trades transacted on the floor of a stock exchange are done on an "agency" basis.
- A *p* means that the firm transacts this type of business only on a "principal" basis. This means that the firm acts as a dealer when buying or selling the security for its customers' accounts, maintaining a position in the security, selling to the customer from its own inventory when the customer wants to buy, and buying from the customer when the customer wants to sell. Over-the-counter (OTC) securities can be traded on a principal basis; exchange-listed securities cannot.
- An *a/p* means that the firm transacts this type of business on either a principal or an agency basis, depending on the specific security involved.

In the section entitled "Can accommodate transactions of:" in the parentheses following mutual funds:

- An *l* means that the firm transacts business in "load" funds only, meaning those that impose a sales charge on purchases.

- An *n* means that the firm transacts business in "no-load" funds only, meaning those that do not impose sales charges on purchases. Some firms may transact this type of business merely as an accommodation to you, whereas others may impose a commission on the transaction.
- An *l/n* means that the firm transacts business in both "load" and "no-load" funds.

In the section entitled "Can accommodate the following types of accounts:"

- *Cash* means the firm requires all securities to be fully paid for.
- *Margin* means the firm will loan customers money to buy securities as per Regulation T of the Federal Reserve rules and/or permit certain types of transactions that must be done in a margin account, such as short sales.
- In the parentheses following IRA and KEOGH is a list of the fees to open/maintain this type of account at the firm. Such fees are typically based on the charges, imposed by the trustee of such plans, to maintain these accounts and prepare the required IRS reports.

In the section entitled "Able to handle the following types of trades:"

- *DVP* means delivery versus payment, meaning securities can be delivered, against payment, to a specific institution, on settlement date. Typically, large institutional accounts require this type of delivery, and the delivery is performed through one of the clearing corporations.
- *DTC* means the depository trust company (usually the one associated with the NYSE), the typical clearing corporation chosen to affect DVP types of transactions.
- *Short sales* means selling a borrowed security. This type of transaction can only occur in a margin account and requires that the firm is capable of finding a lender for the security so that normal delivery can occur on settlement date. Investors who trade in this fashion hope that the price of the security will fall so that they can buy it back cheaper, return it to the lender, and thereby make a profit on the transaction.

Cash Accounts

Next is an assessment of cash account balances left at the firm, and the manner in which the firm treats them. Studies have shown that customers who leave money with their brokers transact more business in the future with the firm, tend to be more active clients in general thereby generating more commission revenue overall, and tend to have a higher degree of allegiance to the firm. In other words, they represent the kind of clientele a firm wants to encourage. These points notwithstanding, properly managed, these cash resources can also generate a nice "spread" for the firm, sometimes representing a very significant source of revenue in the whole scheme of things.

All in all, firms have adopted various methods to encourage investors to leave money with them, ranging from paying interest on credit balances, to offering a choice of money market funds, to even offering cash management accounts.

For the sake of clarity, credit balances with a firm are covered by SIPC, whereas money market funds and cash management types of accounts are not. *Credit balances* are defined as cash left on account with a brokerage firm, not unlike a checking account balance left on deposit at your bank (sans checks, of course). Where such information was provided, the formula used by the firm to set these interest rates is presented.

On the other hand, a *money market fund* is a specialized version of a mutual fund that invests exclusively in short-term, interest-bearing instruments in order to earn as high a current yield as possible while maintaining instantaneous liquidity. When an investment is made in a money market fund, dollars are converted into shares at net asset value (NAV), and when a withdrawal is made, shares are converted back into dollars again at NAV. As long as NAV remains constant, typically "set" at $1, then the account works just like a savings account earning a high day-to-day rate of interest. However, in the event that the NAV were to ever decline from the $1 mark (which has never as yet happened but is theoretically possible), investors would thus be redeeming shares for less than what they were purchased for, and a loss would result. From a legalistic point of view, SIPC does not cover this kind of a loss because the loss did not occur due to the insolvency of the brokerage firm holding the securities but rather from an "injudicious" investment decision.

Various money funds are available through brokerage firms, some managed by the firm itself and only available to the firm's customers, and some managed by third parties but integrated into the firm's computer system. Some require active participation by the broker or the client, and some automatically "sweep" free credit balances into the account. Some invest exclusively in certain types of securities such as tax-free bonds or Treasury bills, whereas other invest in a variety of instruments, ranging from certificates of deposits to banker's acceptances. Each firm typically has its own unique set of restrictions that apply to the fund. Where such information was provided, their characteristics are listed here.

Cash management accounts are slightly more complex versions of a straight money market fund, typically integrated with a check writing feature and a "credit card." For all practical purposes these accounts work just like the money market fund, except they have the additional flexibility that the credit card affords the user. Two types of these credit card accounts exist: those that use debit cards and those that truly use credit cards. With the former, the money is debited from the account immediately upon the use of the card and therefore no longer draws interest or begins to accrue finance charges, whichever is applicable. In the case of a true credit card, the customer has the normal thirty days to pay before the charge actually is added to the account. Typically, these types of accounts have an annual fee, and where this information has been provided, it is included for your review.

If a firm makes margin accounts available to its customers, the pertinent information has also been included in this section for your review. The broker loan rate or call money rate (as quoted in the Money Rates section of *The Wall Street Journal*) is the rate charged on loans to brokers on stock exchange collateral. Typically, a firm bases the margin rates it charges its clientele on this rate, plus or minus some percentage (depending on the size of the margin balance). Where available, the formula or range of rates is listed here.

Account Representatives versus Order Takers

The next section of the questionnaire reviews the interface between the customer and the firm. Some of the discounters assigned specific account representatives to handle each account, whereas others merely staffed their phones with order takers, each of whom could handle any and all transactions for any account. Some of the firms offered free investment advice; others offered it only on a fee basis; and still others offered no advice whatsoever. Some made in-house research reports available, while others had only general research to offer, and still others had none to offer.

Transaction Processing

The next item on the questionnaire deals with processing security transactions, including how trades are cleared, where customer securities are held, where checks would be received and mailed from, and how customers are advised of a trade confirmation. Interestingly enough, every form of the clearing arrangements previously described is represented in this sample, which should help you draw some inferences regarding the size and the sophistication of each responding firm.

To clarify the subject of trade confirmations, be aware that all firms are obliged to send out written confirmations on each trade. What this section is more accurately addressing is how a trade will be confirmed at the time an order is places—that is, on the original phone call, on a subsequent phone call made by the broker back to the client, or in some other fashion (such as the customer having to call the broker back to find out how and when a trade has been filled).

Commission Rates

The questionnaire next deals with commission rates for listed securities. Over the years, each firm has developed its own specific formula for determining what commission it will charge on each transaction. As one might expect, some of the formulas described were so complex that they were unprintable. Others for all intents and purposes were unknown, except to the computer system that determines them on a trade-by-trade basis. Therefore, in an effort to present accurate data for your comparison purposes, I have included a grid that should cover most typical transactions, complete enough to provide you with the tools necessary to do your own interpolation as need be.

Additionally, this section includes a table outlining the minimum commission charged by each firm on the more nominal transactions, in an effort to provide the smaller investor with some basis by which to pick a discount firm. Where available, a maximum transaction cost per 100 hundred shares of stock and per option contract is listed, irrespective of the price of the issue.

Brokerage Contact Information

Finally, the locations and phone numbers of each of the firms' offices are given. It is hoped that this list will assist you in determining not only the size and sophistication of the firm, but also which offices may be convenient for you to do your trading in.

Brown & Company Securities Corp.   **(800) 225-6707 Nat'l**
20 Winthrop Square
Boston, MA 02110

Ownership:
> Subsidiary of Chemical New York Corp.

Member firm of:
> NASD, NYSE, ASE, PhSE, OCC

Can accommodate transactions of:
> Stocks(a), corporate bonds(a), government bonds(a), treasury bills, options

Can accommodate the following types of accounts:
> Cash, Margin, IRA, Keogh

Able to handle the following types of trades:
> DVP/DTC, short sales, GTC orders, Day orders

Cash balances/Margin rates:
> Interest paid on average credit balances above $1,000. Rate varies but is usually less than money
> market fund rate.
> No money market or cash management accounts offered.
> Interest charged on margin accounts: Broker loan rate—½% to 0%

Accounts insured to:
> $500,000 through SIPC

Account executive:
> No assigned representative—order processed by first available.

Availability of advice:
> No advice available

Availability of research:
> No in-house research reports available.
> No general research available.

Transaction processing:
> Trades cleared in-house
> Securities held in-house
> Checks originate from main office only.
> Securities/monies are sent to local/main office.

Trade confirmation:
> Follow-up phone call.

Sample commission rates for listed stocks:

Price Qty	$1	$5	$10	$25	$50	$75	$100
10	25.40	25.40	25.40	25.60	25.80	25.80	25.80
25	26.00	26.00	26.00	26.50	27.00	27.00	27.00
50	27.00	27.00	27.00	28.00	29.00	29.00	29.00
100	29.00	29.00	29.00	31.00	33.00	33.00	33.00
200	33.00	33.00	33.00	37.00	41.00	41.00	41.00
500	45.00	45.00	45.00	55.00	65.00	65.00	65.00
1000	65.00	65.00	65.00	85.00	105.00	105.00	105.00
2500	117.50	117.50	117.50	167.50	217.50	217.50	217.50

Note: If monthly commission total exceeds $350.00, a rebate of 10% is given.
Lower rates available for OTC trades.

Minimum commission level is:

Stocks:	$25.04 (100 share maximum is $33.00)
Corporate Bonds:	25.00
Government Bonds:	25.00
Treasury Bills:	37.50 (maximum commission is $75.00)
Options:	21.00 (contract maximum is $21.00)

Offices located in:

Boston, MA	(800) 225-6707
New York, NY	(800) 223-5566
Orlando, FL	(800) 327-4798
Philadelphia, PA	(800) 334-1200

William C. Burnside & Company, Inc.

111 N. Vermilion Street
Danville, IL 61832

(217) 443-3310
(800) 624-7631 Midwest
(800) 252-1678 IL

Ownership:
Privately owned

Member firm of:
NASD, MCC

Can accommodate transactions of:
Stocks(a/p), corporate bonds(a/p), government bonds(a/p), treasury bills, options, mutual funds (l/n),
annuities, life insurance, CDs, financial planning services, tax-shelters, commodities, financial
futures, stock index futures, underwritings.

Can accommodate the following types of accounts:
Cash, Margin, IRA ($25 annual), Keogh ($25 annual)

Able to handle the following types of trades:
DVP/DTC, short sales, GTC orders, Day orders

Cash balances/Margin rates:
Interest paid on credit balances; rate varies
No automatic sweep feature, $100 to open.
Regular, government, and tax-free money market funds available.
Regular, government, and tax-free cash management account with free checking, free debit VISA,
$50 annual or setup fees, $5,000 cash to open.
Interest charged on margin accounts: Broker loan rate + ½ to 2%

Accounts insured to:
$500,000 through SIPC.

Account executive:
An assigned representative will always service the account.

Availability of advice:
Free advice available.

Availability of research:
No in-house research reports available.
Value-Line, Standard & Poor's, Argus, Merrill Lynch Letter, and Bear Stearns Research reports
available.

Transaction processing:
Trades cleared in-house.
Securities held in-house or at Midwest Securities Trust Company.
Checks originate from main office.
Securities/monies are sent to main office.

Trade confirmation:
Follow-up phone call.

Sample commission rates for listed stocks:

Price Qty	$1	$5	$10	$25	$50	$75	$100
10	30.00	30.00	30.00	30.00	30.00	30.00	30.00
25	30.00	30.00	30.00	30.00	33.56	43.21	52.87
50	30.00	30.00	30.00	33.56	52.87	66.23	80.73
100	30.00	30.00	30.00	52.87	80.73	80.73	80.73
200	30.00	30.00	50.00	89.00	100.00	100.00	100.00
500	100.00	100.00	100.00	100.00	100.00	100.00	100.00
1000	120.00	120.00	120.00	120.00	120.00	120.00	120.00
2500	300.00	300.00	300.00	300.00	300.00	300.00	300.00

Note: Some restrictions apply to these rates.

Minimum commission level is:

Stocks:	$30.00 (100 share maximum is $80.73)
Corporate Bonds:	30.00
Government Bonds:	30.00
Treasury Bills:	30.00
Options:	40.00 (no contract maximum)

Items worth mentioning:

Computer access available for quotes, account information, commission calculations, bond yield to maturities, compound rates based on yields, option writing screens, etc.

Offices located in:

Auburn, IL	(217) 438-3982
Casey, IL	(217) 932-5777
Champaign, IL	(217) 352-0011
Danville, IL (main)	(217) 443-3310, (800) 624-7631(MW), (800) 252-1678(IL)
Decatur, IL	(217) 424-2660, (800) 447-2307(IL)
Harrisburg, IL	(618) 252-7319
Oakbrook, IL	(312) 571-3343
Oakland, IL	(800) 252-2013
Shelbyville, IL	(217) 774-2163
South Bend, IN	(219) 287-8625
Spencer, IA	(712) 262-9400
Springfield, IL	(800) 252-8907
Staunton, IL	(618) 635-8408
Wichita, KS	(316) 267-1061

Clayton, Polleys & Co., Inc.
50 Federal Street
Boston, MA 02110

(617) 357-5474
(800) 252-9765 Nat'l
(800) 882-1452 MA

Ownership:
> Privately owned

Member firm of:
> NASD, BSE

Can accommodate transactions of:
> Stocks(a/p), corporate bonds(a), government bonds(a), treasury bills, options, mutual funds(l)

Can accommodate the following types of accounts:
> Cash, Margin, IRA ($25 annual), Keogh ($25 annual)

Able to handle the following types of trades:
> DVP/DTC, short sales, GTC orders, Day orders

Cash balances/Margin rates:
> Interest paid on credit balances. Rate varies
> No money market or cash management accounts offered.
> Interest charged on margin accounts: Broker loan rate—⅛ to + 1%

Accounts insured to:
> $500,000 through SIPC

Account executive:
> No assigned representative—order processed by first available.
> Assigned representative will always service customers who qualify for the frequent traders program (six trades per month).

Availability of advice:
> No advice available

Availability of research:
> No in-house research reports available.
> No general research available.

Transaction processing:
> Trades cleared in-house
> Securities held in-house or at Depository Trust Company
> Checks originate from main office
> Securities/monies are sent to main office.

Trade confirmation:
> Follow-up phone call.

Sample commission rates for listed stocks:

Price Qty	$1	$5	$10	$25	$50	$75	$100
10	24.00	24.00	24.00	24.00	24.00	24.00	24.00
25	24.00	24.00	24.00	24.00	24.00	24.00	24.00
50	24.00	24.00	24.00	24.00	24.00	24.00	24.00
100	24.00	24.00	24.00	24.00	24.00	24.00	24.00
200	24.00	36.00	40.00	40.00	40.00	40.00	40.00
500	24.00	53.00	60.00	77.00	77.00	77.00	77.00
1000	35.00	84.00	86.00	116.00	116.00	116.00	116.00
2500	87.50	120.00	145.00	210.00	210.00	210.00	210.00

Minimum commission level is:

Stocks:	$24.00 (100 share maximum is $24.00)
Corporate Bonds:	24.00
Government Bonds:	35.00
Treasury Bills:	35.00
Options:	24.00 (contract maximum is $24.00)

Offices located in:

Boston, MA	(617) 357-5474, (800) 252-9765(N), (800) 882-1452(MA)
Fairfield, CT	(203) 367-2311

Ira Epstein Stocks & Options   **(800) 621-1155 Nat'l**
Ira Epstein & Co. Commodities
566 W. Adams
Chicago, IL 60606

Ownership:
 Ira Epstein Stocks & Options: a division of Shatkin Financial Services
 Ira Epstein & Co. Commodities: privately owned.

Member firm of:
 NASD, NFA, OFTC

Can accommodate transactions of:
 Stocks(a/p), corporate bonds(a), government bonds(a), treasury bills, options, mutual funds(l/n),
  commodities, financial futures, stock index futures, commodity options

Can accommodate the following types of accounts:
 Cash, Margin, IRA ($50 annual), Keogh

Able to handle the following types of trades:
 DTC, short sales, GTC orders, Day orders

Cash balances/Margin rates:
 Interest paid on credit balances: Broker loan rate—2%
 Regular, government, and tax-free money market funds and cash management accounts available,
  with automatic sweep feature, $2,500 to open.
 Interest charged on margin accounts: Broker loan rate + ¼ to 2%

Accounts insured to:
 $500,000 through SIPC

Account executive:
 Stock/option accounts: No assigned representative—order processed by first available.
 Commodity accounts: Assigned representative will always service the account.

Availability of advice:
 Free advice available for stock & option accounts. Fee based advice for commodity accounts.

Availability of research:
 No in-house research reports available for stock & options accounts; in-house research available
  for commodity accounts.
 Investment strategist and specialty reports available.

Transaction processing:
 Trades cleared through Adler Coleman & Co., Inc.
 Securities held by Adler Coleman & Co., Inc.
 Checks originate from main office: Adler Coleman & Co., Inc.
 Securities/monies are sent to local office: Ira Epstein Stocks & Options

Trade confirmation:
 On original or follow-up phone call.

Sample commission rates for listed stocks:

Price Qty	$1	$5	$10	$25	$50	$75	$100
10	20.00	20.00	20.00	20.00	20.00	20.00	20.00
25	20.00	20.00	20.00	20.00	20.00	20.00	20.00
50	20.00	20.00	20.00	20.00	20.00	20.00	20.00
100	25.00	25.00	25.00	25.00	25.00	25.00	25.00
200	25.00	25.00	27.00	32.00	32.00	32.00	32.00
500	35.00	35.00	37.50	45.00	45.00	45.00	45.00
1000	50.00	50.00	60.00	75.00	75.00	75.00	75.00
2500	100.00	100.00	125.00	137.50	150.00	150.00	150.00

Minimum commission level is:

Stocks:	$20.00 (100 share maximum is $25.00)
Corporate Bonds:	35.00
Government Bonds:	35.00 ($21.00 day trade in commodity account)
Treasury Bills:	35.00 ($21.00 day trade in commodity account)
Options:	20.00 (contract maximum is $20.00)

Items worth mentioning:

Ira Epstein Stock & Options is a separate entity from Ira Epstein Commodities. Money can instantly be transfered between accounts at the two firms. Free market letters, charts, and futures magazine available. Sponsors nationally syndicated investment television show.

Offices located in:

Beverly Hills, CA	(Opening soon)
Chicago, IL	(800) 621-1155
New York, NY	(800) 621-1155

Haas Securities Corp.
208 S. LaSalle Street
Chicago, IL 60604

(312) 443-1660
(800) 621-1410 Nat'l
(800) 572-1139 IL

Ownership:
>   Privately owned.

Member firm of:
>   NASD, NYSE, ASE, MSE, CBOE

Can accommodate transactions of:
>   Stocks(a/p), corporate bonds(a/p), government bonds(a/p), treasury bills, options, mutual funds(l/n), commodities, financial futures, stock index futures, underwritings.

Can accommodate the following types of accounts:
>   Cash, Margin, IRA ($30 to open), Keogh

Able to handle the following types of trades:
>   DVP/DTC, short sales, GTC orders, Day orders

Cash balances/Margin rates:
>   Interest paid on credit balances.
>   Regular and tax-free money market funds available with automatic sweep, $1000 to open, $100 subsequent deposits.
>   No cash management account offered.
>   Interest charged on margin accounts: Broker loan rate + ½ to 1¾%

Accounts insured to:
> $500,000 through SIPC; additional $2,000,000 through AETNA

Account executive:
>   No assigned representative—order processed by first available.

Availability of advice:
>   No advice available

Availability of research:
>   No in-house research reports available.
>   Value Line research available.

Transaction processing:
>   Trades cleared by L.F. Rothschild, Unterberg, Towbin.
>   Securities held by L.F. Rothschild, Unterberg, Towbin.
>   Checks originate from main office.
>   Securities/monies are sent to main office.

Trade confirmation:
>   On original or follow-up phone call. Report is immediate.

Sample commission rates for listed stocks:

Price Qty	$1	$5	$10	$25	$50	$75	$100
10	25.00	25.00	25.00	25.00	25.00	25.00	25.00
25	25.00	25.00	25.00	25.00	25.00	25.00	25.00
50	25.00	25.00	25.00	25.00	25.00	25.00	25.00
100	25.00	25.00	25.00	25.00	36.00	40.50	40.50
200	25.00	25.00	28.00	43.00	77.00	81.00	81.00
500	25.00	32.50	42.50	82.50	130.00	160.00	162.50
1000	30.00	45.00	65.00	110.00	150.00	185.00	225.00
2500	50.00	100.00	125.00	187.50	287.50	375.00	475.00

Minimum commission level is:

Stocks:	$25.00 (100 share maximum is $40.50)
Corporate Bonds:	35.00
Government Bonds:	35.00
Treasury Bills:	25.00 (available on auction only)
Options:	25.00 (contract maximum is $25.00)

Items worth mentioning:
Free trading rooms with desks and equipment, are available in each office for active traders.

Offices located in:

Chicago, IL (main)	(312) 443-1660, (800) 621-1410(N), (800) 572-1139(IL)
Chicago, IL	(312) 670-0191
Highland Park, IL	(312) 433-6200
Oak Brook, IL	(312) 789-1333
Louisville, KY	(502) 583-5422
Cleveland, OH	(216) 765-1270

Heartland Securities Inc.

208 S. LaSalle Street
Chicago, IL 60606

(312) 372-0075
(800) 621-0662 Nat'l
(800) 972-0580 IL

Ownership:
> Privately owned.

Member firm of:
> NASD, MSE

Can accommodate transactions of:
> Stocks(a), corporate bonds(a), options, mutual funds(l), tax shelters.

Can accommodate the following types of accounts:
> Cash, Margin, IRA (no fees)

Able to handle the following types of trades:
> DVP/DTC, short sales, GTC orders, Day orders

Cash balances/Margin rates:
> Interest paid on credit balances: treasury bill rate—$\frac{1}{2}$%.
> Regular and tax-free money market funds available with automatic sweep.
> No cash management account offered.
> Interest charged on margin accounts: Broker loan rate + $\frac{1}{2}$ to $1\frac{1}{2}$%

Accounts insured to:
> $500,000 through SIPC.

Account executive:
> An assigned representative will always service the account.

Availability of advice:
> No advice available

Availability of research:
> No in-house research reports available.
> No general research available.

Transaction processing:
> Trades cleared in-house.
> Securities held in-house.
> Checks originate from main office only.
> Securities/monies are sent to main office.

Trade confirmation:
> On original or follow-up phone call. Report in 10–15 minutes.

Sample commission rates for listed stocks:

Price Qty	$1	$5	$10	$25	$50	$75	$100
10	16.50	16.50	16.50	16.50	16.50	16.50	16.50
25	18.75	18.75	18.75	18.75	18.75	18.75	18.75
50	22.50	22.50	22.50	22.50	22.50	22.50	22.50
100	30.00	30.00	30.00	30.00	30.00	30.00	30.00
200	30.00	30.00	35.00	45.00	45.00	45.00	45.00
500	35.00	40.00	65.00	90.00	90.00	90.00	90.00
1000	55.00	65.00	115.00	125.00	125.00	125.00	125.00
2500	115.00	140.00	190.00	200.00	200.00	200.00	200.00

Note: If stock sale takes place within 60 days of purchase, commission is discounted an additional 50%.

Minimum commission level is:

Stocks:	$15.00 (100 share maximum is $30.00)
Corporate Bonds:	30.00
Government Bonds:	n/a
Treasury Bills:	n/a
Options:	30.00

Offices located in:
   Chicago, IL   (312) 372-0075, (800) 621-0662(N), (800) 972-0580(IL)

Barry W. Murphy & Company, Inc.
125 High Street
Boston, MA 02110

(617) 426-1770
(800) 225-2494 Nat'l
(800) 882-1610 MA

Ownership:
Privately owned

Member firm of:
NASD

Can accommodate transactions of:
Stocks(a), corporate bonds(a), government bonds(a), treasury bills, options, mutual funds(l0, CDs, tax-shelters, stock index futures

Can accommodate the following types of accounts:
Cash, Margin, IRA ($25 annual), Keogh ($25 annual). Accounts subject to an inactive account fee ($25 annual).

Able to handle the following types of trades:
DVP/DTC, short sales, GTC orders, Day orders

Cash balances/Margin rates:
No interest paid on credit balances.
Regular and government, and tax-free money market funds available, with automatic sweep feature, $250 to open.
Interest charged on margin accounts: Broker loan rate + ½ to 2¼%

Accounts insured to:
$500,000 through SIPC; additional $2,000,000 through AETNA.

Account executive:
No assigned representative—order processed by first available.

Availability of advice:
Advice available.

Availability of research:
No in-house research reports available.
No general research available.

Transaction processing:
Trades cleared by Broadcort Capital Corp.
Securities held by Broadcort Capital Corp.
Checks originate from main office.
Securities/monies are sent to main/local branch office.

Trade confirmation:
On original or follow-up phone call.

Sample commission rates for listed stocks:

Price Qty	$1	$5	$10	$25	$50	$75	$100
10	25.10	25.35	25.35	25.55	25.75	25.75	25.75
25	25.25	25.88	25.88	26.38	26.88	26.88	26.88
50	25.50	26.75	26.75	27.75	28.75	28.75	28.75
100	26.00	28.50	28.50	30.50	32.50	32.50	32.50
200	27.00	32.00	32.00	36.00	40.00	40.00	40.00
500	30.00	42.50	42.50	52.50	62.50	62.50	62.50
1000	35.00	60.00	60.00	80.00	100.00	100.00	100.00
2500	50.00	112.50	112.50	162.50	212.50	212.50	212.50

Minimum commission level is:

Stocks:	$25.00 (100 share maximum is $32.50)
Corporate Bonds:	25.00
Government Bonds:	25.00
Treasury Bills:	25.00
Options:	20.00 (contract maximum is $20.00)

Offices located in:

Boston, MA   (617) 426-1770, (800) 225-2494(N), (800) 882-1610(MA)

Oberweis Securities

841 N. Lake Street
Aurora, IL 60506

(312) 897-7100
(800) 323-6166 Nat'l
(800) 942-0850 IL

Ownership:
>Privately owned

Member firm of:
>NASD, MSE

Can accommodate transactions of:
>Stocks(a/p), corporate bonds(a/p), government bonds(a/p), treasury bills, options, mutual funds(l/n), annuities, life insurance, CDs, precious metals, financial planning services, tax-shelters, managed equity accounts, underwritings

Can accommodate the following types of accounts:
>Cash, Margin, IRA ($25 annual), Keogh ($25 annual)

Able to handle the following types of trades:
>DVP/DTC, short sales, GTC orders, Day orders

Cash balances/Margin rates:
>Interest paid on credit balances: Broker loan rate—2%
>Regular, government, and tax-free money market funds available, no automatic sweep feature, $1,000 to open, $100 subsequent additions.
>Interest charged on margin accounts: Broker loan rate + ½ to 1½%

Accounts insured to:
>$500,000 through SIPC

Account executive:
>Assigned representative will always service the account.

Availability of advice:
>Advice available on free and fee basis.

Availability of research:
>In-house research reports available.
>Value Line and Standard & Poor's reports available.

Transaction processing:
>Trades cleared in-house
>Securities held in-house or at Midwest Securities Trust Company
>Checks originate from local branch/main office
>Securities/monies are sent to local branch/main office.

Trade confirmation:
>Original or follow-up phone call.

Sample commission rates for listed stocks:

Price Qty	$1	$5	$10	$25	$50	$75	$100
10	34.60	35.00	35.50	36.00	36.50	36.50	36.50
25	35.50	36.50	37.75	39.00	40.25	40.25	40.25
50	37.00	39.00	41.50	44.00	46.50	46.50	46.50
100	40.00	44.00	49.00	54.00	59.00	59.00	59.00
200	46.00	54.00	64.00	74.00	84.00	84.00	84.00
500	64.00	84.00	109.00	134.00	159.00	159.00	159.00
1000	79.00	109.00	146.00	184.00	221.00	221.00	221.00
2500	124.00	184.00	259.00	334.00	409.00	409.00	409.00

Minimum commission level is:

Stocks:	$34.00
Corporate Bonds:	34.00
Government Bonds:	34.00
Treasury Bills:	34.00
Options:	34.00

Items worth mentioning:
Complimentary copy of monthly investment advisory letter.

Offices located in:

Aurora, IL	(312) 897-7100
Barrington, IL	(312) 382-3900
Birmingham, MI	(313) 642-0711
Chicago, IL	(312) 263-5400
Grand Rapids, MI	(616) 451-0200
Indianapolis, IN	(317) 846-6166
Lima, OH	(419) 227-1000
Munster, IN	(219) 836-2590
Oakbrook, IL	(312) 789-2500
Oconomowoc, WI	(414) 567-1700
Palm Harbor, FL	(813) 785-6600
Rockford, IL	(815) 229-3700
Sarasota, FL	(813) 953-7700
Toledo, OH	(419) 535-1600
Waukegan, IL	(312) 249-1000

Pace Securities, Inc.
225 Park Avenue
New York, NY 10017

(212) 490-6363
(800) 221-1660 Nat'l

Ownership:
   Privately owned

Member firm of:
   NASD, NYSE, ASE, MSRB

Can accommodate transactions of:
   Stocks(a/p), corporate bonds(a/p), government bonds(a/p), treasury bills, options, mutual funds(l/n), annuities, life insurance, financial planning services, financial futures, stock index futures, venture capital, underwritings

Can accommodate the following types of accounts:
   Cash, Margin, IRA ($30 annual), Keogh ($50 annual)

Able to handle the following types of trades:
   DVP/DTC, short sales, GTC orders, Day orders

Cash balances/Margin rates:
   Interest paid on credit balances: rate varies with account balance
   Regular, government, and tax-free money market funds available, with automatic sweep feature, $2,000 to open, $100 subsequent deposits.
   Interest charged on margin accounts: Broker loan rate + ½ to 1½%

Accounts insured to:
   $500,000 through SIPC; additional $2,000,000 through Lloyds of London

Account executive:
   No assigned representative—order processed by first available.

Availability of advice:
   Free advice available

Availability of research:
   In-house research reports available.
   Value Line and Standard & Poor's reports available.

Transaction processing:
   Trades cleared Edward A. Viner & Co., Inc.
   Securities held by Edward A. Viner & Co., Inc.
   Checks originate from main office
   Securities/monies are sent to main office.

Trade confirmation:
   Follow-up phone call.

Sample commission rates for listed stocks:

Price Qty	$1	$5	$10	$25	$50	$75	$100
10	35.00	35.00	35.00	35.00	35.00	35.00	35.00
25	35.00	35.00	35.00	35.00	35.00	35.00	35.00
50	35.00	35.00	35.00	35.00	35.00	35.00	35.00
100	35.00	35.00	35.00	35.00	35.00	35.00	35.00
200	35.00	35.00	35.00	35.00	35.00	35.00	35.00
500	60.00	60.00	60.00	60.00	60.00	60.00	60.00
1000	60.00	60.00	60.00	60.00	60.00	60.00	60.00
2500	125.00	125.00	125.00	125.00	125.00	125.00	125.00

Minimum commission level is:

Stocks:	$35.00 (100 share maximum is $15.00)
Corporate Bonds:	35.00
Government Bonds:	35.00
Treasury Bills:	50.00
Options:	35.00 (contract maximum is $5.00)

Offices located in:

New York, NY   (212) 490-6363, (800) 221-1660

Pacific Brokerage Services, Inc.
5757 Wilshire Blvd, Suite 3
Los Angeles, CA 90036

(213) 939-1100
(800) 421-8395 Nat'l

Ownership:
Privately owned

Member firm of:
NASD, NYSE, ASE (associate), PSE, DTC, OCC, PCC

Can accommodate transactions of:
Stocks(a/p), corporate bonds(a/p), government bonds(a/p), options

Can accommodate the following types of accounts:
Cash, Margin, IRA

Able to handle the following types of trades:
DVP/DTC, short sales, GTC orders, Day orders

Cash balances/Margin rates:
Interest paid on credit balances: money market rate.
No money market or cash management accounts offered
Interest charged on margin accounts: Broker loan rate + 0% to ½%

Accounts insured to:
$500,000 through SIPC; additional $2,000,000 through Lloyds of London

Account executive:
No assigned representative—order processed by first available.

Availability of advice:
No advice available

Availability of research:
No in-house research reports available.
Standard & Poor's reports available.

Transaction processing:
Trades cleared in-house
Securities held by Depository Trust Company
Checks originate from local branch/main office
Securities/monies are sent to main office; local office by request only.

Trade confirmation:
On original or follow-up phone call. Report in 5–15 minutes.

Sample commission rates for listed stocks:

Price Qty	$1	$5	$10	$25	$50	$75	$100
10	25.00	25.00	25.00	25.00	25.00	25.00	25.00
25	25.00	25.00	25.00	25.00	25.00	25.00	25.00
50	25.00	25.00	25.00	25.00	25.00	25.00	25.00
100	25.00	25.00	25.00	25.00	25.00	25.00	25.00
200	25.00	25.00	25.00	25.00	25.00	25.00	25.00
500	32.00	42.00	42.00	42.00	42.00	42.00	42.00
1000	42.00	53.00	78.00	78.00	78.00	78.00	78.00
2500	74.00	93.00	125.00	125.00	125.00	125.00	125.00

Minimum commission level is:

Stocks:	$25.00 (100 share maximum is $25.00)
Corporate Bonds:	25.00
Government Bonds:	25.00
Treasury Bills:	n/a
Options:	25.00 (max. per add'l contract is $6.25)

Offices located in:

Boca Raton, FL	(305) 395-3444
Chicago, IL	(312) 444-1082
Dallas, TX	(214) 696-3992
Los Angeles, CA	(213) 939-1100, (800) 421-8395(N)
New York, NY	(212) 509-3880

Quick & Reilly, Inc.
120 Wall Street
New York, NY 10005

(800) 672-7220 Nat'l
(800) 522-8712 NY

Ownership:
> Publicly owned

Member firm of:
> NASD, NYSE, ASE

Can accommodate transactions of:
> Stocks(a), corporate bonds(a/p), government bonds(a/p), treasury bills, options, mutual funds(l/n)

Can accommodate the following types of accounts:
> Cash, Margin, IRA ($25 annual), Keogh ($25 annual)

Able to handle the following types of trades:
> DVP/DTC, short sales, GTC orders, Day orders

Cash balances/Margin rates:
> No interest pad on credit balances.
> No automatic sweep feature, $1,000 to open.
> Regular, government, and tax-free money market funds available.
> Interest charged on margin accounts: Broker loan rate + ½ to 2%

Accounts insured to:
> $500,000 through SIPC; additional $1,500,000 through AETNA.

Account executive:
> Assigned representative will always service the account.

Availability of advice:
> No advice available

Availability of research:
> No in-house research reports available.
> Standard & Poor's reports available.

Transaction processing:
> Trades cleared in-house through a subsidiary firm.
> Securities held in-house
> Checks originate from local branch office
> Securities/monies are sent to local branch office.

Trade confirmation:
> Follow-up phone call.

Sample commission rates for listed stocks:

Price Qty	$1	$5	$10	$25	$50	$75	$100
10	35.00	35.00	35.00	35.00	35.00	35.00	35.00
25	35.00	35.00	35.00	35.00	35.00	35.00	35.00
50	35.00	35.00	35.00	35.00	35.00	38.32	46.32
100	35.00	35.00	35.00	35.00	46.32	48.44	48.44
200	35.00	35.00	35.64	56.31	92.41	96.88	96.88
500	35.00	44.25	57.62	102.16	162.70	199.96	201.83
1000	50.00	45.26	64.09	108.80	149.78	187.04	224.30
2500	62.19	98.55	134.88	194.50	287.65	380.80	473.95

Minimum commission level is:

Stocks:	$35.00 (100 share maximum is $48.44)
Corporate Bonds:	30.00
Government Bonds:	30.00
Treasury Bills:	35.00
Options:	35.00 (no contract maximum)

Items worth mentioning:

Quick Way computer trading available through Compuserve.

Offices located in:

Please refer to Appendix B for a complete list of offices.

Robinson Securities
11 S. LaSalle Street
Chicago, IL 60603

(312) 346-7710
(800) 621-2840 IL

Ownership:
Privately owned

Member firm of:
NASD, MSE

Can accommodate transactions of:
Stocks(a/p), corporate bonds(a/p), government bonds(a/p), treasury bills, options, mutual funds(l), CDs, financial planning, tax-shelters

Can accommodate the following types of accounts:
Cash, Margin, IRA ($50 annual), Keogh ($75 annual)

Able to handle the following types of trades:
DVP/DTC, short sales, GTC orders, Day orders

Cash balances/Margin rates:
Interest paid on credit balances: Broker loan rate—1½%
Regular, government, and tax-free money market funds available with automatic sweep feature, $500 to open, $100 subsequent deposits.
Interest charged on margin accounts: Broker loan rate + ½ to 1½%

Accounts insured to:
$500,000 through SIPC.

Account executive:
No assigned representative—order processed by first available.

Availability of advice:
Advice available on a fee basis.

Availability of research:
No in-house research reports available.
No general research available.

Transaction processing:
Trades cleared in-house.
Securities held by Midwest Clearing Corp.
Checks originate from main office
Securities/monies are sent to main office.

Trade confirmation:
On original phone call.

Sample commission rates for listed stocks:

Price Qty	$1	$5	$10	$25	$50	$75	$100
10	22.50	22.50	22.50	22.50	22.50	22.50	22.50
25	22.50	22.50	22.50	22.50	22.50	25.00	25.00
50	22.50	22.50	22.50	22.50	25.00	25.00	25.00
100	22.50	22.50	22.50	25.00	25.00	25.00	25.00
200	22.50	22.50	30.00	50.00	50.00	50.00	50.00
500	22.50	30.00	60.00	90.00	125.00	125.00	125.00
1000	40.00	60.00	90.00	125.00	200.00	200.00	200.00
2500	100.00	100.00	125.00	200.00	250.00	375.00	500.00

Minimum commission level is:

Stocks:	$22.50 (100 share maximum is $25.00)
Corporate Bonds:	22.50
Government Bonds:	22.50
Treasury Bills:	22.50
Options:	22.50 (max. per add'l contract is $10.00)

Items worth mentioning:

Commission calculator available upon request.

Offices located in:

Chicago, IL   (312) 346-7710, (800) 621-2840

Charles Schwab & Co., Inc.
101 Montgomery Street
San Francisco, CA 94104

(415) 398-1000
(800) 227-4444 Nat'l
(800) 792-0988 CA

Ownership:
> Subsidiary of BankAmerica Corp.

Member firm of:
> NASD, NYSE, ASE, MSE, PSE, CBOE, PhSE

Can accommodate transactions of:
> Stocks(a), corporate bonds(a), government bonds(a), treasury bills, options, mutual funds(l/n), CDs, tax-shelters, financial planning services (via software)

Can accommodate the following types of accounts:
> Cash, Margin, IRA (no fees), Keogh (annual fee)

Able to handle the following types of trades:
> DVP/DTC, short sales, GTC orders, Day orders

Cash balances/Margin rates:
> Interest paid on credit balances: based on market rate for insured funds
> Regular, government, and tax-free money market funds available, with automatic sweep feature, $2,000 to open, no minimum on subsequent deposits.
> Tax free cash management account with free checking, free debit VISA card, no annual or setup fees, $5,000 cash/securities to open.
> Interest charged on margin accounts: Broker loan rate + ¼ to 1½%

Accounts insured to:
> $500,000 through SIPC; additional $9,500,000 through AETNA.

Account executive:
> No assigned representative—order processed by first available.

Availability of advice:
> Investment advice available, on fee basis, via computer only.

Availability of research:
> No in-house research reports available.
> Standard & Poor's and Dow Jones News Retrieval reports available.

Transaction processing:
> Trades cleared in-house.
> Securities held by DTC or Pacific Coast DTC
> Checks originate from local branch/main office
> Securities/monies are sent to local branch/main office.

Trade confirmation:
> On original or follow-up phone call.

Sample commission rates for listed stocks:

Price Qty	$1	$5	$10	$25	$50	$75	$100
10	34.00	34.00	34.00	34.00	34.00	34.00	35.00
25	34.00	34.00	34.00	34.00	39.00	49.00	49.00
50	34.00	34.00	34.00	34.00	49.00	49.00	49.00
100	34.00	34.00	35.00	49.00	49.00	49.00	49.00
200	34.00	35.00	51.00	74.00	92.00	94.00	94.00
500	40.00	59.00	74.00	99.50	134.00	159.00	184.00
1000	76.00	76.00	92.00	134.00	184.00	209.00	234.00
2500	136.00	136.00	136.00	196.50	259.00	321.50	384.00

Minimum commission level is:

Stocks:	$34.00 (100 share maximum is $49.00)
Corporate Bonds:	34.00
Government Bonds:	34.00
Treasury Bills:	34.00
Options:	31.50 (contract maximum is $34.00)

Items worth mentioning:

Orders can be placed 24 hours per day, 7 days per week.

A software program called Equalizer is available which combines trading, research, recordkeeping, quotes, news, etc.

SchwabQuotes, a touch tone access to Dow Jones news retreival and stock quotes is available.

VIP service available to active clients.

Offices located in:

Please refer to Appendix C for a complete list of offices.

StockCross, Inc.
One Washington Mall
Boston, MA 02108

(617) 367-5700
(800) 225-6196 Nat'l
(800) 392-6104 MA

Ownership:
Privately owned

Member firm of:
NASD, NYSE, ASE, BSE

Can accommodate transactions of:
Stocks(a), corporate bonds(a), treasury bills, options

Can accommodate the following types of accounts:
Cash, Margin, IRA ($25 to open, $25 annual), Keogh ($25 to open, $25 annual plus $25 per participant)

Able to handle the following types of trades:
DVP/DTC, short sales, GTC orders, Day orders

Cash balances/Margin rates:
Interest paid on credit balances above $3,000 at money market rate
No money market or cash management accounts offered.
Interest charged on margin accounts: Broker loan rate + 0% to 1%

Accounts insured to:
$500,000 through SIPC.

Account executive:
No assigned representative—order processed by first available.

Availability of advice:
No advice available

Availability of research:
No in-house research reports available.
No general research available.

Transaction processing:
Trades cleared in-house
Securities held in-house/Depository Trust Company
Checks originate from main back office
Securities/monies are sent to main office.

Trade confirmation:
Follow-up phone call.

Sample commission rates for listed stocks:

Price Qty	$1	$5	$10	$25	$50	$75	$100
10	25.85	25.85	25.85	25.85	25.85	25.85	25.85
25	27.13	27.13	27.13	27.13	27.13	27.13	27.13
50	29.25	29.25	29.25	29.25	29.25	29.25	29.25
100	33.50	33.50	33.50	33.50	33.50	33.50	33.50
200	42.00	42.00	42.00	42.00	42.00	42.00	42.00
500	67.50	67.50	67.50	67.50	67.50	67.50	67.50
1000	110.00	110.00	110.00	110.00	110.00	110.00	110.00
2500	237.50	237.50	237.50	237.50	237.50	237.50	237.50

Minimum commission level is:
Stocks: $25.00 (100 share max. is $33.50 for market orders)
Corporate Bonds: 25.00
Government Bonds: —
Treasury Bills: —
Options: 20.00 (max. per add'l contract is $8.00)

Items worth mentioning:
Commission charges are slightly higher for limit orders.

Offices located in:
Boston, MA   (617) 367-5700, (800) 225-6196(N), (800) 392-6104(MA)

York Securities, Inc.
160 Broadway
New York, NY 10038

(212) 349-9700
(800) 221-3154 Nat'l

Ownership:
 Privately owned

Member firm of:
 NASD, NYSE, ASE

Can accommodate transactions of:
 Stocks(a/p), corporate bonds(a/p), government bonds(a/p), treasury bills, options, mutual funds(l/n), life insurance, CDs, financial planning services, tax-shelters, financial futures, stock index futures

Can accommodate the following types of accounts:
 Cash, Margin, IRA, Keogh

Able to handle the following types of trades:
 DVP/DTC, short sales, GTC orders, Day orders

Cash balances/Margin rates:
 No interest paid on credit balances.
 Regular, government, and tax-free money market funds available, no automatic sweep feature.
 Interest charged on margin accounts: Broker loan rate + ½ to 2½%

Accounts insured to:
 $500,000 through SIPC; additional $1,500,000 through AETNA.

Account executive:
 Assigned representative will always service the account.

Availability of advice:
 No advice available

Availability of research:
 No in-house research reports available.
 Value Line and Standard & Poor's reports available.

Transaction processing:
 Trades cleared through Q & R Clearing Corp.
 Securities held by Q & R Clearing Corp.
 Checks originate from Q & R Clearing Corp.
 Securities/monies are sent Q & R Clearing Corp.

Trade confirmation:
 Follow-up phone call.

Sample commission rates for listed stocks:

Price Qty	$1	$5	$10	$25	$50	$75	$100
10	35.00	35.00	35.00	35.00	35.00	35.00	35.00
25	35.00	35.00	35.00	35.00	35.00	35.00	35.00
50	35.00	35.00	35.00	35.00	35.00	35.00	35.00
100	35.00	35.00	35.00	35.00	35.00	35.00	35.00
200	35.00	35.00	35.00	35.00	46.20	47.56	48.44
500	35.00	35.00	35.00	50.00	70.00	70.00	70.00
1000	35.00	45.00	60.00	70.00	80.00	80.00	80.00
2500	75.00	100.00	125.00	137.50	150.00	150.00	150.00

Minimum commission level is:

Stocks:	$35.00 (100 share maximum is $35.00)
Corporate Bonds:	35.00
Government Bonds:	35.00
Treasury Bills:	35.00
Options:	35.00 (contract maximum is $35.00)

Items worth mentioning:

Stock guides and tear sheets available upon request.

Offices located in:

New York, NY   (212) 349-9700, (800) 221-3154(N)

DATABASES

A *database* is a collection of information, stored and organized so that retrieval of any specific data item(s) is fast and easy. The collection can be large or small, the organization of the data can be simple or complex, and the method of retrieval can be sophisticated or unsophisticated. The fact remains that a database is nothing more than a collection of data organized in some form or fashion.

Databases have been around since humans first started recording history. In fact, the recording of history itself is nothing more than a database of events organized in chronological order. A dictionary is another example of a database. It is nothing more than a collection of the words that compose a language, organized alphabetically. Likewise, the card catalog found in the library is nothing more than a database of books organized in some fashion, usually by author, title, and/or subject. And a newspaper is still another example of a database—representing a collection of news items organized by chronological order (published daily), by subject (placement within the various sections of the paper) and by importance (page placement within each section). The point is, any collection of data, organized in some fashion as to allow for retrieval of specific information can be thought of as a database.

Over the years, ownership and control of data has grown into a big business. For example, over half of this country's gross national product is derived from some form of service: be that the creation, maintenance, interpretation, sale, application, or use of information known by someone and useful to somebody else. Database information is used by virtually everyone, from the school child researching a paper, to the consumer evaluating a product, to the businessperson doing strategic planning, to the government evaluating the effects of a legislative proposal. Data is used to make decisions, solve problems, and plan for the future. In fact, it is used in virtually every aspect of our daily lives.

To satisfy this voracious appetite for information, thousands of databases have come into existence in a variety of fields. Subjects covered by databases range from literature to history, news to travel, and consumer services to business and finance. Today, most databases are created and maintained on computers. The reasons for this are simple:

1. Computers are capable of storing and accessing an enormous amount of information.
2. Computers can quickly and easily manipulate data, handling many more variables with greater consistency than people can.

3. Computer databases can be updated continuously, with the new data instantaneously available to a network of users.
4. Computer databases can be linked and integrated with other computer databases with relative ease, allowing for virtually unlimited expansion of available information.
5. Computer databases can be accessed from diverse geographical locations through a variety of means, making access to data conveniently available to even the remotest locations.

Despite the fact that the actual data resides on computers, most database information is still available in two formats: hard copy and electronic. Data may be physically distributed on paper, tape, or disk; it may be distributed electronically through broadcast media such as hardwire, FM radio, and satellites; or it may be distributed through a dial-up phone network. Each database is organized differently, determined by the specific types of data available, the urgency of the information, and the requirements of the subscribers.

Some databases are controlled and organized by nonprofit enterprises such as libraries and schools, whereas others are organized and maintained strictly for profit. Some databases restrict access to a designated group of users; others are available to the general public. Some databases charge a flat fee for unlimited use; others charge a fee for usage based on the time of the day, the amount of computer time used, the speed of data transmission, and the types of information requested. Some databases provide only raw data for transmission to remote computers for on-site analysis; others provide extensive on-line data manipulation and analysis services.

In fact, about the only thing that can be said about databases in general is that they are all unique. They differ with respect to the types of data they contain, the manner by which the data is organized, the method by which the user is charged, and the manner by which the data is delivered. But these points notwithstanding, there is virtually no better way to evaluate huge amounts of data than to have it organized and maintained on computer, available on request.

As investors, we are concerned only with a small subset of the databases available, so the remaining discussion focuses on this subset.

Investor databases, or *business and financial databases* as they are sometimes called, are designed to serve one of two purposes:

- to provide up-to-the-minute security pricing information with which to monitor securities portfolios;
- to provide background information by which to select, evaluate, and construct portfolios.

The former category of databases, called *quote databases,* provide subscribers with access to current pricing information on various security issues. This type of database is typically used by amateur and professional investors, institutions, and money management personnel such as financial planners, investment advisors, and stockbrokers. Many of the vendors of this kind of database offer two types of quote delivery services: a real-time pricing option and a delayed pricing option. With the delayed pricing option, pricing information is delayed fifteen minutes before it is transmitted to subscribers, and no restrictions are placed on who can qualify for this service. Under the real-time option, pricing information is transmitted immediately, but permission must be obtained from the appropriate exchanges and exchange fees must be paid before a subscriber can qualify for this service.

The other category of databases, here called *historical databases,* provide subscribers with historical company data, balance sheets, income statements, current and historical security pricing information, industry and market statistical data, general and proprietary research opinions, and/or news items. They may also provide specialty information items such as government econometric data, tax, court, and legislative transcripts, insider trading, and a host of other items that could help in the investment decision-making process. The target market for this type of database is more general in nature, providing information to both amateur and professional investors as well as academicians, corporate executives, lawyers, accountants, and the like.

Some database suppliers have even linked together both types of databases, hoping to garner a larger share of the subscribers' research dollars and tighter control over subscribers in general. Some suppliers have even gone so far as to link the whole service into the back office computer of a brokerage firm, providing subscribers with an on-line order execution service. Other vendors have branched out in different directions, providing airline schedules, computer software/hardware forums, electronic mail services, consumer shopping "catalogs," and a host of other items to attract a larger market share.

All in all, just about any need investors might have can be satisfied by selecting among the many databases. The data is available so long as you have the means to "capture" it and the money to pay for it.

HOW DATA IS DELIVERED

In general, databases deliver information to subscribers in one of three ways: via continuous broadcast, through dial-up, and on magnetic media.

Broadcast Databases

Broadcast databases transmit data to the subscriber in a continuous mode, requiring the subscriber to have equipment dedicated to the task of receiving and storing the data as it arrives. Typically, data is delivered by a hardwired phone line (one dedicated to these transmissions) or satellite transmission, though some databases have chosen to use FM radio band to transmit the data stream. Data transmission is unidirectional in that it always originates from the data supplier and is always received by the subscriber's unit.

In essence, the subscriber's unit acts as a data storage device for the data being broadcasted. The unit basically serves four functions:

1. It "captures" the data which is being broadcast.
2. It stores the data in memory or on disk.
3. It takes requests for specific data items from the user.
4. It responds to the requests by searching its "own" data store to find the appropriate responses, displaying the answers.

This type of database normally requires a highly sophisticated receiving device at least as powerful as an IBM PC-XT, or a "black box" built by the vendor specifically for this purpose. Because of the design used, this type of database is limited by the speed and data storage capabilities of the selected device, therefore limiting future expansion capabilities for both the vendor and the subscriber. Unfortunately, this type of data delivery method more or less obligates the subscriber to dedicate a piece of equipment to the task, often requiring the subscriber to either buy or rent the necessary hardware. By the same token, the vendor is also obliged to make a very substantial investment in equipment, whether it be hardwiring terminals, setting up an FM transmitter, or dedicating a satellite transponder.

For all intents and purposes, this type of delivery mode is used exclusively for quote database services. The reasons are simple—quote databases require:

- a static amount of storage space (be that as it may, a large amount of storage space, but reasonably static);
- instantaneous data delivery; and,
- continuous updating.

Basically, the broadcast method represents the only reasonable alternative to accomplish these objectives, because with it subscribers can be "connected" to the vendor ad infinitum and responses to data requests can be instantaneous. With this method, there is no need to wait for a modem line into the vendor's mainframe to become available, no need to wade through a sophisticated log-on procedure, and no need to wait for a response to come down a phone line at 300 or 1200 baud—the data is already stored on-site in the "black box" or is accessible through a hardwired network at speeds far faster than could ever be achieved on a nonconditioned phone line.

Dial-up Databases

Dial-up databases transmit data to the subscriber through the use of phone lines and modems. Typically, this type of database transmits data only in response to a specific request for information, charging the subscriber on a piecemeal basis for every item requested plus a time charge for delivery.

From the subscriber's point of view, there are several major benefits to this type of database, including:

1. the ability to access enormous amounts of data obtained from diverse sources;
2. the speed of data retrieval and manipulation afforded by a mainframe computer system;
3. the cross-reference and index maintenance done by the vendor;
4. the pay-per-use billing structure, typically with no minimum monthly charges; and,
5. the minimal equipment requirements placed on the subscriber by the vendor.

In addition, many of the dial-up databases are linked to other dial-up databases to provide for even greater data selection. Some also carry on-line versions of research opinions and investment newsletters, so subscribers can buy the information they require on an as-needed basis.

By virtue of the dial-up method of communication, vendors have been forced to overcome several basic difficulties that result when one computer attempts to communicate with another. Specifically, in order for communication to be successful, the computers must:

1. talk through a quiet phone line (clear of noise and distortion);
2. talk at the same speed (also known as baud rate);
3. talk in the same language (using the same number of data bits and stop bits);
4. correctly confirm what has been said (using the same parity); and,
5. display the information received in the proper fashion on the subscriber's terminal (using the correct terminal definition for screen input and output).

To be sure, most vendors have adopted one of two solutions to these communication problems; either they require you to purchase the specific hardware and software combination they intend to support, or they design their interface system so it properly communicates with the least sophisticated piece of hardware expected to be used by their target market. In the former scenario, you may be forced to buy the communications hardware and software the database vendor recommends—a potentially costly process for you. Given the latter alternative, you can be sure that the system will not implement any sophisticated screen-handling features or handle data speeds exceeding 1200 baud. And, on the rare occasion you find a vendor who may be willing to let you try to interface nonstandard equipment into the network, be prepared for what could become a struggle of monumental proportions.

Other disadvantages of a dial-up database service are:

1. limited numbers of access lines (forcing subscribers to wait until such become available);
2. lengthy sign-on procedures;
3. slow data transmission (typically not exceeding 1200 baud); and,
4. long distance phone charges or local network surcharges.

While some database vendors only provide a long distance phone number to connect into the service, others have gone to the opposite extreme of providing a toll-free 800 number for subscribers to call. Most vendors, however, have taken a more moderate stance, tying the database into one of the nation's phone-linking services such as Autonet, Dialnet, Telenet, or Tymnet. To be sure, whichever method is chosen, subscribers ultimately pay for the phone call, whether it's directly through their own phone bills or indirectly through telephone link surcharges or higher vendor connect charges.

Magnetic Media Databases

Magnetic media databases transmit data to the subscriber by physically delivering data on magnetic media such as disks or tape. The subscriber can then analyze the information on-site as needed, in any fashion as desired, using proprietary techniques with absolute security. Obviously, data transmitted in this fashion cannot be as timely as data transmitted through broadcast or dial-up means, making this method of data delivery reasonable only when the information need not be updated continuously or instantaneously.

Probably the biggest advantage to this method of data delivery is that it represents the only reasonable method to deliver the enormous quantities of data that are sometimes required. Bearing in mind that data transmission through broadcast means or dial-up rarely exceeds 9600 baud (typically it doesn't exceed 1200 baud), magnetic media data transmission is tens to hundreds of times faster once the data tape or disk has been physically delivered.

Another advantage of this method of delivery is that neither the subscriber nor the vendor is required to dedicate equipment exclusively to the task of data transmission and retrieval. Additionally, subscribers are able to use whatever equipment they choose to analyze the data, so long as the tape or disk drive can read the media. Plus, vendors will not be required to support any specific hardware configurations except those required to write the data correctly. Finally, subscribers can analyze the data to their heart's content, with no restrictions placed on methodology, no charges assessed for time and usage, and no phone line charges or network surcharges to worry about.

These points notwithstanding, most magnetic media databases designed for use by the general public tend to restrict the media on which the information is stored. The reasons for this are simple: as a rule, the general public does not have access to equipment that reads magnetic tape, so the medium used by vendors is floppy disks. Since subscribers use a wide variety of personal computers, which in turn use a wide variety of incompatible disk formats, vendors are forced to place some restrictions on their target markets. Typically, they choose to support the data formats used by IBM and Apple. By the same token, since most of the general public does not do its own programming, vendors have been forced to write software to work in conjunction with their data or make their data work in conjunction with existing popular software. This, too, may cause some limitations on the vendor's ability and willingness to support a specific machine, but generally vendors try to support Apple, IBM, and a wide variety of compatible and near compatible machines, including most computers that run MS-DOS.

All in all, vendors have made every attempt to select the method of data delivery that best suits the information contained in their databases, with an eye towards efficient, cost effective, timely service. After all, database vendors are in business, too, and serving the needs of subscribers is the best way to stay in business. By the same token, vendors are also forced to make decisions regarding what information is to be included in the database and what charges are to be applied for the use of such data. It is in review of these latter points that the remainder of this discussion is devoted.

DATABASE QUESTIONNAIRES—BACKGROUND

The following information has been obtained from a survey of more than sixty firms identifying themselves as database suppliers. Unfortunately, as with the discount brokerage houses, several firms felt they had insufficient need to publicize their services. Therefore, several databases are not represented herein.

Just as has been done throughout the book, every attempt has been made to report all responses consistently; the same terminology was used across respondents so that comparisons can be made and conclusions drawn. Additionally, each respondent has been asked exactly the same questions in exactly the same manner. I hope that in this way it will make it easier for you to compare and contrast the services offered by each vendor with respect to your own specific needs, making it easier for you to draw your own conclusions. Additionally, the information is presented in a consistent fashion page by page, so that you can easily flip through the pages comparing response with response. Finally, I have adopted the default position that the database includes only those items that are expressly stated by the vendor. In the event no statements have been to the contrary, the presumption is that no data is included, and this fact will be signified by the use of a dash (—). By the same token, if the vendor includes information about specialty items unique to the database, they are reported in the appropriate section in the same fashion as the standard items, but their titles are preceded with an asterisk (*) so you can quickly identify them.

Supplier Contact Information

The name, address, and phone number of the database supplier is reported in the upper left-hand corner of the page. The name of the database, the type of database, the method of data delivery, the available phone links, and the number of current subscribers are reported in the upper right-hand corner of the page. Be aware that in order for you to use one of the phone link services to your advantage, it must have a local phone number for your area—otherwise you will end up paying for a long distance charge to the phone company for access plus a surcharge to the phone link network for their services.

Subscriber Levels

You should also note that the number of subscribers using the database service is generally proprietary information, so I was forced to offer large categories as potential responses in order to get any vendor to even consider answering the question. Unfortunately, even with the available choices, several vendors still refused to answer the question. In any case, the possible choices that were offered were:

1. under 25,000
2. 25,000 to 50,000
3. 50,000 to 100,000
4. 100,000 to 250,000

5. 250,000 to 500,000
6. 500,000 to 1,000,000
7. over 1,000,000

In most cases, vendors chose the answer "under 25,000," which unfortunately tells us little about the relative size of each vendor's client list. However, it does tell us that the concept is still reasonably new to consumers, that there is a lot of room for growth, and that the eventual shakeout which usually results when larger vendors (with economies of scale) begin to pressure smaller vendors may still be several years away. Furthermore, it also tells us that we, as potential subscribers, may still have some bargaining power left since there are a lot of vendors clamoring for our potential business.

Database Description

Next is a paraphrased version of what the vendor says the database contains. Every attempt has been made to remove boastful, sales-oriented comments by replacing them with simple, straightforward, descriptive phrases. Wherever possible, equivalent terminology has been used.

Types of Data Included

The next section overviews the type of data contained in the database:
- first, by generalizing information by security type;
- then by looking at the exchanges for which security data has been included; and,
- finally by identifying the specific items of information available for each security contained in the database.

Where appliable, comments have been included to more clearly describe the information that the database covers. For instance, if *only* the closing price of common stocks listed on the New York Stock Exchange are included in the database, and they are available for each day of the last five years, then:

1. Yes would appear under STOCKS in the securities portion of this section.
2. NYSE would appear in the COMMENTS portion of this section.
3. Yes would only appear under NYSE in the EXCHANGE portion of this section.
4. Yes would appear under the heading CLOSING PRICES (STOCKS) in the available information portion of this section.
5. (1) would appear under the heading CLOSING PRICES (STOCKS) in the available information portion of this section, referencing footnote (1) found immediately below, which would indicate "Data is available for the last five years."
6. All other items would contain a dash (—), signifying that they are not included in the database and therefore no data is available.

Quotes

Listed next are the availability of quotes and the forms in which they are available. Please remember, delayed pricing is available to anyone without restriction, and current pricing is available only by permission of the appropriate exchanges and upon payment of exchange fees. Most vendors who handle current quotes will supply you with the necessary documents to apply for exchange approval and will also assist you in completing them properly.

Hardware Requirements

This section details the equipment required to use the database as determined by the vendor. Remember, functionally equivalent machines may also work. That is, if the database states that it supports an IBM-PC, then most likely all PC clones will also work. If the database computer communicates with your hardware as if your hardware were "any terminal," this means that no special screen-handling protocol is used and that you can use virtually any terminal emulation program to operate your hardware.

Customer Support

Next, the availability of customer support by the vendor and the forms it takes are listed. Depending on the complexity of the database and thoroughness of the vendor, it may range from nonexistent, to on-line help, to a customer service phone number, to full documentation, to a training program.

Subscription Rates

The next section details the applicable subscription charges. At best, comparison of vendors on the basis of cost alone is difficult and probably should be avoided, since each database has a slightly different mix of information.

Note that aside from the fact that vendors really do not want to make it easy for us to compare their charges with that of their competitors, they often have a unique cost of data themselves. The reason for this is simple: some of their data is self-originated, and some of it is purchased. Thus, subscription charges must be a function of the vendor's costs of acquisition, their mix of the data, and their investment in storage hardware and delivery equipment. Basically, the vendor's costs are complex, so they make ours complex.

Where applicable, setup charges, basic rates for prime time and nonprime time usage, specialty charges, surcharges, and minimum monthly or flat rates charges have all been identified. To make your cost assessment more complete, you should also include the cost of your own equipment, phone-link charges, and telephone charges, where applicable, into your analysis.

Other Data

The Other Data section overviews more related information contained in the database, including:
- market statistics;
- company data;
- research opinions; and,
- new items.

If current data is contained in the database, a Yes will appear in the Current Data column. If historic data is available, a phrase describing how far back the data is available for will be found in the Historic Data column. As indicated previously, in the event that specialty items are available in the database, such as another research opinion or news service that the vendor chose to highlight, they are reported in the same fashion as the standard items, but their titles are preceded with an asterisk (*) so that you may quickly identify them as such.

Data Manipulation Capabilities

Next, the listings cover whether each database can manipulate data on request, such as the ability to construct charts/graphs, project trends, run regressions, and so forth. Here too, clarifying comments are included where applicable, and specialty items are preceded with an asterisk. By way of further clarification, some databases allow subscribers a certain amount of memory space to use for anything the subscriber wants. Clients can use the space for functions like saving sample portfolios, writing manipulation programs, and setting up security screening characteristics. If the database is set up in this fashion, a subscriber can save an enormous amount of clerical work not having to continually re-enter the same information. Typically, such memory space is functionally tied to the database information as well, so that sample portfolios can be automatically updated to current prices, and programs and screens can access database information. Finally, some databases allow subscribers to create windows or split columns on the screen, allowing for several functions to operate simultaneously.

Other Features

The final section, "Also worth mentioning," describes other items pertinent to the database that you should be aware of. Depending on the database, this section may contain no information, or it may describe specialty programs or services available to subscribers.

Argus Research Corp.
42 Broadway
New York City, NY 10006
(212) 425-7500

Argus On-Line
Historical
Dial-Up
Telenet/Tymnet
Less than 25,000 subscribers

Description of database:
    Argus On-Line is a menu-driven database providing access to economic, market, industry, and individual stock analyses prepared by the portfolio strategists, economists, and analysts at Argus Research.

The database contains CURRENT data for:

Securities:	Included	Comments
Stocks	Yes	400 selected companies
Corporate Bonds	—	—
GNMA/FNMA	—	—
Treasury Bills	—	—
Government Bonds	—	—
Options	—	—
Commodities	—	—
Financial Futures	—	—
Stock Index Futures	—	—

The exchanges included are:

American (ASE)	Yes	KCBT	—	Pacific (PSE)	—
Boston	—	MidAm	—	Philadelphia	—
Cincinnati	—	Midwest (MSE)	—	OTC-NASDAQ	Yes
CBOE	—	MnGE	—	OTC-NME	—
CBT	—	Montreal	—	Toronto	—
CME	—	NYFE	—	Vancouve	—
CEC	—	NYSE	Yes		

The available information is:

	Stocks	Bonds	Options	Commod	Fin'l Futures	Stk Indx Futures
Closing Prices:	—	—	—	—	—	—
Daily High-Low:	—	—	—	—	—	—
Yearly High-Low:	—	—	—	—	—	—
Bid-Ask:	—	—	—	—	—	—
Volume:	—	—	—	—	—	—

Availability of quotes:
    Not available.

The equipment required to use this database is:

Computer:	Any terminal
Operating system:	—
Monitor:	Mono or color
Disk drives:	Required only for terminal emulation program
Memory:	Required only for terminal emulation program
Modem:	300 or 1200 baud
Software:	—

Support services available:
    Users guide.

The charges for the service are:
    (1) Set-up charges: —
    (2) Basic rate: $1.00 per minute
    (3) Specialty charges: $100 annual charge

The database also contains:

Market Statistics:	Current	Historic Data
Market volume	—	—
Advancing issues	—	—
Advancing volume	—	—
Declining issues	—	—
Declining volume	—	—
Most active	—	—
Most up (%)	—	—
Most down (%)	—	—
Tick by volume	—	—
Trading indices (TRIN)	—	—
Dow Jones indices	—	—
NYSE indices	—	—
ASE indices	—	—
Nasdaq indices	—	—
Standard & Poor's indices	—	—
Financial future indices	—	—

Company data:		
Dividend $ amounts	Yes	—
Dividend yield	Yes	—
Dividend ex-dates	—	—
Dividend pay-dates	—	—
Earnings per share	Yes	—
Price Earnings ratio	Yes	—
Balance sheet	—	—
Income statement	—	—
Financial Ratios	Yes	—
Annual Reports	—	—
10-K's	—	—

Research opinions:		
Value Line	—	—
Standard & Poor's	—	—
Moody's	—	—
Argus	Yes	—

News:		
Dow Jones News Ticker	—	—
Reuters	—	—
Barrons	—	—
Wall Street Journal	—	—
* Miscellaneous sources	Yes	—

The database will:

	Capabilities	Comments
Construct charts/graphs	—	—
Project trends	—	—
Run regressions	—	—
Run other statistics	—	—
Create/Save my own portfolios	—	—
Window or split the screen	—	—
Write/run my own programs	—	—
Screen on certain characteristics	Yes	Up to 28 characteristics

It is also worth mentioning that:

"Argus On-Line" contains the same information which is available to subscribers of Argus' many investment publications.

Companies included in database are large capitalization, utility, and emerging growth companies as determined by Argus.

Bridge Inc.
10050 Manchester Road
St. Louis, MO 63122
(314) 821-5660
(800) 325-DATA

Bridge Information Systems
Quote/Historical
Dial-Up/Hardwire/Satellite
Local/Telenet/Tymnet
Number of subscribers is not available

Description of database:

Bridge Information System was developed by Bridge Inc. The database is designed to deliver a complete range of financial information, including real-time, last sale, quote data, technical and fundamental information, charts, news, market indices and more. Additionally, three levels of service are available to satisfy the needs of traders, strategists, and arbitragers.

The database contains CURRENT data for:

Securities:	Included	Comments
Stocks	Yes	—
Corporate Bonds	Yes	NYSE, ASE, and some OTC
GNMA/FNMA	Yes	—
Treasury Bills	Yes	—
Government Bonds	Yes	Treasury Bonds only
Options	Yes	—
Commodities	Yes	—
Financial Futures	Yes	—
Stock Index Futures	Yes	—

The exchanges included are:

American (ASE)	Yes	KCBT	Yes	Pacific (PSE)	Yes
Boston	Yes	MidAm	Yes	Philadelphia	Yes
Cincinnati	Yes	Midwest (MSE)	Yes	OTC-NASDAQ	Yes
CBOE	Yes	MnGE	Yes	OTC-NME	Yes
CBT	Yes	Montreal	Yes	Toronto	Yes
CME	Yes	NYFE	Yes	Vancouver	Yes
CEC	Yes	NYSE	Yes	* Australian	Yes
* European	Yes	* London	Yes	* Pacific/Far East	Yes

The available information is:

	Stocks	Bonds	Options	Commod	Fin'l Futures	Stk Indx Futures
Closing Prices:	Yes (1)	Yes	Yes (3)	Yes (2)	Yes (2)	Yes (2)
Daily High-Low:	Yes (1)	Yes	Yes (3)	Yes (1)	Yes (1)	Yes (1)
Yearly High-Low:	Yes (2)	Yes	Yes (3)	Yes (2)	Yes (2)	Yes (2)
Bid-Ask:	Yes (3)	Yes	Yes (3)	Yes	Yes	Yes
Volume:	Yes (2)	Yes	Yes (3)	Yes	Yes	Yes

Historical data available varies a great deal.
(1) Historical data available for 6 months.
(2) Historical data available for 10 years.
(3) Historical data available for 5 days.

Availability of quotes:

Real time basis only.

The equipment required to use this database is:

Computer:	IBM-AT or hardware provided by vendor
Operating system:	MS-DOS
Monitor:	Enhanced color screen and adaptor
Disk drives:	1 hard disk
Memory:	2+ megabytes
Modem:	300 or 1200 baud
Software:	Specialty software required

Support services available:

Seminars, on-line and printed documentation, sales/service technical hotline, and quarterly newsletter.

The charges for the service are:

(1) Set-up charges: $50
(2) Basic rate:
    (a) Prime time: Weekdays: 7 AM-6 PM $60 per hour
    (b) Non-prime time: Weekdays: 6 PM-7 AM $12 per hour
                                Weekends & Holidays
(3) Specialty charges: $50 monthly minimum for after-hour dial-up service
                               $200 monthly minimum for prime-time dial-up service

NOTE: Charges vary depending on the type of service chosen and the method of data delivery.

The database also contains:

Market Statistics:	Current Data	Historic Data
Market volume	Yes	10 years (weekly/monthly data)
Advancing issues	Yes	10 years (weekly/monthly data)
Advancing volume	—	—
Declining issues	Yes	10 years (weekly/monthly data)
Declining volume	—	—
Most active	Yes	5 days
Most up (%)	Yes	5 days
Most down (%)	Yes	5 days
Tick by volume	Yes	10 years (weekly/monthly data)
Trading indices (TRIN)	Yes	—
Dow Jones indices	Yes	10 years (weekly/monthly data)
NYSE indices	Yes	10 years (weekly/monthly data)
ASE indices	Yes	10 years (weekly/monthly data)
Nasdaq indices	Yes	10 years (weekly/monthly data)
Standard & Poor's indices	Yes	10 years (weekly/monthly data)
Financial future indices	Yes	10 years (weekly/monthly data)
* Dozens of market statistics *(See "It is also worth mentioning")	Yes	10 years (weekly/monthly data)

Company data:		
Dividend $ amounts	Yes	5 years
Dividend yield	Yes	5 years
Dividend ex-dates	Yes	5 years
Dividend pay-dates	Yes	5 years
Earnings per share	Yes	5 years
Price Earnings ratio	Yes	5 years
Balance sheet	—	—
Income statement	—	—
Financial Ratios	—	—
Annual Reports	—	—
10-K's	—	—

Research opinions:		
Value Line	—	—
Standard & Poor's	—	—
Moody's	—	—
Argus	—	—
* From various brokerage houses	Yes	—
* Fitch research	Yes	—
* DSI indices	Yes	—

News:		
Dow Jones News Ticker	Yes	3 months
Reuters	—	—
Barrons	Yes	3 months
Wall Street Journal	Yes	3 months
* Associated Press	Yes	—
* Business Wire	Yes	3 months
* Capital Market Reports	Yes	—

The database will:	Capabilities	Comments
Construct charts/graphs	Yes	—
Project trends	—	—
Run regressions	Yes	—
Run other statistics	Yes	—
Create/Save my own portfolios	Yes	Many
Window or split the screen	Yes	Up to 4 windows
Write/run my own programs	Yes	Using the Bridge Interface
Screen on certain characteristics	Yes	—

It is also worth mentioning that:

Bridge computes and is a primary source for many indices, a partial subset of which is listed below:

- AMEX (ASE) Indices (Various)
- AMEX (ASE) Transportation
- Gold & Silver
- High Tech (PSE)
- NYCE U.S. Dollar
- NYFE Commodity Research Bureau
- NYSE Double
- OTC 100; OTC 250
- S&P 100; S&P 500
- Value Line

Bridge Market Data offers several other database services including:

- *Bridge Speech System* — offering telephone dial-up for a computer generated verbal quote on over 30,000 securities;
- *Bridge Commodity Quotation Service* — offering a data stream of information on commodities and options;
- *Bridge Money Market* — offering prices and yields on domestic/international money market instruments and fixed income securities; spot and forward foreign exchange quotations; and financial future prices;
- *Bridge European* — offering prices and yields on the London and European markets; and,
- *Bridge Pacific* — offering prices and yields on the Australian and Pacific markets.

Commodity Information Service Co.

327 S. LaSalle
Suite 800
Chicago, IL 60604
(312) 922-3661

CISCO
Historical
Dial-Up
Local/Telenet/Timenet
Less than 25,000 subscribers

Description of database:
CISCO is a historical database covering futures, options on futures, government bonds, and selected money rates. Users have three modes of access:
- an on-line interactive mode which allows subscribers to use the power of a mainframe computer to analyze and screen the data, complete with a library of over 200 custom analysis programs;
- an "express" mode which allows subscribers to view over 3500 pages of data which are computed and updated on a daily basis; and,
- a data downloading mode which allows subscribers to capture and analyze data on their own personal computers.

The database contains CURRENT data for:

Securities:	Included	Comments
Stocks	—	—
Corporate Bonds	—	—
GNMA/FNMA	—	—
Treasury Bills	Yes	All
Government Bonds	Yes	All
Options	Yes	Options on futures only
Commodities	Yes	All
Financial Futures	Yes	All
Stock Index Futures	Yes	All

The exchanges included are:

American (ASE)	—	KCBT	Yes	Pacific (PSE)	—
Boston	—	MidAm	—	Philadelphia	—
Cincinnati	—	Midwest (MSE)	—	OTC-NASDAQ	—
CBOE	—	MnGE	Yes	OTC-NME	—
CBT	Yes	Montreal	—	Toronto	—
CME	Yes	NYFE	Yes	Vancouver	—
CEC	Yes	NYSE	—		

The available information is:

	Stocks	Bonds	Options	Commod	Fin'l Futures	Stk Indx Futures
Closing Prices:	—	—	—	Yes	Yes	Yes
Daily High-Low:	—	—	—	Yes	Yes	Yes
Yearly High-Low:	—	—	—	Yes	Yes	Yes
Bid-Ask:	—	—	—	—	—	—
Volume:	—	—	—	Yes	Yes	Yes

Historical data available from 1970.

Availability of quotes:
Not available.

The equipment required to use this database is:

Computer:	Any terminal
Operating system:	—
Monitor:	Mono or color
Disk drives:	Required only for terminal emulation program
Memory:	Required only for terminal emulation program
Modem:	300 or 1200 baud
Software:	Any terminal emulation program

Support services available:
Training, manual, and phone support.

The charges for the service are:
(1) Set-up Charges: $50
(2) Basic rate: $10 per hour plus $ .35 per CPU second
(3) Specialty charges: $100 minimum monthly charge applies

Note: Two other pricing services are available. See "It is also worth mentioning that:"

The database also contains:

Market Statistics:	Current Data	Historic Data
Market volume	—	—
Advancing issues	—	—
Advancing volume	—	—
Declining issues	—	—
Declining volume	—	—
Most active	—	—
Most up (%)	—	—
Most down (%)	—	—
Tick by volume	—	—
Trading indices (TRIN)	—	—
Dow Jones indices	—	—
NYSE indices	—	—
ASE indices	—	—
Nasdaq indices	—	—
Standard & Poor's indices	—	—
Financial future indices	Yes	Beginning of trading
* CBT Liquidity Data Bank	Yes	5 days-soon to be expanded

Company data:		
Dividend $ amounts	—	—
Dividend yield	—	—
Dividend ex-dates	—	—
Dividend pay-dates	—	—
Earnings per share	—	—
Price Earnings ratio	—	—
Balance sheet	—	—
Income statement	—	—
Financial Ratios	—	—
Annual Reports	—	—
10-K's	—	—

Research opinions:		
Value Line	—	—
Standard & Poor's	—	—
Moody's	—	—
Argus	—	—

News:		
Dow Jones News Ticker	—	—
Reuters	—	—
Barrons	—	—
Wall Street Journal	—	—

The database will:

	Capabilities	Comments
Construct charts/graphs	Yes	—
Project trends	Yes	—
Run regressions	Yes	—
Run other statistics	Yes	
Create/Save my own portfolios	Yes	Unlimited number
Window or split the screen	—	—
Write/run my own programs	Yes	—
Screen on certain characteristics	Yes	—

It is also worth mentioning that:

Two other pricing services are available:

- Express mode has a $50 set-up charge but no basic rate usage charges. Access is allowed to over 3500 pages of data with a specialty charge of $.75 to view each page.
- Data downloading mode has no set-up and no basic rate usage charges. Access is allowed to pre-arranged data only, and the specialty charge to capture the data is $.31 per contract per month. Data downloading is typically done over the phone lines, but data can also be delivered on diskettes.

CISCO also offers a computer software package for personal computers, called Futuresoft, which allows users to analyze data and create graphics in an operating environment similar to CISCO's mainframe environment. The cost for this program is $295.

CompuServe Information Service

P.O. Box 20212
Columbus, OH 43220
(614) 457-0802
(800) 848-8199

CompuServe
Quote/Historical
Dial-Up
Local
250,000 to 500,000 subscribers

Description of database:

CompuServe Information Service combines the information found in more than 400 databases which cover thousands of subject areas. General services include electronic mail, interactive games, news, weather, shopping, and special interest forums. Financial products include Standard and Poor's data, SEC information, on-line brokerage services, stock screening capabilities, Value Line data, and a variety of financial newsletters.

The database contains CURRENT data for:

Securities:	Included	Comments
Stocks	Yes	All
Corporate Bonds	—	—
GNMA/FNMA	—	—
Treasury Bills	—	—
Government Bonds	—	—
Options	—	—
Commodities	Yes	North American
Financial Futures	Yes	All
Stock Index Futures	Yes	All

The exchanges included are:

American (ASE)	Yes	KCBT	Yes	Pacific (PSE)	Yes
Boston	Yes	MidAm	Yes	Philadelphia	Yes
Cincinnati	Yes	Midwest (MSE)	Yes	OTC-NASDAQ	Yes
CBOE	Yes	MnGE	Yes	OTC-NME	Yes
CBT	Yes	Montreal	Yes	Toronto	Yes
CME	Yes	NYFE	Yes	Vancouver	—
CEC	Yes	NYSE	Yes	* IMM	Yes
* Winnipeg	Yes				

The available information is:

	Stocks	Bonds	Options	Commod	Fin'l Futures	Stk Indx Futures
Closing Prices:	Yes	Yes	Yes (1)	Yes (2)	Yes	Yes
Daily High-Low:	Yes	Yes	Yes (1)	Yes (2)	Yes	Yes
Yearly High-Low:	Yes	Yes	Yes (1)	Yes (2)	Yes	Yes
Bid-Ask:	Yes	Yes	Yes (1)	—	—	—
Volume:	Yes	Yes	Yes (1)	Yes (2)	Yes	Yes

Data available from 1974.

(1) Data available up to 3 months after expiration.

(2) Data available from 1979.

NOTE: Open interest data is also available for options, commodities, and futures.

Availability of quotes:

Delayed basis only.

The equipment required to use this database is:

Computer:	Any terminal
Operating system:	—
Monitor:	Mono or color
Disk drives:	Required only for terminal emulation program
Memory:	Required only for terminal emulation program
Modem:	300 or 1200 baud
Software:	Any terminal emulation program

Support services available:

Toll-free customer service, on-line "Feedback" service, and a monthly magazine, "Online Today."

The charges for the service are:

(1) Set-up charges: $39.95

(2) Basic rate:

    (a) Prime time: Weekdays: 8 AM-6 PM @ $12.50 per hour

    (b) Non-prime time: Weekdays: 6 PM-8 AM @ $6.00 per hour
                                       Weekends & Holidays

(3) Specialty charges: $25 per hour communications charge if using CompuServe network

The database also contains:

Market Statistics:	Current Data	Historic Data
Market volume	Yes	8 years
Advancing issues	Yes	8 years
Advancing volume	Yes	8 years
Declining issues	Yes	8 years
Declining volume	Yes	8 years
Most active	Yes	Previous day
Most up (%)	Yes	Previous day
Most down (%)	Yes	Previous day
Tick by volume	—	—
Trading indices (TRIN)	—	—
Dow Jones indices	Yes	12 years
NYSE indices	Yes	12 years
ASE indices	Yes	12 years
Nasdaq indices	Yes	12 years
Standard & Poor's indices	Yes	12 years
Financial future indices	Yes	7 years
* Dozens of market statistics	Yes	Various

Company data:		
Dividend $ amounts	Yes	22 years
Dividend yield	Yes	—
Dividend ex-dates	Yes	22 years
Dividend pay-dates	Yes	22 years
Earnings per share	Yes	1 year
Price Earnings ratio	Yes	—
Balance sheet	Yes	21 years
Income statement	Yes	21 years
Financial Ratios	Yes	21 years
Annual Reports	Yes	—
10-K's	Yes	—
* Ownership Filings	Yes	18 days

Research opinions:		
Value Line	Yes	—
Standard & Poor's	Yes	—
Moody's	—	—
Argus	—	—
* I B E S Consensus	Yes	—
* Money Market Services	Yes	6 weeks

News:		
Dow Jones News Ticker	—	—
Reuters	—	—
Barrons	—	—
Wall Street Journal	—	—
* Associated Press	Yes	30 days
* Washington Post	Yes	30 days
* OTC Newsalert	Yes	1 year

The database will:

	Capabilities	Comments
Construct charts/graphs	Yes	—
Project trends	—	—
Run regressions	—	—
Run other statistics	Yes	—
Create/Save my own portfolios	Yes	Unlimited number
Window or split the screen	—	—
Write/run my own programs	—	—
Screen on certain characteristics	Yes	Up to 44 characteristics

It is also worth mentioning that:

CompuServe's set-up charge includes a manual and $25 worth of free time.

CompuServe Information Service also offers:
- an interconnect with MCI Mail;
- an electronic news clipping service—covering the Associated Press Newswire and the "Washington Post"; and,
- IQuest—an access gateway to 700 additional databases, including Dialog.

Commodity Quotations Inc.

670 White Plains Road
Scarsdale, NY 10583
(914)725-3477
(800) 431-2602

Comstock

Quote
Satellite/FM Radio/Hardwire
Less than 25,000 subscribers

Description of database:

Comstock is a real-time quotation system that utilizes satellite, FM radio, or hardwire to deliver data tick-by-tick. Comstock is designed to work with virtually every type of PC or "dumb" terminal. Comstock covers stocks, options, and futures. Optional charting packages are also available.

The database contains CURRENT data for:

Securities:	Included	Comments
Stocks	Yes	—
Corporate Bonds	—	—
GNMA/FNMA	Yes	—
Treasury Bills	Yes	—
Government Bonds	—	—
Options	Yes	—
Commodities	Yes	—
Financial Futures	Yes	—
Stock Index Futures	Yes	—

The exchanges included are:

American (ASE)	Yes	KCBT	—	Pacific (PSE)	Yes
Boston	Yes	MidAm	—	Philadelphia	Yes
Cincinnati	Yes	Midwest (MSE)	Yes	OTC-NASDAQ	Yes
CBOE	Yes	MnGE	Yes	OTC-NME	Yes
CBT	Yes	Montreal	—	Toronto	—
CME	Yes	NYFE	—	Vancouver	—
CEC	Yes	NYSE	Yes		

The available information is:

	Stocks	Bonds	Options	Commod	Fin'l Futures	Stk Indx Futures
Closing Prices:	Yes	—	Yes	Yes	Yes	Yes
Daily High-Low:	Yes	—	Yes	Yes	Yes	Yes
Yearly High-Low:	—	—	—	—	—	—
Bid-Ask:	Yes	—	Yes	Yes	Yes	Yes
Volume:	Yes	—	Yes	Yes	Yes	Yes

Current prices available only. No historical data available.

Availability of quotes:

Both real time and delayed basis.

The equipment required to use this database is:

Computer:	Any terminal
Operating system:	—
Monitor:	Mono or color
Disk drives:	Required only for terminal emulation program
Memory:	Required only for terminal emulation program
Modem:	—
Software:	Any terminal emulation program

Support services available:

Training, documentation and technical hotline.

The charges for the service are:

(1) Set-up charges: $350
(2) Basic rate: —
(3) Specialty charges: $275 monthly fee which includes all transmission hardware
$300 equipment deposit required

The database also contains:

Market Statistics:	Current Data	Historic Data
Market volume	Yes	—
Advancing issues	Yes	—
Advancing volume	Yes	—
Declining issues	Yes	—
Declining volume	Yes	—
Most active	—	—
Most up (%)	Yes	—
Most down (%)	Yes	—
Tick by volume	Yes	—
Trading indices (TRIN)	Yes	—
Dow Jones indices	Yes	—
NYSE indices	Yes	—
ASE indices	Yes	—
Nasdaq indices	Yes	—
Standard & Poor's indices	Yes	—
Financial future indices	Yes	—

Company data:		
Dividend $ amounts	—	—
Dividend yield	—	—
Dividend ex-dates	—	—
Dividend pay-dates	—	—
Earnings per share	—	—
Price Earnings ratio	—	—
Balance sheet	—	—
Income statement	—	—
Financial Ratios	—	—
Annual Reports	—	—
10-K's	—	—

Research opinions:		
Value Line	—	—
Standard & Poor's	—	—
Moody's	—	—
Argus	—	—

News:		
Dow Jones News Ticker	—	—
Reuters	—	—
Barrons	—	—
Wall Street Journal	—	—

The database will:

	Capabilities	Comments
Construct charts/graphs	Yes	—
Project trends	Yes	—
Run regressions	Yes	—
Run other statistics	Yes	—
Create/Save my own portfolios	Yes	Up to 15 portfolios
Window or split the screen	Yes	Up to 4 windows/split screens
Write/run my own programs	Yes	—
Screen on certain characteristics	Yes	—

It is also worth mentioning that:

Software packages are optionally available which allow subscribers to save historical data.

Data Broadcasting Corporation

8300 Old Courthouse Road
Suite 200
Vienna, VA 22180
(703) 790-3570

DBC/Marketwatch™ Services
Quote
Broadcast
FNN Cable/Satellite
Number of subscribers is not available

Description of database:

DBC/Marketwatch™ Services is a real-time/delayed quote service for stocks and options. The database also allows subscribers to simultaneously view tickers, portfolios, monitors, and a newswire service. Subscription prices include the cost of the decoder (required for receiving the data signal) and all necessary decoding software.

The database contains CURRENT data for:

Securities:	Included	Comments
Stocks	Yes	All
Corporate Bonds	—	—
GNMA/FNMA	—	—
Treasury Bills	—	—
Government Bonds	—	—
Options	Yes	All
Commodities	—	—
Financial Futures	—	—
Stock Index Futures	—	—

The exchanges included are:

American (ASE)	Yes	KCBT	—	Pacific (PSE)	Yes
Boston	Yes	MidAm	—	Philadelphia	Yes
Cincinnati	Yes	Midwest (MSE)	Yes	OTC-NASDAQ	Yes
CBOE	Yes	MnGE	—	OTC-NME	Yes
CBT	—	Montreal	—	Toronto	—
CME	—	NYFE	—	Vancouver	—
CEC	—	NYSE	Yes		

The available information is:

	Stocks	Bonds	Options	Commod	Fin'l Futures	Stk Indx Futures
Closing Prices:	Yes	—	Yes	—	—	—
Daily High-Low:	Yes	—	Yes	—	—	—
Yearly High-Low:	—	—	—	—	—	—
Bid-Ask:	—	—	Yes	—	—	—
Volume:	Yes	—	Yes	—	—	—

Current prices available only. No historical data available.

Availability of quotes:

Both real time and delayed basis.

The equipment required to use this database is:

Computer:	IBM-PC, IBM-XT, IBM-AT
Operating system:	MS-DOS 2.0 or higher
Monitor:	Mono or color
Disk drives:	Two disk drives (floppies or hard)
Memory:	256K for stocks; 640K for stocks and options
Modem:	Supplied by vendor*
Software:	Supplied by vendor*

*NOTE: The proprietary decoder requires either a FNN cable or satellite signal.

Support services available:

Documentation, and technical hotline.

The charges for the service are:

(1) Set-up charges: $50 deposit
(2) Basic rate: —
(3) Specialty charges: $36 per month for delayed stock quotes only ranging to $89 month for real-time stock and option quotes, respectively.

The database also contains:

Market Statistics:	Current Data	Historic Data
Market volume	Yes	—
Advancing issues	Yes	—
Advancing volume	Yes	—
Declining issues	—	—
Declining volume	Yes	—
Most active	Yes	—
Most up (%)	Yes	—
Most down (%)	Yes	—
Tick by volume	—	—
Trading indices (TRIN)	Yes	—
Dow Jones indices	Yes	—
NYSE indices	Yes	—
ASE indices	Yes	—
Nasdaq indices	Yes	—
Standard & Poor's indices	Yes	—
Financial future indices	—	—

Company data:		
Dividend $ amounts	—	—
Dividend yield	—	—
Dividend ex-dates	—	—
Dividend pay-dates	—	—
Earnings per share	—	—
Price Earnings ratio	—	—
Balance sheet	—	—
Income statement	—	—
Financial Ratios	—	—
Annual Reports	—	—
10-K's	—	—

Research opinions:		
Value Line	—	—
Standard & Poor's	—	—
Moody's	—	—
Argus	—	—

News:		
Dow Jones News Ticker	—	—
Reuters	—	—
Barrons	—	—
Wall Street Journal	—	—

The database will:

	Capabilities	Comments
Construct charts/graphs	*	—
Project trends	*	—
Run regressions	*	—
Run other statistics	*	—
Create/Save my own portfolios	Yes	—
Window or split the screen	Yes	—
Write/run my own programs	*	—
Screen on certain characteristics	*	—

*NOTE: Outside vendors sell programs which can do many of these functions.

It is also worth mentioning that:

DBC/Marketwatch™ provides subscribers with unlimited access to the service for one flat monthly fee.

Disclosure
5161 River Road
Bethesda, MD 20816
(301) 951-1300

Disclosure Online Database
Historical
Dial-Up
Dialnet/Telenet
Number of subscribers is not available

Description of database:

Disclosure Online contains financial and management information on 11,000 publicly held U.S. and non-U.S. companies. Information is extracted from reports filed with the U.S. Securities and Exchange Commission. Data includes:
- annual and quarterly balance sheets, sources and uses of funds, and income statements;
- 32 annual financial ratios;
- information on subsidiaries, officers, directors, management discussions, and summary stock ownership data;
- citations to all exhibits, 8-K's filed, and the President's annual report letter to shareholders;
- weekly price earnings information;
- 30 identifying elements including Forbes, Fortune, CUSIP, and DUNS numbers, SIC codes, and ticker symbols;
- company address, telephone number; and,
- a brief description of the company's business.

The database contains CURRENT data for:

Securities:	Included	Comments
Stocks	Yes	—
Corporate Bonds	—	—
GNMA/FNMA	—	—
Treasury Bills	—	—
Government Bonds	—	—
Options	—	—
Commodities	—	—
Financial Futures	—	—
Stock Index Futures	—	—

The exchanges included are:

American (ASE)	Yes	KCBT	—	Pacific (PSE)	—
Boston	—	MidAm	—	Philadelphia	—
Cincinnati	—	Midwest (MSE)	—	OTC-NASDAQ	Yes
CBOE	—	MnGE	—	OTC-NME	Yes
CBT	—	Montreal	—	Toronto	—
CME	—	NYFE	—	Vancouver	—
CEC	—	NYSE	Yes		

The available information is:

	Stocks	Bonds	Options	Commod	Fin'l Futures	Stk Indx Futures
Closing Prices:	Yes	—	—	—	—	—
Daily High-Low:	Yes	—	—	—	—	—
Yearly High-Low:	Yes	—	—	—	—	—
Bid-Ask:	Yes	—	—	—	—	—
Volume:	Yes	—	—	—	—	—

Data compiled on a weekly basis only.

Availability of quotes:

Not available.

The equipment required to use this database is:

Computer:	Any terminal
Operating system:	—
Monitor:	Mono or color
Disk drives:	Required only for terminal emulation program
Memory:	Required only for terminal emulation program
Modem:	300 or 1200 baud
Software:	Any terminal emulation program

Support services available:

Training, manual, phone support, and bi-monthly newsletter.

The charges for the service are:

(1) Set-up charges: —
(2) Basic rate: —
(3) Specialty charges: Service is primarily available through outside vendors. Charges vary depending on which vendor is used, and charges are typically computed on a piecemeal basis.

The database also contains:

Market Statistics:	Current Data	Historic Data
Market volume	—	—
Advancing issues	—	—
Advancing volume	—	—
Declining issues	—	—
Declining volume	—	—
Most active	—	—
Most up (%)	—	—
Most down (%)	—	—
Tick by volume	—	—
Trading indices (TRIN)	—	—
Dow Jones indices	—	—
NYSE indices	—	—
ASE indices	—	—
Nasdaq indices	—	—
Standard & Poor's indices	—	—
Financial future indices	—	—
Company data:		
Dividend $ amounts	Yes	1 year
Dividend yield	—	—
Dividend ex-dates	Yes	1 year
Dividend pay-dates	Yes	1 year
Earnings per share	Yes	5 years
Price Earnings ratio	Yes	1 year
Balance sheet	Yes	5 years
Income statement	Yes	5 years
Financial Ratios	Yes	3 years
Annual Reports	Yes	5 years
10-K's	Yes	5 years
Research opinions:		
Value Line	—	—
Standard & Poor's	Yes	5 years
Moody's	Yes	5 years
Argus	—	—
News:		
Dow Jones News Ticker	—	—
Reuters	—	—
Barrons	—	—
Wall Street Journal	—	—

The database will:

	Capabilities	Comments
Construct charts/graphs	Yes	Through services of Compuserve
Project trends	Yes	Depends on database carrier used
Run regressions	Yes	Depends on database carrier used
Run other statistics	Yes	Depends on database carrier used
Create/Save my own portfolios	Yes	Depends on database carrier used
Window or split the screen	Yes	Depends on database carrier used
Write/run my own programs	Yes	Depends on database carrier used
Screen on certain characteristics	Yes	Up to 250 characteristics

It is also worth mentioning that:

All documents filed with the SEC as far back as 1966 are available on paper or microfiche. Documents can be delivered same day or overnight. Document prices vary.

Vendors which carry the Disclosure Online Database are:

- ADP
- BRS Information Technologies
- Compuserve
- Control Data Corp.
- DATEXT
- Dialog
- Dow Jones News Retrieval®
- IP Sharp
- Lotus Development Corp.
- Mead Data Central
- Quotron
- Savant Investor Services
- Warner Computer Service
- VU/TEXT®

Disclosure is also available through the Electronic Company Filing Index ($4200 per year) and on compact disks (prices range from $2200 to $4500 per year—compact disk reader included).

Dow Jones & Company, Inc.

P.O. Box 3000
Princeton, NJ 08543
(609) 452-2000

Dow Jones News/Retrieval®
Quote/Historical
Dial-Up
Telenet/Tymnet/DowNet/Datapac
Number of subscribers is not available

Description of database:
Dow Jones News/Retrieval® provides access to up-to-the minute news and information on a broad range of topics, including data contained in 40 other databases. It provides selected items from several news, financial, and investment services; research reports; on-line access to brokerage services; portfolio tracking systems; headlines and full-text reports of several important business publications and newswires; and a host of other items. Special features include security and futures quotes, combined with a news alert feature which indicates the occurrence of any late breaking news stories.

The database contains CURRENT data for:

Securities:	Included	Comments
Stocks	Yes	All
Corporate Bonds	Yes	—
GNMA/FNMA	—	—
Treasury Bills	Yes	—
Government Bonds	Yes	—
Options	Yes	—
Commodities	Yes	—
Financial Futures	—	—
Stock Index Futures	—	—

The exchanges included are:

American (ASE)	Yes	KCBT	Yes	Pacific (PSE)	Yes
Boston	—	MidAm	Yes	Philadelphia	Yes
Cincinnati	—	Midwest (MSE)	Yes	OTC-NASDAQ	Yes
CBOE	—	MnGE	Yes	OTC-NME	Yes
CBT	Yes	Montreal	—	Toronto	—
CME	Yes	NYFE	Yes	Vancouver	—
CEC	—	NYSE	Yes	* IMM	Yes
* Winnipeg	Yes				

The available information is:

	Stocks	Bonds	Options	Commod	Fin'l Futures	Stk Indx Futures
Closing Prices:	Yes (1)	Yes	Yes	Yes (2)	—	—
Daily High-Low:	Yes (3)	Yes	Yes	Yes	—	—
Yearly High-Low:	Yes (4)	—	—	—	—	—
Bid-Ask:	Yes	Yes	Yes	—	—	—
Volume:	Yes (4)	Yes	Yes	Yes	—	—

    Data available for current day only.
(1) Data available from 1978.
(2) Data available from 1970.

(3) Data available from 1985.
(4) Data available from 1981.

Availability of quotes:
    Both real time and delayed basis.

The equipment required to use this database is:

Computer:	Any terminal
Operating system:	—
Monitor:	Mono or color
Disk drives:	Required only for terminal emulation program
Memory:	Required only for terminal emulation program
Modem:	300 or 1200 baud
Software:	Any terminal emulation program

Support services available:
    Training seminars, manual, technical hotline, and ''Dowline,'' a monthly magazine.

The charges for the service are:
    (1) Set-up charges: $29.95
    (2) Basic rate:
        (a) Prime time: Weekdays: 6 AM-6 PM @ $ .30 to $1.20/min
        (b) Non-prime time: Weekdays: 6 PM-6 AM @ $ .10 to $ .80/min
                           Weekends & Holidays
    (3) Specialty charges: Dow Jones News/Retrieval® is available through several membership options. Per minute charges vary depending on the type of data used.

The database also contains:

Market Statistics:	Current Data	Historic Data
Market volume	Yes	—
Advancing issues	Yes	—
Advancing volume	Yes	—
Declining issues	Yes	—
Declining volume	Yes	—
Most active	Yes	—
Most up (%)	Yes	—
Most down (%)	Yes	—
Tick by volume	—	—
Trading indices (TRIN)	Yes	—
Dow Jones indices	Yes	4 years
NYSE indices	Yes	4 years
ASE indeces	Yes	4 years
Nasdaq indices	Yes	4 years
Standard & Poor's indices	Yes	4 years
Financial future indices	Yes	4 years
Company data:		
Dividend $ amounts	Yes	7 years
Dividend yield	Yes	—
Dividend ex-dates	Yes	—
Dividend pay-dates	Yes	—
Earnings per share	Yes	7 years
Price Earnings ratio	Yes	7 years
Balance sheet	Yes	2 years
Income statement	Yes	3 years
Financial Ratios	Yes	5 years
Annual Reports	Yes	5 years
10-K's	Yes	5 years
Research opinions:		
Value Line	—	—
Standard & Poor's	Yes	1 week
Moody's	—	—
Argus	—	—
* Investext	Yes	6 months
News:		
Dow Jones News Ticker	Yes	7 years
Reuters	—	—
Barrons	Yes	7 years
Wall Street Journal	Yes	7 years
* Financial World	Yes	1 year
* Forbes	Yes	1 year
* Inc.	Yes	1 year
* Washington Post	Yes	2 years

The database will:

	Capabilities	Comments
Construct charts/graphs	—	—
Project trends	Yes	—
Run regressions	—	—
Run other statistics	—	—
Create/Save my own portfolios	Yes	Up to 5
Window or split the screen	Yes	—
Write/run my own programs	—	—
Screen on certain characteristics	—	—

It is also worth mentioning that:

Dow Jones Market Manager Plus and Dow Jones Market Analyzer Plus, software packages for microcomputers, are also available.

Dow Jones News/Retrieval® provides access to data available through a number of other database vendors, including:
- Disclosure
- Insider Trading Monitor
- INVESTEXT
- Standard & Poor's Online
- Quicksearch

Charles Schwab & Co., Inc.
Investor Information Services
101 Montgomery Street
San Francisco, CA 94104
(415) 627-8665
(800) 334-4455

The Equalizer
Quote/Historical
Dial-Up
Tymnet/800-number
Less than 25,000 subscribers

Description of database:

The Equalizer is a database software package which:
- provides simplified access to research and news services found in several other databases including Dow Jones, Warner, and Standard & Poor's;
- enables investors to place security trades; and,
- automatically updates pricing on investment portfolios.

The database contains CURRENT data for:

Securities:	Included	Comments
Stocks	Yes	All
Corporate Bonds	Yes	Listed only
GNMA/FNMA	—	—
Treasury Bills	Yes	—
Government Bonds	Yes	—
Options	Yes	—
Commodities	Yes	—
Financial Futures	Yes	—
Stock Index Futures	Yes	—

The exchanges included are:

American (ASE)	Yes	KCBT	Yes	Pacific (PSE)	Yes
Boston	Yes	MidAm	Yes	Philadelphia	Yes
Cincinnati	Yes	Midwest (MSE)	Yes	OTC-NASDAQ	Yes
CBOE	Yes	MnGE	Yes	OTC-NME	Yes
CBT	Yes	Montreal	—	Toronto	—
CME	Yes	NYFE	Yes	Vancouver	—
CEC	Yes	NYSE	Yes	* IMM	Yes
* Winnipeg	Yes				

The available information is:

	Stocks	Bonds	Options	Commod	Fin'l Futures	Stk Indx Futures
Closing Prices:	Yes	Yes (1)	Yes (2)	Yes (4)	—	Yes
Daily High-Low:	Yes	Yes (1)	Yes (2)	Yes (3)	—	Yes
Yearly High-Low:	Yes	—	—	—	—	—
Bid-Ask:	Yes	Yes (3)	Yes (3)	—	—	—
Volume:	Yes	Yes (3)	Yes (3)	Yes (3)	—	—

    Data available for the past 10 years.
(1) Data available for the past month.
(2) Data available for the life of the option.

(3) Data available for current day only.
(4) Data available for 16 years.

Availability of quotes:

Both real time and delayed basis.

The equipment required to use this database is:

Computer:	IBM PC, IBM-XT, Apple IIe, Apple IIc
Operating system:	UCSDP System (DOS version available soon)
Monitor:	Mono or color
Disk drives:	—
Memory:	128K
Modem:	300 or 1200 baud
Software:	"The Equalizer"

Support services available:

Complete manual and quick reference card, toll-free customer service available (12 hours per day, 5 days per week), and a quarterly newsletter.

The charges for the service are:

(1) Set-up charges: —
(2) Basic rate:
   (a) Prime time: Weekdays: 6 AM-6 PM ranging to $ .90/min
   (b) Non-prime time: Weekdays: 6 PM-6 AM ranging to $ .20/min
               Weekends & Holidays
(3) Specialty charges: $199 for software package "The Equalizer"
            Per page and per report usage charges apply to Standard & Poor's data

The database also contains:

Market Statistics:	Current Data	Historic Data
Market volume	Yes	10 years
Advancing issues	Yes	10 years
Advancing volume	Yes	10 years
Declining issues	Yes	10 years
Declining volume	Yes	—
Most active	Yes	—
Most up (%)	Yes	—
Most down (%)	Yes	—
Tick by volume	—	—
Trading indices (TRIN)	Yes	—
Dow Jones indices	Yes	10 years
NYSE indices	Yes	10 years
ASE indices	Yes	10 years
Nasdaq indices	Yes	10 years
Standard & Poor's indices	Yes	10 years
Financial future indices	Yes	4 years

Company data:		
Dividend $ amounts	Yes	10 years
Dividend yield	Yes	10 years
Dividend ex-dates	Yes	10 years
Dividend pay-dates	Yes	10 years
Earnings per share	Yes	10 years
Price Earnings ratio	Yes	10 years
Balance sheet	Yes	20 years
Income statement	Yes	20 years
Financial Ratios	Yes	10 years
Annual Reports	Yes	5 years
10-K's	Yes	5 years

Research opinions:		
Value Line	—	—
Standard & Poor's	Yes	1 week
Moody's	—	—
Argus	—	—
* Investext	Yes	6 months

News:		
Dow Jones News Ticker	Yes	7 years
Reuters	—	—
Barrons	Yes	7 years
Wall Street Journal	Yes	7 years
* American Banker	Yes	1 year
* Financial World	Yes	1 year
* Forbes	Yes	1 year
* Inc.	Yes	1 year
* The PR Newswire	Yes	1 year
* Washington Post	Yes	2 years

The database will:

	Capabilities	Comments
Construct charts/graphs	Yes	—
Project trends	Yes	—
Run regressions	—	—
Run other statistics	Yes	—
Create/Save my own portfolios	Yes	Up to 5
Window or split the screen	Yes	—
Write/run my own programs	Yes	—
Screen on certain characteristics	Yes	—

It is also worth mentioning that:

The firm also offers:
- Schwab Quotes—an automated news and quotes service available from any touch tone phone;
- Schwabline—a new and unique printer service that provides automatic personalized printouts of current news, quotes and portfolio valuations; and,
- a full range of brokerage services.

Mead Data Central, Inc.
9393 Springboro Pike, P.O. Box 933
Dayton, OH 45401
(513) 865-7466
(513) 865-7209

Exchange®
Historical
Dial-Up
Local/Telenet/Tymnet/Meadnet/800-number
100,000 to 250,000 subscribers

Description of database:
Exchange® is a database of full-text research reports on U.S. and international companies and industries prepared by analysts at investment banking, brokerage, and research firms. Company reports include: an overview of each company, earnings per share figures, price earnings ratios, yield, and dividend information; assessment of strength within the industry; and an analysis of the company's plans and the impact of these plans. Exchange® also includes 10-Q's and 10-K's filed by over 1500 companies; extracted information from SEC filings on 10,000 companies; market share and other information on 250,000 companies; transcripts of presentations to The New York Society of Security Analysts; information on limited partnerships; and a host of additional information. Information is basically organized in narrative form using tabular data.

The database contains CURRENT data for:

Securities:	Included	Comments
Stocks	—	—
Corporate Bonds	—	—
GNMA/FNMA	—	—
Treasury Bills	—	—
Government Bonds	—	—
Options	—	—
Commodities	—	—
Financial Futures	—	—
Stock Index Futures	—	—

The exchanges included are:

American (ASE)	—	KCBT	—	Pacific (PSE)	—
Boston	—	MidAm	—	Philadelphia	—
Cincinnati	—	Midwest (MSE)	—	OTC-NASDAQ	—
CBOE	—	MnGE	—	OTC-NME	—
CBT	—	Montreal	—	Toronto	—
CME	—	NYFE	—	Vancouver	—
CEC	—	NYSE	—		

The available information is:

	Stocks	Bonds	Options	Commod	Fin'l Futures	Stk Indx Futures
Closing Prices:	—	—	—	—	—	—
Daily High-Low:	—	—	—	—	—	—
Yearly High-Low:	—	—	—	—	—	—
Bid-Ask:	—	—	—	—	—	—
Volume:	—	—	—	—	—	—

Availability of quotes:
Not available.

The equipment required to use this database is:

Computer:	IBM-PC, IBM-XT, IBM-AT, Apple II, IIc, IIe, any MS-DOS PC
Operating system:	PC-DOS, MS-DOS, Apple-DOS
Monitor:	Mono or color
Disk drives:	Required only for terminal emulation program
Memory:	Required only for terminal emulation program
Modem:	300 or 1200 baud
Software:	Any terminal emulation program

Support services available:
Manuals, newsletter, applications brochures, training in MDC offices, and toll-free customer service (24 hours per day, 7 days per week).

The charges for the service are:

			Regular	WATS	
(1) Set-up charges:	—				
(2) Basic rate:					
(a) Prime time:	Weekdays: 7:30 AM-7:30 PM @		$30.00	35.00	per hour
(b) Non-Prime time:	Weekdays: 7:30 PM-7:30 AM @		$21.00	24.50	per hour
	Weekends & Holidays.				
(3) Specialty:	$50 per month subscription fee				
	File charges ranging from $7 to $23				

The database also contains:

Market Statistics:	Current Data	Historic Data
Market volume	—	—
Advancing issues	—	—
Advancing volume	—	—
Declining issues	—	—
Declining volume	—	—
Most active	—	—
Most up (%)	—	—
Most down (%)	—	—
Tick by volume	—	—
Trading indices (TRIN)	—	—
Dow Jones indices	—	—
NYSE indices	—	—
ASE indices	—	—
Nasdaq indices	—	—
Standard & Poor's indices	—	—
Financial future indices	—	—

Company data:		
Dividend $ amounts	Yes	Varies
Dividend yield	Yes	Varies
Dividend ex-dates	Yes	Varies
Dividend pay-dates	Yes	Varies
Earnings per share	Yes	5 years
Price Earnings ratio	Yes	—
Balance sheet	Yes	5 years
Income statement	Yes	5 years
Financial Ratios	Yes	2 years
Annual Reports	Yes	5 years
10-K's	Yes	3 years
10-Q's	Yes	3 years

Research opinions:		
Value Line	—	—
Standard & Poor's	—	—
Moody's	—	—
Argus	Yes	4 years

News:		
Dow Jones News Ticker	—	—
Reuters	Yes	8 years
Barrons	—	—
Wall Street Journal	Yes	13 years
* Reuters North European	Yes	6 years

The database will:

	Capabilities	Comments
Construct charts/graphs	—	—
Project trends	—	—
Run regressions	—	—
Run other statistics	—	—
Create/Save my own portfolios	—	—
Window or split the screen	—	—
Write/run my own programs	—	—
Screen on certain characteristics	—	—

It is also worth mentioning that:

Mead Data Central provides other database services:
- *LEXIS®* — a computer assisted legal research service;
- *NAARS* — an accounting database for CPA's; and,
- *NEXIS®* — composed of the full text of more than 160 information sources, newspapers, magazines, professional journals, and wire services.

Automatic Data Processing (ADP)
175 Jackson Plaza
Ann Arbor, MI 48106
(313) 769-6800

Fastock II
Historical
Dial-Up
Local/Telenet/Tymnet/Datapac/Hardwire/800-number
Number of subscribers is not available

Description of database:
Fastock II contains both current and historical, trading and descriptive information on over 100,000 issues. The database covers options; market and security statistics; dividend, interest, and stock distribution data; common stocks; preferred and convertible preferred stocks and bonds; warrants and rights; government, municipal, and corporate bonds; mutual and money market funds; and when-issued securities.

The database contains CURRENT data for:

Securities:	Included	Comments
Stocks	Yes	—
Corporate Bonds	Yes	—
GNMA/FNMA	Yes	—
Treasury Bills	Yes	—
Government Bonds	Yes	—
Options	Yes	—
Commodities	—	—
Financial Futures	Yes	—
Stock Index Futures	Yes	—
* Municipal Bonds	Yes	3500 issues

The exchanges included are:

America (ASE)	Yes	KCBT	—	Pacific (PSE)	Yes
Boston	Yes	MidAm	—	Philadelphia	Yes
Cincinnati	Yes	Midwest (MSE)	Yes	OTC-NASDAQ	Yes
CBOE	Yes	MnGE	—	OTC-NME	Yes
CBT	—	Montreal	Yes	Toronto	Yes
CME	—	NYFE	Yes	Vancouver	—
CEC	Yes	NYSE	Yes		

The available information is:

	Stocks	Bonds	Options	Commod	Fin'l Futures	Stk Index Futures
Closing Prices:	Yes	Yes	Yes (1)	—	Yes (2)	Yes
Daily High-Low:	Yes	Yes	Yes (1)	—	Yes (2)	Yes
Yearly High-Low:	Yes (3)	Yes (3)	Yes (3)	—	Yes (3)	Yes (3)
Bid-Ask:	Yes	Yes	Yes (1)	—	Yes (2)	Yes
Volume:	Yes	Yes	Yes (1)	—	Yes (2)	Yes

Historical data available for 12 years.
(1) Data available for 1 year.
(2) Data available for 2 years.
(3) Data calculated and updated nightly.

Availability of quotes:
Not available.

The equipment required to use this database is:

Computer:	Any terminal (VT-100 emulation)
Operating system:	—
Monitor:	Mono or color
Disk drives:	Required only for terminal emulation program
Memory:	Required only for terminal emulation program
Modem:	300 through 9600 baud
Software:	—

Support services available:
Training, documentation, and technical hotline.

The charges for the service are:
(1) Set-up charges: $100
(2) Basic rate:
    (a) Primetime: Mon-Sat: 6 AM-6 PM @ $35/hour + $.03/CRU*
    (b) Non-prime time: Mon-Sat: 6 PM-6 AM @ $35/hour + $.013/CRU*
        Sundays & Holidays
(3) Specialty charges: $500 monthly minimum charge

*NOTE: A CRU is a Computer Resource Unit which is a measure of the computing power used.

The database also contains:

Market Statistics:	Current Data	Historic Data
Market volume	Yes	12 years
Advancing issues	Yes	12 years
Advancing volume	Yes	12 years
Declining issues	Yes	12 years
Declining volume	Yes	12 years
Most active	—	—
Most up (%)	—	—
Most down (%)	—	—
Tick by volume	—	—
Trading indices (TRIN)	Yes	12 years
Dow Jones indices	Yes	12 years
NYSE indices	Yes	12 years
ASE indices	Yes	12 years
Nasdaq indices	Yes	12 years
Standard & Poor's indices	Yes	12 years
Financial future indices	Yes	12 years

Company data:		
Dividend $ amounts	Yes	17 years
Dividend yield	Yes	17 years
Dividend ex-dates	Yes	17 years
Dividend pay-dates	Yes	17 years
Earnings per share	Yes	17 years
Price Earnings ratio	Yes	17 years
Balance sheet	Yes	17 years
Income statement	Yes	—
Financial Ratios	Yes	—
Annual Reports	Yes	—
10-K's	Yes	—

Research opinions:		
Value Line	—	—
Standard & Poor's	—	—
Moody's	—	—
Argus	—	—

News:		
Dow Jones News Ticker	—	—
Reuters	—	—
Barrons	—	—
Wall Street Journal	—	—

The database will:

	Capabilities	Comments
Construct charts/graphs	Yes	—
Project trends	Yes	—
Run regressions	Yes	—
Run other statistics	Yes	—
Create/Save my own portfolios	Yes	Unlimited number
Window or split the screen	Yes	—
Write/run my own programs	Yes	—
Screen on certain characteristics	Yes	Unlimited number

Engineering Management Consultants

P.O. Box 312
Fairfax, VA 22030
(703) 791-4675

FOURCAST™
Quote/Historical
Dial-Up
Local/Tymnet
Less than 25,000 subscribers

Description of database:

FOURCAST™ covers historical data on securities, options, commodities, market indices, and statistics. Data can be analyzed, transformed, plotted, and used in trend and change-in-trend forecasting.

The database contains CURRENT data for:

Securities:	Included	Comments
Stocks	Yes	All Standard & Poor's issues
Corporate Bonds	Yes	—
GNMA/FNMA	—	—
Treasury Bills	Yes	—
Government Bonds	Yes	—
Options	Yes	—
Commodities	Yes	—
Financial Futures	—	—
Stock Index Futures	—	—

The exchanges included are:

American (ASE)	Yes	KCBT	Yes	Pacific (PSE	Yes
Boston	Yes	MidAm	—	Philadelphia	Yes
Cincinnati	—	Midwest (MSE)	—	OTC-NASDAQ	Yes
CBOE	Yes	MnGE	Yes	OTC-NME	—
CBT	Yes	Montreal	—	Toronto	—
CME	Yes	NYFE	Yes	Vancouver	—
CEC	Yes	NYSE	Yes	* IMM	Yes
* LCME	Yes	* NCE	Yes	* WGE	Yes

The available information is:

	Stocks	Bonds	Options	Commod	Fin'l Futures	Stk Indx Futures
Closing Prices:	Yes	Yes	Yes (1)	Yes (2)	—	—
Daily High-Low:	Yes	Yes	Yes (1)	Yes (2)	—	—
Yearly High-Low:	—	—	—	—	—	—
Bid-Ask:	—	—	—	—	—	—
Volume:	Yes	Yes	Yes (1)	Yes (2)	—	—

Data available from 1970.
(1) Data available from 1984.
(2) Data available from 1966.

Availability of quotes:

Delayed basis only.

The equipment required to use this database is:

Computer:	IBM-PC
Operating system:	PC-DOS or MS-DOS
Monitor:	Mono or color
Disk drives:	Two disk drives (floppies or hard)
Memory:	190K
Modem:	300 or 1200 baud
Software:	FOURCAST™ $30

Support services available:

Manual, phone support.

The charges for the service are:

(1) Set-up charges: —
(2) Basic rate:
    (a) Prime time: 10 AM-8 PM @ $ .01 per issue per day
    (b) Non-prime time: 8 PM-10 AM @ $ .005 per issue per day
(3) Specialty charges: $15 monthly access charge
                                  FOURCAST™ software @ $30

The database also contains:

Market Statistics:	Current Data	Historic Data
Market volume	Yes	—
Advancing issues	—	—
Advancing volume	—	—
Declining issues	—	—
Declining volume	—	—
Most active	—	—
Most up (%)	—	—
Most down (%)	—	—
Tick by volume	—	—
Trading indices (TRIN)	—	—
Dow Jones indices	Yes	—
NYSE indices	Yes	—
ASE indices	Yes	—
Nasdaq indices	Yes	—
Standard & Poor's indices	Yes	—
Financial future indices	—	—
* Advance/Declines	Yes	—
* New Highs/Low	Yes	—
* New York Financial indices	Yes	—
* Over the counter indices	Yes	—
* Currency	Yes	—

Company data:		
Dividend $ amounts	—	—
Dividend yield	—	—
Dividend ex-dates	—	—
Dividend pay-dates	—	—
Earnings per share	—	—
Price Earnings ratio	—	—
Balance sheet	—	—
Income statement	—	—
Financial Ratios	—	—
Annual Reports	—	—
10-K's	—	—

Research opinions:		
Value Line	—	—
Standard & Poor's	—	—
Moody's	—	—
Argus	—	—

News:		
Dow Jones News ticker	—	—
Reuters	—	—
Barrons	—	—
Wall Street Journal	—	—

The database will:

	Capabilities	Comments
Construct charts/graphs	Yes	—
Project trends	Yes	—
Run regressions	Yes	—
Run other statistics	Yes	—
Create/Save my own portfolios	—	—
Window or split the screen	—	—
Write/run my own programs	Yes	—
Screen on certain characteristics	—	—

It is also worth mentioning that:

FOURCAST™ offers three regression analysis options for forecasting:

- 1 variable for $300;
- 2 variables for $495; and,
- 7 variables for $995.

Tick Data Inc.
10260 W. 13th Ave.
Lakewood, CO 80215
(303) 232-3701

Historical Tick Data For Futures
Historical
Magnetic Media/Dial-Up
Local number only
Less than 25,000 subscribers

Description of database:

Historical Tick Data For Futures provides time and sales data for futures contracts. Data is distributed on floppy disks, with one year of data per standard 5¼″ diskette. Tick update data is available on a daily basis through a dial-up service. Software for analyzing data is also available, allowing the user to list, graph, sample, model, and "real-time" trade commodities and futures.

The database contains CURRENT data for:

Securities:	Included	Comments
Stocks	—	—
Corporate Bonds	—	—
GNMA/FNMA	—	—
Treasury Bills	—	—
Government Bonds	—	—
Options	—	—
Commodities	Yes	—
Financial Futures	Yes	—
Stock Index Futures	Yes	—

The exchanges included are:

American (ASE)	—	KCBT	Yes	Pacific (PSE)	—
Boston	—	MidAm	—	Philadelphia	—
Cincinnati	—	Midwest (MSE)	—	OTC-NASDAQ	—
CBOE	—	MnGE	—	OTC-NME	—
CBT	Yes	Montreal	—	Toronto	—
CME	Yes	NYFE	—	Vancouver	—
CEC	—	NYSE	—		

The available information is:

	Stocks	Bonds	Options	Commod	Fin'l Futures	Stk Indx Futures
Closing Prices:	—	—	—	Yes	Yes	Yes
Daily High-Low:	—	—	—	Yes	Yes	Yes
Yearly High-Low:	—	—	—	—	—	—
Bid-Ask:	—	—	—	—	—	—
Volume:	—	—	—	—	—	—

Data available from 1982, tick-by-tick.

Availability of quotes:

Not available.

The equipment required to use this database is:

Computer:	IBM-PC, any MS-DOS PC, Apple IIe
Operating system:	PC-DOS, MS-DOS, Apple, CPM-86
Monitor:	Mono or color
Disk drives:	One 5¼″ DS/DD floppy
Memory:	256K
Modem:	300 or 1200 baud
Software:	Any terminal emulation program

Support services available:

Manual, and phone support.

The charges for the service are:

(1) Set-up charges:	—
(2) Basic rate:	—
(3) Specialty charges:	$75 minimum monthly charge applies
	$15 per month per contract of data

The database also contains:

Market Statistics:	Current Data	Historic Data
Market volume	—	—
Advancing issues	—	—
Advancing volume	—	—
Declining issues	—	—
Declining volume	—	—
Most active	—	—
Most up (%)	—	—
Most down (%)	—	—
Tick by volume	—	—
Trading indices (TRIN)	—	—
Dow Jones indices	—	—
NYSE indices	—	—
ASE indices	—	—
Nasdaq indices	—	—
Standard & Poor's indices	—	—
Financial future indices	—	—
Company data:		
Dividend $ amounts	—	—
Dividend yield	—	—
Dividend ex-dates	—	—
Dividend pay-dates	—	—
Earnings per share	—	—
Price Earnings ratio	—	—
Balance sheet	—	—
Income statement	—	—
Financial Ratios	—	—
Annual Reports	—	—
10-K's	—	—
Research opinions:		
Value Line	—	—
Standard & Poor's	—	—
Moody's	—	—
Argus	—	—
News:		
Dow Jones News Ticker	—	—
Reuters	—	—
Barrons	—	—
Wall Street Journal	—	—

The database will:

	Capabilities	Comments
Construct charts/graphs	Yes	—
Project trends	Yes	—
Run regressions	Yes	—
Run other statistics	Yes	—
Create/Save my own portfolios	—	—
Window or split the screen	—	—
Write/run my own programs	Yes	—
Screen on certain characteristics	Yes	—

It is also worth mentioning that:

Programs which facilitate graphing, listing, sampling, and modeling are available for sale.

E. F. Hutton & Company, Inc.

One Battery Park Place
New York, NY 10004
(212) 742-5000

Huttonline
Quote/Historical
Dial-Up
Local
Less than 25,000 subscribers

Description of database:

Huttonline, an on-line financial information service, features stock quotes, securities, futures, and economic forecast research. E. F. Hutton, Moody's, and Market News contributes information to the database. Electronic mail and personal account information is also included.

The database contains CURRENT data for:

Securities:	Included	Comments
Stocks	Yes	All
Corporate Bonds	Yes	Previous close, if held in account
GNMA/FNMA	Yes	Previous close, if held in account
Treasury Bills	Yes	Previous close, if held in account
Government Bonds	Yes	Previous close, if held in account
Options	Yes	Listed only
Commodities	Yes	Previous close, if held in account
Financial Futures	Yes	Previous close, if held in account
Stock Index Futures	Yes	Previous close, if held in account

The exchanges included are:

American (ASE)	Yes	KCBT	—	Pacific (PSE)	Yes
Boston	Yes	MidAm	—	Philadelphia	Yes
Cincinnati	Yes	Midwest (MSE)	Yes	OTC-NASDAQ	Yes
CBOE	—	MnGE	—	OTC-NME	Yes
CBT	—	Montreal	—	Toronto	—
CME	—	NYFE	—	Vancouver	—
CEC	—	NYSE	Yes		

The available information is:

	Stocks	Bonds	Options	Commod	Fin'l Futures	Stk Indx Futures
Closing Prices:	Yes	Yes (1)	Yes (1)	Yes (1)	Yes (1)	Yes (1)
Daily High-Low:	Yes	Yes (1)	Yes (1)	Yes (1)	Yes (1)	Yes (1)
Yearly High-Low:	Yes	Yes (1)	Yes (1)	Yes (1)	Yes (1)	Yes (1)
Bid-Ask:	Yes	Yes (1)	Yes (1)	Yes (1)	Yes (1)	Yes (1)
Volume:	Yes	Yes (1)	Yes (1)	Yes (1)	Yes (1)	Yes (1)

Stock prices are updated continously.
(1) Previous close pricing is available only if held in your account.

Availability of quotes:

Delayed basis only.

The equipment required to use this database is:

Computer:	Any terminal
Operating system:	—
Monitor:	Mono or color; minimum 40 columns
Disk drives:	Required only for terminal emulation program
Memory:	Required only for terminal emulation program
Modem:	300 or 1200 baud
Software:	Any terminal emulation program

Support services available:

Manual, toll-free customer service available from 9:00 AM to 6:00 PM (weekdays only), and a monthly magazine.

The charges for the service are:

(1) Set-up charges: $25
(2) Basic rate:
    (a) Prime time: Weekdays: 8 AM-6 PM @ $ .25 per minute
    (b) Non-prime time: Weekdays: 6 PM-8 AM @ $ .10 per minute
                              Weekends & Holidays
(3) Specialty charges: —

The database also contains:

Market Statistics:	Current Data	Historic Data
Market volume	Yes	—
Advancing issues	Yes	—
Advancing volume	Yes	—
Declining issues	Yes	—
Declining volume	Yes	—
Most active	Yes	—
Most up (%)	—	—
Most down (%)	—	—
Tick by volume	Yes	—
Trading indices (TRIN)	—	—
Dow Jones indices	Yes	—
NYSE indices	Yes	—
ASE indices	Yes	—
Nasdaq indices	Yes	—
Standard & Poor's indices	Yes	—
Financial future indices	Yes	—

Company data:		
Dividend $ amounts	Yes	1 year
Dividend yield	Yes	1 year
Dividend ex-dates	Yes	1 year
Dividend pay-dates	Yes	1 year
Earnings per share	Yes	3 years
Price Earnings ratio	Yes	3 years
Balance sheet	—	—
Income statement	—	—
Financial Ratios	—	—
Annual Reports	—	—
10-K's	—	—

Research opinions:		
Value Line	—	—
Standard & Poor's	—	—
Moody's	Yes	—
Argus	—	—
* E.F. Hutton	Yes	—

News:		
Dow Jones News Ticker	—	—
Reuters	—	—
Barrons	—	—
Wall Street Journal	—	—

The database will:

	Capabilities	Comments
Construct charts/graphs	—	—
Project trends	—	—
Run regressions	—	—
Run other statistics	—	—
Create/Save my own portfolios	—	—
Window or split the screen	—	—
Write/run my own programs	—	—
Screen on certain characteristics	—	—

It is also worth mentioning that:

Subscribers must have an account with E. F. Hutton in order to have access to "Huttonline."

Invest/Net Group, Inc.
99 NW 183rd Street
North Miami, FL 33169
(305) 652-1721

Insider Trading Monitor
Specialty
Dial-Up
Autonet
Less than 25,000 subscribers

Description of database:

Insider Trading Monitor is a comprehensive on-line database containing trading information on all open market purchases, sales, and option exercises made by corporate officers, directors, and other insiders. Users can retrieve information by company name, industry group, and insider name. Each transaction is recorded by trade date, name of the insider, price, and number of shares both in the transaction and remaining in the hands of the individual.

The database contains CURRENT data for:

Securities:	Included	Comments
Stocks	Yes	All reporting stocks included
Corporate Bonds	—	—
GNMA/FNMA	—	—
Treasury Bills	—	—
Government Bonds	—	—
Options	—	—
Commodities	—	—
Financial Futures	—	—
Stock Index Futures	—	—

The exchanges included are:

American (ASE)	Yes	KCBT	—	Pacific (PSE)	Yes
Boston	Yes	MidAm	—	Philadelphia	Yes
Cincinnati	Yes	Midwest (MSE)	Yes	OTC-NASDAQ	Yes
CBOE	—	MnGE	—	OTC-NME	Yes
CBT	—	Montreal	—	Toronto	Yes
CME	—	NYFE	—	Vancouver	—
CEC	—	NYSE	Yes		

The available information is:

	Stocks	Bonds	Options	Commod	Fin'l Futures	Stk Indx Futures
Closing Prices:	—	—	—	—	—	—
Daily High-Low:	—	—	—	—	—	—
Yearly High-Low:	—	—	—	—	—	—
Bid-Ask:	—	—	—	—	—	—
Volume:	—	—	—	—	—	—

Availability of quotes:
Not available.

The equipment required to use this database is:

Computer:	Any terminal
Operating system:	—
Monitor:	Mono or color
Disk drives:	Required only for terminal emulation program
Memory:	Required only for terminal emulation program
Modem:	300 or 1200 baud, full duplex
Software:	Any terminal emulation program

Support services available:
Manual, on-line manual, weekly magazine called "Periscope."

The charges for the service are:
   (1) Set-up charges: —
   (2) Basic rate: $60 per hour
   (3) Specialty charges: $35 monthly minimum

The database also contains:

Market Statistics:	Current Data	Historic Data
Market volume	—	—
Advancing issues	—	—
Advancing volume	—	—
Declining issues	—	—
Declining volume	—	—
Most active	—	—
Most up (%)	—	—
Most down (%)	—	—
Tick by volume	—	—
Trading indices (TRIN)	—	—
Dow Jones indices	—	—
NYSE indices	—	—
ASE indices	—	—
Nasdaq indices	—	—
Standard & Poor's indices	—	—
Financial future indices	—	—

Company data:		
Dividend $ amounts	—	—
Dividend yield	—	—
Dividend ex-dates	—	—
Dividend pay-dates	—	—
Earnings per share	—	—
Price Earnings ratio	—	—
Balance sheet	—	—
Income statement	—	—
Financial Ratios	—	—
Annual Reports	—	—
10-K's	—	—

Research opinions:		
Value Line	—	—
Standard & Poor's	—	—
Moody's	—	—
Argus	—	—

News:		
Dow Jones News Ticker	—	—
Reuters	—	—
Barrons	—	—
Wall Street Journal	—	—
* Independent News Channel	—	—

* Other:

	Current Data	Historic Data
* Insider trading information	Yes	6 years

The database will:

	Capabilities	Comments
Construct charts/graphs	—	—
Project trends	—	—
Run regressions	—	—
Run other statistics	—	—
Create/Save my own portfolios	Yes	Unlimited number of alert screens
Window or split the screen	—	—
Write/run my own programs	Yes	—
Screen on certain characteristics	Yes	Up to 4 characteristics

It is also worth mentioning that:

Insider Trading Monitor is also available through the Dow Jones News Retrieval® Service.

Business Research Corp.
12 Farnsworth Street
Boston, MA 02210
(617) 350-4044

INVESTEXT
Historical
Dial-Up
Local/Telenet/Tymnet
Number of subscribers is not available

Description of database:

INVESTEXT contains the full text of brokerage research reports prepared by securities analysts at 44 leading investment banking firms. The reports contain current analysis, opinions, and forecasts on 7,500 U.S. and foreign companies including some non-NASDAQ and OTC firms. The combined research of over 600 analysts who work for these firms provides subscribers with a thorough overview of the companies covered by the database, including current and projected financial health, market positions, and corporate goals. The database is updated with 400 to 500 new reports each week.

The database contains CURRENT data for:

Securities:	Included	Comments
Stocks	Yes	7500 U.S. and foreign companies
Corporate Bonds	—	—
GNMA/FNMA	—	—
Treasury Bills	—	—
Government Bonds	—	—
Options	—	—
Commodities	—	—
Financial Futures	—	—
Stock Index Futures	—	—

The exchanges included are:

American (ASE)	Yes	KCBT	—	Pacific (PSE)	Yes
Boston	—	MidAm	—	Philadelphia	—
Cincinnati	—	Midwest (MSE)	Yes	OTC-NASDAQ	Yes
CBOE	—	MnGE	—	OTC-NME	Yes
CBT	—	Montreal	—	Toronto	—
CME	—	NYFE	—	Vancouver	—
CEC	—	NYSE	Yes		

The available information is:

	Stocks	Bonds	Options	Commod	Fin'l Futures	Stk Indx Futures
Closing Prices:	—	—	—	—	—	—
Daily High-Low:	—	—	—	—	—	—
Yearly High-Low:	—	—	—	—	—	—
Bid-Ask:	—	—	—	—	—	—
Volume:	—	—	—	—	—	—

Availability of quotes:

Not available.

The equipment required to use this database is:

Computer:	Any terminal
Operating system:	—
Monitor:	Mono or color
Disk drives:	Required only for terminal emulation program
Memory:	Required only for terminal emulation program
Modem:	300 or 1200 baud
Software:	Any terminal emulation program

Support services available:

Training, documentation, technical hotline, and quarterly newsletter.

The charges for the service are:

(1) Set-up charges: $75
(2) Basic rate: $95 per hour
(3) Specialty charges: $4.50 per report page

The database also contains:

Market Statistics:	Current Data	Historic Data
Market volume	Yes	Varies
Advancing issues	—	—
Advancing volume	—	—
Declining issues	—	—
Declining volume	—	—
Most active	Yes	Varies
Most up (%)	Yes	Varies
Most down (%)	Yes	Varies
Tick by volume	—	—
Trading indices (TRIN)	Yes	Varies
Dow Jones indices	Yes	Varies
NYSE indices	Yes	Varies
ASE indices	Yes	Varies
Nasdaq indices	Yes	Varies
Standard & Poor's indices	Yes	Varies
Financial future indices	—	—

Company data:		
Dividend $ amounts	Yes	Varies
Dividend yield	Yes	Varies
Dividend ex-dates	Yes	Varies
Dividend pay-dates	Yes	Varies
Earnings per share	Yes	Varies
Price Earnings ratio	Yes	Varies
Balance sheet	Yes	Varies
Income statement	Yes	Varies
Financial Ratios	Yes	Varies
Annual Reports	Yes	Varies
10-K's	—	—

Research opinions:		
Value Line	—	—
Standard & Poor's	—	—
Moody's	—	—
Argus	—	—

News:		
Dow Jones News Ticker	—	—
Reuters	—	—
Barrons	—	—
Wall Street Journal	—	—

The database will:

	Capabilities	Comments
Construct charts/graphs	—	—
Project trends	—	—
Run regressions	—	—
Run other statistics	—	—
Create/Save my own portfolios	—	—
Window or split the screen	—	—
Write/run my own programs	—	—
Screen on certain characteristics	—	—

It is also worth mentioning:

INVESTEXT also offers:

- user guides—$50 extra, updated annually;
- quick reference guides;
- a publication listing most of the new company and industry reports added to the database; and,
- a catalog of new research reports—$45 per year for 25 issues.

Commodity Systems, Inc.
200 W. Palmetto Park Road
Boca Raton, FL 33432
(305) 392-8663

MARSTAT® Data Base
Historical
Dial-Up
Local/Telenet/Tymnet
Less than 25,000 subscribers

Description of database:

CSI MARSTAT® Data Base offers a large collection of data covering: commodity futures, market indicators, cash prices, optionable stocks, commodity options, and rates on various financial instruments. The data base includes data from 1949 through the present. Each record includes open, high, low, and closing prices. Other data includes total volume of sales and total open interest.

The database contains CURRENT data for:

Securities:	Included	Comments
Stocks	Yes	Optionable
Corporate Bonds	—	—
GNMA/FNMA	—	—
Treasury Bills	—	—
Government Bonds	—	—
Options	Yes	Index options
Commodities	Yes	—
Financial Futures	Yes	—
Stock Index Futures	Yes	—
* Commodity Options	Yes	—

The exchanges included are:

American (ASE)	Yes	KCBT	Yes	Pacific (PSE)	Yes
Boston	—	MidAm	Yes	Philadelphia	Yes
Cincinnati	—	Midwest (MSE)	—	OTC-NASDAQ	Yes
CBOE	Yes	MnGE	Yes	OTC-NME	Yes
CBT	Yes	Montreal	—	Toronto	Yes
CME	Yes	NYFE	Yes	Vancouver	Yes
CEC	Yes	NYSE	Yes		

The available information is:

	Stocks	Bonds	Options	Commod	Fin'l Futures	Stk Indx Futures
Closing Prices:	Yes	—	Yes (1)	Yes (2)	Yes (3)	Yes
Daily High-Low:	Yes	—	Yes (1)	Yes (2)	Yes (3)	Yes
Yearly High-Low:	—	—	—	—	—	—
Bid-Ask:	—	—	Yes	—	—	—
Volume:	Yes	—	Yes (1)	Yes (2)	Yes (3)	Yes

       Historical data available for 5 years.
(1) Index data available for 3 years; futures for 1 year.
(2) Historical data available for 21 years.
(3) Historical data available for 9 years.

Availability of quotes:
       Not available.

The equipment required to use this database is:

Computer:	IBM-PC, IBM-XT, IBM-AT, Apple II, Commodore 64
Operating system:	MS-DOS, Apple-DOS, Commodore-DOS
Monitor:	Mono or color
Disk drives:	2 required except for Commodore 64
Memory:	IBM-256K; Apple-48K; Commodore 64-64K
Modem:	300 or 1200 baud
Software:	Software free with subscription

Support services available:
       Manuals, customer service technical hotline (84 hours per week) and a monthly CSI News Journal.

The charges for the service are:

(1) Set-up charges:	$195
(2) Basic rate:	
(a) Prime time:	Weekdays: 8 AM-6 PM @ $45 per month
(b) Non-prime time:	Weekdays: 6 PM-8 AM @ $33 per month
	Weekends & Holidays
(3) Specialty charges:	Basic rate covers 20 stocks/10 contracts.

The database also contains:

Market Statistics:	Current Data	Historic Data
Market volume	Yes	9 years
Advancing issues	Yes	6 years
Advancing volume	Yes	6 years
Declining issues	Yes	6 years
Declining volume	Yes	6 years
Most active	Yes	9 years
Most up (%)	—	—
Most down (%)	—	—
Tick by volume	—	—
Trading indices (TRIN)	—	—
Dow Jones indices	Yes	9 years
NYSE indices	Yes	18 years
ASE indices	Yes	3 years
Nasdaq indices	Yes	2 years
Standard & Poor's indices	Yes	3 years
Financial future indices	Yes	4 years
* Oil index	Yes	3 years
* OTC index	Yes	1 year
* CBOE 100 index	Yes	4 years
* Major Market index	Yes	3 years
* Gold & Silver index	Yes	2 years
* Computer Technology index	Yes	3 years
* Pacific Technology index	Yes	2 years
* Value Line index	Yes	1 year
* CSI composite index	Yes	17 years
* Various commodity indices	Yes	17 years

Company data:		
Dividend $ amounts	—	—
Dividend yield	—	—
Dividend ex-dates	—	—
Dividend pay-dates	—	—
Earnings per share	—	—
Price Earnings ratio	Yes	4 years
Balance sheet	—	—
Income statement	—	—
Financial Ratios	—	—
Annual Reports	—	—
10-K's	—	—

Research opinions:		
Value Line	—	—
Standard & Poor's	—	—
Moody's	—	—
Argus	—	—

News:		
Dow Jones News Ticker	—	—
Reuters	—	—
Barrons	—	—
Wall Street Journal	—	—

The database will:

	Capabilities	Comments
Construct charts/graphs	Yes	—
Project trends	Yes	—
Run regressions	Yes	—
Run other statistics	Yes	—
Create/Save my own portfolios	Yes	One only
Window or split the screen	Yes	Two windows only
Write/run my own programs	Yes	Available through outside vendors
Screen on certain characteristics	—	—

It is also worth mentioning that:

The following data is also available:

- opening prices for all securities except options;
- high, low, settlement, closing bid/ask for options;
- price earnings for all optionable stocks; and,
- open interest for commodity and financial futures.

Commodity Systems also sells an IBM compatible computer for $1195.

PC Quote

401 South LaSalle Street
Chicago, IL 60605
(312) 786-5400
(800) 772-2945/(800) 225-5657

PC Quote
Quote
Satellite
Less than 25,000 subscribers

Description of database:

PC Quote is a real-time quotation system that utilizes the economies and efficiencies of satellite communications to deliver trade data tick-by-tick. PC Quote covers most stock, option, commodity, and stock index futures exchanges.

The database contains CURRENT data for:

Securities:	Included	Comments
Stocks	Yes	—
Corporate Bonds	—	—
GNMA/FNMA	Yes	—
Treasury Bills	—	—
Government Bonds	—	—
Options	Yes	—
Commodities	Yes	—
Financial Futures	—	—
Stock Index Futures	Yes	—

The exchanges included are:

American (ASE)	Yes	KCBT	Yes	Pacific (PSE)	Yes
Boston	Yes	MidAm	Yes	Philadelphia	Yes
Cincinnati	Yes	Midwest (MSE)	Yes	OTC-NASDAQ	Yes
CBOE	Yes	MnGE	Yes	OTC-NME	Yes
CBT	Yes	Montreal	—	Toronto	—
CME	Yes	NYFE	Yes	Vancouver	—
CEC	Yes	NYSE	Yes		

The available information is:

	Stocks	Bonds	Options	Commod	Fin'l Futures	Stk Index Futures
Closing Prices:	Yes	—	Yes	Yes	Yes	Yes
Daily High-Low:	Yes	—	Yes	Yes	Yes	Yes
Yearly High-Low:	Yes	—	—	—	—	Yes
Bid-Ask:	Yes	—	Yes	Yes	Yes	Yes
Volume:	Yes	—	Yes	Yes	Yes	Yes

Current prices available only. No historical data available (except yearly high-low for stocks).

Availability of quotes:

Real time basis only.

The equipment required to use this database is:

Computer:	IBM-AT
Operating system:	PC-DOS
Monitor:	Color
Disk drives:	Two disk drives (one floppy, one hard: 10mb)
Memory:	640K
Modem:	Supplied by vendor
Software:	Supplied by vendor

Support services available:

User manual and toll-free customer service.

The charges for the service are:

(1)	Set-up charges:	$500 ($250-Self installed)
(2)	Basic rate:	—
(3)	Specialty charges:	$295 monthly for the first unit
		$100 monthly for second unit
		$75 monthly for third and fourth units
		$50 monthly for all additional units

The database also contains:

Market Statistics:	Current Data	Historic Data
Market volume	Yes	—
Advancing issues	Yes	—
Advancing volume	—	—
Declining issues	Yes	—
Declining volume	—	—
Most active	Yes	—
Most up (%)	Yes	—
Most down (%)	Yes	—
Tick by volume	Yes	—
Trading indices (TRIN)	Yes	—
Dow Jones indices	—	—
NYSE indices	Yes	—
ASE indices	Yes	—
Nasdaq indices	Yes	—
Standard & Poor's indices	Yes	—
Financial future indices	—	—

Company data:		
Dividend $ amounts	Yes	Current quarter only
Dividend yield	Yes	Current quarter only
Dividend ex-dates	Yes	—
Dividend pay-dates	—	—
Earnings per share	Yes	Current quarter only
Price Earnings ratio	Yes	Current quarter only
Balance sheet	—	—
Income statement	—	—
Financial Ratios	—	—
Annual Reports	—	—
10-K's	—	—

Research opinions:		
Value Line	—	—
Standard & Poor's	—	—
Moody's	—	—
Argus	—	—

News:		
Dow Jones News Ticker	—	—
Reuters	—	—
Barrons	—	—
Wall Street Journal	—	—
* Associated Press	Yes	—
* Dow Jones News Service	Yes	—

The database will:

	Capabilities	Comments
Construct charts/graphs	—	—
Project trends	—	—
Run regressions	—	—
Run other statistics	—	—
Create/Save my own portfolios	Yes	—
Window or split the screen	—	—
Write/run my own programs	Yes	—
Screen on certain characteristics	—	—

It is also worth mentioning that:

PC Quote also offers:

- *CompuTrac Intra Day Analyst*—a graphics package which directly interfaces into the database and is operational on a real-time basis;
- *Advent software*—a portfolio management software package; and,
- *Spreadsheet Utility*—a spreadsheet interface package for integrating quotes into spreadsheets such as Lotus 1-2-3.

Quotron Systems
P.O. Box 66914
5454 Beethoven Street
Los Angeles, CA 90066
(213) 827-4600

Quotdial
Quote
Dial-Up
Tymnet
Less than 25,000 subscribers

Description of database:
> Quotdial is a dial-up financial information service for use with a personal computer. It features security quotes in a "real-time," delayed, and "after-market-hours" time frame.

The database contains CURRENT data for:

Securities:	Included	Comments
Stocks	Yes	All
Corporate Bonds	Yes	—
GNMA/FNMA	Yes	—
Treasury Bills	Yes	—
Government Bonds	Yes	—
Options	Yes	—
Commodities	Yes	—
Financial Futures	Yes	—
Stock Index Futures	Yes	—

The exchanges included are:

American (ASE)	Yes	KCBT	Yes	Pacific (PSE)	Yes
Boston	Yes	MidAm	Yes	Philadelphia	Yes
Cincinnati	Yes	Midwest (MSE)	Yes	OTC-NASDAQ	Yes
CBOE	Yes	MnGE	Yes	OTC-NME	Yes
CBT	Yes	Montreal	Yes	Toronto	Yes
CME	Yes	NYFE	Yes	Vancouver	Yes
CEC	Yes	NYSE	Yes	* Osaka	Yes
* Tokyo	Yes	* Winnipeg	Yes		

The available information is:

	Stocks	Bonds	Options	Commod	Fin'l Futures	Stk Indx Futures
Closing Prices:	Yes	Yes	Yes	Yes	Yes	Yes
Daily High-Low:	Yes	Yes	Yes	Yes	Yes	Yes
Yearly High-Low:	Yes	Yes	Yes	Yes	Yes	Yes
Bid-Ask:	Yes	Yes	Yes	Yes	Yes	Yes
Volume:	Yes	Yes	Yes	Yes	Yes	Yes

> Current prices available only. No historical data available.

Availability of quotes:
> Real time, delayed, and after-market-hours basis.

The equipment required to use this database is:

Computer:	Any terminal
Operating system:	—
Monitor:	Mono or color
Disk drives:	Required only for terminal emulation program
Memory:	Required only for terminal emulation program
Modem:	300 or 1200 baud
Software:	Any terminal emulation program

Support services available:
> Manual, and toll-free customer service.

The charges for the service are:
(1) Set-up charges: $50
(2) Basic rate:
    (a) Prime time: Weekdays: 7 AM-6 PM @ $ .50 per minute
    (b) Non-prime time: Weekdays: 6 PM-7 AM @ $ .17 per minute
                       Weekends & Holidays
(3) Specialty charges: $10 minimum monthly charge applicable

The database also contains:

Market Statistics:	Current Data	Historic Data
Market volume	Yes	—
Advancing issues	Yes	—
Advancing volume	Yes	—
Declining issues	Yes	—
Declining volume	Yes	—
Most active	Yes	—
Most up (%)	Yes	—
Most down (%)	Yes	—
Tick by volume	Yes	—
Trading indices (TRIN)	Yes	—
Dow Jones indices	Yes	—
NYSE indices	Yes	—
ASE indices	Yes	—
Nasdaq indices	Yes	—
Standard & Poor's indices	Yes	—
Financial future indices	Yes	—
* Quotron specialty indices	Yes	—

Company data:		
Dividend $ amounts	Yes	—
Dividend yield	Yes	—
Dividend ex-dates	Yes	—
Dividend pay-dates	—	—
Earnings per share	Yes	—
Price Earnings ratio	Yes	—
Balance sheet	—	—
Income statement	—	—
Financial Ratios	—	—
Annual Reports	—	—
10-K's	—	—

Research opinions:		
Value Line	—	—
Standard & Poor's	—	—
Moody's	—	—
Argus	—	—

News:		
Dow Jones News Ticker	—	—
Reuters	—	—
Barrons	—	—
Wall Street Journal	—	—

The database will:

	Capabilities	Comments
Construct charts/graphs	—	—
Project trends	—	—
Run regressions	—	—
Run other statistics	—	—
Create/Save my own portfolios	—	—
Window or split the screen	—	—
Write/run my own programs	—	—
Screen on certain characteristics	—	—

It is also worth mentioning that:

Quotron is a major supplier of quote equipment for the brokerage industry.

Telemet America

325 First Street
Alexandria, VA 22304
(703) 548-2042

Radio Exchange®

Quote
Broadcast
FM Radio

Number of subscribers is not available

Description of database:

Telemet broadcasts quotes and news on stock, options, futures, and market indices via FM radio. Subscribers receive unlimited access to the broadcast, 24 hours a day, for only $25 per month. Quotes are available on a real-time or delayed basis. In addition, a software package called "Personal Gains" allows subscribers to set limits, news alerts, display intra-day and historical graphs, track portfolio positions, and transfer data into any program capable of reading DIF files.

The database contains CURRENT data for:

Securities:	Included	Comments
Stocks	Yes	—
Corporate Bonds	—	—
GNMA/FNMA	—	—
Treasury Bills	—	—
Government Bonds	—	—
Options	Yes	—
Commodities	Yes	—
Financial Futures	Yes	—
Stock Index Futures	Yes	—

The exchanges included are:

American (ASE)	Yes	KCBT	Yes	Pacific (PSE)	Yes
Boston	—	MidAm	—	Philadelphia	Yes
Cincinnati	—	Midwest (MSE)	—	OTC-NASDAQ	Yes
CBOE	Yes	MnGE	—	OTC-NME	Yes
CBT	Yes	Montreal	—	Toronto	—
CME	Yes	NYFE	Yes	Vancouver	—
CEC	Yes	NYSE	Yes		

The available information is:

	Stocks	Bonds	Options	Commod	Fin'l Futures	Stk Indx Futures
Closing Prices:	Yes	—	Yes	Yes	Yes	Yes
Daily High-Low:	Yes	—	Yes	Yes	Yes	Yes
Yearly High-Low:	Yes	—	—	—	—	—
Bid-Ask:	Yes	—	—	—	—	—
Volume:	Yes	—	Yes	Yes	Yes	Yes

Current prices broadcast only. Personal Gains software can save to data disk, allowing subscribers to build their own histories.

Availability of quotes:

Both real time and delayed basis.

The equipment required to use this database is:

Computer:	IBM-PC, IBM-XT, IBM-AT, Apple IIe, IIc, II+
Operating system:	PC-DOS, MS-DOS, Apple-DOS
Monitor:	Mono or color
Disk drives:	Two disk drives (floppies or hard)
Memory:	IBM-192K, Apple-64K
Modem:	Hardware connects directly to serial port
Software:	Personal Gains

Support services available:

Manual, phone support, and quarterly newsletter.

The charges for the service are:

(1) Set-up charges:	$395
(2) Basic rate:	—
(3) Specialty charges:	$25 monthly access charge

The database also contains:

Market Statistics:	Current Data	Historic Data
Market volume	Yes	—
Advancing issues	Yes	—
Advancing volume	Yes	—
Declining issues	Yes	—
Declining volume	Yes	—
Most active	Yes	—
Most up (%)	Yes	—
Most down (%)	Yes	—
Tick by volume	Yes	—
Trading indices (TRIN)	Yes	—
Dow Jones indices	Yes	—
NYSE indices	Yes	—
ASE indices	Yes	—
Nasdaq indices	Yes	—
Standard & Poor's indices	Yes	—
Financial future indices	Yes	—
* 30 additional indices	Yes	—

Company data:		
Dividend $ amounts	—	—
Dividend yield	—	—
Dividend ex-dates	—	—
Dividend pay-dates	—	—
Earnings per share	—	—
Price Earnings ratio	—	—
Balance sheet	—	—
Income statement	—	—
Financial Ratios	—	—
Annual Reports	—	—
10-K's	—	—

Research opinions:		
Value Line	—	—
Standard & Poor's	—	—
Moody's	—	—
Argus	—	—

News:		
Dow Jones News Ticker	—	—
Reuters	—	—
Barrons	—	—
Wall Street Journal	—	—
* Independent News Channel	Yes	—

The database will:

	Capabilities	Comments
Construct charts/graphs	Yes	—
Project trends	—	—
Run regressions	—	—
Run other statistics	—	—
Create/Save my own portfolios	Yes	—
Window or split the screen	Yes	—
Write/run my own programs	Yes	—
Screen on certain characteristics	—	—

It is also worth mentioning that:

Telemet offers an Independent News Channel which provides breaking news on individual companies and economic developments for only $60 per quarter.

Telemet offers Pocket Quote Pro™, a hand held receiver that provides instant quotes and news, and can also be interfaced to a personal computer.

Source Telecomputing Corp.
1616 Anderson Road
McLean, VA 22102
(703) 734-7500

The Source
Quote/Historical
Dial-Up
Telenet/Sourcenet
50,000 to 100,000 subscribers

Description of database:
The Source is an on-line, information and communication network providing several different categories of services, including:
- Communications—electronic mail and computer conferencing;
- Business & Finance—stock and bond quotations; analysis; portfolios; trading;
- News & Information—UPI, AP, and Washington Post newswires;
- Travel—Official Airline Guide and Accuweather;
- Personal Computing Special Interest groups—Microsearch for PC equipment and software; and,
- Consumer Services—bulletin boards, electronic shopping, games, and entertainment guides.

The database contains CURRENT data for:

Securities:	Included	Comments
Stocks	Yes	NYSE, AMEX, OTC only
Corporate Bonds	Yes	NYSE, AMEX only
GNMA/FNMA	Yes	15 & 30 year
Treasury Bills	Yes	—
Government Bonds	Yes	—
Options	Yes	Stock options only
Commodities	Yes	Most active only
Financial Futures	Yes	Most active only
Stock Index Futures	Yes	Selected
* Mutual & Money Funds	Yes	—
* Precious Metals	Yes	Silver, Gold, Platinum, Coins

The exchanges included are:

American (ASE)	Yes	KCBT	—	Pacific (PSE)	Yes
Boston	Yes	MidAm	—	Philadelphia	Yes
Cincinnati	Yes	Midwest (MSE)	Yes	OTC-NASDAQ	Yes
CBOE	Yes	MnGE	—	OTC-NME	Yes
CBT	Yes	Montreal	—	Toronto	Yes
CME	Yes	NYFE	Yes	Vancouver	—
CEC	—	NYSE	Yes		

The available information is:

	Stocks	Bonds	Options	Commod	Fin'l Futures	Stk Indx Futures
Closing Prices:	Yes	Yes	Yes	Yes	Yes	Yes
Daily High-Low:	Yes	Yes	—	Yes	Yes	Yes
Yearly High-Low:	Yes	—	—	—	—	—
Bid-Ask:	Yes	—	—	—	—	—
Volume:	Yes	Yes	Yes	Yes	Yes	Yes

Data available on a daily basis only. No historic data available.

Availability of quotes:
Both real time and delayed basis.

The equipment required to use this database is:

Computer:	Any terminal
Operating system:	—
Monitor:	Mono or color
Disk drives:	Required only for terminal emulation program
Memory:	Required only for terminal emulation program
Modem:	300, 1200, or 2400 baud
Software:	Any terminal emulation program

Support services available:
Manual, and toll-free customer service.

The charges for the service are:
(1) Set-up charges: $49.95
(2) Basic rate:

	BAUD		
	300	1200	1200
(a) Prime time: Weekdays: 7 AM-6 PM @	.36	.43	.46 per minute
(b) Non-prime time: Weekdays: 6 PM-7 AM @	.14	.18	.20 per minute

Weekends & Holidays
(3) Specialty charges: $10 minimum monthly charge applicable

The database also contains:

Market Statistics:	Current Data	Historic Data
Market volume	Yes	—
Advancing issues	Yes	—
Advancing volume	—	—
Declining issues	Yes	—
Declining volume	—	—
Most active	Yes	—
Most up (%)	—	—
Most down (%)	—	—
Tick by volume	—	—
Trading indices (TRIN)	—	—
Dow Jones indices	Yes	—
NYSE indices	Yes	—
ASE indices	Yes	—
Nasdaq indices	Yes	—
Standard & Poor's indices	Yes	—
Financial future indices	Yes	—

Company data:		
Dividend $ amounts	Yes	1 year
Dividend yield	Yes	1 year
Dividend ex-dates	Yes	1 year
Dividend pay-dates	—	—
Earnings per share	Yes	1 year
Price Earnings ratio	Yes	1 year
Balance sheet	Yes	1 year
Income statement	Yes	1 year
Financial Ratios	Yes	1 year
Annual Reports	—	—
10-K's	—	—

Research opinions:		
Value Line	—	—
Standard & Poor's	—	—
Moody's	—	—
Argus	—	—
* INVESTEXT	Yes	1 year

News:		
Dow Jones News Ticker	Yes	1 year
Reuters	—	—
Barrons	—	—
Wall Street Journal	—	—

The database will:

	Capabilities	Comments
Construct charts/graphs	—	—
Project trends	—	—
Run regressions	—	—
Run other statistics	—	—
Create/Save my own portfolios	Yes	Unlimited
Window or split the screen	—	—
Write/run my own programs	Yes	—
Screen on certain characteristics	—	—

It is also worth mentioning that:

Free, on-line, four-part tutorial is available to subscribers.

Telescan, Inc.

2900 Wilcrest
4th Floor
Houston, TX 77042
(713) 952-1060

Telescan Database
Historical
Dial-Up
Local/Telenet
Number of subscribers is not available

Description of database:

Telescan Database covers 13 years of historical stock price/volume history on over 10,000 stocks, indices, and mutual funds. Information is transmitted graphically. The database also contains up-to-the-minute financial news. Information is also available on corporate insiders—who they are, what their holdings are, what recent trades they've made, and how successful they have been (presented graphically).

The database contains CURRENT data for:

Securities:	Included	Comments
Stocks	Yes	8,000 issues
Corporate Bonds	—	—
GNMA/FNMA	—	
Treasury Bills	Yes	90/180 day T-bills only
Government Bonds	—	—
Options	—	—
Commodities	—	—
Financial Futures	—	—
Stock Index Futures	—	—
* Mutual Funds	Yes	2,000 issues

The exchanges included are:

American (ASE)	Yes	KCBT	—	Pacific (PSE)	—
Boston	—	MidAm	—	Philadelphia	—
Cincinnati	—	Midwest (MSE)	—	OTC-NASDAQ	Yes
CBOE	—	MnGE	—	OTC-NME	Yes
CBT	—	Montreal	—	Toronto	—
CME	—	NYFE	—	Vancouver	—
CEC	—	NYSE	Yes		

The available information is:

	Stocks	Bonds	Options	Commod	Fin'l Futures	Stk Indx Futures
Closing Prices:	Yes	—	—	—	—	—
Daily High-Low:	Yes	—	—	—	—	—
Yearly High-Low:	Yes	—	—	—	—	—
Bid-Ask:	Yes	—	—	—	—	—
Volume:	Yes	—	—	—	—	—

Historical data available from 1973.

Availability of quotes:

Not available.

The equipment required to use this database is:

Computer:	IBM-PC, IBM-JR, IBM-XT, IBM-AT
Operating system:	MS-DOS 2.1 or higher
Monitor:	Mono or color
Disk drives:	One disk drive
Memory:	256K
Modem:	1200 or 2400 baud Hayes modem
Software:	Telescan Analyzer, $49.95

Support services available:

Manual, phone support, and bi-monthly newsletter.

The charges for the service are:

(1) Set-up charges:	—	
(2) Basic rate:		
(a) Prime time:	Weekdays: 7 AM-6 PM @ $.50 per minute
(b) Non-prime time:	Weekdays: 6 PM-7 AM @ $.25 per minute
	Weekends & Holidays
(3) Specialty charges:	Telescan software @ $49.95

The database also contains:

Market Statistics:	Current Data	Historic Data
Market volume	Yes	14 years
Advancing issues	Yes	14 years
Advancing volume	—	—
Declining issues	Yes	14 years
Declining volume	—	—
Most active	Yes	—
Most up (%)	Yes	—
Most down (%)	Yes	—
Tick by volume	—	—
Trading indices (TRIN)	—	—
Dow Jones indices	Yes	14 years
NYSE indices	Yes	14 years
ASE indices	Yes	14 years
Nasdaq indices	Yes	14 years
Standard & Poor's indices	Yes	14 years
Financial future indices	—	—

Company data:		
Dividend $ amounts	Yes	14 years
Dividend yield	Yes	14 years
Dividend ex-dates	—	—
Dividend pay-dates	—	—
Earnings per share	Yes	14 years
Price Earnings ratio	Yes	14 years
Balance sheet	—	—
Income statement	—	
Financial Ratios	—	—
Annual Reports	—	—
10-K's	—	—
* Sales	Yes	14 years
* Cash flow	Yes	14 years
* Capital spending	Yes	14 years

Research opinions:		
Value Line	—	—
Standard & Poor's	—	—
Moody's	—	—
Argus	—	—

News:		
Dow Jones News Ticker	—	—
Reuters	—	—
Barrons	—	—
Wall Street Journal	—	—
* Associated Press	Yes	—
* Business Newswire	Yes	—
* Comtex OTC Newswire	Yes	—
* Garvin Guybutler	Yes	—
* Kyodo Newswire	Yes	—
* OPEC Newswire	Yes	—
* The PR Newswire	Yes	—
* UPI Newswire	Yes	—

* Other:		
* Insider trading information	Yes	—

The database will:

	Capabilities	Comments
Construct charts/graphs	Yes	—
Project trends	Yes	—
Run regressions	Yes	—
Run other statistics	—	—
Create/Save my own portfolios	Yes	—
Window or split the screen	—	—
Write/run my own programs	—	—
Screen on certain characteristics	Yes	—

It is also worth mentioning that:

Telescn database transmits information in a graphic form as opposed to a raw data format. The information is sent within seconds, thereby minimizing on-line usage. A built-in save feature also allows information to be viewed off-line.

National Computer Network Corp.

175 West Jackson, Suite A-1038
Chicago, IL 60604
(312) 427-5125

Tradeline/Nite-Line®
Quote/Historical
Dial-Up
Local
Less than 25,000 subscribers

Description of database:

Tradeline/Nite-Line® is a menu-driven, on-line, data down-loading service covering all markets: stocks, bonds, treasuries, and futures. Costs vary with usage, but for most markets charges are based exclusively on connect time. However, the history option, which includes over seven years of data on over 50,000 issues, does cost extra.

The database contains CURRENT data for:

Securities:	Included	Comments
Stocks	Yes	All
Corporate Bonds	Yes	All
GNMA/FNMA	Yes	All
Treasury Bills	Yes	All
Government Bonds	Yes	Federal only
Options	Yes	All
Commodities	Yes	All
Financial Futures	Yes	All
Stock Index Futures	Yes	All

The exchanges included are:

American (ASE)	Yes	KCBT	Yes	Pacific (PSE)	Yes
Boston	Yes	MidAm	Yes	Philadelphia	Yes
Cincinnati	Yes	Midwest (MSE)	Yes	OTC-NASDAQ	Yes
CBOE	Yes	MnGE	Yes	OTC-NME	Yes
CBT	Yes	Montreal	Yes	Toronto	Yes
CME	Yes	NYFE	Yes	Vancouver	—
CEC	Yes	NYSE	Yes	* London	Yes

The available information is:

	Stocks	Bonds	Options	Commod	Fin'l Futures	Stk Indx Futures
Closing Prices:	Yes	Yes	Yes (1)	Yes (2)	Yes (3)	Yes (4)
Daily High-Low:	Yes	Yes	Yes (1)	Yes (2)	Yes (3)	Yes (4)
Yearly High-Low:	Yes	Yes	Yes (1)	—	—	—
Bid-Ask:	—	—	Yes (1)	—	—	—
Volume:	Yes	Yes	Yes (1)	Yes (2)	Yes (3)	Yes (4)

Historical data available from 1974.
(1) Historical data available from 1978.
(2) Historical data available from 1976, opening price also included.
(3) Historical data available from 1980.
(4) Historical data available from 1984.

Availability of quotes:

Both real time and delayed basis.

The equipment required to use this database is:

Computer:	Any terminal
Operating system:	—
Monitor:	Mono or color
Disk drives:	Required only for terminal emulation program
Memory:	Required only for terminal emulation program
Modem:	300 or 1200 baud
Software:	Any terminal emulation program

Support services available:

Manual, technical hotline.

The charges for the service are:

(1) Set-up charges: $30

(2) Basic rate:

	BAUD RATE	
	300	*1200*
(a) Prime time:	Weekdays: 8 AM-6 PM @ $26	$34 per hour
(b) Non-prime time:	Weekdays: 6 PM-8 AM @ $13	$19 per hour
	Weekends & Holidays	

(3) Specialty charges: Charges for extended history option are $.02 per close plus a reduced time charge

Note: Reduced pricing is available for calls from Area Code (312).

The database also contains:

Market Statistics:	Current Data	Historic Data
Market volume	Yes	13 years
Advancing issues	Yes	13 years
Advancing volume	Yes	13 years
Declining issues	Yes	13 years
Declining volume	Yes	13 years
Most active	Yes	13 years
Most up (%)	Yes	13 years
Most down (%)	Yes	13 years
Tick by volume	—	—
Trading indices (TRIN)	Yes	13 years
Dow Jones indices	Yes	13 years
NYSE indices	Yes	13 years
ASE indices	Yes	13 years
Nasdaq indices	Yes	13 years
Standard & Poor's indices	Yes	26 years
Financial future indices	Yes	13 years

Company data:		
Dividend $ amounts	Yes	18 years
Dividend yield	Yes	18 years
Dividend ex-dates	Yes	18 years
Dividend pay-dates	Yes	18 years
Earnings per share	Yes	7 years
Price Earnings ratio	Yes	7 years
Balance sheet	—	—
Income statement	—	—
Financial Ratios	—	—
Annual Reports	—	—
10-K's	—	—

Research opinions:		
Value Line	—	—
Standard & Poor's	—	—
Moody's	—	—
Argus	—	—

News:		
Dow Jones News Ticker	—	—
Reuters	—	—
Barrons	—	—
Wall Street Journal	—	—

The database will:

Capabilities	Comments	
Construct charts/graphs	—	—
Project trends	—	—
Run regressions	Yes	—
Run other statistics	Yes	—
Create/Save my own portfolios	Yes	Unlimited
Window or split the screen	—	—
Write/run my own programs	Yes	Fortran
Screen on certain characteristics	Yes	—

It is also worth mentioning that:

The database contains several additional services:

- *Banking Industry Products/CD Infoline*—which reports rates on over two hundred jumbo CD's, updated daily;
- *Tradeline*—which allows stock screening, portfolio graphing services, etc.; and,
- *Option Evaluation*—which provides information on options and optionable stocks.

Gregg Corporation

100 Fifth Avenue
Waltham, MA 02154
(617) 890-7227

Tradeline™ Securities Database System

Historical
Dial-Up
Local/Autonet/Telenet/Tymnet
Less than 25,000 subscribers

Description of database:

Tradeline™ Securities Database System is a complete system for managing, retrieving, and analyzing historical securities data. The database includes technical, selected fundamental, and descriptive data on over 70,000 issues from all major North American exchanges. The database provides over 12 years of price, volume, and dividend history. A library of subroutines and a number of application programs is also available to users.

The database contains CURRENT data for:

Securities:	Included	Comments
Stocks	Yes	—
Corporate Bonds	Yes	—
GNMA/FNMA	Yes	Selected issues only
Treasury Bills	Yes	—
Government Bonds	Yes	—
Options	Yes	—
Commodities	—	—
Financial Futures	—	—
Stock Index Futures	—	—

The exchanges included are:

American (ASE)	Yes	KCBT	—	Pacific (PSE)	Yes
Boston	Yes	MidAm	—	Philadelphia	Yes
Cincinnati	—	Midwest (MSE)	Yes	OTC-NASDAQ	Yes
CBOE	Yes	MnGE	—	OTC-NME	Yes
CBT	—	Montreal	Yes	Toronto	Yes
CME	—	NYFE	—	Vancouver	—
CEC	—	NYSE	Yes		

The available information is:

	Stocks	Bonds	Options	Commod	Fin'l Futures	Stk Indx Futures
Closing Prices:	Yes	Yes	Yes (1)	—	—	—
Daily High-Low:	Yes	Yes	Yes (1)	—	—	—
Yearly High-Low:	Yes	Yes	Yes (1)	—	—	—
Bid-Ask:	Yes	Yes	—	—	—	—
Volume:	Yes	Yes	Yes (1)	—	—	—

Data available from 1974.
(1) Data available for one year rolling history.

Availability of quotes:

Not available.

The equipment required to use this database is:

Computer:	Any terminal
Operating system:	—
Monitor:	Mono or color
Disk drives:	Required only for terminal emulation program
Memory:	Required only for terminal emulation program
Modem:	300 or 1200 baud
Software:	Any terminal emulation program

Support services available:

Training and manual availability.

The charges for the service are:

(1) Set-up charges:	—
(2) Basic rate:	—
(3) Specialty charges:	By license agreement only.

The database also contains:

Market Statistics:

	Current Data	Historic Data
Market volume	Yes	13 years
Advancing issues	Yes	9 years
Advancing volume	Yes	8 years
Declining issues	Yes	9 years
Declining volume	Yes	8 years
Most active	Yes	By request only
Most up (%)	Yes	By request only
Most down (%)	Yes	By request only
Tick by volume	—	—
Trading indices (TRIN)	—	—
Dow Jones indices	Yes	13 years
NYSE indices	Yes	13 years
ASE indices	Yes	13 years
Nasdaq indices	Yes	13 years
Standard & Poor's indices	Yes	13 years
Financial future indices	—	—

Company data:

	Current Data	Historic Data
Dividend $ amounts	Yes	18 years
Dividend yield	Yes	—
Dividend ex-dates	Yes	18 years
Dividend pay-dates	Yes	15 years
Earnings per share	Yes	—
Price Earnings ratio	Yes	—
Balance sheet	—	—
Income statement	—	—
Financial Ratios	—	—
Annual Reports	—	—
10-K's	—	—
* Beta coefficient	Yes	—
* SIC codes	Yes	—
* Shares outstanding	Yes	—

Research opinions:

	Current Data	Historic Data
Value Line	—	—
Standard & Poor's	—	—
Moody's	—	—
Argus	—	—

News:

	Current Data	Historic Data
Dow Jones News Ticker	—	—
Reuters	—	—
Barrons	—	—
Wall Street Journal	—	—

The database will:

Capabilities

		Comments
Construct charts/graphs	—	—
Project trends	—	—
Run regressions	Yes	—
Run other statistics	Yes	—
Create/Save my own portfolios	Yes	—
Window or split the screen	—	—
Write/run my own programs	Yes	—
Screen on certain characteristics	Yes	Up to 24 characteristics

It is also worth mentioning that:

This database is licensed to a number of vendors and is redistributed by them under the following names:

- ADP Network Services (Fastock II)
- Citicorp Information Services (Citiquote)
- Compuserve (Micro Quote II)
- Electronic Data Systems, formerly National Data Co. (Rapidquote II)
- National Computer Network, Inc. (Tradeline/Nite-Line®)
- Tymshare/McDonnell Douglas (Tymquote)

Historical stock, bond, and option pricing is also available on floppy diskettes and magnetic tape, formatted for use with a number of popular financial software packages.

Investment Technologies, Inc.

Metropark
510 Thornall Street
Edison, NJ 08837
(201) 494-1200
(800) 524-0831

Vestor
Historical
Dial-Up
Local/Telenet
Less than 25,000 subscribers

Description of database:

Vestor is a twenty-four hour per day, on-line, investment advisory service which works with any PC or computer terminal equipped with a modem. Vestor offers historical price information, evaluations, and buy-sell signals for over 6000 securities traded on the major exchanges.

The database contains CURRENT data for:

Securities:	Included	Comments
Stocks	Yes	—
Corporate Bonds	—	—
GNMA/FNMA	Yes	—
Treasury Bills	Yes	—
Government Bonds	—	—
Options	Yes	—
Commodities	Yes	—
Financial Futures	Yes	—
Stock Index Futures	Yes	—

The exchanges included are:

American (ASE)	Yes	KCBT	—	Pacific (PSE)	—
Boston	—	MidAm	—	Philadelphia	—
Cincinnati	—	Midwest (MSE)	—	OTC-NASDAQ	Yes
CBOE	—	MnGE	—	OTC-NME	Yes
CBT	—	Montreal	—	Toronto	—
CME	—	NYFE	—	Vancouver	—
CEC	—	NYSE	Yes		

The available information is:

	Stocks	Bonds	Options	Commod	Fin'l Futures	Stk Indx Futures
Closing Prices:	Yes	—	Yes	Yes	—	Yes
Daily High-Low:	Yes	—	Yes(1)	Yes(1)	Yes	—
Yearly High-Low:	Yes	—	—	—	—	—
Bid-Ask:	—	—	—	—	—	—
Volume:	Yes	—	—	—	—	Yes

Historical data available for one year.
(1) Data available for 295 days only.

Availability of quotes:

Not available.

The equipment required to use this database is:

Computer:	Any terminal
Operating system:	—
Monitor:	Mono or color: minimum 24 rows × 79 columns
Disk drives:	Required only for terminal emulation program
Memory:	Required only for terminal emulation program
Modem:	300 or 1200 baud
Software:	Any terminal emulation program

Support services available:

Manual, and toll-free customer service.

The charges for the service are:

(1)	Set-up charges:	$295
(2)	Basic rate:	—
(3)	Specialty charges:	$24 minimum monthly usage charge

The database also contains:

Market Statistics:	Current Data	Historic Data
Market volume	—	—
Advancing issues	—	—
Advancing volume	—	—
Declining issues	—	—
Declining volume	—	—
Most active	—	—
Most up (%)	—	—
Most down (%)	—	—
Tick by volume	—	—
Trading indices (TRIN)	—	—
Dow Jones indices	Yes	1 year
NYSE indices	Yes	1 year
ASE indices	—	—
Nasdaq indices	—	—
Standard & Poor's indices	Yes	1 year
Financial future indices	—	—
* Vestor's proprietary indices	Yes	1 year

Company data:		
Dividend $ amounts	—	—
Dividend yield	Yes	—
Dividend ex-dates	—	—
Dividend pay-dates	—	—
Earnings per share	Yes	—
Price Earnings ratio	Yes	—
Balance sheet	—	—
Income statement	—	—
Financial Ratios	—	—
Annual Reports	—	—
10-K's	—	—

Research opinions:		
Value Line	—	—
Standard & Poor's	—	—
Moody's	—	—
Argus	—	—
* Vestor's proprietary opinions	Yes	1 year

News:		
Dow Jones News Ticker	—	—
Reuters	—	—
Barrons	—	—
Wall Street Journal	—	—

The database will:

	Capabilities	Comments
Construct charts/graphs	Yes	—
Project trends	Yes	—
Run regressions	Yes	—
Run other statistics	Yes	—
Create/Save my own portfolios	Yes	Unlimited number
Window or split the screen	—	—
Write/run my own programs	—	—
Screen on certain characteristics	Yes	Up to 15 characteristics

It is also worth mentioning that:

Thirty, easy to use, cost effective, forecasting and evaluation programs are available in the database.

Vestor's research opinions are also distributed through Quotron.

Any customer with an account at Charles Schwab & Co. is given a $100 discount off the normal set-up charges.

Vickers Stock Research Corp.

226 New York Avenue
Huntington, NY 11743
(516) 423-7710

Vickers Online
Specialty
Dial-Up
Local/Telenet/Tymnet
Less than 25,000 subscribers

Description of database:

Vickers Online monitors institutional holdings, insider transactions, and shareholder intentions as reported to the Securities and Exchange Commission through several required filings. The database covers:

- Form 13F—Institutional Holdings;
- Form 13D—5% Equity Ownership;
- Form 144—Proposed Sale of Securities; and,
- Form 4—Change in Beneficial Ownership of Securities

Vestor Online is also tied to Argus On-Line which features:

- Argus' industry and market commentary;
- Argus' economic and investment policy opinions; and,
- Descriptions, analyses, news, recommendations, and financial data on all of the stocks followed by Argus.

The database contains CURRENT data for:

Securities:	Included	Comments
Stocks	Yes	All
Corporate Bonds	Yes	All
GNMA/FNMA	—	—
Treasury Bills	—	—
Government Bonds	—	—
Options	—	—
Commodities	—	—
Financial Futures	—	—
Stock Index Futures	—	—

The exchanges included are:

American (ASE)	Yes	KCBT	Yes	Pacific (PSE)	Yes
Boston	Yes	MidAm	Yes	Philadelphia	Yes
Cincinnati	Yes	Midwest (MSE)	Yes	OTC-NASDAQ	Yes
CBOE	Yes	MnGE	Yes	OTC-NME	Yes
CBT	Yes	Montreal	Yes	Toronto	Yes
CME	Yes	NYFE	Yes	Vancouver	Yes
CEC	Yes	NYSE	Yes		

The available information is:

	Stocks	Bonds	Options	Commod	Fin'l Futures	Stk Indx Futures
Closing Prices:	—	—	—	—	—	—
Daily High-Low:	—	—	—	—	—	—
Yearly High-Low:	—	—	—	—	—	—
Bid-Ask:	—	—	—	—	—	—
Volume:	—	—	—	—	—	—

Availability of quotes:

Not available.

The equipment required to use this database is:

Computer:	Any terminal
Operating system:	—
Monitor:	Mono or color
Disk drives:	Required only for terminal emulation program
Memory:	Required only for terminal emulation program
Modem:	300 or 1200 baud
Software:	Any terminal emulation program

Support services available:

Technical hotline, documentation.

The charges for the service are:

(1)	Set-up charges:	—
(2)	Basic rate:	$1.00 per minute
(3)	Specialty charges:	$50 annual fee

The database also contains:

Market Statistics:	Current Data	Historic Data
Market volume	—	—
Advancing issues	—	—
Advancing volume	—	—
Declining issues	—	—
Declining volume	—	—
Most active	—	—
Most up (%)	—	—
Most down (%)	—	—
Tick by volume	—	—
Trading indices (TRIN)	—	—
Dow Jones indices	—	—
NYSE indices	—	—
ASE indices	—	—
Nasdaq indices	—	—
Standard & Poor's indices	—	—
Financial future indices	—	—

Company data:		
Dividend $ amounts	Yes	—
Dividend yield	Yes	—
Dividend ex-dates	Yes	—
Dividend pay-dates	—	—
Earnings per share	Yes	—
Price Earnings ratio	Yes	—
Balance sheet	Yes	—
Income statement	Yes	—
Financial Ratios	Yes	—
Annual Reports	Yes	—
10-K's	Yes	—
* 400 Stocks thru Argus On-Line	Yes	—

Research opinions:		
Value Line	—	—
Standard & Poor's	—	—
Moody's	—	—
Argus	—	—

News:		
Dow Jones News Ticker	—	—
Reuters	—	—
Barrons	—	—
Wall Street Journal	—	—

The database will:

	Capabilities	Comments
Construct charts/graphs	—	—
Project trends	—	—
Run regressions	—	—
Run other statistics	—	—
Create/Save my own portfolios	—	—
Window or split the screen	—	—
Write/run my own programs	—	—
Screen on certain characteristics	—	—

It is also worth mentioning that:

All information is available in hard copy and machine readable format.

VU/TEXT Information Service, Inc.

1211 Chestnut St., Suite #205
Philadelphia, PA 19107
(215) 665-8080

VU/TEXT® Financial Database

Quote/Historical
Dial-Up
Telenet/Tymnet
Less than 25,000 subscribers

Description of database:

VU/TEXT® Financial Database is actually five databases combined into one:

- *VU/QUOTE*—a delayed stock and futures quote services;
- *Disclosure*—a financial and management information service on over 10,000 publically held companies;
- *The PR Newswire*—an electronic news service covering news releases issued by trade associations, labor unions, U.S. and foreign corporations and government agencies, colleges and universities, and civic and cultural institutions;
- *Associated Press Newswire*—the world's leading news service; and,
- *The Wall Street Transcript*—a weekly publication covering interviews, research, announcements, speeches, and discussions of interest to Wall Street professionals.

The database contains CURRENT data for:

Securities:	Included	Comments
Stocks	Yes	All
Corporate Bonds	—	—
GNMA/FNMA	—	—
Treasury Bills	—	—
Government Bonds	—	—
Options	—	—
Commodities	Yes	Except CME
Financial Futures	Yes	Except CME
Stock Index Futures	Yes	Except CME

The exchanges included are:

American (ASE)	Yes	KCBT	Yes	Pacific (PSE)	Yes
Boston	Yes	MidAm	Yes	Philadelphia	Yes
Cincinnati	Yes	Midwest (MSE)	Yes	OTC-NASDAQ	Yes
CBOE	—	MnGE	Yes	OTC-NME	Yes
CBT	Yes	Montreal	—	Toronto	—
CME	Yes	NYFE	Yes	Vancouver	—
CEC	Yes	NYSE	Yes		

The available information is:

	Stocks	Bonds	Options	Commod	Fin'l Futures	Stk Indx Futures
Closing Prices:	Yes	—	—	Yes	Yes	Yes (1)
Daily High-Low:	Yes	—	—	Yes	Yes	Yes (1)
Yearly High-Low:	—	—	—	—	—	—
Bid-Ask:	Yes	—	—	Yes	Yes	Yes (1)
Volume:	Yes	—	—	Yes	Yes	Yes (1)

Current prices available only. No historical data available.
(1) CME data not available.

Availability of quotes:

Delayed basis only.

The equipment required to use this database is:

Computer:	Any terminal
Operating system:	—
Monitor:	Mono or color
Disk drives:	Required only for terminal emulation program
Memory:	Required only for terminal emulation program
Modem:	300 or 1200 baud
Software:	Any terminal emulation program

Support services available:

Training seminars, technical hotline, and bi-monthly newsletter "VU/TEXT Newsline."

The charges for the service are:

(1) Set-up charges:	—
(2) Basic rate:	—
(3) Specialty charges:	Each subset of data is priced separately. See "It is also worth mentioning that:" for details.

The database also contains:

Market Statistics	Current Data	Historic Data
Market volume	Yes	—
Advancing issues	Yes	—
Advancing volume	Yes	—
Declining issues	Yes	—
Declining volume	Yes	—
Most active	Yes	—
Most up (%)	Yes	—
Most down (%)	Yes	—
Tick by volume	—	—
Trading indices (TRIN)	Yes	—
Dow Jones indices	Yes	—
NYSE indices	Yes	—
ASE indices	Yes	—
Nasdaq indices	Yes	—
Standard & Poor's indices	—	—
Financial future indices	—	—
* Net Tick	Yes	

Company data:		
Dividend $ amounts	Yes	—
Dividend yield	Yes	—
Dividend ex-dates	Yes	—
Dividend pay-dates	Yes	—
Earnings per share	Yes	—
Price Earnings ratio	Yes	—
Balance sheet	Yes	—
Income statement	Yes	—
Financial Ratios	Yes	—
Annual Reports	—	—
10-K's	Yes	—
* Quarterly Balance Sheets	Yes	—
* Ratio Balance Sheets	Yes	—
* Corporate Profiles	Yes	—

Research opinions:		
Value Line	—	—
Standard & Poor's	—	—
Moody's	—	—
Argus	—	—
* Wall Street Transcript	Yes	5 years

News:		
Dow Jones News Ticker	—	—
Barrons	—	—
Wall Street Journal	—	—
* Associated Press	Yes	2 years
* The PR Newswire	Yes	2 years

The database will:

	Capabilities	Comments
Construct charts/graphs	—	—
Project trends	—	—
Run regressions	—	—
Run other statistics	—	—
Create/Save my own portfolios	—	—
Window or split the screen	—	—
Write/run my own programs	—	—
Screen on certain characteristics	—	—

It is also worth mentioning that:

There are two pricing options available.

Option I Contract rate pricing: lower hourly charges, $60 monthly minimum contract rate; and,
Option II Open rate: higher hourly charges, $10 monthly minimum.

Data Type	Option I	Option II
VU/QUOTE	$ 50 per hour	$ 50 per hour
* Disclosure	25 per hour	25 per hour
Associated Press	85 per hour	100 per hour
The PR Newswire	75 per hour	90 per hour
Wall Street Transcript	250 per hour	295 per hour

* An additional $12 document charge also applies.

Warner Computer Systems
1 University Plaza - Suite 300
Hackensack, NJ 07601
(201) 489-1580

Warner's Financial Database
Historical
Dial-Up
Local/Telenet
Less than 25,000 subscribers

Description of database:

Warner's Financial Database covers technical and fundamental security information. Both current and historic data is available— technical information is available for the past 10 years and fundamental information is available for the past 20 years.

The database contains CURRENT data for:

Securities:	Included	Comments
Stocks	Yes	—
Corporate Bonds	Yes	—
GNMA/FNMA	Yes	—
Treasury Bills	Yes	—
Government Bonds	Yes	—
Options	Yes	—
Commodities	—	—
Financial Futures	—	—
Stock Index Futures	—	—

The exchanges included are:

American (ASE)	Yes	KCBT	—	Pacific (PSE)	Yes
Boston	—	MidAm	—	Philadelphia	Yes
Cincinnati	—	Midwest (MSE)	Yes	OTC-NASDAQ	Yes
CBOE	—	MnGE	—	OTC-NME	Yes
CBT	—	Montreal	Yes	Toronto	Yes
CME	—	NYFE	—	Vancouver	—
CEC	—	NYSE	Yes		

The available information is:

	Stocks	Bonds	Options	Commod	Fin'l Futures	Stk Indx Futures
Closing Prices:	Yes	Yes (1)	Yes (2)	—	—	—
Daily High-Low:	Yes	Yes (1)	Yes (2)	—	—	—
Yearly High-Low:	Yes	—	—	—	—	—
Bid-Ask:	Yes	—	—	—	—	—
Volume:	Yes	—	—	—	—	—

Data available for the past 10 years.
(1) Current end of week and end of month data available only.
(2) Data available for one month following the expiration of the option.

Availability of quotes:

Not available.

The equipment required to use this database is:

Computer:	Any terminal
Operating system:	—
Monitor:	Mono or color
Disk drives:	Required only for terminal emulation program
Memory:	Required only for terminal emulation program
Modem:	300 or 1200 baud
Software:	Any terminal emulation program

Support services available:

Training, manual, and phone support.

The charges for the service are:

(1) Set-up charges: $48
(2) Basic rate:
    (a) Prime time: Weekdays: 8 AM-6 PM @ $.85 per minute
    (b) Non-prime time: Weekdays: 6 PM-8 AM @ $.30 per minute
        Weekends & Holidays
(3) Specialty charges: Historical prices over one year old:

Prime time:	@ $1.50 per minute
Non-prime time:	@ $.60 per minute

NOTE: 1200 baud rates are billed at twice the 300 baud rate.

The database also contains:

Market Statistics:	Current Data	Historic Data
Market volume	Yes	10 years
Advancing issues	Yes	10 years
Advancing volume	Yes	10 years
Declining issues	Yes	10 years
Declining volume	—	—
Most active	—	—
Most up (%)	—	—
Most down (%)	—	—
Tick by volume	—	—
Trading indices (TRIN)	Yes	10 years
Dow Jones indices	Yes	10 years
NYSE indices	Yes	10 years
ASE indices	Yes	10 years
Nasdaq indices	Yes	10 years
Standard & Poor's indices	Yes	10 years
Financial future indices	—	—

Company data:		
Dividend $ amounts	Yes	10 years
Dividend yield	Yes	10 years
Dividend ex-dates	Yes	10 years
Dividend pay-dates	Yes	10 years
Earnings per share	Yes	10 years
Price Earnings ratio	Yes	10 years
Balance sheet	Yes	20 years
Income statement	Yes	20 years
Financial Ratios	Yes	10 years
Annual Reports	Yes	4 years
10-K's	Yes	4 years

Research opinions:		
Value Line	—	—
Standard & Poor's	—	—
Moody's	—	—
Argus	—	—

News:		
Dow Jones News Ticker	—	—
Reuters	—	—
Barrons	—	—
Wall Street Journal	—	—

The database will:

	Capabilities	Comments
Construct charts/graphs	Yes	—
Project trends	—	—
Run regressions	—	—
Run other statistics	Yes	—
Create/Save my own portfolios	Yes	—
Window or split the screen	—	—
Write/run my own programs	Yes	—
Screen on certain characteristics	Yes	—

It is also worth mentioning that:

Custom programs are available to facilitate use with microcomputers and mainframes. LOTUS templates are also available.

INVESTMENT PUBLICATIONS

Investment publications are written for a variety of purposes and contain a host of different investment opinions and perspectives covering a wide range of investment topics. Thus, as a subscriber, you can choose newsletters that concentrate on fundamental analysis, technical analysis, or techno-fundamental analysis. You can find publications that periodically review a subset of securities. Or, you can find publications designed solely to increase your level of investment knowledge without giving you specific investment recommendations to follow. Whatever "flavor" you desire is available, and it is usually offered by a host of different publishers. In fact, if you just want to know what everyone else is thinking, you can get publications that do nothing more than monitor a host of other publications.

The reasons investors subscribe to investment publications are as varied as the publications themselves. Some use these services to obtain background information, whereas others manage their portfolios based on the recommendations of their favorite Wall Street "gurus." Some investors choose publications that cover a wide variety of investment topics in an effort to broaden their investment education, while others choose publications that concentrate on a specific investment area, telling all there is to know about it. Whatever the reason, there are a host of publications out there designed to satisfy each and every need.

PUBLICATION QUESTIONNAIRES—BACKGROUND

Once again, I have conducted a survey. This time, the better known, better respected, investment newsletter and publication vendors responded to questionnaires. The pages that follow recap the results of this survey. As usual, despite repeated attempts to cajole several organizations to respond, the respondents listed here do not represent the total range of investment publications queried.

Every attempt has been made to present the information contained in this chapter in a fair and unbiased fashion. To ensure this policy, several conventions have been adopted. Each respondent has been asked exactly the same questions in exactly the same fashion. In attempting to paraphrase the responses, exactly the same terminology was used across respondents so that comparisons can be made and conclusions drawn. Additionally, information is presented in a consistent fashion page by page, so that you can easily flip through the pages comparing response with response. Finally, I have arranged permission with each publisher to allow me to reproduce a sample page (in some cases, pages) of my choosing, so that you see a representative sample of the format and style used by the publication to convey its investment message. Each sample is included as an exhibit and is found on the page opposite the survey results.

Publisher Contact Information

The name, address, and phone number of the publisher is reported in the upper left-hand corner of the page. The name of the publication, the topical area covered by the publication, and the current number of subscribers are reported in the upper right-hand corner of the page.

Categories of Publications

For the sake of simplicity, I have categorized publications into seven topical areas. They are:
  • *Investment Advisory Bulletins*—containing specific investment advice for use in managing investment portfolios;
  • *Advisory Condensation Services*—containing a condensation of the thoughts and recommendations being published by a host of investment advisory bulletins;
  • *Topical Education Services*—containing investment information covering a wide range of topics;
  • *Concentrated Education Services*—containing in-depth investment information covering a specific investment topic;
  • *Statistical Services*—containing raw statistical data covering a subset of securities **without** giving investment advice;
  • *Research Bulletins*—containing general investment advice of a fundamental nature for use in timing portfolio transactions **without** giving specific investment advice; and,
  • *Market Timing Bulletins*—containing general investment advice of a technical nature for use in timing portfolio transactions **without** giving specific investment advice.

Subscriber Levels

Generally, the number of subscribers to a periodical is regarded as proprietary information. Thus, in order to encourage publishers to answer this question, the survey offered large categories as potential responses. Unfortunately, even with the available choices, several publishers refused to respond. In any case, the possible choices that were offered were:

  1. under 25,000
  2. 25,000 to 50,000
  3. 50,000 to 100,000
  4. 100,000 to 250,000
  5. 250,000 to 500,000
  6. 500,000 to 1,000,000
  7. over 1,000,000

In most cases, publishers chose the answer "under 25,000," which unfortunately tells us little about the relative size of each specific publication. However, it does tell us that there is still a lot of room for growth within the industry. Furthermore, noting that oligopolies have already started to form—as evidenced by the fact that most publishers currently offer more than one publication—one can determine the relative size of each publishing organization by summing circulation across all of their publications.

Content Description

The description of the publication is a paraphrased version of what the publisher says the publication contains. Every attempt has been made to remove boastful, sales-oriented comments by replacing them with simple, straightforward, descriptive phrases. Wherever possible, equivalent terminology has been used.

Methodology Used in Investment Selection

The next section highlights the method used to determine what investment selections are to be included in the publication.

For investment advisory bulletins, the results describe how security recommendations are arrived at, such as through fundamental analysis, technical analysis, or the like. Be cognizant that publications stating "fundamental analysis for selection, technical analysis for timing" use a different methodology than those stating "fundamental and technical analysis." In the former case, only fundamental selection criteria are used to determine what selections are made, and then technical analysis is employed to determine the timing to be used. In the latter case, selections are based on fundamental and technical criteria. That is, selections that have exceptional chart patters and only average fundamentals could be included in "fundamental and technical analysis" whereas they would not be included in the former case.

In the case of the other six types of publications, this section refers to the manner by which selections were chosen for review—whether through some periodic review of a subset of securities, through the concentration on some specialty topic area, through the selection of other investment advisory publications, or another means.

Publication Track Record

Next is a summary of the track record of investment advisory bulletins. Three types of phraseology are used to present this information:
- *Not applicable*—the appropriate response for all publications other than investment advisory bulletins;
- *Not available*—the response used by those investment advisory bulletins which were unwilling to disclose their track record; and
- *The track record*—the response used by those investment advisory bulletins which were proud enough of their track record to report it. Please be aware that information contained herein is "as reported by the publication" on whatever terms the publication has chosen to report it. No attempt has been made to verify these reports.

Other Features

The next three sections report the longevity, the cost, and the number of issues per year for the publication. The next identifies whether the publication makes a hotline service available, and if so, the cost of this service. And the next identifies the manner in which the publication is delivered to U.S. residents.

Finally, the last section describes other pertinent information about the publication and the publisher that may be helpful for you to know.

Investor's Analysis, Inc.   **The Astute Investor**™
P.O. Box 988   Investment Advisory Bulletin
Paoli, PA 19301   Less than 25,000 subscribers
(215) 296-2411

Description of the publication:
　　The Astute Investor™ is a comprehensive financial newsletter which discusses and analyzes invest-
　　ment expectations for the economy, monetary policy, interest rates, and corporate earnings. The
　　newsletter provides specific stock market strategy and tactics, stock recommendations with buy
　　ranges, support and resistance levels, and stop points. "Chief Elf," Bob Nurock, of Wall Street
　　Week fame, discusses the technical market index, its current position, and what could change it
　　in the future.

Investment selections in the publication are determined:
　　Using fundamental analysis for selection, technical analysis for timing.

The track record for the publication, as reported by the publication, is:
　　24% average annual gain over past three years.

The publication has been published continuously since: 1983

The cost of a subscription is: $197

The number of issues per year is: 17

A HOTLINE telephone service is: Available
　　Cost for this service: $200/annually plus $20/minute for a personal telephone consultation.

The publication can be delivered: Via first class mail

WRITTEN BY
ROBERT J. NUROCK

© Investor's Analysis, Inc. June 5, 1986

Trip or Trap?

That's what investors would like to know.

Is the market's recent sharp rally the beginning of a much broader and longer lasting upmove? Or, is it a snare for the unwary prior to another downturn?

While the evidence is mixed, there is one thing that we do know. It is extremely difficult to resist joining the rampant bulls who believe we've begun a new stampede to much higher levels.

Mainly, that is the result of the conditioning of the market cycle since late last summer. At that time, the skeptics and pessimists missed out on the beginning of an historic rally. Then, after the market consolidated its prior gains in mid December to late January, those who believed it had gone too far too fast were left in the stampeding bull's dust.

Now that the market has erupted from a period similar to that earlier consolidation, it is hard to fight the apparent trend. Especially in view of the rapidity with which the market has made its upmove, leaving the impression that if you didn't act immediately, you'd be left behind once again.

We admit to a sense of uneasiness as a result of these circumstances; however, we are not yet ready to abandon caution. That is because our analysis of the dynamics of the market rally to date, and the expectational background to decision making, lead us to believe the corrective process which began in late March still has further to run.

It is quite obvious that the recent rally has not been broad based. While there has been some relative improvement in the performance of OTC issues, overall the number of stocks advancing versus those declining has lagged the strength in

In Brief

Trip or Trap? –

Narrowness of rally, expectational background point to further correction. Greater investor uncertainty likely to create conditions for future positive surprise.

Stock Market Outlook –

Rally result of short squeeze. Wider array of improving issues would signify market bottom.

Technical Picture –

Deteriorating again. Breadth, momentum, volume divergences and decreasing skepticism negative. Wall $treet Week TMI turning bearish. Sell signal possible if deterioration continues.

Market Strategy/Tactics –

Remain cautious, maintain reserves. Look for broadening participation, increased skepticism to confirm end of correction. Downside target to DJIA 1721/1739 still valid.

Next Issue – June 26, 1986.

the blue chip indices. On both a daily and weekly basis, many fewer stocks are reaching new highs now than in mid March when the market indices were much lower. And, as many analysts have noted, both the Dow Jones Transportation and Utility averages have failed to confirm the new high in the Industrials.

While these signs of non–confirmation do not necessarily spell immediate disaster, and can be

Copyright ©

Investor's Analysis, Incorporated   P.O. Box 988 Paoli, Pa. 19301 (215) 296-2411

Reprinted with permission.

Davis/Zweig Futures, Inc.
P.O. Box 5345
New York City, NY 10150
(212) 753-7710

Business Timing Guide
Statistical Service
Less than 25,000 subscribers

Description of the publication:
The Business Timing Guide tracks macro-economic statistics, provides an economic checklist based on the outlook of business trends, and recommends suitable generic investment strategies. The newsletter does not make specific investment recommendations nor maintain a buy/sell list but rather it advises when to: buy houses, cars, financial assets, money market assets, and inflation hedges; borrow money; start a business, add to inventory, and expand plant and equipment; or liquidate all assets accordingly.

Investment selections in the publication are determined:
By regularly reviewing business trends.

The track record for the publication, as reported by the publication, is:
Not applicable.

The publication has been published continuously since: 1985

The cost of a subscription is: $150

The number of issues per year is: 24

A HOTLINE telephone service is: Not Available

The publication can be delivered: Via first class mail

It is also worth mentioning that:
Davis/Zweig Futures, Inc., and Zweig Securities Advisory Service, Inc., a related organization, publish several other newsletters covering a variety of topics.

Issue #62
29 October 1986

Business Timing Guide

Researched and Reported by Ned Davis and Martin Zweig

Economic Checklist
WHAT TO DO NOW

BUY A HOUSE	OK
BUY A CAR	OK
BUY FINANCIAL ASSETS	YES
BUY MONEY MARKET ASSETS	OK
BUY INFLATION HEDGES	NO
BORROW MONEY	OK
START A NEW BUSINESS	OK
ADD TO INVENTORY	OK
EXPAND PLANT AND EQUIPMENT . .	OK
BAIL OUT "Liquidate All Assets"	NO

The Business Trend Outlook

The BTG Inflation Timing Model rose two points to -6 this month, reflecting slight increase in food costs but still well within the low inflationary pressure region. The BTG Economic Timing Model is holding steady at +14 maintaining its accurate moderate growth assessment of the economy.

The focus of this issue of BTG is inflation. We begin on page 2 with a discussion of the Morosani Index and then a look at the new American Eagle gold coin on page 3. On page 4, we introduce our new Housing Starts Model and on page 5, we discuss the power of compound interest. We conclude this issue with an update on Marty Zweig's Stock and Bond Models and some quotes of economic interest.

Strategy

As monotonous as it may be beginning to sound, our moderate economic growth outlook has nonetheless been right on the money. With signs of a possible turn-around in the trade deficit, things are looking up for the economy. Until we get further confirmation from our BTG Economic Timing Model, however, we'll remain loyal and retain our moderate economic growth outlook. We have downgraded our "Buy A Car" recommendation in the checklist as the recent wave of buyer incentives for new cars has come to a close.

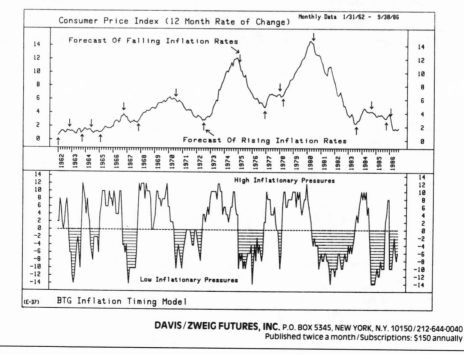

DAVIS/ZWEIG FUTURES, INC. P.O. BOX 5345, NEW YORK, N.Y. 10150/212-644-0040
Published twice a month/Subscriptions: $150 annually

Reprinted with permission.

Wiesenberger Financial Services
Division of Warren, Gorham & Lamont
1 Penn Plaza
New York City, NY 10119
(212) 971-5000

Current Performance & Dividend Record
Statistical Service
Number of subscribers is not available

Description of the publication:
Current Performance & Dividend Record is a sixteen page report reviewing dividend payments and short-term performance of over 750 mutual funds. Also included in this publication is a section comprised of comprehensive data covering over 280 money market funds.

Investment selections in the publication are determined:
By periodically reviewing all major mutual funds.

The track record for the publication, as reported by the publication, is:
Not applicable.

The publication has been published continuously since: 1940

The cost of a subscription is: $150

The number of issues per year is: 12

A HOTLINE telephone service is: Not Available

The publication can be delivered: Via first class mail

It is also worth mentioning that:
Wiesenberger Financial Services publishes several other investment publications covering mutual funds.

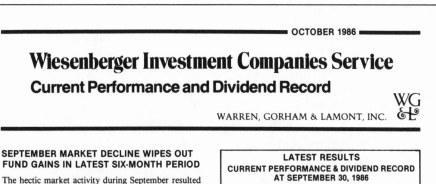

OCTOBER 1986

Wiesenberger Investment Companies Service
Current Performance and Dividend Record

WARREN, GORHAM & LAMONT, INC.

W G & L

SEPTEMBER MARKET DECLINE WIPES OUT FUND GAINS IN LATEST SIX-MONTH PERIOD

The hectic market activity during September resulted in a one-month decline of 6.9 percent for the Dow Jones Industrial Average, 8.2 per cent for the New York Stock Exchange Composite and 8.5 per cent for the Standard & Poor's 500-Stock Index. Gains were wiped out for the first time in over two years for both the funds and the broad market during the six-month period ended September 30. The DJIA dropped 2.8 percent while the NYSE Composite and the S&P-500 declined 3.1 percent and 3.2 percent, respectively. The nation's mutual funds, bettering the broad market over the six-month period for the first time since September 1985, lost an average 2.1 percent from their asset values.

While the market was tumbling, the glitter of gold brought three of these funds into the ranks of "Top-10" performers over the period. In a dramatic turnaround, on average, they outpaced every category of fund, gaining 17.5 per cent over the six months' time frame. Retreating from their steller position of the past year, the International funds, as a group, turned in the second best performance gaining an average 11.8 per cent. They still remained the heavy hitters, contributing seven to the "Top-10" roster which, in order of rank, include:

G.T. Pacific Growth Fund, up 44.2 per cent; **Merrill Lynch Pacific Fund,** up 30.8 per cent; **Financial Strategic-Pacific Basin,** up 30.5 per cent; **USAA Gold Fund,** up 28.2 per cent; **Keystone International Fund,** up 25.2 per cent; **Fidelity Overseas Fund,** up 21.9 per cent; **Golconda Investors,** up 21.0 per cent; **Colonial Advanced Strategic Gold Fund,** up 20.8 percent; **T. Rowe Price International Fund,** up 20.7 per cent; **FT International Fund,** up 20.0 per cent.

Over the 12-month period, gains were trimmed during the September slide for both the market and the funds. The DJIA continued to outpace the broader

LATEST RESULTS
CURRENT PERFORMANCE & DIVIDEND RECORD AT SEPTEMBER 30, 1986
AVERAGE PERCENT CHANGE IN NET ASSET VALUE

No. of Funds	Primary Objective	Avg. Adj. % Chg. in NAV 6 Mos. to September 30, 1986	12 Mos. to September 30, 1986	% Yield Last 12 Mos.
81	Maximum Capital Gains	– 6.9	22.8	1.3
206	Long-Term Growth of Capital—Income secondary	– 4.6	23.8	1.8
65	Growth and Current Income	– 2.9	24.6	3.1
19	Income—Common Stock	– 2.6	14.4	3.7
57	Income—Flexible Policy	– 2.2	11.6	7.5
95	Income—Senior Securities Policy	– 2.0	5.7	9.4
21	Balanced	– 1.4	22.0	4.8
28	Spec.—Canadian/International	11.8	51.9	1.1
13	Spec.—Gold and Prec. Metals	17.5	23.1	2.4
27	Spec.—Industry	– 1.3	24.8	2.2
41	Spec.—Gov't Securities	– 1.3	3.9	9.3
114	Spec.—Tax-Exempt	0.2	12.2	7.1
6	Spec.—Technology	– 8.1	19.5	0.5
7	Spec.—Other	– 0.2	15.4	5.3
780	Average	– 2.1	18.6	4.5
219	Money Market Funds	NA	NA	5.3*
68	Money Market Tax-Exempt	NA	NA	4.0*

*Avg. 30 Day Yield
NA—Not Applicable

MARKET INDICATORS

	Latest Value	% Change 6 Mos.	% Change 12 Mos.
Dow Jones Industrial Average	1767.58	– 2.8	33.0
NYSE Composite Index	133.44	– 3.1	26.9
Standard & Poor's 500-Stock Index	231.32	– 3.2	27.0

market indexes with an increase of 33.0 per cent while the average mutual fund appreciated 18.6 per cent. While on a lesser scale than in the previous month's tabulation, funds investing overseas made a clean sweep of the "Top-10" performers over the period.

Since capturing first place in March 1986, **Fidelity Overseas Fund** has not relinquished its position, leading again with a gain of 106.8 per cent. **G.T. Pacific Growth Fund** was second, increasing 82.0 per cent, followed by **FT International Fund,** up 80.4 per cent; **Merrill Lynch Pacific Fund,** up 78.1 per cent; **Transatlantic Fund,** up 77.4 per cent; **Alliance International Fund,** up 75.8 per cent; **T. Rowe Price International Fund,** up 72.8 per cent; **Kemper International Fund,** up 69.9 per cent; **IDS International Fund,** up 69.5 per

Continued on page 12

This monthly tabulation is intended primarily as a current source of reference to investment income and capital gains distributions declared, and asset value changes, during the preceding six and 12 months. Funds are listed alphabetically, but next to each name is a letter designation indicating into which of six broad categories of investment objective each fund falls. Objectives shown represent the considered judgment of the editors based on prospectuses, reports, and other data, and may or may not coincide with the objectives stated by the funds themselves.

The summary table above illustrates by primary objective the average percent change in asset value during the periods indicated, adjusted in the same manner as are the figures shown for individual funds. Under no circumstances should the data shown here be construed as an indication of future results. It should be recognized that the funds vary widely in their objectives and policies and that comparisons between funds of different types can be misleading.

This tabulation includes all mutual funds with assets in excess of $1 million for which data were obtainable. Investment income dividends are shown for the calendar quarter in which the record date occurred. Percentage return is based upon the month-end offering prices and dividends declared from investment income in the latest 12-month period. Adjustments have been made to reflect the effect of capital gains distributed. Percent changes in net asset values are also after adjustment for capital gains paid to stock of record during the period. The adjustment is made by assuming acceptance of such payments in additional shares. Income dividends paid during the indicated periods are not taken into account.

Wiesenberger Investment Companies Service. Copyright © 1986 by Warren, Gorham & Lamont, Inc., Boston, Mass. All rights reserved.

Reprinted with permission.

Wm. O'Neil & Co., Inc.   **Daily Graphs**
11915 LaGrange Avenue   Statistical Service
Los Angeles, CA 90025   25,000 to 50,000 subscribers
(213) 820-7011

Description of the publication:
Daily Graphs is a primary research and reference tool that provides comprehensive stock market information on over 7,500 securities. Daily Graphs is totally factual in nature, and includes over 41 fundamental measurements (earnings and value) and 26 technical statistics of market action (price and volume) presented in graphical and tabular format.

Daily Graphs provides two basic services:
- the New York Stock Exchange edition which includes 50 specially selected Over-the-Counter growth stocks; and,
- the American Stock Exchange edition, which includes 150 different specially selected Over-the-Counter stocks.

Investment selections in the publication are determined:
By periodically reviewing a subset of securities.

The track record for the publication, as reported by the publication, is:
Not applicable.

The publication has been published continuously since: 1972

The cost of a subscription is: $345/315/580*
* Note: Each service is sold separately—the NYSE version is priced at $345; the ASE version is priced at $315; both versions are priced at $580.

The number of issues per year is: 52

A HOTLINE telephone service is: Not Available

The publication can be delivered: Via first class, and
express mail/airfreight

It is also worth mentioning that:
Wm. O'Neil & Co. also publishes:
- Long Term Values ($195—48 issues per year) which covers 4000 stocks (broken into 200 industry groups), graphically depicting the monthly trading pattern of each stock for the past 15 years.
- Stock Option Guide ($185—52 issues per year) which provides graphic and statistical data on all active call and put options and their underlying stocks.

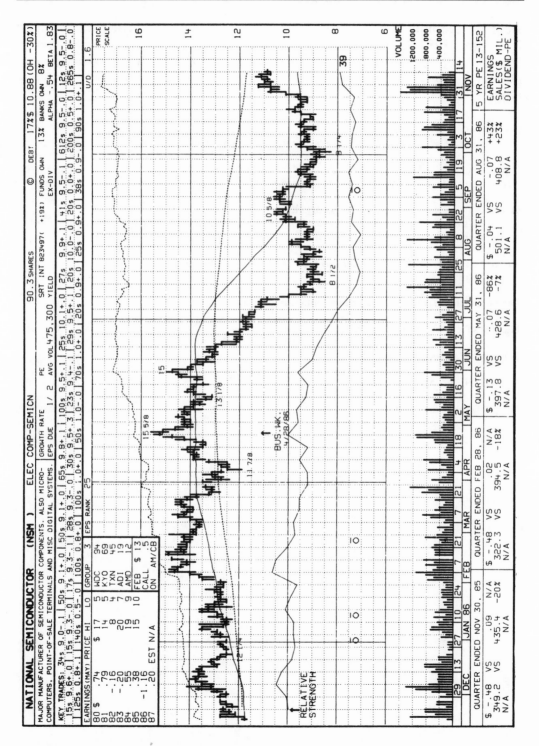

Reprinted with permission.

Dick Davis Publishing

P.O. Box 2828, Ocean View Station
Miami Beach, FL 33140
(305) 531-7777
(800) 422-9299

Dick Davis Digest

Advisory Condensation Service
25,000 to 50,000 subscribers

Description of the publication:
Dick Davis Digest is a bi-weekly, twelve page, compilation of over 300 investment advisory services. Its purpose is to present a condensed overview of what the best minds on Wall Street are thinking and recommending. Though this format does not allow the newsletter to contain a model portfolio, the newsletter does contain the recommendations from hundreds of investment advisors.

Investment selections in the publication are determined:
Using fundamental, technical, and other forms of analysis as determined by the investment advisors who are covered by the newsletter.

The track record for the publication, as reported by the publication, is:
Not applicable.

The publication has been published continuously since: August 1982

The cost of a subscription is: $120

The number of issues per year is: 24

A HOTLINE telephone service is: Not Available

The publication can be delivered: Via first class mail

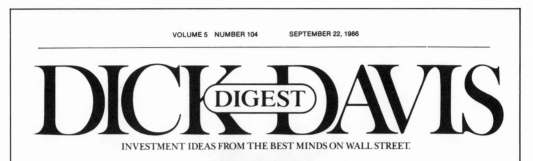

VOLUME 5   NUMBER 104   SEPTEMBER 22, 1986

DICK·DAVIS
DIGEST
INVESTMENT IDEAS FROM THE BEST MINDS ON WALL STREET.

Personal Note:

Bigger Than Life

Everything about this market is "bigger than life". Its gains are spectacular, its losses are spectacular, its volume is spectacular, its volatility is spectacular. Because it moves in such giant strides, it triggers unusually intense emotions. On the downside -- anguish, fear, even panic and hysteria. One of the purposes of this column is to strip away those emotions, to step back from the scary headlines and from the often misleading attempt of the media to provide simple answers to very complex questions, and put what has happened in the market in some perspective.

1) There have been few stock market corrections as widely predicted as this one. As we said in our last issue with the Dow at 1900, "Almost everyone expects a substantial correction, everyone sees it coming. My guess is that it will be accompanied by a temporary rise in interest rates and rising inflationary expectaions." Sharp moves telescoped into very brief time periods have characterized this bull. During the month of July, just two months ago, the Dow fell

(cont. on page 2)

ON THE INSIDE:

Spotlight Stock:

Heinz: More Than Just Ketchup

A "safe" investment usually implies a reduced return. But with Heinz (HNZ 40 NYSE) there is no sacrifice of appreciation potential, or so says The Value Line Investment Survey (711 Third Ave., New York, NY 10017, weekly, $425, 9/5/86): "Heinz packs a double punch -- our highest ranking for both investment timeliness and safety." Of the 1700 stocks followed by Value Line, only 8 other issues fall into this category: Becton, Dickinson; Coca-Cola; Hillenbrand; Johnson & Johnson; Marsh & McLennan; Merck; J.P. Morgan; and Philip Morris.   Says Value Line, "Heinz has an earnings record as rich and consistent as its ketchup.   In fact, HNZ has a growth record unmatched by any company that carries our highest safety rating."   While food processing can hardly be called a high growth industry, Heinz has scored an average 15% gain in per share earnings over the last decade, with annual dividend increases of almost 25%.   Value Line recommends Heinz as its "stock highlight" at 47.

"Two key factors drive Heinz's success. First, management invests aggressively in the future and has never taken prosperity for granted. New products are usually expensive, but they provide the invigorating lifeblood for packaged food companies. Heinz has introduced many low-calorie and convenience foods under such brand names as Weight Watchers and Ore-Ida. In addition, the company has bolstered its leading position in the fast-growing cat food market with 9-Lives and Amore, and its Star-Kist subsidiary has captured a record 36% of the U.S. canned tuna market. Heinz Ketchup, the company's biggest moneymaker, holds over 50% of the U.S. ketchup market for the first time.

(cont. on page 9)

Reprinted with permission.

Dow Theory Forecasts, Inc.
7412 Calumet Avenue
Hammond, IN 46323
(219) 931-6480

Dow Theory Forecasts®
Investment Advisory Bulletin
Number of subscribers is not available

Description of the publication:
Dow Theory Forecasts® examines market trends as interpreted by the Dow Theory. The newsletter also provides recommendations on individual stocks, primarily those traded on the NYSE. Conservative by nature, the newsletter focuses on a "value" approach to investing. Regular features include industry reviews, IRA information, and an examination of income stocks and mutual funds.

Investment selections in the publication are determined:
Using fundamental and technical analysis.

The track record for the publication, as reported by the publication, is:
Not available.

The publication has been published continuously since: 1946

The cost of a subscription is: $168

The number of issues per year is: 52

A HOTLINE telephone service is: Not Available

The publication can be delivered: Via first or second class mail

It is also worth mentioning that:
- An 8-week trial subscription is available for $5.
- Consultation and portfolio review services are available to full-term subscribers.
- Dow Theory Forecasts, Inc. publishes several other newsletters covering a variety of topics.

Dow Theory Forecasts.

STOCK MARKET TRENDS AND SECURITIES REPORTS

September 22, 1986   **Vol. 42, No. 38**

DOW JONES AVERAGES

INDUSTRIALS

TRANSPORTATION

VOLUME
(Millions)

Intermediate
Potential Risk

Timely Investment Values In This Week's *Forecasts*

———— Companies With "Kickers" ————

The following Forecasts *recommended issues have "kickers," or special beneficial characteristics in the way of potential restructurings, cash-rich balance sheets, or new products. The stocks have good long-term potential aside from any benefits that may "kick in" from these factors and may be held in portfolios.*

Ametek — *Strong R&D keys growth.*

Bristol-Myers — *New drug boosts profit potential.*

Dennison Mfg. — *Has restructuring possibilities.*

EDO — *Cash-heavy finances provide opportunities.*

Eastman Kodak — *Sets its sights on biotechnology.*

Genuine Parts — *Office products provide kicker.*

Golden Nugget — *Gaming concern wants to expand.*

Lubrizol — *Ventures enhance prospects.*

Lucky Stores — *Has takeover potential.*

Pennwalt — *Expands health-care sector.*

RJR Nabisco — *Cash flow opens doors.*

Raytheon — *Could streamline certain operations.*

Safeguard Scientifics — *Profits from spin-offs.*

Sargent-Welch Scientific — *Holds plenty of cash.*

——— Highlights Of Current Selections ———

AMR	Du Pont (E.I.)
American Home Prod.	Lawter International
BellSouth	Sears, Roebuck & Co.

——————— Analysts' Choice ———————

American Cyanamid — *Health-Care "Kicker"*

Dow Theory Forecasts is an independent Investment Adviser and makes no commissions on the stock transactions of its subscribers.

Reprinted with permission.

Dow Theory Letters, Inc.   **Dow Theory Letters**
P.O. Box 1759   Market Timing Bulletin
La Jolla, CA 92038   Less than 25,000 subscribers
(619) 454-0481

Description of the publication:

Dow Theory Letters is the oldest investment newsletter continuously written by one person—Richard Russell. Each issue reviews price movements in the market to determine appropriate investment positioning. Issues include charts, tables, and investment commentary on a variety of subjects ranging from stocks and bonds to collectibles and economic news.

Investment selections in the publication are determined:

Not applicable.

The track record for the publication, as reported by the publication, is:

Not applicable.

The publication has been published continuously since: 1958

The cost of a subscription is: $225

The number of issues per year is: 26

A HOTLINE telephone service is: Not Available

The publication can be delivered: Via first class mail

It is also worth mentioning that:

Dow Theory Letters, Inc. also publishes chart books covering the Dow-Jones Averages and the Advance-Decline ratios. Each year of data comprises one page of the book.

RICHARD RUSSELL'S **DOW THEORY LETTERS** INCORPORATED

SINCE 1958 ·

POST OFFICE BOX 1759, LA JOLLA, CALIFORNIA 92038
26 LETTERS PER YEAR · $225 ANNUALLY

Oct. 8, 1986   **LETTER 949**

Sept. 26   DJIA 1769.69;   PTI 2376;   A-D Ratio -7.45
Oct. 3   DJIA 1774.18;   PTI 2386;   A-D Ratio -7.41

A STUDY OF THE PRICE MOVEMENT: There are a thousand studies of the stock market, and there are hundreds (in many cases, thousands) of loyal followers for each study. Through the years the various stock market techniques and studies gain and lose in popularity, and consequently they tend to come and go. But there is only one study that has withstood the TEST OF TIME. That study is the Dow Theory. When the going gets tough and the stock market picture becomes obscure, I always turn to the Dow Theory.

With this in mind, I feel it is important that we review the recent price action of the D-J Averages as interpreted under Dow Theory. The following section should provide subscribers with an excellent example of the way the Dow Theory works. I have lettered significant points on the page 1 chart, and for the purposes of clarity I will refer to these points.

For new readers, and for many of my friends in this business, I want to repeat that a trend (in the current instance, the BULL trend) is taken to REMAIN IN FORCE until proved otherwise. Then how would the Averages in today's market signal a reversal to a primary bear trend? According to Dow Theory, a bear market is signaled as follows: the two D-J Averages (Industrials and Transports) undergo a full secondary reaction. The Averages then rally. If both Averages can advance to new highs, the bull market will be reconfirmed. But if one or both Averages fail to make new highs, and they turn down -- and BOTH Averages then violate the previous lows a bear market will be signaled.

With the above paragraph in mind, let's follow the recent price action. At point A (late March) the two Averages, Industrials and Transports, recorded their last joint highs (note: there has not been a single day in which BOTH Averages closed higher). Next a decline carried to April 7, followed by a rise to April 19. Here at point B Industrials recorded a new high of 1855.03 -- but Transports failed to confirm (the weak Transport action was the first hint of trouble in the price structure).

A decline then took Tranports to a new low of 771.10 on May 19 (point C), but here Industrials refused to confirm. Triggered by this non-confirmation, a rally then carried Industrials to another record high (point D) of 1882.35. Again Transports refused to confirm on the upside. A minor decline ensued, followed by yet another record Industrial high (point E) on July 2 of 1909.03. But note at point E that the Transports flattened out (here they appeared terribly weak) and again refused to confirm.

Up to this point we had witnessed no decline in the Averages that I could call of sufficient proportions to be labeled a secondary correction. But following point E the Averages broke badly with Transports sinking to a new low of 709.13 (F) on August 4. At the same time Industrials dropped to a low of 1763.64 (note that at point F the Industrial Average was 5 points above its April 19 low of 1758.18). Nevertheless, at point F I felt that BOTH Averages had dropped far enough so that the decline could be labeled A FULL SECONDARY REACTION.

The non-confirmation by Industrials (at F) triggered a new advance which by September 4 took Industrials to yet another record high of 1919.71. As might be expected, the still-weak Transportation Average halted its rise at 790.13, thereby failing again to confirm the new record Industrial high.

The price action at that point presented us with an IMPORTANT PICTURE UNDER DOW THEORY. Here, for the first time, we had a full secondary correction down to point F, and then a rally back to point G (at which time Transports refused to confirm). This then was the price pattern which would tell us (in due time) whether a bear market had started or whether the bull market was still in force.

If following the highs at point G, the two Averages turned down and violated their lows recorded at point F, a primary bear market would be signaled. Remember, under Dow Theory not one but BOTH Averages must penetrate critical levels before we can draw valid conclusions. A study of history shows that a penetration of a single Average through an important point is meaningless for predictive purposes -- and more often than not is deceptive.

So what happened next? Following the unconfirmed Industrial high, the Averages turned down. And then something dramatic occurred. The Average which had been weaker all along -- turned strong. And, of course, I am referring to the Transportation Average. On September 29 (point H) Industrials dropped to 1755.20, their lowest closing since April. But surprisingly the Transportation Average REFUSED by a wide margin to confirm! At point H the Transports halted their decline a full 28 points ABOVE their August 4 level of 709.13.

This surprising turn-about (i.e., the non-confirmation by Transports at point H) set off a rally, and by October 1 the Transports closed at 815.13, their highest level since June. If a

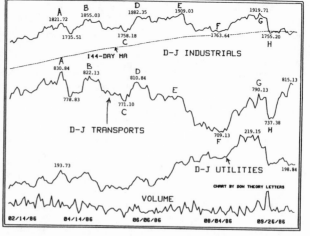

D-J INDUSTRIALS

A 1821.72   B 1855.03   D 1882.35   E 1909.03   1919.71   F   G   1755.20   H
1735.51   1758.18   1763.64

144-DAY MA

D-J TRANSPORTS

A 830.84   B 822.13   D 810.84   E   G 790.13   815.13
778.83   771.10   C   737.38   709.13 F   219.15 H

D-J UTILITIES

193.73   198.84

CHART BY DOW THEORY LETTERS

VOLUME

02/14/86   04/14/86   06/06/86   08/04/86   09/26/86

Reprinted with permission.

Argus Research Corp.
42 Broadway
New York City, NY 10004
(212) 425-7500

Electric Utility Rankings & Spotlight
Investment Advisory & Research Bulletins
Less than 25,000 subscribers

Description of the publication:
Both the Electric Utility Rankings and the Electric Utility Spotlight are designed as monthly fold-out booklets focusing on electric utilities.

Electric Utility Rankings rates 50 leading utility companies on the basis of five quality categories ranging from "Lowest" to "Highest." Then, within each category, each company's stock is rated as a buy, hold, or sell.

Electric Utility Spotlight focuses on subjects of broad investor interest concerning utility companies and the investment merits of their securities. Each report contains a detailed discussion of pertinent subjects, supporting viewpoints with extensive tabulations—sometimes examining as many as 15 parameters for up to 75 companies. Subjects of continual interest include: quarterly earnings performances; fuel sources and costs; construction expenditures; and company interests in nuclear power.

Investment selections in the publication are determined:
Using fundamental analysis.

The track record for the publication, as reported by the publication, is:
Not available.

The publication has been published continuously since: 1950

The cost of a subscription is: $225

The number of issues per year is: Each-12

A HOTLINE telephone service is: Available
Cost for this service: Negotiable with subscription.

The publication can be delivered: Via first class mail

It is also worth mentioning that:
Argus Research Corp. also publishes several other investment publications designed for both individual investors and investment professionals covering a wide range of topics. These reports include the:

- Weekly Staff Report
- Weekly Economic Review
- Viewpoint
- Portfolio Selector
- Investment Portfolio Guide
- Investment Analysis
- Energy Update

- Special Analysis
- Special-Theme Report
- Electric Utility Ranking
- Electric Utility Spotlight
- Special Situations Report
- Master List

All of the above reports can be bought separately or purchased as a group for a combined discount price of $125 per month. Of special interest is a premium service available to brokers which allows for an unlimited amount of analyst contact, live conference calls, and research opinions written on the broker's own letterhead.

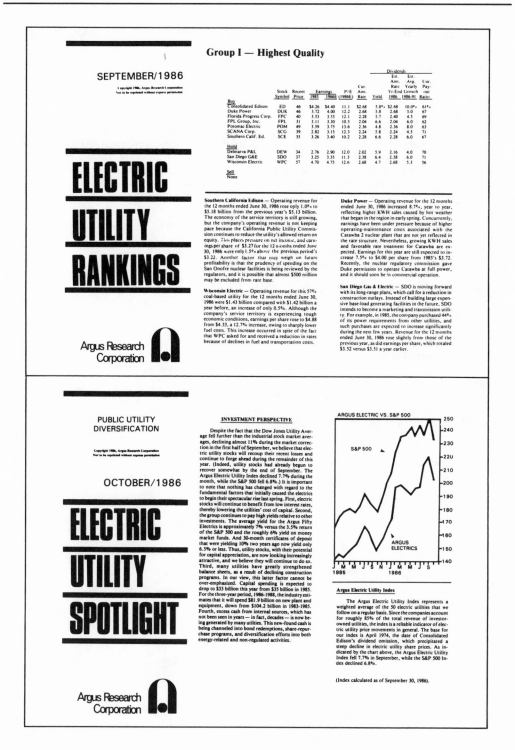

SEPTEMBER/1986

Copyright 1986, Argus Research Corporation
Not to be reprinted without express permission

Group I — Highest Quality

	Stock Symbol	Recent Price	Earnings 1985	1986E	P/E (1986E)	Cur. Ann. Rate	Yield	Dividends Est. Ann. Rate Yr-End 1986	Est. Avg. Yearly Growth 1986-91	Cur. Pay-out Ratio
Buy										
Consolidated Edison	ED	46	$4.26	$4.40	11.1	$2.68	5.8%*	$2.68	10.0%*	61%*
Duke Power	DUK	46	3.72	4.00	12.2	2.68	5.8	2.68	5.0	67
Florida Progress Corp.	FPC	40	3.53	3.55	12.1	2.28	5.7	2.40	4.5	69
FPL Group, Inc.	FPL	31	3.11	3.30	10.5	2.04	6.6	2.04	6.0	62
Potomac Electric	POM	49	3.59	3.75	13.6	2.36	4.8	2.36	8.0	63
SCANA Corp.	SCG	39	2.82	3.15	12.3	2.24	5.8	2.24	4.5	71
Southern Calif. Ed.	SCE	35	3.26	3.40	10.2	2.28	6.6	2.28	6.0	67
Hold										
Delmarva P&L	DEW	34	2.76	2.90	12.0	2.02	5.9	2.16	4.0	70
San Diego G&E	SDO	37	3.25	3.35	11.3	2.38	6.4	2.38	6.0	71
Wisconsin Electric	WPC	57	4.70	4.75	12.6	2.68	4.7	2.68	5.3	56

Sell
None

ELECTRIC UTILITY RANKINGS

Argus Research Corporation

Southern California Edison — Operating revenue for the 12 months ended June 30, 1986 rose only 1.0% to $5.18 billion from the previous year's $5.13 billion. The economy of the service territory is still growing, but the company's operating revenue is not keeping pace because the California Public Utility Commission continues to reduce the utility's allowed return on equity. This places pressure on net income, and earnings per share of $3.27 for the 12 months ended June 30, 1986 were only 1.5% above the previous period's $3.22. Another factor that may weigh on future profitability is that the prudence of spending on the San Onofre nuclear facilities is being reviewed by the regulators, and it is possible that almost $500 million may be excluded from rate base.

Wisconsin Electric — Operating revenue for this 57% coal-based utility for the 12 months ended June 30, 1986 were $1.43 billion compared with $1.42 billion a year before, an increase of only 0.5%. Although the company's service territory is experiencing tough economic conditions, earnings per share rose to $4.88 from $4.33, a 12.7% increase, owing to sharply lower fuel costs. This increase occurred in spite of the fact that WPC asked for and received a reduction in rates because of declines in fuel and transportation costs.

Duke Power — Operating revenue for the 12 months ended June 30, 1986 increased 8.7%, year to year, reflecting higher KWH sales caused by hot weather that began in the region in early spring. Concurrently, earnings have been under pressure because of higher operating-maintenance costs associated with the Catawba 2 nuclear plant that are not yet reflected in the rate structure. Nevertheless, growing KWH sales and favorable rate treatment for Catawba are expected. Earnings for this year are still expected to increase 7.5% to $4.00 per share from 1985's $3.72. Recently, the nuclear regulatory commission gave Duke permission to operate Catawba at full power, and it should soon be in commercial operation.

San Diego Gas & Electric — SDO is moving forward with its long-range plans, which call for a reduction in construction outlays. Instead of building large expensive base-load generating facilities in the future, SDO intends to become a marketing and transmission utility. For example, in 1985, the company purchased 44% of its power requirements from other utilities, and such purchases are expected to increase significantly during the next few years. Revenue for the 12 months ended June 30, 1986 rose slightly from those of the previous year, as did earnings per share, which totaled $3.52 versus $3.51 a year earlier.

OCTOBER/1986

Copyright 1986, Argus Research Corporation
Not to be reprinted without express permission

PUBLIC UTILITY DIVERSIFICATION

ELECTRIC UTILITY SPOTLIGHT

Argus Research Corporation

INVESTMENT PERSPECTIVE

Despite the fact that the Dow Jones Utility Average fell further than the industrial stock market averages, declining almost 11% during the market correction in the first half of September, we believe that electric utility stocks will recoup their recent losses and continue to forge ahead during the remainder of this year. (Indeed, utility stocks had already begun to recover somewhat by the end of September. The Argus Electric Utility Index declined 7.7% during the month, while the S&P 500 fell 6.8%.) It is important to note that nothing has changed with regard to the fundamental factors that initially caused the electrics to begin their spectacular rise last spring. First, electric stocks will continue to benefit from low interest rates, thereby lowering the utilities' cost of capital. Second, the group continues to pay high yields relative to other investments. The average yield for the Argus Fifty Electrics is approximately 7% versus the 3.5% return of the S&P 500 and the roughly 6% yield on money market funds. And 30-month certificates of deposit that were yielding 10% two years ago now yield only 6.5% or less. Thus, utility stocks, with their potential for capital appreciation, are now looking increasingly attractive, and we believe they will continue to do so. Third, many utilities have greatly strengthened balance sheets, as a result of declining construction programs. In our view, this latter factor cannot be over-emphasized. Capital spending is expected to drop to $33 billion this year from $35 billion in 1985. For the three-year period, 1986-1988, the industry estimates that it will spend $81.9 billion on new plant and equipment, down from $104.2 billion in 1983-1985. Fourth, excess cash from internal sources, which has not been seen in years — in fact, decades — is now being generated by many utilities. This new-found cash is being channeled into bond redemptions, share-repurchase programs, and diversification efforts into both energy-related and non-regulated activities.

ARGUS ELECTRIC VS. S&P 500

Argus Electric Utility Index

The Argus Electric Utility Index represents a weighted average of the 50 electric utilities that we follow on a regular basis. Since the companies account for roughly 85% of the total revenue of investor-owned utilities, the index is a reliable indicator of electric utility price movements in general. The base for our index is April 1974, the date of Consolidated Edison's dividend omission, which precipitated a steep decline in electric utility share prices. As indicated by the chart above, the Argus Electric Utility Index fell 7.7% in September, while the S&P 500 Index declined 6.8%.

(Index calculated as of September 30, 1986.)

Reprinted with permission.

New Classics Library
P.O. Box 1618
Gainsville, GA 30503
(404) 536-0309

The Elliott Wave Commodity Letter
Market Timing Bulletin
Less than 25,000 subscribers

Description of the publication:
The Elliott Wave Commodity Letter is designed for speculators and hedgers who wish to recognize tradable turning points in agricultural and industrial commodities, currencies, and the CRB index. On a monthly basis, editor David Weis studies charts of 35 commodities, currencies, and indices using the Wave Principle, Fibonacci calculations, and supporting technical methods, in order to identify those markets with the best emerging profit potential.

Investment selections in the publication are determined:
Using technical analysis, Elliott Wave theory, and Wyckoff methodology.

The track record for the publication, as reported by the publication, is:
Available, but has not been provided.

The publication has been published continuously since: June 1983

The cost of a subscription is: $199

The number of issues per year is: 12*
*Plus special reports.

A HOTLINE telephone service is: Available
Cost for this service: $249 per year.

The publication can be delivered: Via first class, and
express mail/airfreight

It is also worth mentioning that:
New Classics Library also offers personalized telephone consultation services.

The Elliott Wave
COMMODITY LETTER

COVERING CURRENCIES AND PHYSICAL COMMODITIES

Written by *David Weis*

New Classics Library
P.O. Box 1618
Gainesville, Georgia 30503

$199 per year
Published as a supplement to
Robert Prechter's **ELLIOTT WAVE THEORIST**

October 27, 1986
©

ON THE FRONT END

Last week's Elliott Wave workshop was a learning experience for everyone as Bob Prechter and Dave Allman explained all aspects of the Wave Principle. The workbook is a great compilation of material illustrating wave patterns, wave counting, Fibonacci ratios, and much more. I especially enjoyed meeting many of you and look forward to talking with more Elliott enthusiasts at the November workshop.

TRADE OF THE MONTH
SELL DECEMBER CRB

In July there was technical evidence that the CRB Index had reached a temporary low. The decline from the December, 1985 high was a five-wave move. This low coincided with a 46-week cycle that has affected the general trend for over 15 years. Furthermore, market sentiment was unanimously

bearish as the Commerce Department had revealed the first farm-trade deficit in over 20 years. The outlook for crude oil was also bearish as no one expected OPEC to agree on production quotas. Despite the prevailing pessimism, we correctly identified the low in the CRB Index and the oil market (see July issue). One of the important clues that pointed to a rally was the position of the six futures groups. At that time, the imported, precious metals, and livestock groups were out performing the general trend. The grains and oilseeds were showing signs of stabilizing. The 1985-86 decline in the industrial index had a (5)-wave form, but it had not turned up. Based on a 61.8% retracement of wave (5) of ③, we expected wave ④ to at least rally into the ara of the "Chernobyl high" at 216.1. The larger potential was for a correction to the previous fourth wave of one lesser degree (231.1).

For the first time since July, the rally in the CRB Index has fulfilled the requirements of a complete

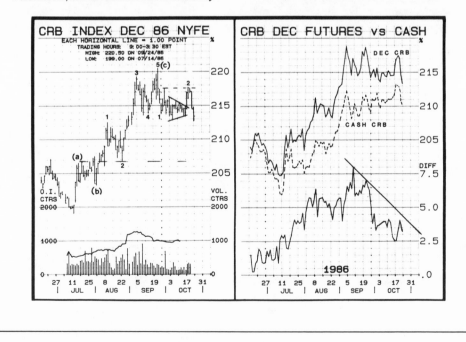

Reprinted with permission.

New Classics Library
P.O. Box 1618
Gainsville, GA 30503
(404) 536-0309

The Elliott Wave Theorist
Market Timing Bulletin
Less than 25,000 subscribers

Description of the publication:
The Elliott Wave Theorist is a ten page, monthly newsletter which uses Elliott waves, Fibonacci relationships, fixed time cycles, momentum, sentiment, and supply-demand factors to predict future price movements in stocks, precious metals, interest rates, and the economy. Forecasts are based on all sizes of trends, from hourly waves to waves lasting over a century.

Investment selections in the publication are determined:
Using technical analysis of the wave principle and time cycles.

The track record for the publication, as reported by the publication, is:
Available, but has not been provided.

The publication has been published continuously since: 1979

The cost of a subscription is: $233

The number of issues per year is: 12*
*Plus special reports.

A HOTLINE telephone service is: Available
Cost for this service: $377 per year.

The publication can be delivered: Via first class, and
express mail/airfreight

It is also worth mentioning that:
New Classics Library also offers personalized telephone consultation services.

ROBERT PRECHTER

THE ELLIOTT WAVE THEORIST

STOCK MARKET
New Classics Library

INTEREST RATES
P.O. Box 1618

PRECIOUS METALS
Gainesville, GA 30503

November 7, 1986

©

$233 per year
12 Monthly issues
plus Special Reports
and Interim Reports

DJIA WAVE STATUS: SUMMARY and OUTLOOK

WAVE DEGREE	DATE BEGAN	WAVE NUMBER	CURRENT DIRECTION	SIGNIFICANCE TO	OPTIMUM STRATEGY	TARGET	ALTERNATE COUNT
GRAND SUPERCYCLE	1789	---	UP, PEAKING	U.S. SURVIVAL	NO ACTION WARRANTED	3686	---
SUPERCYCLE	JULY 8, 1932	(V)	UP	ECONOMIC CONDITIONS	RECESSION APPROACHING	3686	---
CYCLE	AUG. 12, 1982	V	UP	INSTITUTIONAL INVESTOR	HOLD LONG	3686	---
PRIMARY	SEPT. 5, 10:00	④	DOWN/ SIDEWAYS	INSTITUTIONAL TRADER	HOLD T-BILLS	1720 ± 5/ 1620 ± 20	③
INTERMEDIATE	SEPT. 29, 2:00	(b)	UP	INDIVIDUAL INVESTOR	HOLD T-BILLS	1900– 2000	(3)
MINOR	NOV. 5, 1:00	X	DOWN	INDIVIDUAL TRADER	HOLD T-BILLS	1840	3
MINUTE	NOV. 5, 1:00	a	DOWN	OPTION/FUTURE TRADER	HOLD T-BILLS	----	v
MINUETTE	----	---	----	SCALPER	HOLD T-BILLS	----	---
SUBMINUETTE	----	---	----	SKIMMER	HOLD T-BILLS	----	---

THE BOTTOM LINE

The stock market is approaching the end of wave (b), a rally within the Primary wave ④ correction which began September 5. Cycles suggest a pullback into mid–November, then a rally into early December, then down into the first quarter. Wave (b) may peak anywhere between 1900 and 2000 before wave (c) to the downside takes over. Bonds are completing wave (d) of a contracting triangle dating from the April top. A drop back to the mid–90's is likely immediately, but as long as 92 basis the nearby contract is not broken, we should then see a run to new highs. The 8 1/2–month cycle in gold is now in the forecasted time zone for a peak. Gold is building a top of major significance.

ITEMS OF NOTE: IMPORTANT! -- A RENEWAL NOW WILL SAVE TAXES! SEE PAGE 10.

The second Elliott Wave Intensive Weekend Workshop scheduled for November 15/16 is nearly sold out. 175 enthusiasts met at the October workshop, and learned Elliott from square one to advanced application. We will probably hold two more some time next year, but if you want to take advantage of the last such opportunity for at least several months, just call (404) 536-0309 and ask for info or a brochure.

Nov. 20 is your last chance to sign up for the Futures Trading Caribbean Cruise, sailing Jan.31–Feb.8, featuring 5 speakers including Bob Nurock and yours truly; includes free newsletter subscriptions. Call Dick Belz for details at 800-233-7214 or 615-524-5270. Space is limited.

Reprinted with permission.

Standard & Poor's Corporation
25 Broadway
New York City, NY 10004
(212) 208-8000

Emerging & Special Situations
Investment Advisory Bulletin
Number of subscribers is not available

Description of the publication:
Emerging & Special Situations is a monthly publication, with periodic supplements, highlighting lesser known stocks determined by Standard & Poor's analysts to be overlooked and undervalued. The newsletter alerts aggressive investors to growth companies, new issues, and special situations that have superior appreciation potential. The publication presents articles of current investor interest such as analyzing growth stocks, industry analyses, performance of new issues in the aftermarket, as well as maintaining a buy/sell list.

Investment selections in the publication is determined:
Using fundamental analysis.

The track record for the publication, as reported by the publication, is:
31% annualized gain since January, 1982, with an average holding period of one year, two months.

The publication has been published continuously since: 1982*
*(Formerly entitled: "New Issue Investor")

The cost of a subscription is: $140

The number of issues per year is: 24

A HOTLINE telephone service is: Not Available

The publication can be delivered: Via first class mail

It is also worth mentioning that:
Standard & Poor's Corporation publishes several other investment publications covering a variety of topics.

Standard & Poor's

Emerging & Special Situations

August 15, 1986 Vol. 5 • No. 8

OTC-new issue market review

Segment discussion
Wading through The Wallflowers

Spotlight recommendation
Nantucket Industries

Roster of major upcoming offerings

Prospective new issues highlighted
Armor All Products
Axlon
Baldwin Piano & Organ
Criterion Group
Gabelli Equity Trust
Lakeland Industries
McCall Pattern
New Line Cinema
Pori International
Stanley Interiors
VTR, Inc.

Portfolio updates
Farr Co.
Interface Flooring Systems
Iomega
Marquest Medical
TRC Cos.
Tyco Toys
USACafes

Portfolio deletion
Whittaker Corp.

Current purchase recommendation

Reports on a recent new issue & spotlight recommendation
L.A. Gear
Nantucket Industries

Spotlight recommendation

NANTUCKET INDUSTRIES (NAN, 10, OTC)

52 week range	13⅞-8	Ind. dividend	Nil
Fiscal 1985-6 EPS	$0.69	Yield	Nil
Fiscal 1986-7 est. EPS	$0.90	P/E on fiscal 1985 EPS	14
Fiscal 1987-8 est. EPS	$1.15	P/E on fiscal 1986 est. EPS	11
Shares outstanding at June 3, 1986	2,787,000	P/E on fiscal 1987 est. EPS	9
		Public share float	1,700,000

Fiscal Year ends Apx. February 28th

Investment Opinion

Since 1977, this manufacturer of hosiery and men's and women's undergarments has achieved compound annual revenue growth above 22%. Its emphasis on efficient manufacturing and its understanding of consumer preferences have helped the company to gain significant market share over the last few years. Its customer list now includes such retail giants as Mervyn's, K-Mart, Wal-Mart and Zayre. Recently, important contracts with new and existing customers have been signed, the most notable being an agreement to supply K-Mart with hosiery for the nationally advertised "Jaclyn Smith" line. In the second half of this year, the company is making a concerted marketing effort to more fully penetrate the West Coast market for men's undergarments. It has already designed several lines specifically for Western tastes. In addition, Nantucket is introducing a full line of apparel under the "Made in the USA" label, producing undergarments for the label and contracting out for outerwear. We believe that these efforts will result in continued sales growth of 15%-20% over the next few years. The possibility of an acquisition improves growth prospects over the long run, although there may be some short term dilution in EPS, depending upon how the deal is structured. Given the outlook for apparel over the next twelve months, we believe this well positioned company can earn $0.90 in the fiscal year ending in March 1987, followed by $1.15 in FY'87-8. We recommend the purchase of these shares, which are trading at 9X our FY'87-8 EPS estimate, by long term oriented, moderately aggressive investors.

Industry Background

Over the past several years, fashion has become an increasingly important factor in the undergarment industry. Bored with bland white briefs, men are purchasing underwear in a variety of styles and colors. At the same time, women's pantyhose have become more stylish and a multitude of patterns and colors have appeared on the scene. As style has become more important, so has quality, in-

Selected financial data

	Year ended Apx. February 28					13 wks. to May 31	
	1982	1983	1984	1985	1986	1985	1986
Revs. ($000s)	18,885	24,155	32,137	37,444	50,164	10,164	13,064
Net Inc. ($000s)	503	923	1,727	1,309	1,890	335	447
Earn. Per Sh. ($)	.23	.43	.75	.47	.69	.12	.16

Current purchase recommendations

Company	Ticker Symbol	Entered Date	Entered Price	8/13/86 Price	Price Action Stk.	Price Action S&P 500	FY	Earnings per share '85A	'86E	'87E	12mth	Ind. Div.	PE Ratio 12mth	PE Ratio '87E	Book Value	ROE	1985-7 Growth
NEW ISSUES																	
American Cruise Lines	ACRL	7/09/86	9½	7½	−21%	Nil	Jun.	0.52	0.80	1.00	0.65	Nil	12	8	NA	NA	38%
Oliver's Stores	OLVR	2/11/86	6	8⅞	48%	13%	Jun.	0.25	0.30	0.48	0.37	Nil	24	18	2.77	36%	39%
SunGard Data	SNDT	5/03/86	11	12	9%	8%	Dec.	0.51	0.65	0.78	0.63	Nil	19	15	2.20	24%	24%
J. Baker	JBAK	6/11/86	15¾	15½	−2%	2%	Jan.	0.60	0.90	1.30	0.71	Nil	22	12	NA	NA	47%
Waterford Glass	WATFY	7/01/86	20	17⅛	−14%	−4%	Dec.	1.39	1.25	1.45	1.28	Nil	9	12			NM
EMERGING GROWTH																	
Electro-Catheter	ECTH	10/29/84	18⅜	5¾	−69%	48%	Aug.	d0.36	d1.00	0.25	d0.90	Nil	NM	23	3.20	NM	NM
Eng. Measurements	EMCO	3/27/86	10⅜	10	−4%	2%	Apr.	0.21	0.25	1.10	0.21	Nil	48	9	1.49	NM	129%
General Ceramics	GCER	07/10/85	13	19	46%	26%	Jun.	0.87	1.15	1.40	0.95	0.05	20	14	7.82	NA	27%
Hazelton Labs	HLC	4/10/86	17	19¾	16%	3%	Jun.	0.53	0.80	1.25	1.08	0.32	18	16	12.57	5%	54%
Iomega Corp.	IOMG	05/14/86	19¼	10	−48%	2%	Dec.	0.53	↓0.65	1.20	0.54	Nil	19	8	3.38	21%	51%
Marquest Medical Products	MMPI	07/01/83	17	7⅝	−55%	44%	Mar.	0.38	0.47	0.75	0.38	Nil	20	10	6.40	9%	40%
TRC Cos.	TRCC	2/11/86	12⅛	11¾	−3%	13%	Jun.	0.08	0.55	0.62	0.36	Nil	33	19	2.81	8%	178%
Triangle Microwave	TRMW	4/10/86	5¾	5	−13%	3%	Dec.	0.23	0.38	0.45	0.32	Nil	16	11	1.86	NA	40%
SPECIAL SITUATIONS																	
Farr Co.	FARC	10/11/85	7¾	11	42%	32%	Dec.	1.14	1.95	1.30	1.16	0.24	9	8	9.40	NA	7%
Interface Flooring	IFSIA	04/10/85	14½	14¾	2%	36%	Dec.	1.19	1.20	1.38	1.41	0.20	10	11	6.95	15%	8%
Tyco Toys	TTOY	5/14/86	7⅛	7⅜	1%	3%	Dec.	0.73	0.60	0.95	0.73	Nil	10	8	2.56	NA	14%
USACafes	USCF	06/12/85	4¼	7	65%	30%	Sep.	0.40	0.55	0.65	0.53	0.28	13	11	1.00	38%	27%

Since inception at January, 1982, 81 issues have been recommended; 47 have advanced, 34 have declined, for an average gain of 32%. The average holding period was one year, two months. The table above shows current buy recommendations. A complete list of all previous recommendations will be published at the end of each quarter. A—Actual. E—Estimate. NM—Not Meaningful. NA—Not Available. NE-No Estimate d—Deficit. def.—Deficit. Earns. for FY end Mar. 31 or earlier are shown under column of preceding calendar year. ↑Estimate raised. ↓Estimate lowered.

Reprinted with permission.

FSA Inc.   **FSA Inc. Funds Outlook**
P.O. Box 6547   Investment Advisory Bulletin
Lake Worth, FL 33466   Less than 25,000 subscribers

Description of the publication:

FSA Inc. Funds Outlook highlights the best performing funds from a group of several hundred, no-load, telephone switch mutual funds. Specific buy/hold/sell recommendations are given in each monthly issue along with a commentary on the economy, the expectations for inflation, the stock market, and the precious metals markets. The newsletter contains charts, a rolling recommended list, and a forum featuring advice from other investment advisory/newsletter sources. A switch signal service is also available free to subscribers to recommend transactions which should be made between newsletter issues.

Investment selections in the publication are determined:

Using fundamental, technical, and cyclical analysis.

The track record for the publication, as reported by the publication, is:

Not available.

The publication has been published continuously since: 1980

The cost of a subscription is: $89

The number of issues per year is: 12

A HOTLINE telephone service is: Not Available

The publication can be delivered: Via first class, and
                                                                    express mail/airfreight

It is also worth mentioning that:

A free sample issue and one year charter subscription is available for $34.

FSA FUNDS OUTLOOK

SEPTEMBER 8, 1986.

FUNDS STRATEGY and WATCH

As you will read under FSA POSITION SUMMARY and STOCK MARKET $CAN elsewhere in this issue, we expect the stock market to advance to new all time highs during this month, therefore we recommend a fully invested mutual funds position. Our MASTER LIST is well positioned for future gains.

During last month, the gold funds were the best performers, closely followed by the funds invested in the Pacific Basin. While we think the record performance of the gold funds is going to be short lived, the Pacific Basin funds will continue to be the top performers due to the worldwide bull market in stocks and the continuing weak U.S. dollar.

During last year, the total number of mutual funds increased over 30% and investors poured in the first six months of 1986 $75 million more into funds than they withdraw. This sum is close to the total investment of all of last year. Skeptics think this frenzy is the signal for the top of the bull market. We believe the growth of the funds will continue into at least 1987 with the continuation of the bull market.

The correct strategy in bull markets is to be fully invested in top performing funds.
During corrections, using our switch signal, switch into money market funds, cashing-in our stock funds profits.

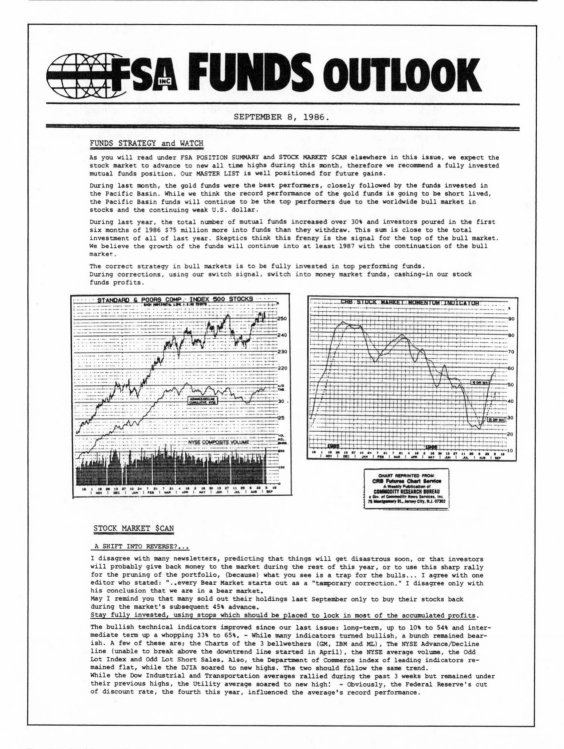

STOCK MARKET $CAN

A SHIFT INTO REVERSE?...

I disagree with many newsletters, predicting that things will get disastrous soon, or that investors will probably give back money to the market during the rest of this year, or to use this sharp rally for the pruning of the portfolio, (because) what you see is a trap for the bulls... I agree with one editor who stated: "..every Bear Market starts out as a "tamporary correction." I disagree only with his conclusion that we are in a bear market.
May I remind you that many sold out their holdings last September only to buy their stocks back during the market's subsequent 45% advance.
Stay fully invested, using stops which should be placed to lock in most of the accumulated profits.

The bullish technical indicators improved since our last issue: long-term, up to 10% to 54% and intermediate term up a whopping 33% to 65%. - While many indicators turned bullish, a bunch remained bearish. A few of these are; the Charts of the 3 bellwethers (GM, IBM and ML), The NYSE Advance/Decline line (unable to break above the downtrend line started in April), the NYSE average volume, the Odd Lot Index and Odd Lot Short Sales. Also, the Department of Commerce index of leading indicators remained flat, while the DJIA soared to new highs. The two should follow the same trend.
While the Dow Industrial and Transportation averages rallied during the past 3 weeks but remained under their previous highs, the Utility average soared to new high! - Obviously, the Federal Reserve's cut of discount rate, the fourth this year, influenced the average's record performance.

Reprinted with permission.

FSA Inc.
P.O. Box 6547
Lake Worth, FL 33466

FSA Inc. Market Outlook
Investment Advisory Bulletin
Less than 25,000 subscribers

Description of the publication:
FSA Inc. Market Outlook is designed as an investment advisory newsletter highlighting specific buy/hold/sell recommendations for stocks, stock options, futures, options on futures, precious metals, and mutual funds. Each issue includes a commentary on the economy and the expectations for inflation. The newsletter contains charts, cyclical analysis, Gann Angles, stochastics, switch signals, a rolling recommended list, and a forum featuring advice from other investment advisory/ newsletter sources.

Investment selections in the publication are determined:
Using fundamental, technical, and cyclical analysis.

The track record for the publication, as reported by the publication, is: Not available.

The publication has been published continuously since: 1980

The cost of a subscription is: $233

The number of issues per year is: 24

A HOTLINE telephone service is: Not Available

The publication can be delivered: Via first class, and express mail/airfreight

It is also worth mentioning that:
A trial subscription is available — 6 issues for $25.

VII/19   SEPTEMBER 24, 1986.

F S A POSITION SUMMARY

The STOCK MARKET remains in a strong bullish uptrend. We may have had an intermediate high on September 5 or it may yet to come during the next two weeks. Our projected Dow 1986$^{\pm}$ is still possible before the decline to Dow 1700$^{\pm}$ by mid-November. After the correction, we expect strong rallies into 1987, to well above Dow 2500. The threat of deflation is great in all of the industrialized countries.
We expect the South African political climate to stabilize, neither inflation nor depression or collapse in the West, therefore we are bearish on the PRECIOUS METALS.
We urge you to stay away from gold and silver since we project lower prices into 1987. We expect lower interest rates and all-time high bond prices. We project a strong U.S. Dollar into late October.
The rise of the GRAIN prices are near and higher SOYBEAN prices are near. We believe MEAT prices climaxed and headed lower.

STOCK MARKET $CAN

DON'T BURY THE BULL.

The correction I was anticipating, arrived ahead of schedule. And the cause was the darling of the Big Boys of the Wall Street; Program Trading. This new game emerged only recently by the birth of index futures and the creation of computer programs, able to track the premium or discount between the cash and the various index futures plus their underlying individual components. There is no indicator or system available to lead or to follow the emergence of divergences. Profit is being made quickly and precisely either by buying stocks and selling futures or, as happened on September 11, selling stocks and buying index futures simultaneously.
The institutions love this new toy, even though the gains are small; however, the individual investors cannot afford it. Simple as that.
Sadly, program trading is changing the marketplace; frightening away capital, rewarding the trading institutions and not the companies' higher sales or profit, or better performance ratios. On the average this type of trading activity may already amount to a third of all transactions.
Before September 11, program trading climaxed on the quarterly "Triple Witching Fridays", when stock index and stock options, plus stock index futures expire together. The Smart Money fooled everyone this time around, by putting on their show one week earlier. This may have happened due to the announced monitoring of large transactions by the New York Stock Exchange on September 19. The two rumors of the day, namely that the Bank of America was illiquid and August retail sales was up 2.5% (inflationary) made fortunes for the few.
Indeed, the marketplace and in particular, the relativity of the short-term trend are changing. Therefore, it is not surprising that many previously successful trading systems and trusted, mostly trend following technical indicators do not perform as before. Also, this phenomena is helping to popularize the no-load, switch mutual funds. I believe that these wide short-term unexpected fluctuations have no influence on the intermediate and long-term trend.
Projecting cycle tops was always more difficult and less reliable than calling the lows. The indicators turned in a dismal performance, sinking the new bullish lows; the long and intermediate-term indicators are down 25% and now both are only 25% bullish. In spite of the overwhelmingly bearish indicators, I am remaining bullish longer term, because of favorable credit balances, margin debt, short sales and short interests, low inflation, interest and monetary data. The Forbes Index is bullish as well.
The looks of the daily index charts are depressing, until one notices that the major supports are holding and more significantly, their 200 day moving averages are rising. Even the laggard NYSE Advance / Decline line stayed above its August low. These and many other signs indicate that the strong major bullish trend cannot be reversed within a few hours.
The monetary indicators are continue to be bullish. The expanding money supply and lower interest rates are very positive for the economy and the stock market. But, at least an intermediate high is near within the ongoing bull market. We may have had this top early on September 5 or, it may yet to come during the next two weeks. So, Dow 1986± is still possible before the decline to Dow 1700± by mid-November. After this correction, I expect the final rally of Superbull to climb to all-time highs, well above Dow 2500 during 1987.
Hold recommended stocks and no-load mutual funds, using our stops and in case of mutual funds, our switch signal. If stopped out or switched, keep cash liquid in money market accounts.
I do not recommend to go short or to buy puts.

RECOMMENDATION FOR HIGH RISK INVESTORS:
BUY NYSE COMPOSITE INDEX DECEMBER 138 PUTS
BUY S&P 500 STOCK INDEX DECEMBER 240 PUTS

Reprinted with permission.

Davis/Zweig Futures, Inc.
P.O. Box 5345
New York City, NY 10150
(212) 753-7710

Futures Hotline
Investment Advisory Bulletin
Less than 25,000 subscribers

Description of the publication:
> Futures Hotline presents market timing models for frequently traded stock index, interest rate, metals, and foreign currency futures.

Investment selections in the publication are determined:
> Using fundamental and technical analysis.

The track record for the publication, as reported by the publication, is:
> An average gain of $1260 per trade for the period beginning January, 1985, and ending October, 1986.

The publication has been published continuously since: 1982

The cost of a subscription is: $400

The number of issues per year is: 24

A HOTLINE telephone service is: Available
> Cost for this service: Free with subscription.

The publication can be delivered: Via first class mail

It is also worth mentioning that:
> Davis/Zweig Futures, Inc., and Zweig Securities Advisory Service, Inc., a related organization, publish several other newsletters covering a variety of topics.

Produced by Ned Davis
with Martin Zweig

*This publication is designed
for sophisticated investors
seeking extraordinary returns
but who are fully aware of the
risks in market forecasting.*

future facts

FUTURES	TRADING MODELS	LONG-TERM TREND	BEARISH SENTIMENT	OVERSOLD INDEX
STOCK INDEX	64%	UP	69%	35%
INTEREST RATE	71%	UP	60%	42%
METALS	67%	UP	40%	55%
CURRENCIES	0%	UP	49%	76%

*TREASURY BOND VALUATIONS
- STILL FAVORABLE*

To determine what bond yields
"should be," we look at a number
of factors including the rate of
inflation and real interest rates,
competitive yields like stock
yields or like short-term interest
rates   and normal cyclical
movements in interest rates
(lows to highs and vice versa).
Using these four factors, we calculate 25-year norms and then add the
four projections. The result is our Bond Yield Normal Valuation Line,
represented by the dotted line in the top clip of this chart.
The bottom clip of this chart shows how many percentage points
current bond yields are above or below our Normal Valuation Line. The
Valuation Line is a valuation indicator, not a timing indicator; it is
best used when it diverges dramatically from widespread predictions
about interest rates (see page 6 for continuation of analysis).

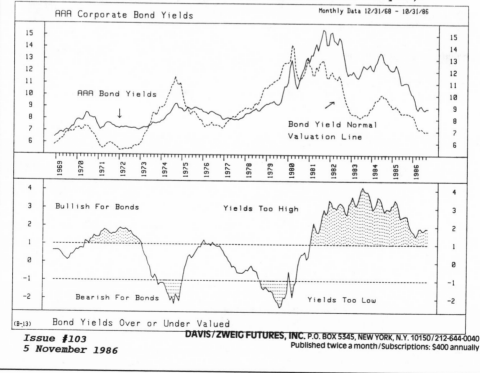

*Issue #103
5 November 1986*

DAVIS/ZWEIG FUTURES, INC. P.O. BOX 5345, NEW YORK, N.Y. 10150/212-644-0040
Published twice a month/Subscriptions: $400 annually

Reprinted with permission.

Newsletter Management Corp.

10076 Boca Entrada Blvd.
P.O. Box 3007
Boca Raton, FL 33431
(305) 483-2600

Growth Stock Report
Investment Advisory Bulletin
Number of subscribers is not available

Description of the publication:
Growth Stock Report is an advisory bulletin specializing in growth stock investing. The newsletter follows and recommends emerging growth stocks in the areas of high technology, medicine, energy, communications, computers, peripherals, and a host of other industries. In each issue stocks are tracked, performance is measured, markets are forecast, and predictions are made.

Investment selections in the publication are determined:
Using fundamental analysis for selection, technical analysis for timing.

The track record for the publication, as reported by the publication, is:
Not available.

The publication has been published continuously since: May 1984

The cost of a subscription is: $96

The number of issues per year is: 12

A HOTLINE telephone service is: Available
Cost for this service: Free with subscription.

The publication can be delivered: Via bulk/third class mail

It is also worth mentioning that:
Newsletter Management Corp. publishes several other newsletters covering a variety of topics.

REPORT

Focusing on Low-Priced Stocks Poised to Double in the Next 12 Months

Volume 3, Number 11   November 1986

Market Pulse: Corrections, Yes — Bull Market Over, No

In early September, we saw the first clear evidence that the market, after having reached new highs, had entered into the long-awaited corrective phase. Quite a bit of damage was done as the Dow fell a record 120 points on record volume in two days. That move scared a lot of people because of its severity. Some of it was caused by institutions trading in blind accordance with what their computerized systems tell them. This is not a bad way for them to go, but it intensifies the size of price swings. Add to this the probability that a great many stop-loss orders and margin calls were triggered, and you can see why downward moves now tend to be greater in magnitude. These large price fluctuations are with us for good, so you might as well get used to seeing them.

The economic numbers are mixed at best, and Wall Street raised the question as to the near-term future of inflation and interest rates. Corporate earnings have been mixed to disappointing. Seemingly, the overall market has outpaced the growth of corporate earnings. It will take more time for earnings to improve. The near-term action of stocks could remain weak, while investors wait for confirmation that the business cycle is again in a period of prosperity.

I view such market weakness as a buying opportunity. Recent government monetary policy and tax legislation are clearly intended to keep the economy moving. Several market advisors do caution, however, that mounting statistics and indicators are giving early warning signs that a recession is just around the corner. Without question, certain industries still have severe problems to solve. The commodity markets have made substantial gains in the last two months, with gold advancing to over $400 once again and other commodity prices moving upward after long-term declines. But inflation still remains low, and a bounce up in interest rates is only just that -- a bounce. There is little reason to suspect there will be a recession of any proportion in the foreseeable future.

In the long term, stocks (especially ones with good fundamentals) will become more attractive. The monetary policies in effect offer a tremendous opportunity for growth. The returns available in good growth stocks should be as viable as ever. Some growth stocks are in the penny stock price range of under $5; to keep up with opportunities regarding these issues, listen to the Penny Stock/New Issues Hotline, which operates 24 hours per day and is updated every morning. For data, call 800/231-2310; from Florida, call 800/433-5565.

Copyright 1986 by Unity Publishers Corp., 82 Wall St., Suite 1105, New York, NY 10005

Reprinted with permission.

The Institute for Econometric Research   **Income and Safety**®
3471 North Federal Highway   Investment Advisory Bulletin
Ft. Lauderdale, FL 33306   Less than 25,000 subscribers
(800) 327-6720

Description of the publication:
Income and Safety® is the most widely-read income newsletter in the country. It is designed to be a complete advisory service for savers and investors who are interested in securing the highest possible yield with the lowest possible risk. Each issue includes a directory of money funds, a directory of income funds, and a survey of the highest-yielding insured money market accounts and certificates of deposit. Special features include safety ratings, yield forecasts, and a buy/sell list.

Investment selections in the publications are determined:
By concentrating on the specialty topic area of: Income funds and money market investments.

The track record for the publication, as reported by the publication, is:
Not available.

The publication has been published continuously since: 1981

The cost of a subscription is: $49

The number of issues per year is: 12

A HOTLINE telephone service is: Available
Cost for this service: Free with subscription.

The publication can be delivered: Via first class mail

It is also worth mentioning that:
- A two-issue trial subscription to this newsletter is available at no charge.
- A 400-page book, ''Stock Market Logic,'' (over 200,000 copies sold) is also available.
- The Institute for Econometric Research also publishes several other newsletters covering a variety of topics.

INCOME & SAFETY®

The Consumer's Guide to High Yields

A Service of The Institute for Econometric Research, 3471 North Federal Highway, Fort Lauderdale, Florida 33306
Norman G. Fosback, President

Glen King Parker, Chairman

Issue No. 63   October 10, 1986

INCOME FUND "BEST BUYS"

Type	Fund	Yield
Treasury	Prudential-Bache Govt. Intermediate	8.8%
Treasury-Zero	Benham Target 2000	7.6%
Govt. Agency	USAA Income	9.4%
Ginnie Mae	Value Line U.S. Government	10.4%
Corporate	Bull & Bear High Yield	12.8%
Pfd. Stock	Vanguard - Qualif. Dividend II	8.9%
Tax-Free	Value Line Municipal	8.3%

INCOME FUND "BUYS"

Treasury	Fidelity Govt. Securities	8.5%
Treasury-Zero	Benham Target 2005	7.5%
Treasury-Zero	Benham Target 2010	7.5%
Govt. Agency	Fidelity Mortgage	9.0%
Govt. Agency	Liberty U.S. Govt. Secur.	9.0%
Ginnie Mae	Benham GNMA Income	9.7%
Ginnie Mae	Vanguard - Fixed-Income GNMA	9.6%
Corporate	Price Rowe High Yield	11.4%
Corporate	Financial Program High Yield	11.3%
Corporate	Vanguard-Fixed Income High Yield	11.2%
Corporate	GIT Maximum Income	11.2%
Tax-Free	Fidelity Aggressive Tax-Free	8.1%
Tax-Free	Kentucky Tax-Free	7.9%
Tax-Free	Vanguard Municipal High Yield	7.7%
Tax-Free	Vanguard Municipal Long-Term	7.6%
Tax-Free	California Muni	7.6%
Tax-Free	Price Rowe Tax-Free High Yield	7.5%

MONEY FUND "BEST BUYS"

Safety Rating	Fund	Tax Status	Yield Fore-cast	30-Day Yield
AAA+	Capital Preservation	Taxable	−1	5.8%
AAA	Shearson Govt. Agencies	Taxable	0	5.9%
AA	Merrill Lynch Ready Assets	Taxable	+2	5.1%
A	Dean Witter - Sears	Taxable	+2	5.9%
AAA	Federated Tax-Free	Tax-Free	0	4.0%
AA	Vanguard Municipal MM	Tax-Free	+1	4.4%
A	Calvert Tax-Free	Tax-Free	+2	4.6%

MONEY FUND "BUYS"

AAA	Vanguard - Federal	Taxable	0	5.7%
AAA	Lazard Government	Taxable	0	5.7%
AAA	Merrill Lynch Government	Taxable	0	5.8%
AAA	Cardinal Government	Taxable	0	5.2%
AAA	DBL Cash Govt.	Taxable	0	5.9%
AAA	N.E. Cash - US Govt.	Taxable	0	5.5%
AAA	Fidelity US Govt. Reserve	Taxable	0	5.5%
AAA	Fund for Govt. Investors	Taxable	0	5.2%
AA	Vanguard - Prime	Taxable	+2	5.9%
AA	Merrill Lynch Institutional	Taxable	+2	5.8%
AA	DBL Cash Money Market	Taxable	+1	5.7%
AA	IDS Cash Management	Taxable	+1	5.6%
A	Kemper Money Market	Taxable	+2	6.0%
A	Transamerica Cash Reserve	Taxable	+2	5.8%
A	Dreyfus Liquid Assets	Taxable	+2	5.8%
AA	Nuveen Tax-Ex. Money Mkt.	Tax-Free	+1	4.3%

Fed to Lower Rates

The money and bond markets were virtually directionless over the past month as traders waited to see whether the Federal Reserve would continue to ease its monetary policy. The key 90-day Treasury Bill rate has been virtually unchanged for a month, even while rates on commercial paper and other money market instruments drifted slightly upward. (Somewhat perversely, yields on money funds fell as older investments matured and the funds rolled over into lower-yielding holdings.) Longer-term, most bond yields rose slightly.

The economy is now sputtering along at barely a 2% rate of growth, well below what central bankers would like to see. The general expectation is that the Fed must push short-term interest rates lower to avoid an imminent recession. Thus, lower money market rates appear in prospect over the next few weeks, and as money fund yields head down, we expect the newly evolved superiority of insured *[Continued on Page 4]*

What To Do Now

LONG-TERM INCOME: *Prudential-Bache Government Intermediate* is the new "Best Buy" in the Treasury category, replacing *Fidelity Government Securities*, which retains a "Buy" recommendation. *Benham Target 2000* has edged out *Benham Target 2005* and *Benham Target 2010* as our "Best Buy" Treasury Zero-Coupon fund, although the latter funds own "Buy" designations. *Value Line U.S. Government* has taken over the "Best Buy" position in the Ginnie Mae group, replacing *Lexington Ginnie Mae Income*, which is now rated "Hold." All other income fund "Best Buys" are unchanged from last issue.

MONEY MARKET: Tax-free money funds are the investment of choice for all investors whose marginal tax bracket is above 24%. *Vanguard Municipal Money Market* and *Calvert Tax-Free* offer particularly attractive yields.

The taxable money fund "Best Buys" shown in the table at left are unchanged from last issue. Investors willing to bank by mail also can boost yields significantly by opening money market accounts or purchasing short-term CDs in any of several federally-insured institutions listed on Page 2 of this issue. The average yield on insured money market accounts now exceeds the national average money fund yield.

See the enclosed letter for your current confidential Hot Line number.

Reprinted with permission.

The Institute for Econometric Research
3471 North Federal Highway
Ft. Lauderdale, FL 33306
(800) 327-6720

The Insiders®
Investment Advisory Bulletin
Less than 25,000 subscribers

Description of the publication:

The Insiders® provides complete guidance on what stocks to buy and sell, and when to buy and sell them based on insider trading trends. A special feature in each issue is a "0-to-10" rating for each of over 2,500 stocks, indicating which stocks have the most insider buying and selling. This newsletter has the largest paid circulation of any insider trading publication, exceeding all other insider services combined.

Investment selections in the publication are determined:

By concentrating on the specialty topic area of: Insider trading.

The track record for the publication, as reported by the publication, is:

The average change of all stocks formally recommended for purchase and subsequently sold, from the initial buy recommendation to the final sell recommendation is +135%—an annual rate of gain of +65%.

The publication has been published continuously since: 1980

The cost of a subscription is: $49

The number of issues per year is: 24

A HOTLINE telephone service is: Available

Cost for this service: Free with subscription.

The publication can be delivered: Via first class mail

It is also worth mentioning that:

- A two-issue trial subscription to this newsletter is available at no charge.
- A 400-page book, "Stock Market Logic," (over 200,000 copies sold) is also available.
- The Institute for Econometric Research also publishes several other newsletters covering a variety of topics.

THE INSIDERS.

America's Most Knowledgeable Investors

A Service of The Institute for Econometric Research

Norman G. Fosback, Editor • 3471 North Federal Highway, Fort Lauderdale, Florida 33306 • Glen King Parker, Publisher

Issue No. 148

See the enclosed letter for
your current confidential
Insider Line number.

October 3, 1986

BAROMETERS MAINTAIN BULLISH STANCE

After stumbling sharply during a brief two-day sinking spell in mid-September, the stock market has stabilized and is once again locked squarely within the trading range that has prevailed since late spring. The buy signals received on our Insider Barometers two weeks ago near the market's current level remain in firm force, as these indexes continue to emit bullish readings today.

The Five-Week Composite Insiders Index (see chart below) stands at 39% insider buyers, still nicely above the 35% normal insider buying proportion.   The Weekly Insiders Index is even stronger at 45% buyers. The Flash Index, which measures especially recent insider trades, is a notch more bullish yet at 46% buyers.

TOP-RATED STOCKS

The Henley Group and Western Capital Investment have both earned the top Insider Rating of "10" on our 0-to-10 rating scale.   From a fundamental standpoint, we do not think highly of Henley's prospects (see *TI*, 6/20/86) and have therefore not recommended it for the Insiders' Portfolio. Western Capital is another story — see our "Buy" recommendation below.

No stocks have the next-to-highest Insider Rating

of "9". However, 18 different stocks have Ratings of "8". All of these are listed on Page 2 ("Highest and Lowest Rated Stocks by Market"), and insider trading details on the stocks with the most significant buying are also shown on Page 2 ("Insider Buy Favorites"). Many of these stocks are good purchase candidates for underinvested portfolios.

At the other end of the scale, **Boeing, Digital Equipment, DuPont, General Motors, Gibson Greetings, IBM, McDonald's, Raytheon, Service Corp. of America,** and **Safeway** all have the lowest possible Insider Rating of "0". While a rising market could send the prices of these stocks higher, as a group their heavy insider selling suggests they will underperform the averages. These issues are therefore best avoided.

BUY WESTERN CAPITAL

Western Capital Investment Corporation (NASDAQ — WECA, $14.00) is a financial conglomerate headquartered in Denver. It engages in retail and commercial banking, mortgage banking, general insurance, real estate brokerage, and financial management services through 85 offices in 18 states. Most importantly, the firm is the holding company for Bank Western, the largest savings and loan association in Colorado with $2.4 billion of deposits. *[Continued on Page 3]*

THE INSIDERS INDEX and Standard & Poor's 500

The Insiders Index   Our Insiders Index measures the number of insider buyers as a percentage of total insiders executing open market trades in NYSE and Amex companies during the last five weeks. Moderately favorable at 39%.

Reprinted with permission.

InvesTech Research
522 Crestview Drive
Kalispell, MT 59901
(406) 755-8527

InvesTech Market Letter®
Investment Advisory Bulletin
Less than 25,000 subscribers

Description of the publication:
The InvesTech Market Letter® is designed for both investors and traders, as well as individuals who invest in mutual funds. Each issue analyzes the outlook for the economy and the stock market and includes detailed, easy to understand charts, specific stock recommendations, and switching advice for no-load mutual funds. A telephone hotline updated twice each week and special research reports are also included as part of the service. As well as maintaining a buy/sell list, the newsletter also is designed to be a topical education service covering a wide range of investment topics.

Investment selections in the publications are determined:
Using fundamental analysis for selection, technical and monetary analysis for timing.

The track record for the publication, as reported by the publication, is:
Available, but has not been provided.

The publication has been published continuously since: 1981

The cost of a subscription is: $185

The number of issues per year is: 24

A HOTLINE telephone service is: Available
Cost for this service: Free with subscription.

The publication can be delivered: Via first class mail

It is also worth mentioning that:
InvesTech Research also offers:
- computerized retrieval of hotline reports and key indicators;
- a daily commodity hotline (as an extra service); and,
- a daily stock index futures and options trading hotline (as an extra service).

INVESTECH ®

MARKET LETTER

V86I09   *TECHNICAL AND MONETARY INVESTMENT ANALYSIS*   SEPT. 26, 1986

4 Wks Ending Sept 26th

	HIGH	LOW	LAST
Financial			
Discount Rate	5.50%	5.50%	5.50%
Federal Funds	5 7/8%	5 5/8%	5 3/4%
90-Day T-Bills	5.27%	5.12%	5.22%
Stock Market			
DJIA	1919.71	1758.72	1803.29
DJTA	794.38	737.38	792.13
DJUA	219.15	198.78	204.16
NASDAQ	382.86	343.67	354.52
Silver (DEC)	6.07	5.23	5.98
Gold (DEC)	445.20	392.00	436.00

Chart: OTC NASDAQ INDEX, 1985–1986

NO TIME FOR HEROES

Aside from a tipsy-teetering Bond market, monetary conditions are near the most favorable levels of the past two years. With key short-term interest rates on their lows and the Federal Reserve not displaying even the slightest inclination of wavering from its 'easy-money' policy of the past 23 months, THIS is the type of climate in which new Bull Markets normally bask and frolic.

However at four years of age (or 12 if you count 1981 only as a mini-bear), this Bull could hardly be called new. Nor would many analysts describe current economic conditions as NORMAL. Lower interest rates, a falling U.S. Dollar, cheap oil prices... all are supposed to point the way to a booming economy. Even the Commerce Department's Index of Leading Economic Indicators has confirmed that prosperity is just around the corner - it's been saying that for almost two years now!

But the debt-ridden consumer (who accounts for 2/3's of GNP growth), has yet to turn these promising forecasts into economic reality. Cut-rate auto financing led to a meager 1.7% gain in mid-September auto sales. And American Motors, who blazed the trail with 0.0% financing, watched their sales drop 28%!

While economic sleuths seek new Truths to resolve this mystery, we will explore several of the riddles confronting investors today: Is this Bull Market Over? What will determine its next move? And finally, we also examine the compelling evidence why we feel that the next couple months will be "NO TIME FOR HEROES".

NOTE: James Stack will be appearing as the featured guest on THE NIGHTLY BUSINESS REPORT with Paul Kangas on October 23rd. Check your local listings for time and PBS channel.

EDITOR: JAMES B. STACK   522 Crestview Drive, Kalispell, MT 59901 (406) 755-8527   **COPYRIGHT 1986 INVESTECH**

Reprinted with permission.

Argus Research Corp.
42 Broadway
New York City, NY 10004
(212) 425-7500

Investment Portfolio Guide
Investment Advisory Bulletin
Less than 25,000 subscribers

Description of the publication:
Investment Portfolio Guide is a monthly forty page narrative and statistical review of the industries and companies regularly monitored by Argus. In addition to such statistical information as reported profits, earnings estimates, price/earnings ratios, dividends, yields, etc., the Guide incorporates Argus' appraisal of the probably market performance of each issue on both a near-term and long-term basis.

Investment selections in the publication are determined:
Using fundamental analysis.

The track record for the publication, as reported by the publication, is:
Not available.

The publication has been published continuously since: 1950

The cost of a subscription is: $235

The number of issues per year is: 12

A HOTLINE telephone service is: Available
Cost for this service: Negotiable with subscription.

The publication can be delivered: Via bulk/third class mail

It is also worth mentioning that:
Argus Research Corp. also publishes several other investment publications designed for both individual investors and investment professionals covering a wide range of topics. These reports include the:

- Weekly Staff Report
- Weekly Economic Review
- Viewpoint
- Portfolio Selector
- Investment Portfolio Guide
- Investment Analysis
- Energy Update

- Special Analysis
- Special-Theme Report
- Electric Utility Ranking
- Electric Utility Spotlight
- Special Situations Report
- Master List

All of the above reports can be bought separately or purchased as a group for a combined discount price of $125 per month. Of special interest is a premium service available to brokers which allows for an unlimited amount of analyst contact, live conference calls, and research opinions written on the broker's own letterhead.

INDUSTRY RATINGS

Earnings prospects for individual industry groups are tabulated by averaging the percentage change between estimated reported full-year 1985 earnings per share and the Argus estimates of 1986 earnings per share for the stocks that comprise the particular group. Extreme fluctuations in company earnings are omitted.

The Price Behavior column indicates the Argus expectation of market price action during the next six-to-12 months of an industry group relative to the broad market averages.

Income ratings are based on a comparison of dividend yields with the S&P 500.

Bullet (●) denotes the standing for the current month, the symbol (○) for the previous month.

Industry	1986 Earnings Prospects — DOWN MORE THAN 15%	DOWN 5-15%	FLAT: +5% to -5%	UP 5-15%	UP MORE THAN 15%	Price Behavior — BELOW AVG.	AVG.	ABOVE AVG.	Dividend Income — 0-3%	3-6%	6%+
AEROSPACE				●			●	○	●		
AIRLINES		●				●	○	●	●		
AUTOMOTIVE			●				●			●	
BROADCASTING					●		●	●	●		
BUILDING				●			●			●	
CHEMICALS				●			●	●		●	
ELEC. & ELECTRONICS			●				●	●	●		
COMPUTER SERVICES					●			●	●		
CON. ELECTRONICS				●			●		●		
ELEC. EQUIP.				●			●			●	
OFFICE EQUIP.				●			●	●	●		
COMPONENTS & INSTR.				●			●		●		
DEFENSE SYSTEMS					●		●	●		●	
FINANCIAL SERVICES			●				●		●		
BANKS				●			●			●	
BROKERAGE & OTHERS				●		○			●		
FOOD, BEV. & TOBACCOS				●			●			●	
BEVERAGES					●		●	●		●	
FOODS				●			●			●	
FOOD DISTRIBUTORS				●			●		●		
TOBACCOS				●		●				●	
HEALTH CARE				●			●		●		
LEISURE TIME				●			●		●		
ENTERTAINMENT				●			●	●	●		
APPAREL				●			●			●	
LODGING & RESTAUR.				●			●	●	●		
METALS & MINING	●						●		●		
OIL SERVICES	●					○			●		
OILS			●				●			●	
DOM. INTEGRATED						○				●	
PRODUCERS	●					○					●
INDEP. REFINERS	●					○					●
INTERNATIONAL						○				●	
PAPER				●			●			●	
RAILROADS				●			●			●	
RETAILING				●			●		●		
UTILITIES				●			●			●	
ELECTRIC				●		○					●
GAS DISTRIBUTION			●				●			●	
GAS PIPELINES		●				○				●	
COMMUNICATIONS				●			●	○		●	

EARNINGS PER SHARE

INDUSTRY AND COMPANY	STOCK SYMBOL	INTERIM MOS	CURR YEAR	PREV YEAR	FULL YEAR 1987E	1986E	1985	GROWTH % 85-90E	90-85	PRICE RECENT	12 MOS RANGE	BETA	P/E 86E	REL TO S&P 500	DIV ANNUAL RATE $	YIELD %	RET EQ 86E	85	FIN'L STRNG	EXPECTED 9-MONTH / 5-YR TOT RET
S&P 500	—	—	—	—	19.00	16.00	14.83	3.7	0.8	236	227-177	1.00	14.8	1.00	7.98	3.4	14	13(c)	H	B/B
AEROSPACE																				
Boeing ● BA		6	0.95	1.88	NA	4.40	3.75	7	(2)	55	55-42	1.51	12.5	0.85	1.20	2.2	16	16	H	C/C
General Dynamics ○ GD		6	2.04	4.54	NA	9.50	9.05	8	20	72	89-62	1.41	7.6	0.52	1.00	1.4	34	25	NL	B/B
Grumman ● GQ		6	4.07	1.91	NA	2.90	2.90	9	17	25	30-23	0.55	9.5	0.64	1.00	4.1	10	12	H	B/A
Lockheed K ○ LK		6	1.13	2.59	NA	6.90	6.10	9	84	45	80-43	1.20	6.8	0.46	0.80	1.8	29	W	NL	A/A
Lear Siegler 6/30F ○ LSI		—	2.50	3.82	NA	5.20	3.02	10	7	57	61-46	1.57	11.0	0.75	2.00	3.5	17	16	H	A/B
● Martin Marietta ○ ML		6	1.84	2.83	NA	3.80	4.36	3	13	42	49-31	1.85	11.7	0.79	1.00	2.4	32	25	NH	A/A
McDonnell Douglas ○ MD		6	3.52	4.43	NA	9.00	8.80	4	19	85	89-64	1.37	9.4	0.64	2.06	2.5	17	13	H	A/A
Northrop ○ NOC		6	1.34	2.97	NA	4.20	4.83	9	18	46	57-38	1.45	10.8	0.74	1.20	2.6	27	17	N	B/B
Rockwell Int'l 9/30F ○ ROK		9	3.01	3.05	NA	4.80	4.30	9	18	38	48-31	1.01	7.8	0.54	1.12	2.9	23	19	NH	B/A
Textron ○ TXT		6	2.71	3.02	NA	5.30	5.99	3	8	55	66-44	1.10	10.4	0.70	1.80	3.3	14	12	NH	C/C
United Technologies K ○ UTX		6	1.37	1.38	NA	4.00	2.25	7	6	45	58-38	1.42	11.2	0.76	1.40	3.1	20	18	H	B/B
AIRLINES																				
AMR Corp. ○ AMR		6	2.16	4.20	6.50	4.80	5.94	15	11	56	61-39	1.36	12.1	0.82	Nil	0.0	13	W	H	A/A
Alaska Airlines ○ ALK		6	0.16d	0.91	2.00	1.00	1.75	17	21	20	23-14	1.58	18.5	1.32	0.16	0.8	5	21	H	A/A
America West Airlines ○ AWAL		6	0.33d	0.32	1.50	0.50	1.01	W	W	8	14-6	—	5.0	0.34	Nil	0.0	W	W	NL	A/A
Delta Air Lines 6/30F ○ DAL		12	1.18	8.50	4.00	4.00	8.50	15	5	44	49-35	1.18	11.1	0.75	1.00	2.3	11	(13)	NH	C/B
Eastern Air Lines EAL		6	2.48d	0.72	—	4.00 d	0.85	W	W	9	10-4	1.81	—	—	Nil	0.0	W	W	L	B/-
Emery Air Freight ○ EAF		6	0.48d	0.41	1.75	0.50	0.85	15	W	14	22-11	1.41	5.0	0.34	0.50	3.7	5	15	H	A/A
● NWA ○ NWA		6	0.34	1.90	6.00	3.50	3.18	12	4	51	55-42	1.25	14.6	0.99	0.90	1.8	10	3	NH	B/A
Pan American ○ PN		6	2.01d	2.09d	3.00	2.00 d	0.45	W	W	6	10-5	1.00	—	—	Nil	0.0	W	W	L	A/A
People Express ○ PEXP		6	5.29d	0.47d	0.50 d	6.50 d	1.80d	W	W	9	18-6	2.02	—	—	Nil	0.0	W	W	NL	C/-
Southwest Airlines ○ LUV		6	0.81	0.89	2.10	1.70	1.54	18	24	24	29-15	1.24	14.0	0.94	0.05	3.5	NA	W	NL	B/B
Trans World Airlines ○ TWA		6	6.47d	2.71d	0.00	3.80 d	1.10d	W	W	25	29-13	1.47	—	0.00	0.13	0.6	14	20	N	A/A
UAL ○ UAL		6	1.97d	2.99d	6.00	2.00	2.09d	10	W	80	85-46	1.80	10.0	0.88	Nil	0.0	NA	W	NL	B/B
AUTOMOTIVE																				
Chrysler ○ C		6	5.54	6.13	NA	9.50	9.38	(3)	W	38	47-24	1.26	4.0	0.27	1.40	3.7	41	W	NL	B/B
Ford Motor ○ F		6	6.72	5.30	NA	7.33	8.06	(3)	W	55	64-29	1.10	7.4	0.50	2.80	4.0	23	W	NH	B/B
General Motors ○ GM		6	5.92	6.90	NA	10.00	12.28	4	W	69	89-64	1.72	6.9	0.47	5.00	7.2	13	13	MH	B/B
TIRES																				
Firestone 10/31F ○ FIR		9	1.40	1.06	NA	2.00	0.14d	5	W	25	27-18	1.04	12.5	0.85	0.80	3.3	W	5	L	C/B
Goodrich (B. F.) ○ GR		6	0.99d	15.01d	NA	2.00	15.79d	5	W	40	48-31	1.25	19.0	1.35	1.56	3.9	W	2	L	B/B
Goodyear ○ GT		6	0.38	1.92	NA	3.50	3.84	2	(2)	33	37-25	1.01	8.3	0.83	1.60	4.8	W	11	H	C/B

Reprinted with permission.

Investor's Daily
1941 Armacost Ave
Los Angeles, CA 90025
(213) 207-1832

Investor's Daily
Topical Education Service
50,000 to 100,000 subscribers

Description of the publication:
Investor's Daily is a daily newspaper, published Monday through Friday covering a wide range of investment topics.

Investment selections in the publication are determined:
Not applicable.

The track record for the publication, as reported by the publication, is:
Not applicable.

The publication has been published continuously since: 1984

The cost of a subscription is: $84

The number of issues per year is: 250

A HOTLINE telephone service is: Not Available

The publication can be delivered: Via home delivery, second class mail,
                                                          newstands, and news racks.

Investor's Daily

America's Business Newspaper

Vol. 3, No. 127 — 1986, Investor's Daily Inc. Los Angeles, Calif 90025 — **Tuesday, October 7, 1986** — Paid Circulation: 64,000 — S&P 500 +1.07 (+0.46%) — ★ — 35¢

Today's News Digest

THE ECONOMY

Treasury Bill Yields Fall To 9-Year Lows

Yields of short-term Treasury bills at the regular weekly auction fell to their lowest levels in more than nine years. The Treasury Department auctioned $7.23 billion in 13-week bills at an average discount rate of 5.08%, down from 5.20% last week. The government sold $7.20 billion in 26-week bills at an average discount rate of 5.13%, down from 5.37% the week before. Both rates were the lowest they have been since 1977, when the 13-week rate was 5.04% on July 1 and the six-month rate was 5.05% on May 2.
See chart / page 30

Gas Spot Prices Fall In First Week Of October

Spot prices for natural gas declined between 3%-6% during the first week of this month because of slack demand and competition among suppliers, according to a monthly survey by the Natural Gas Clearinghouse Inc. in Houston. The industry monitoring group said prices ranged between $1.25-$1.45 per million British Thermal Units.

Trade Surpluses Double In West Germany, Japan

The trade surpluses of Japan and West Germany doubled between mid-1985 and mid-1986, while the U.S. trade deficit rose by 21%, the International Monetary Fund reported. The study also noted total trade deficits are declining for industrial countries, but imbalances among them are increasing.
Japan's surplus rose to $34.4 billion in first-half 1986 from $1.78 billion a year earlier, while West Germany's surplus rose to $22 billion from $10.2 billion. The U.S. deficit rose to $83.8 billion from $69.3 billion, the IMF said.

Few Americans Expect To Pay Lower Taxes

Only 16% of all American families expect to buy lower taxes as a result of tax reform legislation, according to a Conference Board survey of 5,000 families across the country. Nearly 44% expect to pay higher taxes and about 40% expect their tax burden to remain about the same.
The survey also reveals opinion is severely split on the fairness of the new legislation. While 36% say the new tax system would be "more fair," 33% claim it will be "less fair." The remaining 31% believe the new law would be neither more nor less fair than the current system.

U.S. Seeks Safeguards In Indian Arms Deal

Concerns over adequate safeguards to protect highly sophisticated technology threaten to delay the pending sale of U.S. fighter aircraft engines and other weapons systems to India, according to Pentagon and industry sources.
See story / page 2

BUSINESS

BankAmerica Names Chief Financial Exec

BankAmerica Corp. named Frank Newman, executive vice president and chief financial officer with Wells Fargo & Co., as vice chairman and chief financial officer. Newman replaces John S. Poelker, who resigned in August after less than six months in the post.
Separately, BankAmerica also confirmed its directors approved severance packages for "fewer than 12 individuals," including Samuel H. Armacost, BankAmerica's embattled president and chief executive — should management be changed as a result of a hostile takeover.
See story / page 34

Viacom Stock Closes Above Offer Price

Viacom International Inc.'s stock yesterday closed at 42½, indicating investors strongly believe a pending 40½-a-share bid by management would be raised. Volume was about eight times the daily average before the Sept. 16 announcement that management offered to take the company private in a $2.8 billion transaction involving cash and preferred stock.
See story / page 9

Cherokee Group's Net Gained 41% In 3rd Qtr

Cherokee Group Inc. said earnings for the fiscal third quarter ended Aug. 30 rose 40.9% to 31 cents a share from 22 cents a year earlier. The results were in line with estimates the company made in a mid-August meeting with analysts. The North Hollywood, Calif.-based apparel and shoe manufacturer said net income rose 73% to $1.74 million from $1.27 million. Sales totaled $26.8 million, up 21.3% from $22.1 million a year earlier.

Steel Production

Estimated weekly raw steel production in millions of short tons.

Week ended Oct. 4
1.28 million tons

Figures in chart compare '85-'86 for same week. Source: American Iron & Steel Institute

STEEL PRODUCTION OFF 1.6%. U.S. steel production fell to 1.28 million short tons the week ended Oct. 4 from 1.3 million tons the previous week, the American Iron and Steel Institute said. Production for 1986 totals 63.23 million tons, down from 66.67 million tons a year earlier.

Allied Stores Still Silent Despite Halt In Trading

Trading in shares of Allied Stores Corp., target of a hostile $66-a-share cash and stock tender offer by Canadian developer Campeau Corp., was halted briefly pending an announcement that hadn't come by late afternoon. After the morning halt, Allied's shares rose to 65½ on anticipation of an announcement, but finished unchanged at 64½ in heavy trading. The company has said it is studying alternatives to the Campeau offer, which sources have valued at about $62 a share, or around $3.3 billion.

IL-3: Potential Weapon In Cancer, AIDS Wars

Genetics Institute Inc., a Cambridge, Mass., genetic engineering firm, said its scientists have identified a human protein — called interleukin-3 — that could prove an important new weapon against cancer, AIDS and blood disorders. Commercialization of IL-3 is probably at least four years away.
See story / page 10

Lucky Rejects Edelman Bid, Studies Alternatives

Lucky Stores Inc. said its directors rejected as inadequate a $35-a-share cash takeover proposal from investor Asher B. Edelman, and instructed management to explore ways of restructuring the company to realize shareholder values. Edelman said he might be willing to raise his $1.79 billion offer if the food, discount and specialty store operator would provide certain data. He also sought a meeting with independent directors. Market sources said Edelman lined up a $2.1 billion war chest with Marine Midland and Banque Paribas banks.

COMB Sees Losses; May Sell Retail Units

COMB Co., the Minneapolis-based marketer controlled in part by investor Irwin Jacobs, said it may shed its marginally profitable 41-store retail operation and expects to post third-quarter operating and net losses. A year earlier, it earned $457,000, or four cents a share, on sales of about $25 million. The operator of the Cable Value Network shop-by-TV service said it will take an after-tax charge of $4.5 million, or about 28 cents, to cover the costs of disposing of its stores. It attributed the operating loss to the retail division, costs of moving to new quarters and CVN investments.

Midlantic Banks Reports 3rd-Qtr Earnings Up 13%

Midlantic Banks Inc., Edison, N.J., reported preliminary fully diluted third-quarter earnings gained 12.9% to $1.31 from $1.16 a year earlier. Consolidated net income rose 16.2% to $29.4 million from $25.3 million. The firm cited higher net interest income resulting largely from increased loan activity and higher fee income, primarily from greater activity in its mortgage banking subsidiary. Midlantic's return on average assets, on an annualized basis, was 1.05% at Sept. 30, up from 1.03% a year earlier.

Kodak Appeal Of Instant Camera Suit Rejected

The U.S. Supreme Court left Eastman Kodak Co. open to billions of dollars in damages when it denied the Rochester, N.Y.-based company's appeal of a ruling that its instant cameras and film infringed on Polaroid Corp.'s patents. Kodak quit the instant photography market in January after a federal appeals court upheld a lower court's ruling that Kodak's designs infringed on seven of Polaroid's patents. An award to Polaroid, which analysts estimate could be as high as $2 billion, will be determined in U.S. District Court in Boston.

WASHINGTON & WORLD

■ A Soviet nuclear-powered submarine, armed with at least 16 nuclear-tipped missiles, sank in the Atlantic about 600 miles east of Bermuda, a few days after being damaged by an explosion and fire.
■ U.S. experts said the sinking should pose no danger of radioactive contamination or explosion of missiles.
■ Israeli warplanes bombed a Palestinian guerrilla headquarters and harassed Lebanese militia training camps in strikes six miles from the Syrian border with northern Lebanon, the deepest air strike ever in Lebanon. Three guerrillas were reported hurt.
■ Lebanese and Palestinian leaders agreed on a cease-fire to end fighting in a major Palestinian refugee camp in Lebanon, Palestinian representatives announced.
■ Three Frenchmen held hostage in Lebanon for more than a year made an impassioned videotaped appeal to their government to negotiate their release from what one called "the slow death" of captivity. And in the U.S., relatives of American hostages continued to talk to the press seeking more U.S. government action to free the prisoners.
■ Reagan began a series of meetings to prepare for his meeting with Soviet leader Mikhail Gorbachev this weekend in Iceland. The administration said Nancy Reagan will remain behind during the meeting, despite a surprise announcement that Raisa Gorbachev will go.
■ Soviet dissident Yuri Orlov arrived in New York and vowed to continue the human rights campaign that landed him in a labor camp and exile in Siberia, and said he feels guilty about those he left behind.
■ Edward Perkins, Reagan's nominee for ambassador to South Africa, told a Senate confirmation hearing he will do all he can to urge Pretoria to end its policy of apartheid. Perkins was well received by members of the committee, who will vote today.
■ Security forces killed a black man and wounded two others in breaking up a crowd of about 600 people who were attacking the home of a black councilor in Soweto, the South African government said. Earlier, a release of official figures showed a dramatic decline in anti-government violence in recent weeks, although peaceful protests such as rent boycotts escalated.
■ Former Philippine President Ferdinand Marcos asked a federal judge for permission to sue the Philippine government for at least $10 million.
■ Torrential rains and high winds lashed the Manila area, and the Red Cross reported at least 11 deaths. Thousands of people were evacuated from flood waters, which reached seven feet in some districts.
■ An army vehicle detonated a land mine near the Mozambique border, wounding six soldiers, officials reported yesterday.
■ The impeachment trial of federal judge Harry E. Claiborne moves to the Senate floor today but will not be the full-scale proceeding sought by the imprisoned Nevada jurist. Majority Leader Bob Dole said.
■ The Indian government asked a district court in Bhopal to bar Union Carbide Corp. from destroying evidence relating to the 1984 toxic chemical disaster in a Union Carbide plant there.
■ A federal judge in Topeka, Kan., heard opening arguments in the re-argued landmark desegregation case, Brown vs. Board of Education of Topeka.
■ Meanwhile, a group of fundamentalist parents in Mobile, Ala., asked a federal court to purge from classrooms 46 books they claim place man before God.
■ Dismissandie, a controversial growth regulator used on apples, does not seem to have caused any cancers in rats examined in a laboratory study, according to Uniroyal Chemical Co., the manufacturer.

Inside The Market

Market Shows Modest Gain; Trading Slows To 88 Million

By Leo Fasciocco, Investor's Daily

The stock market moved modestly higher yesterday but with very little conviction as trading slowed to 88.25 million shares — the smallest turnover in five months.
"It's almost like the cat does not know which way to jump," said equity strategist Donald Carver of First Pennsylvania Bank of Philadelphia. "There's confusion among investors over monetary and fiscal policy and the strength of the economy and it's been going on for several months."
The Dow Jones industrial index, which has been trading in a range between 1920 and 1750 the past six months (see chart on page 8), closed at 1784.45, up 10.27, or 0.58%. The Investor's Daily Stock Index advanced 0.38, or 0.25%, to 153.99.

Groups With The Greatest % Of Stocks Making New Highs

Retail-major dept stores.	11%
Tools-hand hand	9%
Office automation	9%
REIT-mortgage trust	9%
Chemicals-plastics	9%

Groups Up Most In Price — % Chg

Chemicals-fibers	+2.3
Machinery-farm	+1.9
Silver mining & proc	+1.8
Office automation	+1.7
Gold mining & proc	+1.6

See Prices Of 198 Industry Groups / page 9

In the broad market, gainers led losers 6 to 5, while up volume topped down volume 2 to 1. The average price of a share increased 14 cents to $37.02.

"I am not looking for a big drop in the stock market," said Carver, who manages $2 billion in equity accounts. "What the market seems to need is three to five months to rebuild investor confidence. We believe the risk is that we'll have a choppy market for an extended period, rather than a 150-point decline."
Carver said the light volume shows there's a lot of investor uncertainty. "I, myself, have no confidence that this rally will last," he said. "If the stock market were to move up, we'd try to raise more cash. We have been fairly fully invested."
The market's strength was centered in the blue chips, railroad and insurance issues. International Business Machines Corp. jumped 2% to 133%. Today, IBM is expected to introduce a new minicomputer. The stock, with a Relative Strength of 35, has been a market laggard.
McDonald's Corp. rose 1% to 59% and American Can Co. 1% to 83. Among the rails, Burlington Northern Inc. was up 1% to 58 and Norfolk Southern Corp. 1% to 82% and in the insurance group, General Re Corp. picked up 1% to 60 and CNA Financial Corp. 1 to 54½.
Polaroid Corp., up 2 Friday, added another 2 to 66% after the Supreme Court refused to hear Eastman Kodak Co.'s appeal of a patent dispute it lost with Polaroid involving instant cameras. Eastman Kodak was unchanged at 55.
The past year, Polaroid has doubled in price. Its Relative Strength is 90. Eastman Kodak, on the other hand, is up 11 points, or 25%, the past year. Its Relative Strength is 63.
News Ltd., a market leader, hit a new high, gaining 1% to close at 41½. The past three sessions, the stock has leaped 5% points. The Australian publishing firm has an Earnings Per Share Rank of 98, reflecting a 27% annual growth in net income the past five years.
Transworld Corp. bounced up 1% to 27%. Analyst Michael Mueller of Montgomery Securities said the rise was a snapback from a recent sell-off triggered by the resignation of Transworld's president in August. "The company has been rumored from time to time as a takeover, but I haven't heard anything," Mueller said.
Kaiser Cement Corp., which said in September it was considering the sale of the company, spurted 2 to 22%. The stock has vaulted 7 points, or 47%, the past five weeks. DCNY Corp., which handles government securities and has shown an erratic earnings record, moved up 1% to 46% after posting a 511% increase in third-quarter net income.
Western Pacific Industries Inc. declined 4 to 162% after accepting a takeover offer of $163 a share from Danaher Corp.
See Stocks At New Highs / page 8

Icahn Makes 'Friendly' Takeover Offer For Struggling USX Corp.

Financier Presents $8.5 Bil Cash Bid For Energy, Steel Conglomerate

NEW YORK (Reuter) — Veteran corporate raider Carl Icahn yesterday announced his long-awaited bid to take over USX Corp., making an $8.5 billion "friendly" cash offer for the huge steel and energy producer.
The flamboyant New York financier, after stalking the company for weeks in the marketplace, said he already owns 9.83% of USX stock, with a total investment of $545.7 million. He estimated he would spend another $8 billion to acquire the remainder of the company.
Icahn, who vowed not to accept greenmail to deter his bid, said in a government filing that he might drop his offer if USX management agreed to restructure the company so as to boost the value of the company's share.
Greenmail is the controversial payment by a corporate raider of a sum of money to end a takeover bid.
The Icahn takeover offer is valued at $31 a share. USX closed at $26.50 yesterday in very heavy trading of 12.7 million shares, some of which was believed to be purchases by Icahn.
In a disclosure statement to the Securities and Exchange Commission, Icahn said he made the offer in a letter to USX Chairman David Roderick.
Icahn told Roderick he would put up about $1 billion for the takeover, with his financial adviser, investment firm Drexel Burnham Lambert Inc., has said it is "highly confident" it can obtain commitments for the balance of the estimated $8.5 billion.
Icahn, 50, who earlier this year took control of Trans World Airlines Inc., offered to drop his offer for the former U.S. Steel if USX management calls up with a better plan for increasing the value of its stock, but only would enhance value for all shareholders.
Icahn said if he is forced to seek control of the company through normal acquisition, he would consider a takeover of less than 51% of the shares.
USX had no immediate comment.
Shares of USX have been climbing sharply due to speculation the company would be the object of a takeover attempt. Prior to the bid, stock was trading at around $16.
Icahn was just one of those well-known investors rumored to be accumulating USX stock. Australian Robert Holmes a Court was believed still interested, but speculators have grown doubtful whether the often-mentioned
See USX TAKEOVER / page 34

U.S. Seen Meeting Gramm-Rudman Goal

Government Report Predicts 1987 Deficit Below $154 Bil Threshold

By Charles W. Pluckhahn, Investor's Daily

WASHINGTON — Officials yesterday said Congress is likely to achieve the budget savings required by the Gramm-Rudman law, although it has missed the deadline for doing so.
A one-page report issued jointly by the Office of Management and Budget and the Congressional Budget Office projected the same $163.4 billion fiscal 1987 deficit that the two agencies had estimated in August.
Technically, lawmakers had until the beginning of the 1987 fiscal year Oct. 1 to meet the Gramm-Rudman deficit target of $144 billion, plus a cushion of $10 billion, or face a vote on across-the-board spending cuts to meet the target.
The across-the-board reductions, detailed in August by OMB and CBO, would cut 7.6% from domestic programs and 5.6% from the military. Authorities have said that such reductions would disrupt both civilian and military programs and force layoffs of hundreds of thousands of government employees, including military personnel.
However, congressional action is pending on a budget reconciliation bill that would trim $10 billion to $15 billion from the deficit. Also, the tax reform bill that cleared Congress in late September and now awaits President Reagan's signature is estimated to increase government revenues by $11 billion.
The reconciliation measure's savings have been questioned, even by its authors, who admit it contains a large dose of accounting gimmickry that will reduce its savings to no more than a few billion dollars.
Even so, the OMB-CBO report said, the combined savings from the reconciliation and tax measures will bring the deficit below the $154 billion threshold and possibly close to the $144 billion target.
"A number of legislative actions ... are currently under way that, if enacted as expected, would reduce the estimated budget deficit for 1987 below $154 billion" and avoid automatic spending cuts, the joint report said.
Yesterday's notice was required by a section of the Gramm-Rudman law that survived June's Supreme Court ruling that invalidated the measure's main enforcement mechanism for keeping budget deficits within targeted levels.
Under the law, CBO and OMB take several "snapshot" estimates of federal deficits during the year, with the August measurement used to determine what action should be taken.
See GRAMM-RUDMAN / page 34

IBM To Unveil Small Mainframe Series

Move Seen As An Attempt To Recapture Share Of Market Lost To DEC

By Edward R. Silverman, Investor's Daily

NEW YORK — International Business Machines Corp. today is expected to release a new series of small mainframe computers that would bolster its position on the midrange market where it's lost ground against Digital Equipment Corp.
Word of the product introduction has caused a stir in the industry because it marks the first time IBM will market midsize machines that can run the same software as its larger and older mainframe computers, the System-370 line, which is used by large corporations.
Although IBM commands the lion's share of the markets for larger mainframe and personal computers, its hold on customers using midsize machines, or minicomputers, has been lessened by DEC's VAX product line. Analysts have attributed DEC's success in the past two years to its ability to offer a complete line of computers — from small workstations to high-powered minicomputers — all running the same software.
The new computers could give IBM "substantial penetration into DEC's accounts," said Marty Gruhn, who follows IBM for the Sierra Group, a Massachusetts firm. "DEC's been very successful pitching systems that all can run the same operating system. It's a very defensive and very aggressive move. DEC is pushing its minicomputers up and IBM is pushing its mainframes down."
Gruhn added that a recent survey found 10% of the information managers in Fortune 500 companies prefer DEC equipment, making it the second most popular supplier, which may in two years ago the company had little presence in the corporate marketplace.
The new computers, dubbed the "Baby 4300s" by industry watchers, extend IBM's existing 4300 line of midsized mainframes. IBM wouldn't comment, but they're expected to cost much less, with base prices between $20,000 and $60,000, versus the
See NEW IBM SERIES / page 34

Inside Daily

NYSE Tables	24	Earnings Reports	22
Market Charts	8	Futures	25,26
Industry Groups	9	Futures Charts	27
Computers & Inds.	...	Mutual Funds	28
Company Profile	34	Preferreds	23
Nat. Mkts Tables	16-18	Credit Markets	30
OTC Tables	19	Industrial News	33
Company News	34	Inside	32
Options	20-22	At The Analysts	33

Reprinted with permission.

Chartcraft, Inc.
1 West Avenue
Larchmont, NY 10538
(914) 834-5181

Investors Intelligence®
Advisory Condensation Service
Less than 25,000 subscribers

Description of the publication:
Investor Intelligence® monitors and condenses the best material from dozens of other newsletters and financial publications. Each issue summarizes investment opinions and sentiment indicators using charts, graphs, and prose.

Investment selections in the publication are determined:
Using fundamental, technical, and other forms of analysis as determined by the investment advisors who are covered by the newsletter.

The track record for the publication, as reported by the publication, is:
Not applicable.

The publication has been published continuously since: 1963

The cost of a subscription is: $108

The number of issues per year is: 26

A HOTLINE telephone service is: Available
Cost for this service: Free with subscription.

The publication can be delivered: Via first class mail

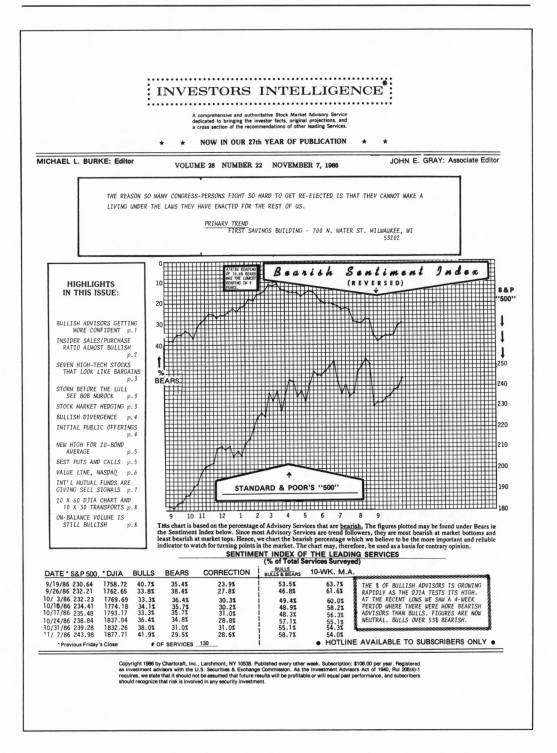

INVESTORS INTELLIGENCE®

A comprehensive and authoritative Stock Market Advisory Service
dedicated to bringing the investor facts, original projections, and
a cross section of the recommendations of other leading Services.

★ ★ NOW IN OUR 27th YEAR OF PUBLICATION ★ ★

MICHAEL L. BURKE: Editor VOLUME 28 NUMBER 22 NOVEMBER 7, 1986 **JOHN E. GRAY: Associate Editor**

THE REASON SO MANY CONGRESS-PERSONS FIGHT SO HARD TO GET RE-ELECTED IS THAT THEY CANNOT MAKE A
LIVING UNDER THE LAWS THEY HAVE ENACTED FOR THE REST OF US.

PRIMARY TREND
FIRST SAVINGS BUILDING - 700 N. WATER ST. MILWAUKEE, WI
53202

HIGHLIGHTS IN THIS ISSUE:

BULLISH ADVISORS GETTING MORE CONFIDENT p.1

INSIDER SALES/PURCHASE RATIO ALMOST BULLISH p.2

SEVEN HIGH-TECH STOCKS THAT LOOK LIKE BARGAINS p.3

STORM BEFORE THE LULL SEE BOB NUROCK p.3

STOCK MARKET HEDGING p.3

BULLISH DIVERGENCE p.4

INITIAL PUBLIC OFFERINGS p.4

NEW HIGH FOR 20-BOND AVERAGE p.5

BEST PUTS AND CALLS p.5

VALUE LINE, NASDAQ p.6

INT'L MUTUAL FUNDS ARE GIVING SELL SIGNALS p.7

20 X 60 DJIA CHART AND 10 X 30 TRANSPORTS p.8

ON-BALANCE VOLUME IS STILL BULLISH p.8

Bearish Sentiment Index (REVERSED)

4/4/86 READING OF 10.6% BEARS WAS THE LOWEST READING IN 9 YEARS.

S&P "500"

% BEARS

STANDARD & POOR'S "500"

THIs chart is based on the percentage of Advisory Services that are **bearish**. The figures plotted may be found under Bears in the Sentiment Index below. Since most Advisory Services are trend followers, they are most bearish at market bottoms and least bearish at market tops. Hence, we chart the bearish percentage which we believe to be the more important and reliable indicator to watch for turning points in the market. The chart may, therefore, be used as a basis for contrary opinion.

SENTIMENT INDEX OF THE LEADING SERVICES
(% of Total Services Surveyed)

DATE * S&P 500	* DJIA	BULLS	BEARS	CORRECTION	BULLS BULLS & BEARS	10-WK. M.A.
9/19/86 230.64	1758.72	40.7%	35.4%	23.9%	53.5%	63.7%
9/26/86 232.21	1762.65	33.8%	38.4%	27.8%	46.8%	61.6%
10/ 3/86 232.23	1769.69	33.3%	36.4%	30.3%	49.4%	60.0%
10/10/86 234.41	1774.18	34.1%	35.7%	30.2%	48.9%	58.2%
10/17/86 235.48	1793.17	33.3%	35.7%	31.0%	48.3%	56.3%
10/24/86 238.84	1837.04	36.4%	34.8%	28.8%	57.1%	55.1%
10/31/86 239.28	1832.26	38.0%	31.0%	31.0%	55.1%	54.3%
11/ 7/86 243.98	1877.71	41.9%	29.5%	28.6%	58.7%	54.0%

* Previous Friday's Close   # OF SERVICES 130

THE % OF BULLISH ADVISORS IS GROWING RAPIDLY AS THE DJIA TESTS ITS HIGH. AT THE RECENT LOWS WE SAW A 4-WEEK PERIOD WHERE THERE WERE MORE BEARISH ADVISORS THAN BULLS. FIGURES ARE NOW NEUTRAL. BULLS OVER 53% BEARISH.

● HOTLINE AVAILABLE TO SUBSCRIBERS ONLY ●

Copyright 1986 by Chartcraft, Inc., Larchmont, NY 10538. Published every other week. Subscription: $108.00 per year. Registered as investment advisors with the U.S. Securities & Exchange Commission. As the Investment Advisors Act of 1940, Rul 206(4)-1 requires, we state that it should not be assumed that future results will be profitable or will equal past performance, and subscribers should recognize that risk is involved in any security investment.

Reprinted with permission.

The Kiplinger Washington Editors, Inc.   **The Kiplinger Tax Letter**
1729 H St., N.W.   Concentrated Education Service
Washington, D.C. 20006   100,000 to 250,000 subscribers
(202) 887-6400

Description of the publication:
> The Kiplinger Tax Letter is a bi-weekly report covering current tax developments such as Treasury regulations, IRS rulings, legislative issues, court decisions, and legal interpretations. Written with the layman in mind, the letter also includes analyses and practical suggestions to help subscribers cope with the impact of these tax changes on their business and personal affairs.

Investment selections in the publication are determined:
> Not applicable.

The track record for the publication, as reported by the publication, is:
> Not applicable.

The publication has been published continuously since: 1925

The cost of a subscription is: $42

The number of issues per year is: 26

A HOTLINE telephone service is: Not Available

The publication can be delivered: Via second class mail

It is also worth mentioning that:
> The Kiplinger Washington Editors, Inc. also publishes several other investment publications, including:
> - The Kiplinger Washington Letter;
> - The Kiplinger Agriculture Letter;
> - The Kiplinger California Letter;
> - The Kiplinger Florida Letter;
> - The Kiplinger Texas Letter; and,
> - Changing Times Magazine.

THE KIPLINGER TAX LETTER

Circulated biweekly to business clients since 1925—Vol. 61 No. 22

THE KIPLINGER WASHINGTON EDITORS

1729 H St., N.W., Washington, D.C. 20006 Tel: 202-887-6400

Cable Address: Kiplinger Washington D C

Dear Client: Washington, Oct. 31, 1986.

Year-end planning is in a familiar setting. For the fourth time
in six years, tax rates in the year ahead are below those in current year.
Rates drop across the board...from a 50% top this year to 38½% next year.

We're devoting this Letter to helping you reduce your personal tax
for this year and next, the total amount of tax you pay for the two years.
Our main emphasis will be on the changes made by the new tax law.
Though mostly taking effect in 1987, they affect what you do this year.

Normally, you defer income when rates are scheduled to fall.
But this time around, it may not pay to defer all income you can.
Income from capital gains will be taxed more heavily next year...
a top of 28% compared with a 1986 peak of 20%. If you are below the top,
then the lower your tax in 1986, the bigger the tax hike on gains in 1987.
Thus, taking gains this year makes more sense in some situations:
Assets you plan to sell in a year or two ought to be sold in 1986
when 60% of your long-term gain is excluded from the regular income tax.
Also appreciated bonds near maturity or likely to be called soon.

But investors for the long haul are better off holding securities
instead of selling and buying them back quickly (the wash-sale rule nixes
deductions for losses within 30 days of a purchase, doesn't affect gains).
Ditto for owners of mutual funds...won't gain much by buying back
because they still would be taxed on any gains that the funds pay them.
Appreciated assets bought since June 30, 1986 also should be held
until 1987 when rates are lower. Short-term gains will remain fully taxed
in both years, but the top rate falls to 38½% in 1987 (it's 50% in 1986).

Buying back makes more sense the bigger your existing profit is.
Also, the more shares or units that are involved (lower sales cost, etc.),
the less time you plan to hold the asset and the higher your state taxes.
Bear in mind that with buybacks, you must pay income tax on gains.
If the proceeds are fully reinvested, the tax must come from other funds.

Three alternatives to your taking gains are worth considering:
Giving long-term assets to charity. You can deduct the full value
without appreciation being taxed. Each dollar saves you up to 50¢ of tax.
But carryovers of donations since Aug. 15, too large to be fully deducted
this year, are subject to the alternative minimum tax beginning next year.
Or giving assets to children who sell them this year and are taxed
on gain at their rate, which is below yours this year and theirs in 1987.
And retaining appreciated assets until death is still sound...
especially for elderly taxpayers or those who are ill. They should sell
only if required by non-tax reasons...pre-death appreciation will escape
income tax. Only gain after death is hit with income tax when heirs sell.
Does not affect estate tax...appreciated assets, cash from a sale
or any property bought with the cash would be part of the eventual estate.

COPYRIGHT 1986 THE KIPLINGER WASHINGTON EDITORS, INC.
QUOTATION NOT PERMITTED. MATERIAL MAY NOT BE REPRODUCED IN WHOLE OR IN PART IN ANY FORM WHATSOEVER

Reprinted with permission.

The Kiplinger Washington Editors, Inc.   The Kiplinger Washington Letter

1729 H St., N.W.   Topical Education Service
Washington, D.C. 20006   250,000 to 500,000 subscribers
(202) 887-6400

Description of the publication:
The Kiplinger Washington Letter is a concise, weekly briefing on business trends. Each issue includes analyses, forecasts, and judgments as to what the future holds for: government policies and programs; politics; legislation; employment; wages; union plans; prices; interest rates; investments; and foreign affairs. The publication is designed to be useful for both business and personal planning.

Investment selections in the publication are determined:
Not applicable.

The track record for the publication, as reported by the publication, is:
Not applicable.

The publication has been published continuously since: 1923

The cost of a subscription is: $48

The number of issues per year is: 52

A HOTLINE telephone service is: Not Available

The publication can be delivered: Via second class mail

It is also worth mentioning that:
The Kiplinger Washington Editors, Inc. also publishes several other investment publications, including:
- The Kiplinger Tax Letter;
- The Kiplinger Agriculture Letter;
- The Kiplinger California Letter;
- The Kiplinger Florida Letter;
- The Kiplinger Texas Letter; and,
- Changing Times Magazine.

THE KIPLINGER WASHINGTON LETTER

Circulated weekly to business clients since 1923—Vol. 63, No. 44

THE KIPLINGER WASHINGTON EDITORS

1729 H St., N.W., Washington, D.C. 20006 Tel: 202-887-6400

Cable Address: Kiplinger Washington D C

Dear Client: Washington, Oct. 31, 1986.

Sure, the trade situation is starting to look a little better, but it will take YEARS to climb out of the deep hole we're in.

<u>Focus in '87 will be on halting the loss of U.S. competitiveness</u> around the world...a series of moves designed to strengthen our economy. <u>Reagan and Congress will be FORCED to act</u> on the trade problems because there has already been severe damage, and much more is in store. Plain fact is, Reagan will lose control unless he takes the initiative, jumps out in front before Congress grabs the ball and runs away with it.

<u>Major trade legislation will pass next year</u> after a rough battle. At a minimum, it'll let Reagan enter a round of talks with other nations to expand world trade by easing up on tariffs, quotas and other barriers. <u>A flood of protectionist proposals</u> will surge through Congress... to keep out imports that compete unfairly with hard-pressed industries.

<u>Legislation will include breaks for business.</u> Less red tape on export licensing. Also rejiggering of the bribery and antitrust laws so that U.S. firms won't be so badly handicapped in overseas competition. And curbs on the use of World Bank loans that subsidize export business.

<u>Reagan will fight extreme protectionism</u> but yield a few points. He'll probably accept some strengthening of rules for limiting imports that injure U.S. industries and for retaliating against those countries that keep out imports of American goods. Congress wants surer action. <u>Tougher enforcement of existing laws</u> also is likely from now on. By using his powers more fully, Reagan probably can head off legislation that he considers damaging to the principles of expanding world trade. <u>And look for closer scrutiny of foreign investment</u> in the U.S. Especially in such sensitive lines as supercomputers, banking & finance. There's growing concern about the long-term implications of such deals. Even the White House feels that the present approach is too free & easy.

<u>"Competitiveness" will be the buzzword</u> in the coming debate. It's true that our dismal trade record in recent years is due in part to unfair tactics of other countries and overvaluation of the dollar. But a more basic cause is the failure of American industry to keep pace with foreigners on productivity, costs, innovation, quality and service. <u>Even high-tech lines are falling behind</u>...imports exceed exports. More than jobs and profits are at stake...nat'l security can be weakened. <u>Reagan wants to rely mainly on business</u> to solve the problem... keeping gov't on the sidelines. Still, he'll accept a limited gov't role in working with industry to stay ahead in semiconductors and other lines. And he'll set up a permanent trade center here to promote U.S. goods. <u>Democrats will push broader programs</u>...using the need to compete as a peg for aid to education, R&D, profit sharing and even public works.

COPYRIGHT 1986 THE KIPLINGER WASHINGTON EDITORS, INC.
QUOTATION NOT PERMITTED. MATERIAL MAY NOT BE REPRODUCED IN WHOLE OR IN PART IN ANY FORM WHATSOEVER

Reprinted with permission.

Dow Theory Forecasts, Inc.
7412 Calumet Avenue
Hammond, IN 46324
(219) 931-6480

The Low Priced Stock Survey®
Investment Advisory Bulletin
Number of subscribers is not available

Description of the publication:
The Low Priced Stock Survey® features attractive low-priced stocks trading primarily in the over-the-counter market.

Investment selections in the publication are determined:
Using fundamental and technical analysis.

The track record for the publication, as reported by the publication, is:
Not available.

The publication has been published continuously since: May 1980

The cost of a subscription is: $82

The number of issues per year is: 26

A HOTLINE telephone service is: Not Available

The publication can be delivered: Via first or second class mail

It is also worth mentioning that:
Dow Theory Forecasts Inc. publishes several other newsletters covering a variety of topics.

THE LOW PRICED STOCK SURVEY®

A SURVEY OF TODAY'S LOW PRICED STOCKS

THAT COULD BE TOMORROW'S LEADERS

Biotechnology Issues Jar NASDAQ Market

September 15, 1986   **Vol. 7, No. 19**

Biotechnology stocks took a sharp tumble last week that jarred the NASDAQ market. Overall, a number of these former highfliers have backed off around 50% in recent weeks, a major switch from the sharp run-ups in price that these issues enjoyed earlier this year. These stocks had been bid up by investors to excessive price-earnings ratios and were prime candidates for sharp sell-offs. This sell-off by the biotechnology group has some positive implications, however. By letting off some of the speculative fervor that had been building in the stock market, this pullback helps lay the groundwork for a future rally by the NASDAQ issues.

Diagnostic Products has been a good performer for subscribers but could be vulnerable to a pullback in price should the retreat of the biotechnology issues spill over to related sectors. This manufacturer of diagnostic test kits has chalked up good gains in the bottom line in recent quarters, boosted by new products, a softer dollar, and greater penetration of the domestic market. Prospects for future quarters appear promising, and the stock remains a good growth holding.

LyphoMed gave back some of its earlier gains when the biotechnology issues took their tumble. This pharmaceutical concern has an outstanding record of growth — revenues have increased more than tenfold over the past five years while profits have risen to $0.27 per share from $0.01 per share during that time — and should show further gains. The company continues to introduce new products, a factor that bodes well for earnings in future quarters. Investors should use any further weakness in this issue as a buying opportunity.

New Brunswick Scientific Co., after rising to a new 52-week high of $13⅜, has pulled back in price recently. This manufacturer of biological shakers and other equipment for the biotechnology field reported a good turnaround in profitability in the June quarter following some earlier sluggishness in the bottom line. The stock offers an attractive selection at current prices and is one of the safer ways to profit from the long-term growth of the biotechnology field.

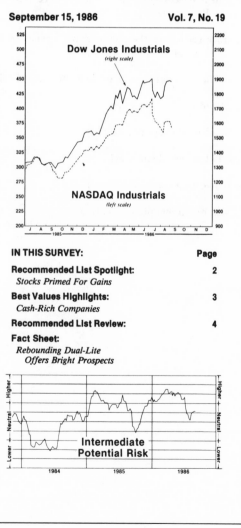

IN THIS SURVEY: **Page**

Recommended List Spotlight: 2
Stocks Primed For Gains

Best Values Highlights: 3
Cash-Rich Companies

Recommended List Review: 4

Fact Sheet:
*Rebounding Dual-Lite
Offers Bright Prospects*

Reprinted with permission.

Wiesenberger Financial Services
Division of Warren, Gorham & Lamont
1 Penn Plaza
New York City, NY 10119
(212) 971-5000

Management Results®
Statistical Service
Number of subscribers is not available

Description of the publication:
 Management Results® is a fifteen page, quarterly update on the long-term performance of over 700 mutual funds and 35 closed-end investment companies, arranged alphabetically and categorized by the investment objectives of the funds.

Investment selections in the publication are determined:
 By periodically reviewing all major mutual funds.

The track record for the publication, as reported by the publication, is:
 Not applicable.

The publication has been published continuously since: 1940

The cost of a subscription is: $100

The number of issues per year is: 4

A HOTLINE telephone service is: Not Available

The publication can be delivered: Via first class mail

It is also worth mentioning that:
 Wiesenberger Financial Services publishes several other investment publications covering mutual funds.

Wiesenberger Investment Companies Service
MANAGEMENT RESULTS [R]

COVERING THE PERIOD ENDING SEPTEMBER 1986

ASSETS GROW TO RECORD HIGHS DESPITE DROP IN THIRD QUARTER PERFORMANCE

Billions of dollars flowed into the bond and income funds (including government bond funds) during the third quarter, both in terms of new money and from the shifting of assets from the equity funds, to bring the total net assets of the 735 funds tabulated here to a record $326.8 billion, up from $314.5 billion at the end of June. The reallocation of resources and the erosion of the value of their shares brought assets of the common stock funds to $110.2 billion, down from $121.5 billion at the end of the previous quarter.

The Dow Jones Industrial Average, best of the market yardsticks, lost 5.7 per cent and the Standard & Poor's 500-Stock Index lost 7.0 per cent during the quarter, trimming year-to-date gains to 17.4 per cent and 12.3 per cent, respectively. The nation's mutual funds gained on the market during the quarter losing an average 2.8 per cent, with 307 or 42 per cent posting gains, but still trailing the market over the nine-month period registering average gains of 11.4 per cent. Funds investing in gold mining issues made a strong recovery, gaining an average 34.1 per cent for the period.

The funds, on average, continued to outpace the market over the 10¾ year period, with the maximum capital gains funds remaining well in the lead, increasing 553.4 per cent. The average of the 337 funds with this long a history gained 395.8 per cent, while the Standard & Poor's 500-Stock Index rose 326.2 per cent and the Dow Jones Industrial Average gained 263.5 per cent. Over the 5¾ year period, only the International funds and the Balanced group of funds outpaced the market, gaining 158.3 per cent and 152.2

PERFORMANCE SUMMARY

MUTUAL FUNDS

No. of Funds		Total Net Assets ($ million)	% Change in Net Assets per Share			% Yield
			9 Mos. 1986	3rd Qtr. 1986	5¾ Years	10¾ Years
79	Max Capital Gains	27,669.9	7.8	− 11.4	93.7	553.4	1.3
189	Long-Term Growth	45,977.5	9.7	− 8.6	109.1	426.5	1.9
64	Growth & Income	31,284.1	12.4	− 5.7	121.7	360.6	3.2
19	Balanced	4,347.0	13.3	− 2.7	152.2	321.2	4.9
17	Income-Com Stk	5,263.3	7.0	− 3.0	114.9	448.7	3.6
55	Income-Flexible	19,012.2	10.2	− 0.8	137.9	310.3	7.8
89	Income-Sen Secs	35,242.4	9.8	0.7	129.6	219.4	9.7
27	Specizd-Canadian	14,100.8	32.6	4.4	158.3	413.5	1.1
11	Specizd-Gold & Prec Metals	1,877.8	34.4	34.1	− 1.9	305.3	2.5
23	Specizd-Industry	4,589.5	10.9	− 7.2	95.3	346.1	2.3
39	Specizd-Gov't Sec	78,960.4	8.5	2.9	113.0	149.3	9.4
112	Spec-Tax-Exempt	57,723.3	12.6	4.4	108.7	1.0	7.1
5	Specizd-Tech	399.3	2.1	− 10.3	69.9	389.2	0.6
6	Specizd-Other	387.4	12.9	0.6	1.0	1.0	4.4
735	Average	326,834.9	11.4	− 2.8	115.0	395.8	4.6

CLOSED-END COMPANIES

No. of Funds		% Disc.	% Change in Net Assets per Share			% Yield
			9 Mos. 1986	3rd Qtr. 1986	5¾ Years	10¾ Years
8	Diversfd Inv Co Avg.	7.4	11.0	− 6.6	103.0	395.0	2.6

MARKET INDICATORS

	9 Mos. 1986	% Change 3rd Qtr. 1986	5¾ Years	10¾ Years
Dow Jones Industrial Avg.*	17.4	− 5.7	144.9	263.5
S&P 500-Stock Index*	12.3	− 7.0	122.1	326.2

*Market Indicators are calculated on a total return basis.

WIESENBERGER MUTUAL FUND INDEXES

	Value 9/30/86	9 Mos. 1986	3rd Qtr. 1986	5¾ Years	10¾ Years
Growth	1,386.75	10.8	− 8.6	94.9	332.4
Growth/Income	1,265.79	14.6	− 5.6	134.5	369.1
Income	1,340.47	13.6	− 2.4	154.6	346.3
Balanced	949.03	13.3	− 2.7	150.0	321.4

12/31/58 = 100.00; data on total return basis

per cent, respectively, while the DJIA was up 144.9 per cent.

Over the longer periods, there were few changes in the complement of top performers, although the

Continued on page 14

The data contained on the following pages supplements the information on management performance of open-end investment companies (mutual funds) and of closed-end investment companies contained in INVESTMENT COMPANIES, the basic reference manual in the Wiesenberger Investment Companies Service.

This is a record of what management accomplished with the money at its disposal; it is not an illustration of shareholder results, since the percentage changes are based on net assets per share and thus do not allow for sales charges on mutual funds, nor for fluctuations in closed-end discounts and premiums, nor for brokerage commissions. For the mutual funds, it is assumed that all capital gains and income dividends were reinvested in additional shares. The closed-end funds assume that all capital gains distributions were accepted in shares. Income dividends are included in the figures shown, as an essential part of overall performance; they are treated as having been taken in cash. For the mutual funds, the "yield" is based on dividends from investment income in the previous 12 months related to the current offering price; in the case of the closed-end companies, dividends on the same basis are related to market price. In both cases, adjustments have been made to reflect the effect of capital gains distributed.

Management results should be considered in the light of each company's objectives and investment policy. Similar results should not be expected from companies whose investment policies and portfolio emphasis may differ widely. The mutual funds listed here are grouped alphabetically in various classifications; the closed-end funds are divided into diversified, nondiversified and specialized companies, and senior securities funds.

Mutual funds in general do not fall into completely homogeneous groups. Rather, they cover a graduated range of emphasis on capital growth, income, and relative price stability, or risk. Exactly where to draw distinguishing lines is, at best, a matter of opinion and frequently may be of little long-term significance. Objectives shown represent the judgment of the Editors as to the individual investor requirements for which the policies of specific funds appear most suited. While these objectives are the same as those stated by many of the funds, this is not true in all instances.

Categories reflect recent policies and characteristics. We have footnoted those funds where a change of policy or management has occurred. These changes should be considered in evaluating longer-term performance data.

As noted above, income dividends have been included in the computation of performance figures. "Yield," therefore, is NOT an additional element in overall results but is already a part of it. It is shown separately, as one indication of objective and policy. The figures are not, of course, a representation of future income results.

IMPORTANT—The explanation above is an essential part of the tabulation that follows.

Copyright © 1986 by Warren, Gorham & Lamont Inc., 1633 Broadway, 23rd Floor, New York, N.Y. 10019. All rights reserved. Reproduction strictly prohibited.

NO PART OF THIS REPORT CAN BE REPRODUCED IN ANY FORM OR THROUGH ANY COPYING DEVICE OR INCLUDED IN ANY INFORMATION RETRIEVAL SYSTEM WITHOUT THE EXPRESS WRITTEN PERMISSION OF THE COPYRIGHT PROPRIETOR. VIOLATIONS OF THIS RESERVATION CAN RESULT IN CRIMINAL SANCTIONS AND CIVIL DAMAGES.

Reprinted with permission.

The Institute for Econometric Research

3471 North Federal Highway
Ft. Lauderdale, FL 33306
(800) 327-6720

Market Logic®
Investment Advisory Bulletin
Less than 25,000 subscribers

Description of the publication:
MarketLogic® is a full service investment advisory newsletter providing complete guidance on what stocks to buy and sell and when to buy and sell them in the market cycle. Every issue includes features on: market timing; stock recommendations and follow ups on prior recommendations; industry group rankings; economic forecasts; market indicator and seasonality patterns; insider trading signals; option recommendations and follow ups on prior recommendations; mutual fund selections; stock index futures; total return market indices; gold price predictions; tax strategies for investors; and a column entitled "Investor's Digest"—a review of over $10,000 worth of other investment advisory service predictions.

Investment selections in the publication are determined:
Using fundamental and technical analysis.

The track record for the publication, as reported by the publication, is:
The average change of all 60 stocks previously recommended for purchase and subsequently sold is +139%, an annual gain of +49%. The average change of the additional 36 stock previously recommended for purchase but not yet sold is +465%, an average annual gain of +33%.

The publication has been published continuously since: 1975

The cost of a subscription is: $95

The number of issues per year is: 24

A HOTLINE telephone service is: Available
Cost for this service: Free with subscription.

The publication can be delivered: Via first class mail

It is also worth mentioning that:
- A two-issue trial subscription to this newsletter is available at no charge.
- A 400-page book, "Stock Market Logic," (over 200,000 copies sold) is also available.
- The Institute for Econometric Research also publishes several other newsletters covering a variety of topics.

MARKET LOGIC®

from THE INSTITUTE FOR ECONOMETRIC RESEARCH
3471 NORTH FEDERAL HIGHWAY, FORT LAUDERDALE, FLORIDA 33306
NORMAN G. FOSBACK, PRESIDENT   **GLEN KING PARKER, CHAIRMAN**

Issue No. 279   October 3, 1986

INSIDE MARKET LOGIC

Sentiment indicators improve; market forecasts
  higher 2

Western Pacific soars amidst looming takeover
  battle. *Maxxam* gets takeover bid, too, but
  stock steady. *Federal Express* jumps as company zaps its Zap program 3

Tax reform act a mixed blessing to investors;
  creates renewal opportunity 5

AXP, FDX calls near expiration 6

Gold model bearish 7

See the enclosed letter for
your current confidential
Hot Line number.

CURRENT FORECASTS
(From The Institute's Econometric Models of the U. S. Stock Market)

Projections of Standard & Poor's 500 Index:

Three Months:	17%	HIGHER
Six Months:	29%	HIGHER
One Year:	28%	HIGHER
Two Years:	1%	LOWER
Three Years:	23%	HIGHER
Five Years:	27%	HIGHER

Projections of the NYSE Total Return Index:

Three Months:	14%	HIGHER
Six Months:	26%	HIGHER
One Year:	28%	HIGHER
Two Years:	13%	LOWER
Three Years:	20%	LOWER
Five Years:	13%	HIGHER

The Major Trend Model is BULLISH at 1.45

SUMMARY & RECOMMENDATION

Secondary stocks withstood the early September collapse much better than the blue chips and have modestly outpaced them on the recovery. Broad market strength confirms our array of bullish monetary and technical indicators, and points to higher prices ahead. With the average stock off less than 5% from its all-time high of four weeks ago, there is no reason to disturb our 100% invested position.

CURRENT POSITION

The September "massacre" shaved 161 points off the Dow Industrials in just six trading days, and left most market participants expecting a lot more action on the downside. Instead, prices stabilized, and some groups are now actually higher than before the break began. Notable in this regard is the Dow Jones Transportation Average, which has already topped its early-September peak and moved within striking distance of the all-time high it established last spring. This is hardly "bear market" action.

Stocks have not been fundamentally cheap for some time, but the Federal Reserve's policy of aggressive monetary ease has kept interest rates trending down — and that was all that was needed to sustain the bull market. With the economy still soft, especially in the manufacturing sector, it is hard to imagine the Fed tightening up at this point. This assures a continuing monetary and interest rate climate favorable to higher stock prices.

Just as importantly, there is now enough popular pessimism about the market's near-term course, and even about whether the bull market has ended, to provide the base for another good rally. In this environment, the appropriate strategy is to be fully invested in our recommended Master Portfolio stocks.

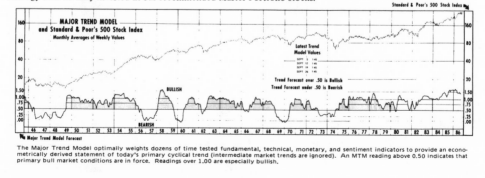

The Major Trend Model optimally weights dozens of time tested fundamental, technical, monetary, and sentiment indicators to provide an econo-metrically derived statement of today's primary cyclical trend (intermediate market trends are ignored). An MTM reading above 0.50 indicates that primary bull market conditions are in force. Readings over 1.00 are especially bullish.

Reprinted with permission.

Moody's Investors Service
99 Church Street
New York City, NY 10007
(212) 553-0300

Moody's® Handbook of Common Stocks
Statistical Service
Number of subscribers is not available

Description of the publication:
Moody's® Handbook of Common Stocks presents a one page historical and financial description on about 900 New York and American Stock Exchange listed companies. Each listing includes:
- a chart depicting trading prices and volume;
- a table highlighting quarterly dividend and earnings information;
- an overview of the company's main lines of business;
- a summary of recent corporate developments;
- a table of selected income and balance sheet items; and,
- various other pertinent corporate information.

Investment selections in the publication are determined:
By periodically reviewing a subset of securities.

The track record for the publication, as reported by the publication, is:
Not applicable.

The publication has been published continuously since:	1956
The cost of a subscription is:	$135
The number of issues per year is:	4
A HOTLINE telephone service is:	Not Available
The publication can be delivered:	Via fourth class mail

It is also worth mentioning that:
Moody's Investors Service publishes several other investment publications covering a variety of topics.

INTERNATIONAL BUSINESS MACHINES CORPORATION

LISTED	SYM.	LTPS•	STPS•	IND. DIV.	REC. PRICE	RANGE (52-WKS.)	YLD.
NYSE	IBM	104.6	89.6	$4.40•	132	162 - 122	3.3%

HIGH GRADE. AGGRESSIVE RESEARCH AND STRONG MARKETING SUGGEST THAT OUTSTANDING GROWTH WILL CONTINUE OVER THE LONG TERM.

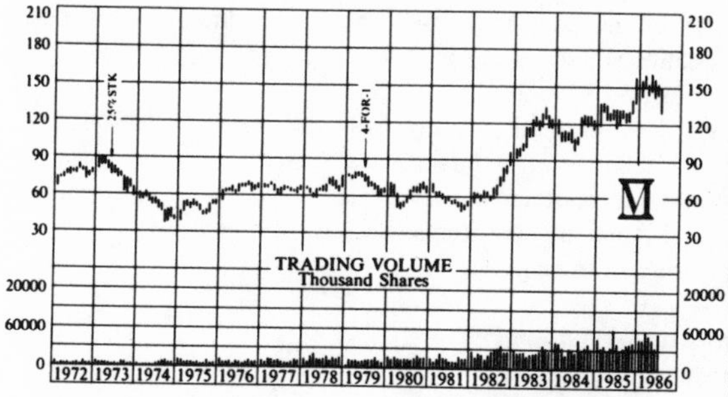

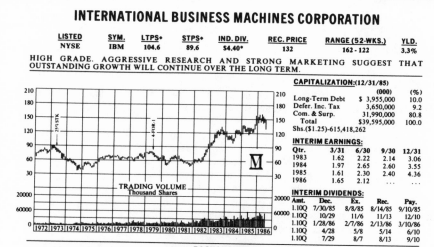

CAPITALIZATION:(12/31/85)

	(000)	(%)
Long-Term Debt	$ 3,955,000	10.0
Defer. Inc. Tax	3,650,000	9.2
Com. & Surp.	31,990,000	80.8
Total	$39,595,000	100.0

Shs.($1.25)-615,418,262

INTERIM EARNINGS:

Qtr.	3/31	6/30	9/30	12/31
1983	1.62	2.22	2.14	3.06
1984	1.97	2.65	2.60	3.55
1985	1.61	2.30	2.40	4.36
1986	1.65	2.12	...	...

INTERIM DIVIDENDS:

Amt.	Dec.	Ex.	Rec.	Pay.
1.10Q	7/30/85	8/8/85	8/14/85	9/10/85
1.10Q	10/29	11/6	11/13	12/10
1.10Q	1/28/86	2/7/86	2/13/86	3/10/86
1.10Q	4/28	5/8	5/14	6/10
1.10Q	7/29	8/7	8/13	9/10

BACKGROUND:

IBM's operations are mainly in the field of information handling systems, equipment and services. Products include data processing machines and systems, telecommunications systems and products, information distributors, office systems, typewriters, copiers, education and testing materials and related supplies and services. Most products are both leased and sold through IBM's worldwide marketing organizations. Selected products are distributed through authorized dealers and remarketers. The 1985 revenue breakdown is as follows: sales, 68.8%; rentals, 8.2%; and services, 23.1%. Foreign operations contributed 39% to earnings. Growth has been vigorous and dividends have been paid since 1916.

RECENT DEVELOPMENTS:

Reflecting the ongoing slump in capital expenditure in North America, net income for the quarter ended 6/30/86 fell 8% to $1.31 billion from a year ago. Earnings were aided by strong sales overseas. Sales rose 7% to $12.27 billion. Revenues from service rose 26% to $3.40 billion while rental revenue fell 36% to $680 million. For the six months, net income fell 3% to 2.32 billion while sales rose 6%. Rental revenue fell 34% to $1.49 billion which was offset by a 29% increase in service revenue to $6.61 billion.

PROSPECTS:

Near-term results should improve, however, domestic sales may lag the strong growth of the rest of, the world. Continued high growth in earnings is expected from the software segment. Furthermore, new product introductions such as the Token-Ring network, more powerful computers, and high-capacity disk storage will also aid results. The 3090 series of mainframes is expected to positively affect earnings over the near term. The continuing interest in telecommunications ensures IBM of an area for growth over the long term.

STATISTICS:

YEAR	GROSS REVS. ($mill.)	OPER. PROFIT MARGIN %	RET. ON EQUITY %	NET INCOME ($mill.)	WORK CAP. ($mill.)	SENIOR CAPITAL ($mill.)	SHARES (000)	EARN. PER SH.$	DIV. PER SH.$	DIV. PAY. %	PRICE RANGE	P/E RATIO	AVG. YIELD %
76	16,304	25.0	18.8	2,398	5,838	275	602,780	3.99	2.00	50	72⅛ - 55⅞	16.0	3.1
77	18,133	25.7	21.6	2,719	4,864	256	589,884	4.58	2.50	54	71½ - 61⅛	14.4	3.7
78	21,076	25.8	23.1	3,111	4,511	287	583,240	5.32	2.88	54	77½ - 58⅜	12.8	4.2
79	22,863	22.9	20.1	3,011	4,406	1,589	583,594	5.16	3.44	67	80½ - 61⅛	14.1	5.0
80	26,213	21.9	21.6	3,562	3,399	2,099	583,807	6.10	3.44	56	72¾ - 50⅜	10.1	5.6
81	29,070	20.7	18.2	3,308	2,983	2,669	592,294	5.63	3.44	61	71½ - 48⅜	10.7	6.0
82	34,364	23.4	22.1	4,409	4,805	2,851	602,406	7.39	3.44	47	98 - 55⅝	10.4	4.5
83	40,180	23.9	23.6	5,485	7,763	2,674	610,725	9.04	3.71	41	134¼ - 92¼	12.5	3.3
84	45,937	24.5	24.8	6,582	10,735	3,269	612,686	10.77	4.10	38	128½ - 99	10.6	3.6
85	**50,056**	**22.4**	**20.5**	**6,555**	**14,637**	**3,955**	**615,418**	**10.67**	**4.40**	**41**	**158½ - 117⅜**	**12.9**	**3.2**

•Long-Term Price Score — Short-Term Price Score; See page 4a. STATISTICS ARE AS ORIGINALLY REPORTED. Adjusted for 4-for-1 stock split 5/79.

INCORPORATED:
June 16, 1911 – New York

PRINCIPAL OFFICE:
Armonk, N Y 10504
Tel.: (914) 765-1900

ANNUAL MEETING:
Last Monday in April

NUMBER OF STOCKHOLDERS:
798,152

TRANSFER AGENT(S):
Company Office, New York, N Y
Trust General du Canada
National Trust Co., Ltd.

REGISTRAR(S):
Morgan Guaranty Trust Co., N.Y.
First National Bank, Chicago, Ill.
Montreal Trust Co.

INSTITUTIONAL HOLDINGS:
No. of Institutions: 1,686
Shares Held: 314,116,081

OFFICERS:
Chairman
J.R. Opel
Vice-Chairman
P.J. Rizzo
Pres. & Ch. Exec. Off.
J.F. Akers
Treasurer
J.W. Rotenstreich
Secretary
J.H. Grady

Reprinted with permission.

Moody's Investors Service
99 Church Street
New York City, NY 10007
(212) 553-0300

Moody's® Handbook of OTC Stocks
Statistical Service
Number of subscribers is not available

Description of the publication:
> Moody's® Handbook of OTC Stocks presents a one page historical and financial description on about 600 over-the-counter companies. Each listing includes:
> - a chart depicting trading prices and volume;
> - a table highlighting quarterly dividend and earnings information;
> - an overview of the company's main lines of business;
> - a summary of recent corporate developments;
> - a table of selected income and balance sheet items; and,
> - various other pertinent corporate information.

Investment selections in the publication are determined:
> By periodically reviewing a subset of securities.

The track record for the publication, as reported by the publication, is:
> Not applicable.

The publication has been published continuously since: 1981

The cost of a subscription is: $90

The number of issues per year is: 4

A HOTLINE telephone service is: Not Available

The publication can be delivered: Via fourth class mail

It is also worth mentioning that:
> Moody's Investors Service publishes several other investment publications covering a variety of topics.

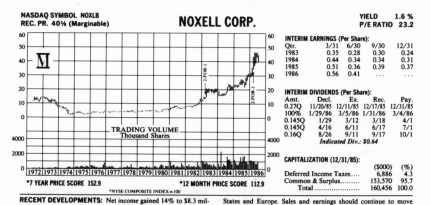

NASDAQ SYMBOL NOXLB
REC. PR. 40⅛ (Marginable)

NOXELL CORP.

YIELD 1.6 %
P/E RATIO 23.2

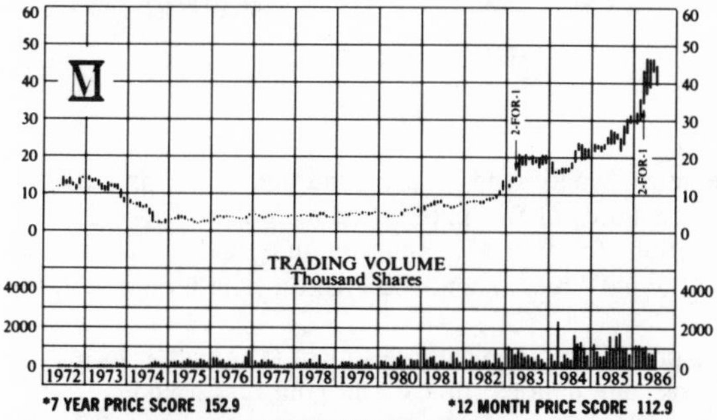

***7 YEAR PRICE SCORE 152.9** ***12 MONTH PRICE SCORE 112.9**

*NYSE COMPOSITE INDEX=100

INTERIM EARNINGS (Per Share):

Qtr.	3/31	6/30	9/30	12/31
1983	0.35	0.28	0.30	0.24
1984	0.44	0.34	0.34	0.31
1985	0.51	0.36	0.39	0.37
1986	0.56	0.41	...	...

INTERIM DIVIDENDS (Per Share):

Amt.	Decl.	Ex.	Rec.	Pay.
0.27Q	11/20/85	12/11/85	12/17/85	12/31/85
100%	1/29/86	3/5/86	1/31/86	3/4/86
0.145Q	1/29	3/12	3/18	4/1
0.145Q	4/16	6/11	6/17	7/1
0.16Q	8/26	9/11	9/17	10/1

Indicated Div.: $0.64

CAPITALIZATION (12/31/85):

	($000)	(%)
Deferred Income Taxes....	6,886	4.3
Common & Surplus.........	153,570	95.7
Total	160,456	100.0

RECENT DEVELOPMENTS: Net income gained 14% to $8.3 million for the quarter ended 6/30/86. Sales increased 10% to $101.7 million. For the six months net income was up 12% to $19.4 million on a 9% increase in sales to $217.3 million. Income before income taxes was up 14% from the prior year six month period. The effective income tax rate for the first half of 1986 was 48.8% versus last year's annual rate of 48.9%. The higher sales benefited mainly from unit growth of Cover Girl cosmetics in the United States and Europe. Sales and earnings should continue to move higher. Aggressive marketing programs, coupled with investments in future manufacturing capacity will aid results. The ongoing emphasis on new product development will contribute to growth. The Company plans to introduce a major new cosmetic line, Clarion, in September. Clarion cosmetics are UltraPure, Fragrance-Free, and sensitivity-tested. The line initially will include 85 items including facial make-up, eye make-ups, and lipsticks.

BUSINESS

NOXELL CORPORATION'S principal line of business is the development, manufacture, and marketing of mass packaged consumer items which are distributed through the Corporation's sales force or brokers directly to food, drug, variety, military, and mass-merchandising stores, and to wholesale distributors. The Corporation's principal products include skin care and shave cream **(Noxzema)**, cosmetics **(Cover Girl)**, a household cleaner **(Lestoil)**, and a new skin moisturizer **(RainTree)**.

Major domestic manufacturing and warehousing facilities are located in Cockeysville, Maryland. Sales in Canada are made through a subsidiary, The Noxzema Chemical Company of Canada, Ltd., which operates its own manufacturing and warehousing facilities in Ontario. Sales in certain foreign countries are made from facilities of contract manufacturers, licensed manufacturers, and the corporation's own warehousing and packaging site located at Wakefield, Yorkshire, in the U.K.

In the United States and Canada, the Company's products are distributed through food, drug, variety, department, mass merchandise and specialty stores.

ANNUAL EARNINGS AND DIVIDENDS PER SHARE

	1985	1984	1983	1982	1981	1980	1979
Earnings Per Share.	**1.63**	**1.43**	**1.17**	**[1] 0.94**	**0.87**	**0.76**	**0.67**
Dividends Per Share	**0.50**	**0.42**	**[2] 0.35**	**0.29**	**0.26**	**0.23**	**0.20**
Dividend Payout %	**30.7**	**29.4**	**29.9**	**30.9**	**29.9**	**30.3**	**29.9**

Note: 100% stk. div., 3/86.
[1] Before extraordinary credit [2] Also a 100% stk. div. 3/83.

ANNUAL FINANCIAL DATA

RECORD OF EARNINGS (IN MILLIONS):							
Net Sales	382.1	349.5	304.3	261.9	233.1	204.2	179.7
Costs and Expenses	315.1	293.8	260.2	226.0	201.9	176.6	154.6
Depreciation	6.2	5.1	4.1	3.1	2.6	2.4	1.9
Operating Profit	60.9	50.6	40.0	32.8	29.5	25.2	23.2
Income Before Taxes	63.3	52.7	42.5	34.2	30.9	27.2	25.2
Income Taxes	30.9	24.4	19.3	15.7	14.0	12.5	11.8
Net Income	32.4	28.3	23.2	[1]18.5	16.9	14.7	13.3
Aver. Com. Shs. (000)	19,901	19,816	19,934	19,660	19,536	19,988	20,248

[1] Bef. extraordinary credit $1,539,000

BALANCE SHEET (IN MILLIONS):							
Cash, Securities, Etc.	43.7	12.6	27.6	23.3	5.1	8.0	16.9
Net Receivables	32.6	28.5	23.7	20.5	20.0	17.2	15.0
Inventories	49.5	49.4	44.0	37.6	39.0	32.2	26.6
Gross Property	92.4	85.7	73.3	58.6	50.8	44.5	38.4
Depreciation Reserve	31.3	25.6	21.9	18.4	15.9	14.8	13.9
Net Stockholders' Equity	153.6	128.9	116.1	98.9	84.9	74.1	65.7
Total Assets	200.2	161.5	157.4	127.1	108.8	94.9	86.3
Total Current Assets	135.0	97.0	101.2	85.9	68.5	59.9	60.2
Total Current Liabilities	39.7	27.7	38.2	25.8	22.2	19.4	19.1
Net Working Capital	95.3	69.3	63.0	60.1	46.3	40.6	41.1
Yr.-End Common Shs. (000)	20,668	19,800	19,882	19,804	19,704	19,484	19,844
STATISTICAL RECORD:							
Operating Profit Margin %	15.9	14.5	13.1	12.5	12.7	12.3	12.85
Book Value Per Share	7.24	6.29	5.56	4.76	4.31	3.77	3.28
Return on Equity %	21.1	22.0	20.0	18.7	19.9	19.8	20.2
Return on Assets %	16.2	17.5	14.7	14.6	15.5	15.5	15.4
Average Yield %	1.9	2.1	2.1	2.7	3.5	4.1	4.1
P/E Ratio	19.4-13.4	17.0-11.0	17.9-10.4	15.0-8.2	10.2-6.8	9.0-5.6	8.4-5.8
Price Range	31⅝-21⅞	24¼-15¾	21-12⅛	14⅛-7¾	8⅞-5⅞	6⅞-4¼	5⅝-3⅞

Statistics are as originally reported.

OFFICERS:
G. L. Bunting, Jr., Chmn. & C.E.O.
M. L. Hathaway, Pres. & C. O.O.
R. W. Lindsay, Vice Pres. & Sec.
R. W. Pierce, Vice Pres.-Fin.

INCORPORATED: Maryland, Sept. 17, 1917

PRINCIPAL OFFICE: 11050 York Road
Hunt Valley, Md 21030

TELEPHONE NUMBER: (301) 628-7300

NO. OF EMPLOYEES: 1,100

ANNUAL MEETING: In March

SHAREHOLDERS: 3,919

INSTITUTIONAL HOLDINGS:
No. of Institutions: 116
Shares Held: 6,318,295

REGISTRAR(S):

TRANSFER AGENT(S): Equitable Bank, N. A., Baltimore, MD 21201

Reprinted with permission.

The Institute for Econometric Research

3471 North Federal Highway
Ft. Lauderdale, FL 33306
(800) 327-6720

Mutual Fund Forecaster®

Investment Advisory Bulletin
50,000 to 100,000 subscribers

Description of the publication:

Mutual Fund Forecaster® is the most widely read mutual fund publication in America. Designed for use by the general public, the features of this publication include:
- risk ratings and profit projections for over 450 equity mutual funds;
- a "buy," "best buy," and "avoid" recommendation list for long-term investors and switch-fund traders to follow;
- a directory of mutual funds providing complete investment information for each fund;
- features on penny stock funds, international funds, and gold funds; and,
- a Fund Timing Index and a special econometric model providing a one year market forecast.

Other topics regularly featured are mutual fund new issues, closed-end funds, and follow-up comments on prior recommendations.

Investment selections in the publication are determined:

By concentrating on the specialty topic area of: Mutual Funds.

The track record for the publication, as reported by the publication, is:

Not available.

The publication has been published continuously since: 1985

The cost of a subscription is: $49

The number of issues per year is: 12

A HOTLINE telephone service is: Available

Cost for this service: Free with subscription.

The publication can be delivered: Via first class mail

It is also worth mentioning that:
- A two-issue trial subscription to this newsletter is available at no charge.
- A 400-page book, "Stock Market Logic," (over 200,000 copies sold) is also available.
- The Institute for Econometric Research also publishes several other newsletters covering a variety of topics.

MUTUAL FUND FORECASTER®

Profit Projections and Risk Ratings for Traders and Investors

Issue No. 21   October 2, 1986

BEST BUY RECOMMENDATIONS
(Mutual funds with highest Profit Projection for each Risk Rating)

Risk Rating	Mutual Funds	1-Year Profit Project.	Combined Sales & Red. Fees
Very High	Engex (closed-end)	+46%	None
High	Gemini II - Capital (closed-end)	+41%	None
Medium	Fidelity OTC	+43%	3.1%
Low	Legg Mason Value Trust	+33%	None
Low	Federated Stock Tr. (banks only)	+34%	None
Very Low	Evergreen Total Return	+30%	None
Very Low	Safeco Income	+30%	None
Very Low	Selected American Shares	+30%	None

BUY RECOMMENDATIONS
(Mutual funds with high Profit Projections in each Risk Rating)

Risk	Mutual Funds	Profit	Sales
Very High	AIM - Weingarten Equity	+37%	5.0%
Very High	AIM - Constellation Growth	+37%	5.0%
Very High	Z-Seven (closed-end)	+35%	None
Very High	Twentieth Century Ultra	+35%	1.0%
Very High	New England Life Growth	+34%	8.6%
Very High	Seligman Capital	+34%	9.3%
Very High	Twentieth Century Growth	+34%	None
High	ABT Midwest Emerging Growth	+37%	9.3%
High	Twentieth Century Select	+36%	None
High	Mass. Finl. - Emerging Growth	+34%	7.8%
High	Founders Mutual	+34%	None
High	Fidelity Freedom	+34%	None
High	Weiss Peck Greer - Tudor	+34%	1.0%
High	Amev Growth	+33%	9.3%
Medium	Fidelity Magellan	+40%	3.1%
Medium	IDS Strategy Aggressive	+38%	5.3%
Medium	Century Shares	+36%	None
Medium	Neuberger - Manhattan	+35%	None
Medium	United Income	+35%	9.3%
Medium	Venture - New York Venture	+35%	9.3%
Low	Phoenix Growth	+33%	9.3%
Low	Merrill Lynch Basic Value	+32%	6.9%
Low	Evergreen Fund	+31%	None
Low	Vanguard-World U.S. Growth	+31%	None
Very Low	Pilgrim Magnacap	+30%	7.8%
Very Low	Oppenheimer Equity Income	+30%	9.3%
Very Low	Liberty - American Leaders	+29%	None
Very Low	AARP Growth and Income	+29%	None
Very Low	Acorn Fund	+29%	2.0%
Very Low	Fid. Qual. Div. (corp. only)	+29%	None
Very Low	Ivy Growth	+29%	None
Very Low	Fidelity Equity - Income	+29%	2.0%
Very Low	Colonial Fund	+29%	7.2%

See the enclosed letter for your current confidential Hot Line number.

New Highs Forecast

After the last issue, the market quickly broke out to the predicted new record high. An uptick in interest rates, coupled with institutional program trading, then set off a correction marked by a record one-day loss. This correction is a short-term reaction within an ongoing bull market and is no reason to disturb our policy of being fully invested in recommended funds.

Higher stock prices are ahead. In fact, we expect new record highs in 1986 *and* in 1987. Investors and traders alike should take advantage of price weakness to institute or add to mutual fund positions.

What To Do Now

INVESTORS: The "Best Buys" in the very high and high Risk Rating categories — *Engex* and *Gemini II - Capital Shares* respectively — are unchanged from last issue. The Risk Rating on *Fidelity OTC* has increased from low to medium and the fund is now the "Best Buy" in the medium risk category. It replaces *Fidelity Magellan*, which nonetheless retains a strong "Buy" recommendation in the medium risk group.

Two new "Best Buys" in the low Risk Rating group are *Federated Stock Trust*, which is available through bank trust departments only, and *Legg Mason Value Trust*, which can be purchased by individual investors. Finally, five funds with very low Risk Ratings are tied with +30% Profit Projections. In the event of ties, our "Best Buy" goes to no-load funds which, in this case, are *Evergreen Total Return, Safeco Income*, and *Selected American Shares*.

TRADERS: The current market correction is a buying opportunity. Switch-fund traders should own no-load and low-load funds with top Profit Projections. These funds are: *Twentieth Century Select, Century Shares, Neuberger - Manhattan, Twentieth Century Ultra, Twentieth Century Growth, Federated Stock Trust, Founders Mutual, Fidelity Freedom,* and *Weiss Peck Greer - Tudor.* Two closed-end funds currently selling at discounts to their net asset values, *Engex* and *Gemini II - Capital Shares,* are also attractive.

GOLD: The Gold Price Model is graded bearish and all gold and hard-asset funds are rated "Avoid."

A Service of The Institute for Econometric Research, 3471 North Federal Highway, Fort Lauderdale, Florida 33306
Norman G. Fosback, President • Telephone: 305-563-9000 • Glen King Parker, Chairman

Reprinted with permission.

Newsletter Management Corp.

10076 Boca Entrada Blvd.
P.O. Box 3007
Boca Raton, FL 33431
(305) 483-2600

Mutual Fund Profit Alert

Investment Advisory Bulletin
Number of subscribers is not available

Description of the publication:
Mutual Fund Profit Alert is designed for readers with little or no technical background. The newsletter's regular features include: a "Best Buy of the Month"; four model portfolios with ratings, profit potential, and specific buy/sell/hold/avoid recommendations; switching advice; and continuous performance updates. The newsletter also reviews specific forecasts and recommendations for gold, penny, international, closed-end and specialized mutual funds.

Investment selections in the publication are determined:
Using fundamental analysis for selection, technical analysis for timing.

The track record for the publication, as reported by the publication, is:
Not available.

The publication has been published continuously since: July 1986

The cost of a subscription is: $119

The number of issues per year is: 12

A HOTLINE telephone service is: Available
Cost for this service: Free with subscription.

The publication can be delivered: Via bulk/third class mail

It is also worth mentioning that:
Newsletter Management Corp. publishes several other newsletters covering a variety of topics.

Mutual Fund
Profit Alert

Volume 1, Number 4   October 1986

Market Forecast...

Economy's Vital Signs Strengthen, Boding Well for Stock Market

I think the economy finally may be strengthening in response to the Federal Reserve Board's easy-money policy. Unemployment is down, and factory orders are up. These early signs suggest the current economic expansion will continue well into 1987, pushing stock prices up -- haltingly -- along the way.

The stock market's wild gyrations promise to persist. In part, these reflect the effect of the options and futures markets. Another factor is the historically high level of share prices.

More important, the stock market -- ever since inflation worsened markedly during the Lyndon Johnson administration -- has developed two warring personalities: an economic side and a monetary side.

On the one hand, stock buyers want corporate earnings growth to be nurtured by vigorous economic expansion because, historically, share prices have followed earnings. On the other hand, the market fears that a strong economy will drive up inflation and interest rates. This is why share prices sometimes fall on news of economic acceleration. A variation of this occurs when the stock market reacts to the favorable economic reports indirectly and declines -- knee-jerk fashion -- in response to sliding bond prices.

These days, Wall Street demands that the economy walk a tightrope between growth that's strong enough to rekindle inflation and growth weak enough to foreshadow a recession. Moreover, at current market levels, the schizophrenia is compounded by high-altitude sickness.

Sorting it all out isn't an easy task for the busy individual investor. I'll try to help.

From the Trading Room...

Fund Managers Forecast New Highs for Stock Prices

The bull market is in a new phase and share prices will push to new record highs, predicts chief investment officer James McClure of Oppenheimer Management. "Over the coming months, we will be concentrating on stock selection rather than broad market movements," adds McClure, who is responsible for all seven Oppenheimer stock funds. "The issue is not when to invest, but where."

Copyright 1986 by Barclay Publishing Corp., 40 Wall St., Suite 2124, New York, NY 10005

Reprinted with permission.

The Institute for Econometric Research

3471 North Federal Highway
Ft. Lauderdale, FL 33306
(800) 327-6720

New Issues®

Investment Advisory Bulletin
Less than 25,000 subscribers

Description of the publication:
New Issues® is an investor's guide to initial public offerings, the largest such service in the country. Each edition of New Issues contains: a calendar of all newly registered initial public offerings; in-depth analyses of up to 20 forthcoming offerings; specific buy recommendations on the one or two best positioned offerings; a Penny Stock and Low-Priced Stock Selector featuring attractive low-priced issues; and a summary of all previous recommendations. A buy/sell list is also maintained.

Investment selections in the publication are determined:
By concentrating on the specialty topic area of: New Issues.

The track record for the publication, as reported by the publication, is:
Not available.

The publication has been published continuously since: 1978

The cost of a subscription is: $95

The number of issues per year is: 12

A HOTLINE telephone service is: Available
Cost for this service: Free with subscription.

The publication can be delivered: Via first class mail

It is also worth mentioning that:
- A two-issue trial subscription to this newsletter is available at no charge.
- A 400-page book, "Stock Market Logic," (over 200,000 copies sold) is also available.
- The Institute for Econometric Research also publishes several other newsletters covering a variety of topics.

NEW ISSUES®

The Investor's Guide to Initial Public Offerings

Norman G. Fosback, Editor • *3471 North Federal Highway, Fort Lauderdale, Florida 33306* • *Glen King Parker, Publisher*

"Rambo" Producer Eyes Public Offering

Issue No. 98	October 10, 1986

What to Do Now

New issues activity is heating up. The 174 offerings in our Calendar of Forthcoming Offerings and Penny Stock Digest (Pages 3-5) is an all-time record. Our featured buy recommendation this month is **Carolco Pictures** (see story at right). We also recommend purchase of **WTD Industries** (Page 8). The featured low-priced stock selection this month is **Saztec** (Page 6).

See the enclosed letter for your current confidential Action Line number.

New Issue Scene: Big Deals in Pipeline

Offerings in the pipeline for the balance of 1986 include both the largest domestic new issue and the largest international new issue in history.

Domestically, **Coca-Cola's** bottling operation will make a $1.5 billion initial public offering, easily topping the largest domestic new issue to date, **Henley Group's** $1.1 billion sale last May.

Ford Motors' $658 million 1956 offering held the record for nearly three decades, but in the past twelve months that record has successively passed to the **Rockefeller Center Properties** $750 million offering, the **Firemans Fund** $825 million issue, the **First Australia Prime Income Fund** $855 million deal, and finally to Henley, which will now surrender the record to Coca-Cola.

The largest initial public offering worldwide was **British Telecom's** late 1984 sale of $4.6 billion of shares, $280 million of which were sold in the U.S. Now, **British Gas** is slating a $10 billion offering, including approximately $1 billion of shares in the United States. British Gas supplies fuel to 16 million customers in the British Isles, each of which will be guaranteed the right to buy at least $375 of the new issue. The exact timing of the British Gas offering is yet to be determined, but the U.S. portion will be underwritten by Prudential-Bache, Salomon Brothers, and Merrill Lynch. We will have a detailed analysis in a forthcoming issue.

Another well-known corporate name in this month's huge offerings calendar is [Continued on Page 4]

CAROLCO PICTURES will offer 6,500,000 shares between $11 and $13 in November. The shares are recommended as a short-term, high-risk, speculative holding.

The hottest-selling motion picture series in the world during the last three years has been "Rambo." Early next month, Carolco Pictures, whose predecessor entities produced these popular movies, hopes to make its own hot offering, a 6½-million-share underwriting scheduled to be priced between $11 and $13 a share.

Carolco was formed in April 1986 to continue the motion picture financing and production activities of

Mario Kassar and Andrew Vajna, producers of the two Rambo movies. The first of those flicks, "First Blood," earned worldwide box office receipts of $120 million. The sequel, "Rambo: First Blood Part II," grossed $270 million. Both pictures starred Sylvester Stallone. Carolco is currently negotiating, and expects to finalize, an agreement

CAROLCO PICTURES INC. — 9255 Sunset Blvd., Suite 910, Los Angeles, CA 90069; (213) 273-0284.

Offering of 6,500,000 common shares @$11-$13 per share; 4,500,000 shares (69%) by the company and balance by existing stockholders, who are selling 8% of their shares. Managing Underwriters: Paine Webber, 1221 Avenue of the Americas, NY 10020; (212) 730-8500; Drexel Burnham Lambert, 60 Broad St., NY 10004; (212) 480-6000; Bear, Stearns, 55 Water St., NY 10041; (212) 952-5000; and Furman Selz Mager Dietz & Birney, 230 Park Avenue, NY 10069; (212) 309-8200.

After the offering, 29,975,000 shares will be outstanding and book value will equal $3.19 per share. Latest 12-month revenues are $2.68 per share for a Price/Revenues ratio of 4.1-4.8, and 12-month earnings equal $1.40 per share for a P/E of 8-9. No dividend. 34 employees. Proposed symbol: CARC.

Year Ended	Revenues	Net Income	Prof. Marg.	Earn./Sh.
Dec. 31, 1981	$ 3,450,000	$ 71,000	2.1%	---
Dec. 31, 1982	12,869,000	5,892,000	45.8%	$ .24
Dec. 31, 1983	18,940,000	7,784,000	41.1%	.32
Dec. 31, 1984	4,006,000	566,000	14.1%	.02
Dec. 31, 1985	82,639,000	44,007,000	53.3%	1.80*
Six Months Ended:				
June 30, 1985	$24,601,000	$13,512,000	54.9%	$ .55
June 30, 1986	22,566,000	11,579,000	51.3%	.47†

(*$1.47 pro forma; †$.39 pro forma; on shares to be outstanding.)

under which it will secure Stallone's acting talents for five motion pictures between 1988 and 1993, and his production abilities for five additional pictures.

Carolco plans to release two or three high-budget (greater than $20 million production cost) motion pictures annually. One of the first of these will be "Rambo III," once again starring Sylvester Stallone. The picture is scheduled for [Continued on Page 2]

Reprinted with permission.

Newsletter Management Corp.

New Issues Alert
Investment Advisory Bulletin
Number of subscribers is not available

10076 Boca Entrada Blvd.
P.O. Box 3007
Boca Raton, FL 33431
(305) 483-2600

Description of the publication:
New Issues Alert reports on significant new stock offerings coming available using a unique 100-point rating system to evaluate each issue on both fundamental and technical factors. Regular features include an aftermarket performance table and an in-depth look at the newsletter's "Pick of the Month." The newsletter is also filled with news, quotes, investment caveats, insights, strategies, and regulations worthy of note.

Investment selections in the publication are determined:
Using fundamental analysis for selection, technical analysis for timing while concentrating on the specialty topic areas of: New Issues.

The track record for the publication, as reported by the publication, is:
Not available.

The publication has been published continuously since: March 1984

The cost of a subscription is: $119

The number of issues per year is: 12

A HOTLINE telephone service is: Available
Cost for this service: Free with subscription.

The publication can be delivered: Via first class mail

It is also worth mentioning that:
Newsletter Management Corp. publishes several other newsletters covering a variety of topics.

NEW ISSUES ALERT

Volume 3, Number 11
November 1986

The Insiders Report on the Month's Strongest New Stock Offerings

Four Reasons Why the New Issues Market Will Remain Strong

1. The 1986 Tax Reform Act has effectively eliminated real estate (other than historic rehabs) and most tax shelters as viable investments. The only tax shelter still available is a working interest in oil and gas production, and that requires that you share unlimited risk (essentially as a general partner instead of sharing limited risk as a limited partner). Now there's a strong incentive to invest in stocks. Incidentally, you will be free to trade without regard to tax-related limitations on holding time, because of the cancellation of the long-term capital-gain advantage. That will bring more people into the market and will tend to create more demand in the new issues aftermarket.

2. The inflation rate is at its lowest level in 25 years and probably will remain low for the next several months. High oil prices in the 1970s raised it to the double-digit area, but it's unlikely OPEC will choose to make any catastrophic moves; it will instead move slowly to increase prices as the economies of the countries it serves heat up. This will cause interest rates to remain at current levels (or go down a bit more) for at least a few more months before beginning to rise again. This in turn will result in a continuation of the overall bull market (with some corrections here and there) and will prolong the even greater bull market in new issues.

3. Investment in stocks, as a percentage of household (and personal trust) assets, is lower now than it has been in the last 40 years (according to charts published by Ned Davis Research, Atlanta, GA). This means stocks are under-owned, resulting in pressure toward more stock investment. This in turn will create more demand in the new issues aftermarket.

4. In addition to these overall considerations, there is the fact that new issues provide an opportunity to get in on the ground floor of real growth situations. The organizers of the companies NIA covers have invested not only their money but also a great deal of "sweat equity." They have usually worked hard to create viable opportunities, and investors can share the benefits of their innovations. NIA's main task is to identify which companies have created the most valid opportunities. You are investing at the effective beginning in most cases -- at a time when the input of public funds may propel a company to attractive profits.

We'll probably see another severe correction before the bullish movement resumes, but bear in mind that the corrections experienced by the overall market do not affect new issues and their aftermarket very much. This segment is truly a market of stocks rather than a stock market. That's why it's so important to make careful selections on the basis of fundamental considerations. (See my comments in NIA, October 1986, Page 1.) I feature every NIA selection on the Penny Stock/New Issues Hotline early enough to permit you to investigate before the issue begins to trade. The hotline also advises you when to close out issues. If you're not presently a subscriber to the PS/NI Hotline, call 800/231-2310; from Florida, call 800/433-5565.

Copyright 1986 by NIA Corp., 82 Wall St., Suite 1105, New York, NY 10005.

Reprinted with permission.

The New Mutual Fund Advisor
Box 1975
Davis, CA 95617
(916) 756-6112

The New Mutual Fund Advisor
Investment Advisory Bulletin
Less than 25,000 subscribers

Description of the publication:
The New Mutual Fund Advisor is an action oriented newsletter identifying:
- low risk/high return mutual funds;
- bull/bear market timing signals;
- economic and technical indicators; and,
- bond and stock funds.

As well as maintaining a buy/sell list, the newsletter also is a topical education service covering a wide range of investment topics.

Investment selections in the publication are determined:
Using fundamental analysis for selection, technical analysis for timing.

The track record for the publication, as reported by the publication, is:
Not available.

The publication has been published continuously since: February 1986

The cost of a subscription is: $45

The number of issues per year is: 10

A HOTLINE telephone service is: Not Available

The publication can be delivered: Via first class mail

It is also worth mentioning that:
- Subscribers may call in at anytime to discuss investment issues, though this availability is not designed to be a "Hotline" service.
- The Editor of this newsletter currently has a book available: *The New Mutual Fund Investment Advisor,* Probus Publishing (1985).

THE
NEW MUTUAL FUND ADVISOR

VOLUME 1, NUMBER 8   SEPTEMBER 1986

Portfolio Recommendations

Fund	% Return 1 Year to 7/31/86	July	Risk-Beta	Action
Growth & Income - Lower Risk				
Wellesley	25.8	0.1	0.49	b
Windsor II	27.6	-4.6	0.75	b
Evergreen Total Return	35.2	0.5	0.63	bb
Stratton Mo. Div.	33.1	2.2	0.50	bb
Price Equity Income	NA	-3.9	0.75	b
Safeco Income	24.4	-5.2	0.77	b
Copley	31.2	3.5	0.47	b
Growth - Market Risk and Return				
Fidelity Financial	38.7	-7.1	0.93	b
Fidelity Leisure	43.1	-9.6	0.90	b
Vanguard Service Econ.	26.4	-9.2	0.90	b
Quest for Value	24.0	-5.2	0.67	h
Price International	77.1	5.4	0.66	bb
Vanguard International	75.0	1.8	0.70	b
Income - Lowest Risk, Lower Return				
Nicholas Inc.	16.6	0.5	0.23	b
Price High Yield	19.8	0.1	0.50	b
No. East Inv. Trust	24.5	0.7	0.28	bb
Vanguard High Yield	19.9	0.1	0.28	b
S & P 500	28.4	-5.6	1.0	

bb = best buy   **b = buy**   **w = watch**   **h = hold**   **s = sell**

Current Recommendation:

Continue to hold growth and income funds as the economy unfolds this autumn, Safeco Income is added to our buy list while Fidelity Growth and Income is moved off to a watch status. Continue to buy or retain an international fund. Avoid technology funds and those aggressive funds that hold low capitalization stocks. Retired persons should buy Northeast Investors Trust.

Reprinted with permission.

Standard & Poor's Corporation
25 Broadway
New York City, NY 10004
(212) 208-8000

The Outlook
Investment Advisory Bulletin
Less than 25,000 subscribers

Description of the publication:
  The Outlook is an investment advisory publication that:
  • reports Standard & Poor's stock market investment policy;
  • comments on the investment merits of a wide range of securities;
  • gives advice on individual stocks, including a "Master List of Supervised Stocks" recommended
    for capital gains and income; and,
  • includes articles on special situations, stock groups, economics, industries, options, and other
    subjects of concern to investors.
  The newsletter maintains a buy/sell list of investment securities.

Investment selections in the publication are determined:
  Using fundamental analysis.

The track record for the publication, as reported by the publication, is:
  Not available.

The publication has been published continuously since: 1922

The cost of a subscription is: $219

The number of issues per year is: 52

A HOTLINE telephone service is: Not Available

The publication can be delivered: Via second class mail

It is also worth mentioning that:
  Standard & Poor's Corporation publishes several other investment publications covering a variety
  of topics.

Dividend Increase Candidates

Selected REITs Attractive for Total Return

Master List: Group 2

What You Want to Know About Mutual Funds

In the Limelight

Vol. 58, No. 38   Pages 526-536

October 15, 1986

Standard & Poor's

The Outlook

ANALYZES AND PROJECTS BUSINESS AND MARKET TRENDS

The Market Last Week

The generally firm showing of the broad market despite IBM's sharp decline was notable. The S&P 500 posted a small net gain.

S&P 500 Index	
Close	*Change*
235.48	+ 1.77

The Current Outlook

While the resiliency shown by the market last week was impressive, we would like to see a further period of base-building and testing of the late-September lows. Higher stock prices ultimately lie ahead, but we would not abandon caution just yet.

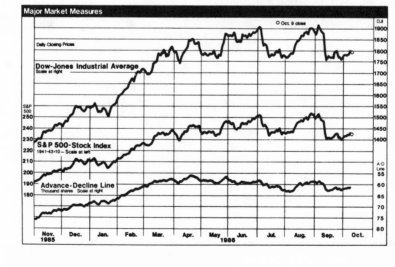

Standard & Poor's Corporation

Reprinted with permission.

Newsletter Management Corp.
10076 Boca Entrada Blvd.
P.O. Box 3007
Boca Raton, FL 33431
(305) 483-2600

Penny Stock Insider
Investment Advisory Bulletin
Number of subscribers is not available

Description of the publication:
Penny Stock Insider provides investors with genuine "insider" advice as well as specific recommendations from a network of highly placed analysts, underwriters, market makers, stockbrokers and other financial insiders who are privy to "behind the scenes" information on low-priced stocks poised for massive gains. Regular features include: "Pick of the Month"; "Hottest Industries"; "Insider Buying and Selling"; news; quotes; and strategies.

Investment selections in the publication are determined:
Using fundamental analysis for selection, technical analysis for timing.

The track record for the publication, as reported by the publication, is:
Not available.

The publication has been published continuously since: March 1986

The cost of a subscription is: $119

The number of issues per year is: 12

A HOTLINE telephone service is: Available
Cost for this service: Free with subscription.

The publication can be delivered: Via bulk/third class mail

It is also worth mentioning that:
Newsletter Management Corp. publishes several other newsletters covering a variety of topics.

Volume 1, Number 8   **October 1986**

Market Pulse: Major Correction Imminent

There is renewed concern on the Street about inflation's increasing, since bonds
have gone down and gold and silver have gone up. Disinflationary stocks, such
as utilities, are weakening. Market leaders, such as pharmaceuticals, are showing some weakness. Many stocks have been hitting their targets and are now
rolling over and beginning to decline, and corporate earnings are not coming in
as well as was expected.

These underlying currents are making the market a bit risky: Witness the record
drop of 86 points in the Dow to 1792 on Sept. 11. That was a record trading
day of 239 million shares, with 226 million going down and only 7 million going
up. The trading index (1 is neutral; less is bullish, more is bearish) went up to
3.04; 1.5 is pretty bearish -- 3.04 is downright bearish! If you have a position
in stocks other than penny stocks, sell in rallies to convert some of your assets
to cash -- up to about 40 percent. Use extreme caution in your investments in
the general market -- I see a major correction coming, perhaps a decline in the
Dow to 1600.

Don't Buy on the Basis of Tips

The easiest way to lose money in this market (and in any market) is to invest on
the basis of tips, no matter how reliable the source. I can't believe how many
readers call me to ask about a stock they purchased because of a tip. Most
stocks that are the subject of hot tips eventually make substantial negative
moves. This is usually the result of an unfavorable set of fundamentals. "In"
stocks also tend to go down, because they are touted until prices reach many
times their book value.

Remember, you can make money in penny stocks regardless of where the Dow is.
The secret is to buy stocks that have good fundamentals. Check them out yourself. I give the address and telephone number of each recommended stock so you
can do just that. Occasionally, as in this issue, I cover situations that have
high risk but substantial potential. I don't pretend they have good normal fundamentals, but I feature them because I think the potential outweighs the risk.
I think they are excellent gambles, but satisfy yourself before putting your
money up!

Most readers answer "no" when I ask them if they applied a stop-loss order when
they bought stock, as I always recommend. Some don't even know what it is.
So I have included a description of stop-loss orders in this issue. For a more-
detailed explanation, see Page 3.

Copyright 1986 by American Stock Market Publications, 82 Wall St., Suite 1105, New York, NY 10005

Reprinted with permission.

Argus Research Corp.
42 Broadway
New York City, NY 10004
(212) 425-7500

Portfolio Selector & Viewpoint
Investment Advisory & Research Bulletins
Less than 25,000 subscribers

Description of the publication:
Portfolio Selector and Viewpoint are monthly publications designed to report highlight specific investment selections and report Argus' investment viewpoint, respectively.

The Portfolio Selector is a monthly fold-out booklet presenting Argus' "Best Buys." Selected common stocks are arranged according to specific investment objectives: Income, Capital Gains & Income, Long-Term Growth, Businessman's Risk, and Emerging Growth. Earnings estimates and key fundamental data are included along with a brief commentary on recommended stocks. The report also features a "Market Outlook" comment, a "Technical View," and the research director's stock selection of the month—"The Director's Choice."

Viewpoint is a monthly, four-page report defining Argus' investment policy and its relationship to economic, political, and market developments. The report also discusses investment strategies for the stock and bond markets and incorporates a tabular update to the stock recommendations carried in the "Portfolio Selector."

Investment selections in the publication are determined:
Using fundamental analysis.

The track record for the publication, as reported by the publication, is:
Not available.

The publication has been published continuously since: 1950

The cost of a subscription is: $390

The number of issues per year is: Each-12

A HOTLINE telephone service is: Available
Cost for this service: Negotiable with subscription.

The publication can be delivered: Via first class mail

It is also worth mentioning that:
Argus Research Corp. also publishes several other investment publications designed for both individual investors and investment professionals covering a wide range of topics. These reports include the:

- Weekly Staff Report
- Weekly Economic Review
- Viewpoint
- Portfolio Selector
- Investment Portfolio Guide
- Investment Analysis
- Energy Update

- Special Analysis
- Special-Theme Report
- Electric Utility Ranking
- Electric Utility Spotlight
- Special Situations Report
- Master List

All of the above reports can be bought separately or purchased as a group for a combined discount price of $125 per month. Of special interest is a premium service available to brokers which allows for an unlimited amount of analyst contact, live conference calls, and research opinions written on the broker's own letterhead.

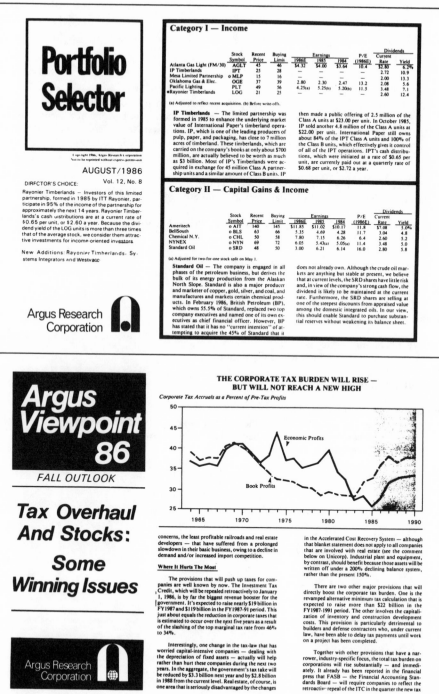

Portfolio Selector

Copyright 1986, Argus Research Corporation
Not to be reprinted without express permission

AUGUST/1986
Vol. 12, No. 8

DIRECTOR'S CHOICE:

Rayonier Timberlands — Investors of this limited partnership, formed in 1985 by ITT Rayonier, participate in 95% of the income of the partnership for approximately the next 14 years. Rayonier Timberlands's cash uistributions are at a current rate of $0.65 per unit, or $2.60 a year. Because the dividend yield of the LOG units is more than three times that of the average stock, we consider them attractive investments for income-oriented investors.

New Additions: Rayonier Timberlands, Systems Integrators and Westvaco

Argus Research Corporation

Category I — Income

	Stock Symbol	Recent Price	Buying Limit	Earnings 1986E	Earnings 1985	Earnings 1984	P/E (1986E)	Dividends Current Rate	Dividends Yield
Atlanta Gas Light (FM/30)	AGLT	45	46	$4.32	$4.00	$3.64	10.4	$2.80	6.2%
IP Timberlands	IPT	25	28	—	—	—	—	2.72	10.9
Mesa Limited Partnership	o MLP	15	16	—	—	—	—	2.00	13.3
Oklahoma Gas & Elec.	OGE	37	39	2.80	2.30	2.47	13.2	2.08	5.6
Pacific Lighting	PLT	49	56	4.25(a)	5.25(b)	5.20(b)	11.5	3.48	7.1
●Rayonier Timberlands	LOG	21	25	—	—	—	—	2.60	12.4

(a) Adjusted to reflect recent acquisition. (b) Before write-offs.

IP Timberlands — The limited partnership was formed in 1985 to enhance the underlying market value of International Paper's timberland operations. IP, which is one of the leading producers of pulp, paper, and packaging, has close to 7 million acres of timberland. These timberlands, which are carried on the company's books at only about $700 million, are actually believed to be worth as much as $3 billion. Most of IP's Timberlands were acquired in exchange for 45 million Class A partnership units and a similar amount of Class B units. IP then made a public offering of 2.5 million of the Class A units at $23.00 per unit. In October 1985, IP sold another 4.8 million of the Class A units at $22.00 per unit. International Paper still owns about 84% of the IPT Class A units and 100% of the Class B units, which effectively gives it control of all of the IPT operations. IPT's cash distributions, which were initiated at a rate of $0.65 per unit, are currently paid out at a quarterly rate of $0.68 per unit, or $2.72 a year.

Category II — Capital Gains & Income

	Stock Symbol	Recent Price	Buying Limit	Earnings 1986E	Earnings 1985	Earnings 1984	P/E (1986E)	Dividends Current Rate	Dividends Yield
Ameritech	o AIT	140	145	$11.85	$11.02	$10.17	11.8	$7.08	5.0%
BellSouth	o BLS	63	66	5.35	4.69	4.28	11.7	3.04	4.8
Chemical N.Y.	o CHL	50	58	7.80	7.15	6.26	6.4	2.60	5.2
NYNEX	o NYN	69	72	6.05	5.43(a)	5.05(a)	11.4	3.48	5.0
Standard Oil	o SRD	48	50	3.00	6.21	6.14	16.0	2.80	5.8

(a) Adjusted for two-for-one stock split on May 1.

Standard Oil — The company is engaged in all phases of the petroleum business, but derives the bulk of its energy production from the Alaskan North Slope. Standard is also a major producer and marketer of copper, gold, silver, and coal, and manufactures and markets certain chemical products. In February 1986, British Petroleum (BP), which owns 55.5% of Standard, replaced two top company executives and named one of its own executives as chief financial officer. However, BP has stated that it has no "current intention" of attempting to acquire the 45% of Standard that it does not already own. Although the crude oil markets are anything but stable at present, we believe that at current levels, the SRD shares have little risk and, in view of the company's strong cash flow, the dividend is likely to be maintained at the current rate. Furthermore, the SRD shares are selling at one of the steepest discounts from appraised value among the domestic integrated oils. In our view, this should enable Standard to purchase substantial reserves without weakening its balance sheet.

Argus Viewpoint 86

FALL OUTLOOK

Tax Overhaul And Stocks: Some Winning Issues

Argus Research Corporation

THE CORPORATE TAX BURDEN WILL RISE — BUT WILL NOT REACH A NEW HIGH

Corporate Tax Accruals as a Percent of Pre-Tax Profits

concerns, the least profitable railroads and real estate developers — that have suffered from a prolonged slowdown in their basic business, owing to a decline in demand and/or increased import competition.

Where It Hurts The Most

The provisions that will push up taxes for companies are well known by now. The Investment Tax Credit, which will be repealed retroactively to January 1, 1986, is by far the biggest revenue booster for the government. It's expected to raise nearly $19 billion in FY1987 and $119 billion in the FY1987-91 period. This just about equals the reduction in corporate taxes that is estimated to occur over the next five years as a result of the slashing of the top marginal tax rate from 46% to 34%.

Interestingly, one change in the tax-law that has worried capital-intensive companies — dealing with the depreciation of fixed assets — actually will help rather than hurt these companies during the next two years. In the aggregate, the government's tax take will be reduced by $3.3 billion next year and by $2.8 billion in 1988 from the current level. Real estate, of course, is one area that is seriously disadvantaged by the changes

in the Accelerated Cost Recovery System — although that blanket statement does not apply to all companies that are involved with real estate (see the comment below on Unicorp). Industrial plant and equipment, by contrast, should benefit because those assets will be written off under a 200% declining balance system, rather than the present 150%.

There are two other major provisions that will directly boost the corporate tax burden. One is the revamped alternative minimum tax calculation that is expected to raise more than $22 billion in the FY1987-1991 period. The other involves the capitalization of inventory and construction development costs. This provision is particularly detrimental to builders and defense contractors who, under current law, have been able to delay tax payments until work on a project has been completed.

Together with other provisions that have a narrower, industry-specific focus, the total tax burden on corporations will rise substantially — and immediately. It already has been reported in the financial press that FASB — the Financial Accounting Standards Board — will require companies to reflect the retroactive repeal of the ITC in the quarter the new tax

Reprinted with permission.

LynaTrace, Inc.
P.O. Box 2133
Pompano Beach, FL 33061-2144
(800) 826-2122

The Professional Investor®
Investment Advisory Bulletin
Less than 25,000 subscribers

Description of the publication:
The Professional Investor® is an eight page publication which forecasts the future direction of the stock market, selects individual stocks, and carries a complete performance record for each stock the newsletter is currently following. In addition, the newsletter: offers advice on options, mutual funds, and stocks; monitors 50 other market letters; and, includes educational articles of investor interest.

Investment selections in the publication are determined:
Using fundamental and technical analysis, with 80% of the emphasis placed on technical.

The track record for the publication, as reported by the publication, is:
Average of +54% annual gain over a 16-year time period.

The publication has been published continuously since: January 1971

The cost of a subscription is: $75

The number of issues per year is: 24

A HOTLINE telephone service is: Available
Cost for this service: Free with subscription.

The publication can be delivered: Via first class mail

It is also worth mentioning that:
- LynaTrace, Inc. arranges, from time to time, to get special discounts on investment books, etc., which are worthwhile for subscribers to have in their own personal libraries.
- The telephone HOTLINE service can best described as a tape recorded update service.

The Financial Magazine Designed To Be Better!

THE PROFESSIONAL INVESTOR ®

Volume 17, Issue 4   *A Financial Magazine Sold By Subscription Or On Newsstands At $15.00 Each.*   October 24, 1986
LYNATRACE, INC.   P.O. BOX 2144   POMPANO BEACH, FL 33061-2144

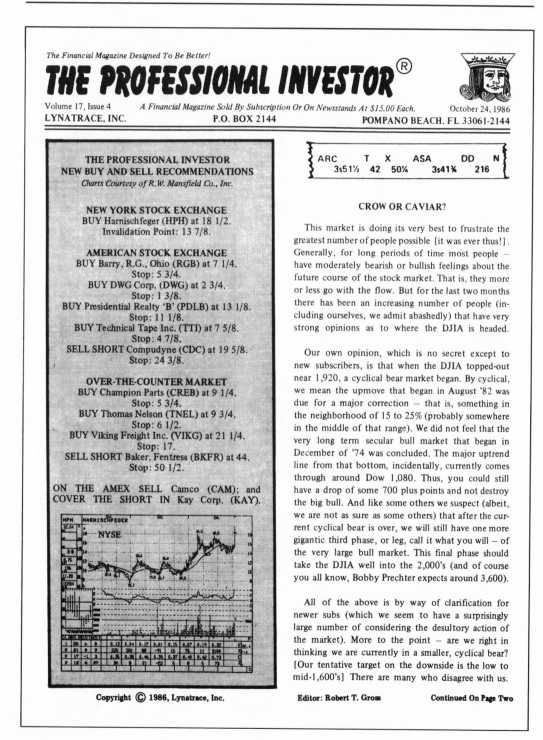

THE PROFESSIONAL INVESTOR
NEW BUY AND SELL RECOMMENDATIONS
Charts Courtesy of R.W. Mansfield Co., Inc.

NEW YORK STOCK EXCHANGE
BUY Harnischfeger (HPH) at 18 1/2.
Invalidation Point: 13 7/8.

AMERICAN STOCK EXCHANGE
BUY Barry, R.G., Ohio (RGB) at 7 1/4.
Stop: 5 3/4.
BUY DWG Corp. (DWG) at 2 3/4.
Stop: 1 3/8.
BUY Presidential Realty 'B' (PDLB) at 13 1/8.
Stop: 11 1/8.
BUY Technical Tape Inc. (TTI) at 7 5/8.
Stop: 4 7/8.
SELL SHORT Compudyne (CDC) at 19 5/8.
Stop: 24 3/8.

OVER-THE-COUNTER MARKET
BUY Champion Parts (CREB) at 9 1/4.
Stop: 5 3/4.
BUY Thomas Nelson (TNEL) at 9 3/4.
Stop: 6 1/2.
BUY Viking Freight Inc. (VIKG) at 21 1/4.
Stop: 17.
SELL SHORT Baker, Fentress (BKFR) at 44.
Stop: 50 1/2.

ON THE AMEX SELL Camco (CAM); and
COVER THE SHORT IN Kay Corp. (KAY).

Copyright © 1986, Lynatrace, Inc.

ARC	T	X	ASA	DD	N
3s51½	42	50¼	3s41¾	216	

CROW OR CAVIAR?

This market is doing its very best to frustrate the greatest number of people possible [it was ever thus!]. Generally, for long periods of time most people — have moderately bearish or bullish feelings about the future course of the stock market. That is, they more or less go with the flow. But for the last two months there has been an increasing number of people (including ourselves, we admit abashedly) that have very strong opinions as to where the DJIA is headed.

Our own opinion, which is no secret except to new subscribers, is that when the DJIA topped-out near 1,920, a cyclical bear market began. By cyclical, we mean the upmove that began in August '82 was due for a major correction — that is, something in the neighborhood of 15 to 25% (probably somewhere in the middle of that range). We did not feel that the very long term secular bull market that began in December of '74 was concluded. The major uptrend line from that bottom, incidentally, currently comes through around Dow 1,080. Thus, you could still have a drop of some 700 plus points and not destroy the big bull. And like some others we suspect (albeit, we are not as sure as some others) that after the current cyclical bear is over, we will still have one more gigantic third phase, or leg, call it what you will — of the very large bull market. This final phase should take the DJIA well into the 2,000's (and of course you all know, Bobby Prechter expects around 3,600).

All of the above is by way of clarification for newer subs (which we seem to have a surprisingly large number of considering the desultory action of the market). More to the point — are we right in thinking we are currently in a smaller, cyclical bear? [Our tentative target on the downside is the low to mid-1,600's] There are many who disagree with us.

Editor: Robert T. Gross

Continued On Page Two

Reprinted with permission.

The Professional Tape Reader
P.O. Box 2407
Hollywood, FL 33022
(305) 923-3733

The Professional Tape Reader®
Investment Advisory Bulletin
Less than 25,000 subscribers

Description of the publication:
The Professional Tape Reader® is a stock market advisory service published twice each month, giving readers eight full pages of charts, investment advice, and information. The newsletter presents forecasts for long and short term market trends, and advice to take advantage of these trends. The newsletter also maintains a buy/sell list highlighting the market's most promising and vulnerable stocks, as well as an unweighted market average and indicator scan.

Investment selections in the publication are determined:
Using technical analysis.

The track record for the publication, as reported by the publication, is:
Not available.

The publication has been published continuously since: 1972

The cost of a subscription is: $250

The number of issues per year is: 24

A HOTLINE telephone service is: Available
Cost for this service: Free with subscription.

The publication can be delivered: Via first class mail*
*Special delivery also available for $50 per year extra.

It is also worth mentioning that:
The Professional Tape Reader will, at no extra charge, send out buy/hold/sell reports for NYSE, ASE,and OTC stocks as determined by its proprietory method of stage analysis. The company also has available a series of eight booklets which comprise a course on technical market analysis.

"The Tape Tells All"

Published & Edited by: *STAN WEINSTEIN*

THE **PROFESSIONAL** TAPE READER ®

RADCAP, Inc.   P.O. Box 2407   Hollywood, Fla. 33022

Issue No. 355   September 12, 1986

FURTHER DETERIORATION

By now it should be obvious why we've urged you to remain in such a cautious and defensive position for the past several weeks. While the crowd has been celebrating each new marginal high in the Dow, the broad market has quietly been deteriorating and heading south almost unnoticed. As we told you last time "for many individual stocks, bear markets have started already....especially in the secondary sector". Now, however, after today's historic drop (the largest point drop in one day in history on the heaviest volume ever), there is nothing quiet about the decline any longer. It looks as if the street is finally taking note of what we've been warning you about all summer—this is a sick and dangerous market—and certainly not one to be 100% invested in on the long side!

After such a shattering decline, the same questions are always asked: Is this selloff a fluke? Is it merely a correction soon to be followed by a move to new highs? Is it time to bargain-hunt among the ruins? Was the decline simply a 'mechanical' move set off totally by the sell programs? To each of those questions, we answer loudly and clearly—NO! Let's therefore work through each trend so you'll see exactly why we feel as we do and how we feel you should deal tactically with the market at this point.

First let's start with the long term pattern which we continue to view far *less* optimistically than most investors and analysts. We continue to feel that the broad market (as measured by the Value Line index of 1700 stocks) topped out in early June and is already in a bear market. This is why few-er and fewer stocks are making new individual highs even when the Dow 30 moves to new marginal highs. And it's also why our NYSE Survey has been acting so poorly. Note how back in the summer of 1982 when we flashed our bull market buy signal, this proprietary gauge was strengthening (A–B) while the Dow continued to head south. This was a clear indication that while the popular averages were still weak and were causing the crowd to be overly pessimistic, the sub-surface technical condition of the market was strengthening. The rest is history as our July 1982 buy signal was followed by one of the great-est advances in history. Now, however, the exact opposite is taking place. While the 30 blue chips made a new marginal high in early July and then another one last week, this excellent forecasting tool was setting a series of lower peaks at each new Dow high (pts. H, I and J). Think about this for a minute. It isn't merely some 'mumbo jumbo' rule of a technician, but rather a common sense concrete fact. Fewer and fewer stocks (we measure every stock on the NY Exchange) are healthy so how can the market put together a broad-based sustainable rally? The answer is simple—it can't until this indicator improves and that's why no rally has really followed through over the past 3 months. To see just how sick this market has become, all we have to do is realize that last spring 90% of all NYSE stocks were healthy by our unique method, but last week, when the Dow hit its new high at 1930, *less than* 50% of all stocks were technically healthy! And to make matters worse, there is even greater weakness on the Amex and OTC markets. On the day when the Dow ran up 38 points to hit its new high, there were actually more stocks hitting new lows than issues hitting new highs Over-the-Counter which is really unbelievable! This is why we warned you so emphatically *not* to become bullish on a new Dow high and why we said "you don't have to be a master technician to know that this is a serious problem and is a clear-cut sign that the Dow is masking an awful lot of sub-surface weakness in the broad market".

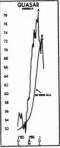

Another sign that the recent rally was a case of 'less than meets the eye' can be seen by studying our chart of Quasar Fund which is acting very poorly as of late. Now don't get us wrong, we aren't 'picking' on Quasar Fund (there are many other funds that look similar). Long term subscribers know that this has been one of our favorite funds over the past 2 years and we've made good money switching with them as their performance has been excellent. Our point is simply that if a fund with such a fine record is now acting so poorly (pt. B was far below pt. A even though pt. B on the Dow was a new high) and has broken below its long term moving

continued on page 8

COPYRIGHT © 1986 RADCAP, INC. Reproduction in whole or in part prohibited except by written permission. All rights reserved.

Reprinted with permission.

The Prudent Speculator	The Prudent Speculator

The Prudent Speculator
P.O. Box 1767
Santa Monica, CA 90406
(213) 395-5275

The Prudent Speculator
Investment Advisory Bulletin
Less than 25,000 subscribers

Description of the publication:

> The Prudent Speculator maintains a buy/sell list of stocks, focusing exclusively on the selection of undervalued common stocks by using a series of fundamental screens. From time to time the newsletter will also recommend stock index puts to hedge portfolios against the risk of a market decline. The newsletter concentrates on fundamental analysis, but employs technical analysis to determine whether the stock market is overbought or oversold. Follow-up advice is provided in every fourth issue of the newsletter covering all stocks previously recommended.

Investment selections in the publication are determined:

> Using fundamental analysis for selection, technical analysis for timing.

The track record for the publication, as reported by the publication, is:

> 1985% gain over nine and one-half years margined, 467% gain over nine and one-half years unmargined.

The publication has been published continuously since: March 1977

The cost of a subscription is: $200

The number of issues per year is: 17

A HOTLINE telephone service is: Not Available

The publication can be delivered: Via first class mail

It is also worth mentioning that:

- The Prudent Speculator will send special market timing bulletins to all subscribers whenever significant buy/sell signals are generated.
- The firm also manages investment accounts (minimum $100,000) for individuals, corporations, pension and retirement plans, IRAs and Keoghs.
- The Prudent Speculator has the best performance record over the six year period ending June 30, 1986, of any newsletter tracked by the authoritative Hulbert Financial Digest of Washington, D.C.

The Prudent Speculator

(213) 395-5275, P.O. Box 1767, Santa Monica, California 90406

TPS 209, October 2, 1986   (213) 395-5275   ISSN 0743-0809

CURRENT APPROACHES

We practice at being lucky. We practice, because "Luck favors the well prepared." There is no certain way to know the future, whether in life or in the stock market. Still, certain probabilities seem to obtain, and if one can discover enough of those probabilities and systematically abide by them, then the chance of catching a desired outcome is enhanced. Common sense, discipline and fundamental analysis are our tools. We keep trying and sharing our conjectures and experience. More we cannot do.

The stock market seems to be at a crossroads. It is oversold and so I expect a rally, although the multi-month correction may well continue on balance for a week or more. BOLD SPECULATORS can take their chances and use margin. I am holding OEX 220 puts for their insurance value. MODERATE SPECULATORS should also hedge portfolios at this time, and might pick up some bargains. CONSERVATIVE INVESTORS should continue to "stand aside," perhaps taking longterm capital gains and also remain hedged. I was wrong in the last issue writing that you need a margin account to buy stock index put options.

REVIEW OF INDEXES	Dow Jones Industrials*	Composite Index*	TPS Portfolio Market Value*	TPS Portfolio Equity Analysis
For the past three weeks:				
Close 9/26/86	1769.69	133.94	$1,497,203	$853,108
Close 9/ 5/86	1899.75	143.89	$1,567,452	$703,235
Changes	-130.06	- 9.95	-$ 49,801^	- $ 50,127^^
Percentages	- 6.85%	- 6.92%	- 3.20%^	- 7.13%^^
For the past 39 weeks:				
Close 12/31/85	1546.67	121.58	$ 877,814	$330,066
Changes	+223.02	+ 12.36	+$ 192,999^	+ $181,705^^
Percentages	+ 14.42%	+ 10.17%	+ 20.17%^	+ 54.85%^^
For the life of TPS:				
Close 3/11/77	947.72	54.72	$ 16,200	$ 8,006
Changes	+822.67	+ 79.22	+$ 525,096^	+ $374,751^^
Percentages	+ 86.87%	+144.77%	+ 466.56%^	+1,985.22%^^

*These "averages" do not include dividends paid during the various periods,
 or reinvestments made with cash generated from tenders and buyouts.
 TPS Portfolio is Al Frank's actual "real time" common stock portfolio.
^Changes reflect adjustments for stocks bought and sold during the periods.
 Equity Analysis accounts for margin expenses, dividends, and paid commissions.
^^Changes reflect adjustments for cash paid in and taken out during the periods.

RECENT STOCK MARKET ACTIVITY

I have not seen such volatility in the stock markets since I started following them in 1969. Of course, today's markets are different beasts than those of 17 years ago, even than those of nine years ago when TPS was started. What can we do in the face of computer programmed arbitrage and trading, which

The Prudent Speculator (TPS) is a stock advisory service produced by Al Frank, an Investment Advisor registered with the Securities & Exchange Commission, and the State of California. Al Frank manages stock portfolios. Information in TPS comes from sources believed reliable, but accuracy is not guaranteed. All material is subject to change without notice. Al Frank or his clients may hold or trade issues recommended or not. Recommendations may not become profitable or equal previous performance. Subscriptions are not assignable: $175, 17-issues; $300, 35-issues; add $10 for overseas airmail.

Reprinted with permission.

Argus Research Corp.
42 Broadway
New York City, NY 10004
(212) 425-7500

Special Situations
Investment Advisory Bulletin
Less than 25,000 subscribers

Description of the publication:
Special Situations is a sixteen page investment advisory bulletin which consolidates the efforts of three other Argus publications (Emerging Growth Stocks, Special Values, and Low-Priced Stocks) into one conveniently organized, monthly report. In addition to an in-depth highlight of one newly recommended stock, each issue also reviews the progress of Argus' two specially selected portfolios: Growth Stocks, and Value Stocks. Each report also contains the results of a computerized "screen" designed to find stocks with outstanding investment characteristics.

Investment selections in the publication are determined:
Using fundamental analysis.

The track record for the publication, as reported by the publication, is:
Not available.

The publication has been published continuously since: 1986

The cost of a subscription is: $390

The number of issues per year is: 12

A HOTLINE telephone service is: Available
Cost for this service: Negotiable with subscription.

The publication can be delivered: Via first class mail

It is also worth mentioning that:
Argus Research Corp. also publishes several other investment publications designed for both individual investors and investment professionals covering a wide range of topics. These reports include the:

- Weekly Staff Report
- Weekly Economic Review
- Viewpoint
- Portfolio Selector
- Investment Portfolio Guide
- Investment Analysis
- Energy Update

- Special Analysis
- Special-Theme Report
- Electric Utility Ranking
- Electric Utility Spotlight
- Special Situations Report
- Master List

All of the above reports can be bought separately or purchased as a group for a combined discount price of $125 per month. Of special interest is a premium service available to brokers which allows for an unlimited amount of analyst contact, live conference calls, and research opinions written on the broker's own letterhead.

SPECIAL SITUATIONS

ARGUS RESEARCH CORPORATION/42 BROADWAY/NEW YORK, N.Y. 10004/(212) 425-7500

ARGUS

INDEPENDENT INVESTMENT RESEARCH SINCE 1934.

October 1986

Copyright 1986, Argus Research Corporation
Not to be reprinted without express permission

In This Issue

Reprinted with permission.

Dow Theory Forecasts, Inc.
7412 Calumet Avenue
Hammond, IN 46323
(210) 931-6480

Special Situations Under $5
Investment Advisory Bulletin
Number of subscribers is not available

Description of the publication:
> Special Situations Under $5 focuses on undervalued stocks and warrants trading at prices under $5. The newsletter makes and follows up on specific recommendations; maintains a buy/sell list, regularly reviews a subset of securities, and provides readers general information on a variety of topics.

Investment selections in the publication are determined:
> Using fundamental and technical analysis.

The track record for the publication, as reported by the publication, is:
> Not available.

The publication has been published continuously since: 1983

The cost of a subscription is: $97

The number of issues per year is: 12

A HOTLINE telephone service is: Not Available

The publication can be delivered: Via first class mail

It is also worth mentioning that:
> Dow Theory Forecasts, Inc. publishes several other newsletters covering a variety of topics.

Special Situations Under $5

PUBLISHED BY
40 Years of Service
1946   1986
DOW THEORY FORECASTS

September 1986   Vol. 4, No. 9

In This Issue Of
Special Situations

The gaming issues have corrected, providing an opportunity in Golden Nugget warrants, the spotlight selection...Page 2 features some of the recommended issues on the American Stock Exchange – Booth, Technical Tape, and Warner Computer Systems ...Page 3 highlights Advanced Computer Techniques, an attractive software and computer-services issue. Two concerns reporting strong profits, Gentex and Visual Electronics, are also reviewed on the page.

SPECIAL SITUATIONS SPOTLIGHT

Golden Nugget Warrant Offers Good Gaming Selection

The gaming group is one of the more attractive areas for special situations, and the Golden Nugget warrant ($2) provides a low-priced way to invest in this sector. The warrant has been volatile in line with the action of the underlying common. Irregular earnings have been a major reason for the volatility. However, profits should improve later this year. The warrant has backed off considerably from its high of $4 per share and offers a good speculation for aggressive investors.

Leader In The Gaming Field

Golden Nugget is one of the leaders in the gaming field. The firm operates casinos in both the Atlantic City and Las Vegas gaming markets along with operating a bus-tour service to its Atlantic City operations. The firm has traditionally been one of the stronger factors in its markets, though it has had its share of volatility.

The major cause for the stock's erratic performance over the last year is its bottom line. Per-share profits lagged in the first quarter, and results were below expectations in the June period. However, Golden Nugget is expected to get its earnings in gear in the second half of the year, which should provide some support to the stock price.

Continued on page 4

News Briefs On
Recommended Stocks

ABM Computer Systems ($2¾) has agreed to acquire Franklin Telecommunications, a maker of computer-peripheral products. The name of the surviving concern following the merger will be Franklin Telecommunications Corp. At this point, ABM Computer stockholders should maintain positions pending further developments...Aspen Ribbons ($2), despite a drop in profitability in the fiscal fourth quarter, managed to show a gain for the fiscal year overall, with per-share profits up 14% to $0.16. The firm added over 20 new products during the year. This manufacturer of computer-printer ribbons expects the favorable earnings trend to continue into the new fiscal year. The stock remains a good holding...Jones & Vining ($4) suffered a poor quarter due to the flood of imports in its footwear markets. Finances continue to be strong, with the firm having over $7 million in cash assets at the end of the quarter. Further irregularities are possible in the near term, but the issue holds rebound potential.

Recent Earnings Results

	Quarter Ended	Net Income	EPS	% Change
Aspen Ribbons	6-30-86	$183,646	$0.06	−25
CACI	6-30-86	477,328	0.05	−17
Care Plus	6-30-86	207,283	0.02	0
Courier Dispatch	6-30-86	179,712	0.06	*
Jones & Vining	6-28-86	119,000	0.03	−86
Quest Medical	6-30-86	31,630	0.01	*

* Reported nil profits during year-earlier period.

Reprinted with permission.

Robert A. Stanger & Co.
P.O. Box 7490
1129 Broad St.
Shrewsbury, NJ 07701
(201) 389-3600

The Stanger Register™
Concentrated Educational Service
Less than 25,000 subscribers

Description of the publication:
The Stanger Register™ is a monthly magazine containing up-to-date, in-depth, technical articles written for serious financial planners. The Register also carries listings covering all SEC registered public partnerships, synopsizing each offering and ranking its terms as to their relative attractiveness for the limited partners.

Investment selections in the publication are determined:
By concentrating on the specialty topic area of: Investment Partnerships.

The track record for the publication, as reported by the publication, is:
Not applicable.

The publication has been published continuously since: 1981

The cost of a subscription is: $225

The number of issues per year is: 12

A HOTLINE telephone service is: Available
Cost for this service: Free with subscription.

The publication can be delivered: Via bulk/third class mail

It is also worth mentioning that:
- The SEC now permits rankings made by Robert A. Stanger & Co. to be included in investment prospectuses.
- Robert A. Stanger & Associates, a company affiliated with Robert A. Stanger & Co., offers consulting services on all aspects of due diligence as well as marketing, executive search, expert witness testimony, and a host of other services related to investment partnerships.

THE STANGER REGISTER™

NOVEMBER 1986/VOL. 5, No. 11

ADVISORY BOARD

Richard G. Wollack
Chairman

William Anthes, PhD
Financial Planning/Education

John Cahill
Financial Planning

Robert E. Frey
Securities and Syndication Law

Robert Goodman, PhD
Economics

John Goodson
Estate Planning/Taxation

Harold W. Gourgues
Financial Planning Theory and Practice Management

Gus Hansch
Financial Planning

Lawrence Krause
Financial Planning/Marketing

Charles Lefkowitz
Financial Planning/
Practice Management

Max B. Lewis
Estate Planning and Tax Law

Richard Loughlin
Real Estate/Housing

Michael Markey
Financial Planning

Lewis G. Mosburg, Jr.
Tax Shelter/Securities and Tax Law

George Nordhaus
Insurance

Chandler Peterson
Financial Planning/ESOPs

Donald Pitti
Bonus/Mutual Funds

Gary Pittsford
Fee-Only Planning

Michael Radde
Taxation/Accounting

Donald Rowe
Stock Market

Eileen Sharkey
Financial Planning

William Shearer
Securities and Tax Law/Estate Planning

Alberto Villoldo, PhD
Human Resources Development

Lewis Walensky
Financial Planning

Wade Webster
Financial Planning and Computers

Rich White
Funds and Securities

Judith Zabalaoui
Financial Planning

Reprinted with permission.

Robert A. Stanger & Co.
P.O. Box 7490
1129 Broad St.
Shrewsbury, NJ 07701
(201) 389-3600

The Stanger Report:™
A Guide to Partnership Investing
Concentrated Education Service
Less than 25,000 subscribers

Description of the publication:
The Stanger Report™ is a monthly newsletter containing in-depth, technical articles on analyzing and evaluating investment partnerships. Industry and investment data are included along with commentary on the tax law's impact in an effort to provide subscribers with all of the necessary information with which to make informed investment decisions.

Investment selections in the publication are determined:
By concentrating on the specialty topic area of: Investment Partnerships.

The track record for the publication, as reported by the publication, is:
Not applicable.

The publication has been published continuously since: 1979

The cost of a subscription is: $325

The number of issues per year is: 12

A HOTLINE telephone service is: Available
Cost for this service: Free with subscription.

The publication can be delivered: Via first class mail

It is also worth mentioning that:
- The SEC now permits rankings made by Robert A. Stanger & Co. to be included in investment prospectuses.
- Robert A. Stanger & Associates, a company affiliated with Robert A. Stanger & Co., offers consulting services on all aspects of due diligence as well as marketing, executive search, expert witness testimony, and a host of other services related to investment partnerships.

THE STANGER REPORT™

A GUIDE TO PARTNERSHIP INVESTING

VOLUME VII, No. 11

NOVEMBER 1986

IN THIS ISSUE

> **TAXES**

The Coming Of The PIG

If you bought a tax shelter that will produce losses in 1987, you need to know how tax reform affects you. Your losses from limited partnerships are now defined as passive activity losses ("PALs"). Tax reform also defines "passive activity income" as the only type of income you can shelter with PALs.

Beginning in 1987, you can't fully deduct limited partnership losses from wages, salaries, divi- dends and interest income. But, you can deduct PALs from passive activity income. Investment vehicles that create passive activity income are called "PIGs" which stands for passive income generators. (The term was coined by Alan Rachap, our good friend from Merrill Lynch, Annapolis, MD.) You net your PALs against income from your PIGs to calculate your net PAL.

THE STANGER REPORT is published monthly for $325 per year by Robert A. Stanger & Co., registered investment advisors, P.O. Box 7490, 1129 Broad Street, Shrewsbury, N.J. 07701. Tel: 201-389-3600. ©COPYRIGHT 1986 by ROBERT A. STANGER & CO. Reproduction, photocopying or incorporation into any information retrieval system for external or internal use is prohibited unless permission is obtained beforehand from the publisher in each case for a specific article. The subscription fee entitles the subscriber to one original only. Unauthorized copying is considered theft. This publication is designed to provide accurate and authoritative information in regard to the subject matter. It is sold with the understanding that the publisher is not engaged in rendering legal or accounting services. If such assistance is required, seek the advice of a competent professional. Editor-in-Chief, Robert A. Stanger; Editor, Keith D. Allaire; Associate Editors, Richard A. Natelson, Nancy T. Schabel, Michele Damen, Daniel W. Horchler; Research, John P. Blake, Donna L. Aumack, Catherine A. Friel; Production Manager, Patricia K. Fogle.

Reprinted with permission.

Standard & Poor's Corporation
25 Broadway
New York City, NY 10004
(212) 208-8000

Stock Guide
Statistical Service
Number of subscribers is not available

Description of the publication:
Stock Guide is a unique pocket-size summary of investment data on over 5,300 common and preferred, listed and over-the-counter stocks. Designed for use by investors and investment professionals, the format of this 260-page monthly publication provides a rapid review of 48 items of data on each security. Data items featured include dividend and earnings estimates, monthly high-low prices and volume, and historical price ranges. A special section also covers mutual fund performance.

Investment selections in the publication are determined:
By periodically reviewing all New York and American Stock Exchange and the most active Over-the-Counter issues.

The track record for the publication, as reported by the publication, is:
Not applicable.

The publication has been published continuously since: 1943

The cost of a subscription is: $88

The number of issues per year is: 12

A HOTLINE telephone service is: Not Available

The publication can be delivered: Via first class mail

It is also worth mentioning that:
Standard & Poor's Corporation also publishes several other publications covering a variety of topics.

8 AAR-Adv

Standard & Poor's Corporation

¶S&P 500 ●Options Index	Name of Issue		Com. Rank. & Pfd. Rating	Par Val.	Inst.Hold		Principal Business	Price Range						Sep. Sales in 100s	September,1986				%Div. Yield	P-E Ratio
	Ticker Symbol	(Call Price of Pfd. Stocks) Market			Cos	Shs. (000)		1971-84		1985		1986				Last Sale Or Bid					
								High	Low	High	Low	High	Low		High	Low	Last	Bid			
1	AIR	AAR Corp ....NY,M	B+	1	68	5825	Mkts aviation parts/service	15¾	1¾	17⅝	10¾	26½	17	9170	24¾	20⅜	21¾		2.0	16
2	ARON	Aaron Rents ....OTC	NR	1	30	1489	Rents & sells furniture	25¾	10¾	23	15½	20	15¾	4444	19¾	17	17¼			16
3●	ABT	Abbott Laboratories ....NY,B,C,M,P,Ph	A+	No	632	116739	Diversified health care prod	26¹¹/₁₆	1⅞	36	19¹⅛	19¹¹/₁₆	31½	104416	49¾	41	41⅞		2.0	18
4	ACAJ	Ace Joe ....OTC	NR	10¢	8	447	Operate/license apparel strs	8⅝	¼	10⅛	1¹/₁₆	8¼	2⅝	11914	3⅞	2⅝	2⅛			d
5	ACIG	Academy Insur Gr ....OTC	C	10¢	18	3569	Accident,health,life insur	17¼	¼	12¼	1¾	3¾	¾	13335	3½	2⅛	2¾			d
6	ACLE	Acceleration Corp ....OTC	NR		16	777	Insurance:credit life/disab	17½	2	13	7¼	16¼	8¾	1798	11¼	8¾	8⅝			18
7	ACO	ACCO World ....NY,M	NR	5¢	82	7638	Mfrs office supply products	23¾	13¾	26¾	19¾	32	25	4486	28¾	25	25¾		2.2	7
8	ACRA	AccuRay Corp ....OTC	B	1	39	1760	Mfr,lease process mgmt sys	38	2	26	18¾	28¾	16	4830	19	16	16¼		1.7	12
9	ACET	Aceto Corp ....OTC	B+	1¢	15	753	Mfrs & dstr chemicals	14¼	⅝	18¼	13¾	20½	16¾	1080	18½	17¾	18½	s0.8		12
10	ACF	ACI Holdings ....AS,M	NR	No			Hldg;air carrier sv'g Calif	14¼	5¾	12	7¾	11¼	6¾	4252	8¾	7¾	8			d
11	Pr	$1.20cm Cv⁴⁵Exch Pfd(⁴⁵11.08)..AS,M	B	1						13¾	9¾	13¾	10	1909	12½	11½	12		10.0	d
12	AMT	Acme-Cleveland ....NY,M	B-	1	50	3006	Mfr automatic mach tools	35¾	7	19½	10	14½	9	2371	11¾	9½	9¾		4.1	d
13	ACE	Acme Electric ....NY	B	1	13	877	Pwr conv eq: transformers	11¾	⅜	9	6¾	9½	6¼	597	7¾	6½	6¾	s4.8		14
14	ACU	Acme Precision Prod ....AS	B	1			Mfr precision cutt'g tools	12¼	⅜	8	6¾	8¾	2½	100	4½	4¼	4⅛			2
15	ACU	Acme United ....AS	B+	2½	14	1334	Medic eq:shears,scissors	19½	1¾	11½	9½	12¼	7⅜	449	8¼	7¾	7¾		4.1	28
16	ACX	Action Indus ....AS	B-	10¢	22	1527	Merchandising programs	16¾	¼	18¼	9¾	15¾	8¼	8392	10¾	9¼	9¼			10
17	AVSN	Activision Inc ....OTC	NR	No	11	1823	Mfr home video game softw	12¾	⅞	1¾	¾	1½	1	19623	1¾	1	1¾	0.6		d
18	ACTM	Actmedia Inc ....OTC	NR	9¢	11	3376	Shop'g cart advert'g displays	16¼	9¾	25	13½	32½	23¼	4757	26½	24	26¼			d
19	ATN	Acton Corp ....OTC	C	66²/₃¢	11	922	Owner,operator CATV systems	18	¼	5⅞	¼	3¾	1¼	1481	2¼	1½	1¾			49
20	WS	Wrrt(Purch 1.15 com at$16.40)...AS		1¢	2		:mfr,dstr electronic tel eqp	6½	¾	1⅝	¾	¾	¼	56	¼	⅛	¼			d
21	ACSN	Acuson Corp ....OTC	NR	No			Medical ultrasound imaging					9½	7½	18113	9½	7½	8¾			44
22	ADAC	ADAC Laboratories ....OTC	C	No	19	1413	Nuclear medicine comput sys	27½	2¾	7¼	1	7¾	1¾	9730	1¾	1⅜	1¾			d
23	ADGE	Adage Inc ....OTC	NR	⅛	26	2933	Computer graphics term sys	20⅜	¼	10¾	6	7¼	2¼	5864	2¾	1¾	2⅛			d
24	ADX	Adams Express ....NY,B,M,Ph	B	1	17	233	Closed-end investment co	18¾	7	19¾	15½	22¾	17¼	2671	23¾	19¾	19¾	3.6		
25	ALL	Adams-Millis ....NY,B,M,Ph	B+	No	26	1322	Hosiery & yarn products	19¾	1¾	22¾	14	33¾	19¾	1543	30	23¼	23¾	1.7		10
26	AE	Adams Res & Energy ....AS	C	10¢	4	385	Oil dstr:transp:coal:o&g	35¼	1½	14	⅝	2¾	1¾	278	2½	2	2½			19
27	AAR	Adams-Russell ....AS	B+	50¢	56	2742	Owns/operates CATV systems	30¾	¼	30¼	23¾	43	18¾	4189	20¼	18¾	20	0.8		d
28	ADCT	ADC Telecommunications ....OTC	B	1⅔¢	47	5275	Telecommunications equip	3	⅜	15	11	19	11	3696	20¼	17	18⅞	2.6		15
29	ADSNB	Addison-Wesley Pub¹⁰ ....OTC	B+	No	7	691	Pub textbooks, prof, ref books	32¾	3¾	36	28	42	33½	150	37½	34½	35¼			23
30	ADE	ADI Electronics ....AS	NR	1¢	5	210	Mfrs electronic components	7¼	1	6¾	3¾	6¾	3¼	2007	1¾	¾	1			d
31	ADIA	Adia Services ....OTC	NR	25¢	20	1180	Temporary personnel service	7¾	6¼	7¾	16¾	16¼	10¼	1012	14½	11¼	13¾	0.7		21
32	JPAC	ADMAC Inc ....OTC	NR	1¢	18	734	Indl/mining cutg,drill sys			13¼	10¼	11¼	3¾	3296	4¾	3¼	3¾			34
33	ADB	Adobe Resources ....NY	NR	1¢	21	1792	Oil & gas exploration,devel-			13¼	9½	9⅜	5¾	1463	7¾	6⅝	6¾			d
34	Pr A	$1.84cm Cv Pfd(⁴⁵21.16) ....NY	NR	20	14	720	opment,production			17¾	14¾	18¾	13¾	651	15½	15	15¼	12.1		
35	Pr B	12% cm Pfd(⁴⁵21.50) ....NY	NR	20	2	58				18	15¾	20¾	16¾	695	18¾	17¾	17½	13.4		
36	ADT	ADT Inc ....NY,M,P	B+	1	81	5855	Electric protection services	34¼	⁷/₁₆	29¾	20	30	21¾	4929	25¾	22	24¾	3.7		d
37	ADVC	Advance Circuits ....OTC	NR	10¢	24	1648	Mfr printed circuit boards	9½		11⅞	6	14¼	3¾	5648	6	4¾	5			d
38	AROS	Advance Ross ....OTC	B-	10¢	6	188	Transp'n pr: metal fabric'n	11¾	⅜	¾	¼	6¾	4¾	2	5¾	5⅝	5¾			d
39	ACTP	Advanced Computer Tech ....OTC	B-	10¢	1	197	Computer services	11¾	¾	4¼	2¼	6¾	2¼	551	5¼	4⅛	4¾			35
40	AGSI	Advanced Genetic Sci⁷ ....OTC	NR	1¢	5	392	Agricultural biotechnology	15	2¼	7¾	3¾	6½	3¾	5582	5¾	4¾	5½			11
41	AVMS	Advanced Mfg Systems ....OTC	NR	4	570	Mfrs industrial robots		⁴²@$1.46,'85, ⁴⁵Co opt fr 4-15-87 exch for $50amt 12% Cv 2005,					465	½	¾	½		d	
42	AMD	Advanced Micro Dev ....NY,B,M,Ph	B	1¢	217	24668	Monolithic integ circuits	14⅛	1¼	36¾	22¾	33½	14¼	86701	20¼	15¼	15¾			d
43	AMSI	Advanced Monit'g Sys ....OTC	NR	No	1		Dev microprobe,damage to PL	11½	¼	2¼	1	2¾	1¼	4080	2½	1¾	1¾			d
44	ASMIF	Advanced Semi Mat's ....OTC	B	1.03	16	819	Eq to mfr semicond devices	38¼	6½	22	7¼	14¼	5¾	3519	9½	5¾	7⅝			d
45	ASY	Advanced Systems ....NY,M	B	10¢	34	2293	Video asst'd train'g courses	19	5¾	17½	8¾	10¾	13¼	2487	16¼	13¼	13¼	s.		12

Uniform Footnote Explanations—See Page 1. Other: ¹Ph:Cycle 2. ²P:Cycle 1 Pilot Program. ¹¹●$1.46,'85. ⁴⁵Co opt fr 4-15-87 exch for $50amt 12% Cv 2005. ¹⁵●$0.07,'82. ¹⁶●0.06,'83. ¹⁷△$0.17,'82. ⁴⁴●$0.21,'84. ⁴²®$0.99,'86. ⁴¹Beltran Corp wrrt. ⁴⁵●$1.18,'85. ⁴⁴●$1.08,'85. ¹⁹⁰$0.56,'83. ²⁵Stk dstr of Adams-Russell Electronics Co. ²⁵△$0.51,'83. ⁴⁴△$0.46,'83. ⁴¹△$0.05,'84. ⁴⁶Cl B. ⁴⁷Fiscal Nov'85 & prior. ¹⁰Fr 11-1-90,scale to $20 in '97. ¹¹Fr 11-1-90,scale to $20 in '98. ²⁵Stk dstr of Aritech Corp. ⁴⁷Cl A. ⁴⁹®$1.04,'85.

Common and Preferred Stocks

AAR-Adv 9

Splits ◆ Index	Cash Divs. Ea. Yr. Since	Dividends						Financial Position				Capitalization			Earnings $ Per Shr.						Interim Earnings			Index
		Latest Payment			Total $			Mil-$			Balance Sheet Date	Lg Trm Debt Mil-$	Shs. 000		Years					Last 12 Mos.		$ Per Shr.		
		Per$	Date	Ex. Div.	So Far 1986	Ind. Rate	Paid 1985	Cash& Equiv.	Curr. Assets	Curr. Liab.			Pfd.	Com.	End	1982	1983	1984	1985	1986		Period	1985	1986	
1	1973	Q0.11	9-3-86	7-28	0.33	0.44	0.346	n/a	148.	59.3	8-31-86	16.2		10480	My	0.22	0.47	0.65	1.01	1.27	1.33	3 Mo Aug	0.27	0.33	1
2		None Since Public			Nil			Equity per shr $7.59			6-30-86	24.2		14126	Mr	0.92	0.92	1.13	1.08		1.10	3 Mo Jul	0.30	0.32	2
3	1926	Q0.21	11-15-86	10-8	0.80½	0.84	0.67½	567.	1903	1103	6-30-86	450		234751	Dc	1.19	1.43	1.67	1.94	E2.30	2.12	6 Mo Jul	0.91	1.09	3
4		None Since Public			Nil			5.34	14.5	7.93	5-4-86	52.1		13724	Ja	d0.02	d0.60	d0.56	0.07		d0.05	6 Mo Jul	0.01	d0.11	4
5	1984	5% Stk	7-15-85	6-24				Equity per shr $0.99			9-30-86			19992	Dc	0.76	...	1.03	d0.79		d1.96	6 Mo Jul	d1.44	d0.55	5
6		4% Stk	12-15-85	11-19			Nil	4% Stk	Equity per shr $7.98			6-30-86	13.2	6	4913	Dc	⁴⁷0.45	⁴⁷0.58	⁴⁷0.62	⁴⁷0.57		0.48	6 Mo Jun	0.33	0.40	6
7	1975	Q0.14	10-10-86	9-24	0.53	0.56	0.47	26.8	112.	44.7	6-30-86	48.0		13809	Dc	0.83	1.07	1.32	1.50		1.53	6 Mo Jun	0.32	0.35	7
8	1981	S0.14	8-10-86	7-25	0.26	0.26	0.22	2.89	91.3	34.3	6-30-86	21.2		4247	Dc	▲1.08	1.31	1.64	1.90		1.31	6 Mo Jun	0.94	0.35	8
9	1985	s0.07	10-29-86	10-7	0.137	0.14	s0.123	8.81	54.6	16.1	3-31-86	3.50	1.20	3135	Dc	0.99	1.02	1.37	⁴⁷1.47	P1.49	1.49				9
10		None Public			Nil			8.59	54.3	78.6	3-31-86	58.7	3680	8524	Dc	d5.93	d0.43	⁴⁷0.54	⁴⁷0.21		d1.81	6 Mo Jun	⁴⁷0.56	d1.46	10
11	1985	Q0.30	10-15-86	9-25	1.20	1.20	0.656	Cv into 0.962 com,$10.40					Red restr to 4-15-88⁴⁴								11				
12	1936	Q0.08	8-15-86	7-29	0.30	0.40	0.40	18.0	103.	60.6	6-30-86	31.9	161	6279	Dc	⁴⁷0.37	d2.11	▲1.90	E0.151	d3.07	9 Mo Jun	q0.57	d1.74	12
13	1939	Q0.08	9-15-86	8-21	s0.236	0.32	s0.300	1.18	24.0	4.74	6-30-86	5.21		4016	Je	0.57	0.04	0.57	0.67	0.47	0.47	9 Mo Jun	d2.17	▲2.64	13
14		None Public			Nil			1.07			3-31-86	8.42		3220	Dc	d0.80	1.19	0.63	0.38		2.28	6 Mo Jun	0.16	0.06	14
15	1947	Q0.08	9-10-86	8-11	0.24	0.32	0.32	0.04	24.6	3.28	6-28-86				Dc	0.80	1.01	0.63	0.38		2.28	6 Mo Jun	0.16	0.06	15
16	1986	0.06	9-15-86	8-11	0.06	0.06		33.4	79.7	37.9	6-28-86	20.7		6150	Je	⁴⁷0.41	1.28	⁴⁷0.44	0.92	⁴⁷1.01	1.01	3 Mo Jun	d0.07	d0.05	16
17		None Since Public			Nil			17.9	31.9	8.65	6-28-86	2.10		35074	Mr	0.64	d0.56	⁴⁷0.32	⁴⁷0.40		d0.15	3 Mo Jun	d0.07	d0.05	17
18		None Since Public			Nil			0.24	23.42	9.42	6-28-86			7779	Dc	0.06	0.23	0.35	0.51		0.54	24 Wk Jun	0.18	0.21	18
19		5% Stk	7-15-82	6-25			Nil		Check terms/trad'g in detail			6-28-86	0.19		1330	Dc	0.15	d1.07	d2.09	Pd1.40		d1.40				19
20		Wrrt	4-1-82	4-2			Nil															Wrrts expire 6-1-86			20
21		None Since Public			Nil			8.72	27.4	7.58	6-30-86	0.70	⁴¹21605	Dc		d0.27	d0.38	d0.04	⁴⁷0.10	0.20	6 Mo Jun	d0.13	0.13	21
22		None Since Public			Nil			3.13	25.4	17.9	6-29-86	11.0	3421	9606	Sp	d0.62	0.51	0.54	d0.11	d0.12	d2.71	6 Mo Jun	d1.50	d1.08	22
23		0.12	10-22-86	10-3	⁴⁷0.72	0.72	⁴⁷0.70	2.45	7478	Net Asset Val $21.92	6-29-86	3.46	Mr	0.83	0.99	1.03	d0.11	d0.12	d1.54	3 Mo Jun	d0.03	d0.45	23	
24	1936	Q0.10	8-29-86	8-11	0.30	0.40	0.34	Net Asset Val $21.92			6-30-86	50.9		2310	Dc	$18.07	$19.27	⁴⁷1.96	2.31		2.42	6 Mo Jun	0.72	0.83	24
25	1977	Q0.10	8-29-86	8-11	0.30	0.40	0.34	0.47	71.9	29.8	6-30-86	50.9		2310	Dc	0.74	⁴⁷0.94	2.50	2.31		2.42	6 Mo Jun	0.72	0.83	25
26		0.10	8-15-78	7-10			Nil	0.93	9.31	9.30	6-30-86	6.80	35	6958	Dc	d0.55	⁴⁷0.59	⁴⁷0.39	⁴⁷0.25		0.11	6 Mo Jun	d0.23	d0.09	26
27	1977	h	7-14-86	7-15	h0.08	0.16	0.15	30.3	54.5	11.7	6-30-86	57.0		6283	Sp	1.00	0.58	1.28	0.63		0.19	9 Mo Jun	0.16	0.01	27
28		None Since Public			Nil			17.3	58.1	27.8	6-30-86	15.86		8594	Sp	0.52	⁴⁷0.50	⁴⁷0.77	⁴⁷0.63		0.52	9 Mo Jun	0.06	d0.21	28
29	1956	Q0.22½	9-30-86	8-25	0.62½	0.90	0.75	10.0			3-31-86	10.0		2558	Dc	2.54	...	...	...		6.51	6 Mo Apr	3.46	3.02	29
30		None Since Public			Nil			0.16	5.79	4.25	4-30-86	4.50		3385	Jl	d0.04	0.08	0.26	0.20		d0.65	6 Mo Apr	0.16	d0.57	30
31	1984	Q0.02½	9-18-86	8-27	0.05½	0.10	0.06	7.13	34.8	23.7	6-30-86	1.88		8058	Dc		0.31	0.60	0.62		0.66	6 Mo Jun	0.32	0.36	31
32		None Since Public			Nil			0.26	22.8	11.8	7-31-86	1.15		4952	Ap			⁴⁷0.08	0.20		d0.02	6 Mo Jul	0.10	d0.19	32
33		None Since Public			Nil			31.1	78.3	60.5	6-30-86	94.4	4005	22196	Dc		pd0.21	pd0.14			1.62	6 Mo Jun	d0.10	d1.58	33
34	1986	Q0.46	8-15-86	7-18	1.47	1.84		Cv into 0.9 com					4159		Dc										34
35	1986	Q0.60	8-15-86	7-18	1.92	2.40							4896		Dc										35
36	1903	Q0.23	9-19-86	8-25	⁴⁷0.69	0.92	0.92	8.90	116.	105.	6-30-86	26.8	13041	Dc	2.14	2.02	0.92	⁴⁷2.67		d2.52	6 Mo May	0.60	0.75	36
37		None Since Public			Nil			0.80	16.5	10.7	5-31-86	16.9	4347	Au	d0.08	0.16	⁴⁷0.16	⁴⁷0.25		d0.18	9 Mo May	0.30	d0.48	37
38		h	11-27-64		Nil			8.74	10.8	1.82	6-30-86		2192	Dc	⁴⁷0.42	d0.38	d0.53	⁴⁷0.77		d0.43	6 Mo Jun	0.36	d0.33	38
39		0.05	8-20-76	6-26			Nil	0.01	4.94	4.02	6-30-86	0.22	210	1716	Dc	0.07	0.16	0.14	0.13		0.16	6 Mo Jun	0.07	0.12	39
40		None Since Public			Nil			1.38	2.39	1.00	6-30-86		¹12935	Dc	d0.06	d0.37	d0.63	d0.73		d0.58	6 Mo Jun	d0.39	d0.24	40
41		None Since Public			Nil			0.92	6.61	4.62	6-30-86	2.57	8560	Mr	0.30	d0.29	d0.08	d0.62	Ed1.00	d0.15	3 Mo Jun	d0.01	Nil	41
42		None Since Public			Nil			11.1	240.	154.	6-29-86	138	57159	Mr	0.39	1.23	2.00	d0.63		d1.05	6 Mo Jun	d0.01	d0.49	42
43		None Since Public			Nil			0.14	0.20	0.07	6-30-86		5408	Dc	d0.42	d0.06	d0.02	d0.15		d0.18	6 Mo Jun	d0.05	d0.11	43
44		None Since Public			Nil			19.2	261.	171.	¹²3-31-85	44.3	6959	Dc	0.23	0.85	⁴⁷0.56	⁴⁷1.05		1.12	9 Mo Jul	0.61	0.74	44
45		5% Stk	10-31-86	10-6	10% Stk	Stk	5% Stk	2.90	42.0	39.0	4-30-86	³¹3.1	5229	Dc	0.69	0.84	⁴⁷0.56	⁴⁷1.05		1.12	9 Mo Jun	0.61	0.68	45

◆ Stock Splits & Divs By Line Reference Index ¹3-for-2,'84. ³3-for-2,'85. ⁴3-for-2,'81. ⁵2-for-1,'86. ⁶2-for-1,'83:Adj for 5%,'85. ⁷Adj for 4%,'85. ⁸3-for-2,'84. ⁹4-for-3,'83:3-for-2,'85:Adj to 4% Mar,'86. ¹⁰10%,'84:Adj to 5%,'84. ¹¹3-for-1,'83. ¹²3-for-1,'83. ¹³3-for-2,'85. ¹⁴Adj for 5%,'82:10%,'83. ¹⁵2-for-1,'82. ¹⁶2-for-1,'83. ¹⁷3-for-2,'82:No adj for stk dstr. ¹⁸3-for-2,'82,'83,'86. ¹⁹2-for-1,'86. ²⁰2-for-1,'83. ²¹3-for-2,'82:2-for-1,'83. ²²3-for-2,'83:Adj to 5%,'86.

Reprinted with permission.

Standard & Poor's Corporation

25 Broadway

New York City, NY 10004

(212) 208-8000

Stock Reports

Statistical Service

Number of subscribers is not available

Description of the publication:

Stock Reports is a library of data covering 3,700 companies, including all those listed on the New York and American Stock Exchanges and more than 1,400 of the most active issues traded over-the-counter. Organized in a succinct two page report format, with extensive statistical data presented in a fashion so as to facilitate quick year-to-year comparison, each company's activity and financial position is reviewed. Stock Reports is published in a loose-leaf version distributed on a weekly basis and in a bound version distributed on a quarterly basis.

Investment selections in the publication are determined:

By periodically reviewing all New York and American Stock Exchange and the most active Over-the-Counter issues.

The track record for the publication, as reported by the publication, is:

Not applicable.

The publication has been published continuously since: 1933

The cost of a subscription is: (1) $820

    (1) For NYSE reports.   (2) $660

    (2) For ASE and OTC reports.

The number of issues per year is: Loose-leaf: 52

Bound: 12

A HOTLINE telephone service is: Not Available

The publication can be delivered: Loose-leaf: Via second class mail

Bound: Via fourth class mail

It is also worth mentioning that:

- Bound volumes represent three volumes per exchange per quarter.
- Standard & Poor's Corporation also publishes several other publications covering a variety of topics.

DWG Corp. 7649

ASE Symbol DWG

Price	Range	P-E Ratio	Dividend	Yield	S&P Ranking
Feb. 2'84 3¼	1983-4 4½-2⅜	3	⁴---	⁴---	B

Summary

Operating through four major subsidiaries, this company distributes liquefied petroleum gas, provides services to utilities and municipalities, operates cold storage facilities, manufactures men's shirts and other apparel and makes fabrics used primarily for utility wear and sportswear. It also has equity interests in various other companies.

Business Summary

DWG Corporation is a holding company that owns 100% of National Propane Corp. and 63% of NYSE-listed Southeastern Public Service Co. Subsequent to 1982-3 year-end, the company increased its ownership of NYSE-listed Graniteville Co. to 85%, from 23%, and ASE-listed Wilson Brothers to 54%, from 42%. Contributions by industry segment in 1982-3 were:

	Revs.	Profits
LP Gas	48%	45%
Utility & municipal services	41%	24%
Refrigeration	8%	16%
Other	3%	15%

National Propane distributes liquefied petroleum gas for household, farm, commercial and industrial use, largely in areas not provided with municipal gas services. Marketing is through company-owned retail outlets, franchised dealers and distributors primarily in the Southeast, Northeast, Midwest, Southwest, and the Virgin Islands.

Southeastern Public Service provides services to utilities and municipalities, operates refrigeration and cold storage facilities, distributes LP gas in Florida and Alabama and owns interests in oil and gas producing properties in seven states. Utility and municipal services include tree maintenance, right-of-way clearance, and protection of power and telephone lines from encroaching vegetation. Refrigeration operations encompass the manufacture and distribution of ice, and providing freezer cooler, dry warehousing and food processing facilities.

Graniteville Co., 85% owned, manufactures, dyes and finishes cotton, synthetic and blended fabrics

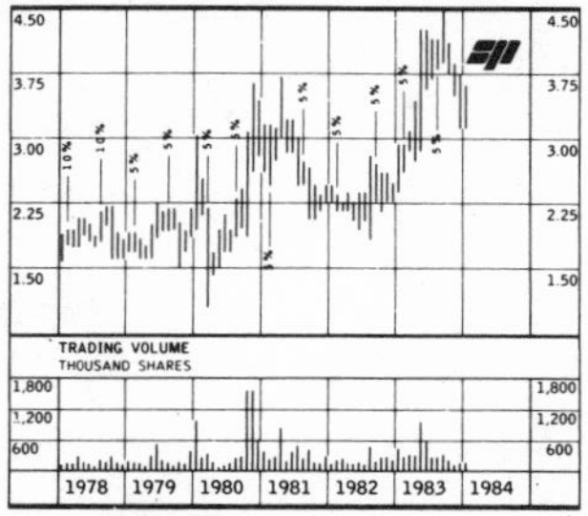

used mainly for utility wear and sportswear.

Wilson Brothers, 54%-owned, primarily manufactures and imports men's and boys' apparel.

Through subsidiaries, DWG has an equity interest in Chesapeake Insurance Co. Ltd., which reinsures policies issued to DWG and affiliates. In January 1984, Chesapeake was bidding to acquire Royal Crown Companies.

As of October 31, 1983, DWG also had marketable securities valued at $18,187,000, equity investments in affiliates of $46,755,000, and $15,731,000 in cash and equivalents.

Employees: 5,800.

Next earnings report due in mid-March.

Per Share Data ($)

Yr. End Apr. 30¹	1982	1981	1980	1979	1978	1977	1976	1975	1974	1973
Book Value	**6.13**	5.47	4.56	4.22	3.74	3.43	3.09	2.70	2.48	2.12
Earnings²	**0.97**	1.03	0.58	0.48	0.25	0.41	0.43	0.40	0.41	0.52
Dividends	**Nil**	Nil	Nil	Nil	Nil	Nil	Nil	Nil	0.02⁷⁄₈	Nil
Payout Ratio	**Nil**	Nil	Nil	Nil	Nil	Nil	Nil	Nil	7%	Nil
Prices³—High	**2¾**	3¾	3⅝	2¼	2¼	2¾	1¾	1⅜	⅞	1⅜
Low	**1⅞**	2	1⅛	1½	1⅝	1½	¾	½	½	⅝
P/E Ratio—	**3-2**	4-2	6-2	5-3	9-6	7-4	4-2	3-1	2-1	3-1

Data as orig. reptd. Adj. for stk. divs. of 5% Aug. 1983, 5% Feb. 1983, 5% Sep. 1982, 5% Apr. 1982, 5% Feb. 1981, 5% Aug. 1980, 5% Mar. 1980, 5% Aug. 1979, 5% Feb. 1979, 10% Aug. 1978, 10% Feb. 1978, 10% Aug. 1977, 10% Feb. 1977, 10% Aug. 1976, 10% Feb. 1976, 10% Aug. 1975, 5% Mar. 1975, 5% Aug. 1974. 1. Of fol. cal. yr. 2. Ful. dil.: 0.57 in 1982, 0.59 in 1981, 0.33 in 1980, 0.27 in 1979, 0.16 in 1978, 0.23 in 1977, 0.23 in 1976, 0.21 in 1975, 0.23 in 1974, 0.37 in 1973. 3. Cal. yr. 4. Pays 5% stk. semiannually.

February 9, 1984

Copyright © 1984 Standard & Poor's Corp. All Rights Reserved

Standard & Poor's Corp.
25 Broadway, NY, NY 10004

7649 DWG Corporation

Income Data (Million $)

Year Ended Apr. 30¹	Revs.	Oper. Inc.	% Oper. Inc. of Revs.	Cap. Exp.	Depr.	Int. Exp.	³Net Bef. Taxes	Eff. Tax Rate	⁴Net Inc.	% Net Inc. of Revs.
1982	**302**	**37.0**	**12.3%**	**20.1**	**15.1**	**17.6**	**24.0**	**31.7%**	**11.9**	**3.9%**
1981	289	38.9	13.5%	22.5	12.9	17.1	33.8	35.2%	12.3	4.3%
1980	267	34.2	12.8%	18.7	11.8	13.6	18.9	38.1%	6.6	2.5%
1979	224	30.8	13.7%	21.7	10.0	8.7	16.6	44.3%	5.3	2.4%
1978	180	25.9	14.4%	14.0	9.1	5.2	11.1	50.9%	3.1	1.7%
1977	173	22.9	13.2%	15.9	8.5	3.3	12.2	44.2%	² 4.7	2.7%
1976	153	22.2	14.6%	10.3	8.1	2.9	12.4	49.8%	4.6	3.0%
1975	134	20.0	15.0%	6.9	8.4	3.4	9.6	48.4%	4.2	3.1%
1974	135	22.0	16.3%	10.0	7.9	4.3	11.1	47.1%	4.1	3.0%
1973	125	22.2	17.8%	13.0	7.1	4.1	12.4	44.8%	4.6	3.7%

Balance Sheet Data (Million $)

Apr. 30¹	Cash	Current Assets	Current Liab.	Current Ratio	Total Assets	Ret. on Assets	Long Term Debt	Common Equity	Total Cap.	% LT Debt of Cap.	Ret. on Equity
1982	**118**	**174**	**56.0**	**3.1**	**362**	**3.5%**	**138**	**93.9**	**303**	**45.5%**	**12.5%**
1981	94	149	52.5	2.8	304	4.4%	102	81.2	249	41.0%	15.3%
1980	56	108	40.4	2.7	252	2.5%	82	69.4	210	39.3%	8.6%
1979	55	101	34.6	2.9	237	2.5%	83	59.6	194	43.0%	8.1%
1978	33	66	23.3	2.8	186	1.8%	58	54.6	158	36.6%	4.7%
1977	14	53	24.2	2.2	169	3.0%	47	52.5	142	32.7%	8.0%
1976	5	38	19.4	2.0	147	3.1%	36	49.1	126	28.9%	8.2%
1975	9	36	18.7	1.9	144	2.9%	41	43.8	122	33.1%	8.3%
1974	12	34	19.5	1.7	143	2.8%	40	40.3	120	33.6%	9.2%

Data as orig. reptd. 1. Of fol. cal. yr. 2. Refl. acctg. change. 3. Incl. equity in earns. of nonconsol. subs. 4. Bef. spec. items.

Revenues (Million $)

Quarter:	1983-4	1982-3	1981-2	1980-1
Jul.	65.0	60.6	59.2	50.5
Oct.	93.1	71.0	68.5	61.7
Jan.		87.5	83.2	77.4
Apr.		82.8	78.0	77.2
		301.9	288.9	266.8

For the six months ended October 31, 1983, revenues advanced 20%, year to year, aided by the consolidation of Wilson Brothers revenues (see Business Summary). A decline in operating profit was more than offset by increased gains on sales of marketable securities and equity in net earnings of affiliates. Net income increased 14%, to $2,074,000 ($0.14 a share; $0.10 fully diluted), from $1,821,000 ($0.13; $0.09). Results exclude an extraordinary credit of $0.07 ($0.04 fully diluted) a share in the 1983 interim.

Common Share Earnings ($)

Quarter:	1983-4	1982-3	1981-2	1980-1
Jul.	0.16	d0.21	0.23	d0.07
Oct.	d0.02	0.34	0.30	0.40
Jan.		0.31	0.19	0.26
Apr.		0.51	0.31	Nil
		¹0.97	1.03	0.59

Dividend Data

No cash dividends have been paid since 1974. A 5% semiannual stock dividend was paid April 1, 1983, and another on October 3, 1983, to holders of record September 6.

Capitalization

Long Term Debt: $153,126,000 (10/83), incl. about $8,500,000 of 5½% debs. (listed PSE; some listed ASE), conv. into com. at $2.26 to $3.36 a sh.

Minority Interest: $37,488,000.

$0.60 Pfd. Stk.: 17,700 shs. ($1 par), conv. into some 107,970 com. shs.

$0.35 Pfd. Stk.: 1,680,518 shs. ($1 par), conv. into some 5,881,813 com. shs.

Common Stock: 11,580,057 shs. ($0.10 par).
V. Posner owns or controls some 15%; such control would increase to about 50% if other DWG securities held were converted or exercised.
Institutions hold about 10%.
Shareholders: 7,264 of record.

1. Does not reconcile because of changes in shs. outstanding. d-Deficit.

Office—6917 Collins Ave., Miami Beach, Fla. 33141. **Tel**—(305) 866-7771. **Chrmn & CEO**—V. Posner. **Vice Chrmn & Chrmn, Exec Comm**—S. Posner. **Pres & COO**—M. A. Orloff. **Secy**—E. A. Christensen. **Sr VP-CFO**—J. Coppersmith. **VP & Investor Contact**—F. E. (Gene) Autrey. **VP, Treas & Asst Secy**—R.C. Griffin. **Dirs**—M. R. Colvin, F. F. Oddi, M. A. Orloff, W. L. Pallot, T. A. Prendergast, B. I. Posner, S. Posner, V. Posner, M. Rosen, A. Sherman, R. Stak4, H. K. Stanford, A. Wildavsky. **Transfer Agent**—National Bank of North America, NYC. **Registrar**—Chase Manhattan Bank, NYC. **Incorporated** in Ohio in 1929.

Information has been obtained from sources believed to be reliable, but its accuracy and completeness are not guaranteed. T. Graves

Reprinted with permission.

Babson-United Investment Advisors, Inc.   **United & Babson Investment Report**
210 Newbury Street   Investment Advisory Bulletin
Boston, MA 02116   25,000 to 50,000 subscribers
(617) 267-8855

Description of the publication:
United & Babson Investment Report is a weekly, 12-page report, summarizing important business and investment developments. Featured topics include: news from Washington, industry surveys, and the outlook for the stock market. The publication also maintains a buy/sell list.

Investment selections in the publication are determined:
Using fundamental analysis.

The track record for the publication, as reported by the publication, is:
Not available.

The publication has been published continuously since: 1919

The cost of a subscription is: $190

The number of issues per year is: 52

A HOTLINE telephone service is: Not Available

The publication can be delivered: Via first class mail

It is also worth mentioning:
Babson-United Investment Advisors, Inc. publishes several other investment publications covering a variety of topics.

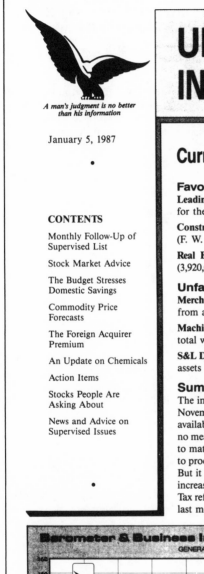

*A man's judgment is no better
than his information*

January 5, 1987

•

CONTENTS

•

UNITED & BABSON INVESTMENT REPORT

Current Business Situation at a Glance

Favorable Factors

Leading Economic Indicators—This barometer of future activity was up for the third straight month in November, increasing 1.2% from October.

Construction Contracts—Rose an adjusted 1% in November from October (F. W. Dodge data), led by a 20% surge in nonresidential awards.

Real Estate—November's adjusted annual sales rate for existing homes (3,920,000) exceeded October by 2.9%, and was highest since September 1979.

Unfavorable Factors

Merchandise Trade Deficit—Widened sharply in November to $19.22 billion from an unrevised $12.06 billion in October.

Machine Tool Orders—Were quite weak in November; the $132.7 million total was down 26% from October and 32% from a year earlier.

S&L Delinquencies—The ratio of "bad" loans and repossessed assets to all assets has risen steadily for over a year, reaching 4.41% in November.

Summary and Forecast

The index of leading economic indicators gave a strong positive reading in November, rising 1.2% from October. Changes in eight of the 11 initially available components (there are 12) were favorable. This barometer is by no means infallible, being famous for predicting several recessions that failed to materialize. Critics also complain that the index gives too much weight to production and not enough to the steadily more important service sector. But it has reasonable validity, and components are periodically changed to increase accuracy. ("Net business formations" will be dropped in March.) Tax reform-related spending may have exaggerated November's rise. Even so, last month's increase has favorable implications.

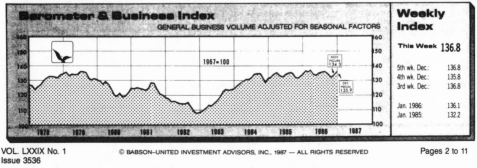

Barometer & Business Index

GENERAL BUSINESS VOLUME ADJUSTED FOR SEASONAL FACTORS

1967=100

NOV FIGURE 134.3

DEC PRELIM 135.9

Weekly Index	
This Week	**136.8**
5th wk. Dec.:	136.8
4th wk. Dec.:	135.8
3rd wk. Dec.:	136.8
Jan. 1986:	136.1
Jan. 1985:	132.2

VOL. LXXIX No. 1
Issue 3536   © BABSON–UNITED INVESTMENT ADVISORS, INC., 1987 — ALL RIGHTS RESERVED   Pages 2 to 11

Reprinted with permission.

Babson-United Investment Advisors, Inc.   **United Mutual Fund Selector®**
210 Newbury Street   Investment Advisory Bulletin
Boston, MA 02116   Less than 25,000 subscribers
(617) 267-8855

Description of the publication:
United Mutual Fund Selector® regularly provides a statistical review of both the short and long-term performance of over 800 funds. Additionally, the publication maintains a supervised list of mutual funds, which in the opinion of the publisher, are best suited for purchase. Also featured is regular commentary on the mutual fund industry, including personal interviews with the top management of selected funds.

Investment selections in the publication are determined:
Using fundamental analysis.

The track record for the publication, as reported by the publication, is:
Not available.

The publication has been published continuously since: 1969

The cost of a subscription is: $110

The number of issues per year is: 24

A HOTLINE telephone service is: Not Available

The publication can be delivered: Via first class mail

It is also worth mentioning that:
Babson-United Investment Advisors, Inc. publishes several other investment publications covering a variety of topics.

A man's judgment is no better than his information

December 16, 1986

A Look At What's To Come

Mutual fund buyers don't like stocks as much as they like bonds. At least, the figures show that roughly 80% of the new money going into funds is going into fixed-income funds and only 20%, therefore, into equity funds. This has been true for several years with a few monthly exceptions, and is still true based on the latest figures we have — October of this year.

And to compound their conservatism, or yen for income now, fixed-income fund buyers have overwhelmingly picked the riskless end of the bond spectrum, U.S. Treasuries, at that. Of course, the drop in interest rates has been severe and has consequently greatly boosted bond prices. So, the bond holders have done pretty well and probably little missed this year's booming stock market which has taken the Dow-Jones Industrials up almost 30%.

So far so good, but what should fund buyers do for income and gain in 1987? We doubt very much if there is much more of a rise in store for the bond market. After all, 20-year Treasury bond yields have dropped from 10.35% to 7.5% in a year. How much more easing can investors reasonably expect? Furthermore, our view of the outlook for the economy next year is for continued modest business expansion which will no where near soak up all of the idle capital, labor and plant capacity. Thus, there should be little upward pressure on interest rates generally. The demand for money will remain modest.

What's Up for 1987?

Let's take a look at some of the economic numbers which appear a reasonable expectation for the year ahead. We look for real GNP growth in the 2%-2 1/2% range, that is without inflation. Although this will make the fifth consecutive year of economic expansion, getting close to some sort of record for such, the rate of growth in the last three of these five years has been under 3%, a mild rate which is easily sustainable.

Whether the stock market can do as well in '87 as it did in '86 is something else again. It will not have the stimulus of falling interest rates. The new tax law will slow up housing activity, and consumers who have been on a plastic spending spree for four years, at least, won't be much of a help. And auto sales, which appear to be a bit ahead of themselves, will probably not prove to be much of a supporting factor, either.

On the Bright Side

There are some strong aspects to next year's business scene. Inventories need some rebuilding. Exports could surge as the cheaper dollar takes effect. It is down now about one-third and could drift off another 5%-10%. Corporate earnings will be picking up and will make equities cheaper. We are looking for a 7%-10% gain, a pretty good number compared to about a zero increase experience in 1986. Dividends should continue to grow.

The Federal deficit, the trade deficit, the farm problem and its drag on the economy, will still all be around to plague the worried investor over coming months. But the stock market should be able to handle these problems. Think of what it handled in addition to these in 1986 — tax reform, program selling panics, insider trading scandals, the Reykjavik summit, and now the Iranian imbroglio. The all-time high recorded by the Dow this month in the face of confusion in Washington D.C. suggests that Wall Street concentrates more on equity value and prospect than on newspaper headlines or instant TV analyses.

To Be Specific

So much for the generalized suggestion that long term investors should buy and hold good equity funds, maybe easing up a bit on the passion for bonds. Just which ones they should buy depends on what their individual needs and objectives happen to be. The timid and conservative should stick to funds that concentrate on "Big Blues," the tried and true leaders of American industry. Our suggestions include such well-known names as **Neuberger & Berman's Guardian Mutual** and the **American Funds' Washington Mutual.** The income-minded should go for the funds which emphasize consistent, steady yield such as **Northeast Investors Trust** and **Vanguard's Wellesley Income Fund.**

We will be bringing many different funds to your attention over the months ahead, something to suit all investment tastes — even those who still want bonds despite the logic of the foregoing. ■

Vol. 18 No. 23   ©United Business Service Co., 1986 — All rights reserved Printed in U.S.A.   **pages 265 through 276**
Issue No. 454

Reprinted with permission.

Value Line Inc.
711 Third Avenue
New York City, NY 10017
(212) 687-3965
(800) 633-2252

Value Line Investment Survey
Investment Advisory Bulletin
100,000 to 250,000 subscribers

Description of the publication:
Value Line Investment Survey is an independent, weekly, investment advisory service registered with the SEC. Value Line systematically evaluates and reviews 1700 stocks in 92 different industries. The Investment Survey provides subscribers with two main investment advisory signals—timeliness and safety.

Investment selections in the publication are determined:
Using fundamental analysis for selection, technical analysis for timing.

The track record for the publication, as reported by the publication, is:
A portfolio invested in equal dollar amounts of Value Line's Group I stocks at the beginning of 1986, and held through July 1, 1986, would have appreciated approximately 37%, compared to a 23% gain in the Dow Jones Industrial Average and a 19% gain in the NYSE Composite Index for the same time period.

The publication has been published continuously since: 1935

The cost of a subscription is: $425

The number of issues per year is: 52

A HOTLINE telephone service is: Not Available

The publication can be delivered: Via second class mail

It is also worth mentioning that:
- Value Line Inc. also offers Value Screen Plus, a microcomputer product (consisting of programs and data) to assist computerized investors with their own analysis of the stocks contained in the Value Line universe. The software package is available for IBM, Apple, and MacIntosh computers.
- Value Line's timeliness ranks have a proven, 17-year record of success in actual forecasting.
- A 10-week trial subscription is available for $55.

PHILIP MORRIS NYSE-MO

| RECENT PRICE | **51** | P/E RATIO | **8.0** (Trailing 8.1 / Median 12.9) | EARN'S YLD | **12.5 %** | DIV'D YLD | **5.0 %** | **340** |

TIMELINESS **2** Above Average
(Relative Price Perform- ance Next 12 Mos.)

SAFETY **2** Above Average
(Scale: 1 Highest to 5 Lowest)

BETA .90 (1.00 = Market)

July 9, 1982 — Value Line

| | 1984 | 1985 | 1986 | 1987 |

1985-87 PROJECTIONS

	Price	Gain	Ann'l Total Return
High	185	(+265%)	40%
Low	135	(+165%)	30%

© Arnold Bernhard & Co., Inc.

BUSINESS: Philip Morris Incorporated is the second largest cigarette producer (32% of domestic consumption). Brands: Marlboro, Benson & Hedges, Parliament, Merit. Acquired Miller, now second-largest beer manufacturer in U.S., in 1970. Sells High Life, Lite and Lowenbrau. Acquired Seven-Up, fourth leading soft drink co. in '78.

Owns Mission Viejo, West Coast real estate developer. '81 deprec. rate: 6.3%. Est'd plant age: 5 yrs. Insiders own 2% of common shares. Has 60,000 ample, 30,300 com. stkhldrs. Est'd labor costs: 11% of sales. Chairman: G. Weissman. Pres.: C. Goldsmith. Incorporated: Virginia. Address: 100 Park Avenue, New York, N.Y. 10017.

Philip Morris has what the consumer wants—cigarettes, beer, and soft drinks. These relatively low-priced items are the little pleasures in life that folks clamor for in good times and bad. That's a major reason for PM's enviable success: twenty-eight consecutive years of higher sales and earnings. Good showings from the tobacco and brewing division are likely to lengthen this string of record-breaking performances to 30 years. We look for earnings gains of about 20% and 15% in 1982 and 1983, respectively.

Pricing is a key determinant of PM's profitability. In the cigarette business, the twice-yearly price hikes that are the industry norm usually exceed cost increases—so margins remain plump. Over at Miller, prices were raised 7.5% in the March quarter. Coupled with a slowdown in raw material cost increases, Miller's operating profits should start looking up.

So, too, are marketing outlays. PM is in the midst of a concerted marketing effort to turn Seven-Up around. The heavy ad spending needed to launch Like, a caffeine-free cola, suggests that Seven-Up will do no better than break even this year, despite a more favorable pricing environment.

Leverage remains high. Long-term debt accounted for about 52% of total capital as of 3/31/82. PM always has been an aggressive user of debt financing. That isn't as much of a problem for the company, given today's high interest rates, as one might expect: About 70% of PM's debt is at fixed rates. With the company's capital spending program near a peak, we expect outstanding debt to decline as a percentage of total capital over the next several years.

This stock is timely. Impressive profit punch in the face of a ho-hum economy should enable these shares to beat the year-ahead averages. Prospects to 1985-87 are excellent, too. The cigarette business, with its exceptional "cash flow", provides a steady earnings base from which Philip Morris can expand, either internally or via the acquisition route. M.L.C./P.F.

(A) Includes Miller Brewing from '70; Seven-Up from 6/78. (B) Based on avg. shs. outst'g. Next earnings report due late July. Est'd constant-dollar egs./sh. '81, $4.00. (C) Next div'd meet'g about Aug. 25. Goes ex about Sept. 9. Approx div'd paym't dates: Jan. 8, Apr. 10, July 10, Oct. 10. ▦ Div'd reinvest. plan av'ble. (D) Incl. intangibles. In '81: $632.2 mill. $5.04/sh. (E) In mill., adj. for stk. splits & div'ds. (F) Restated to reflect acct'ng change.

Company's Financial Strength	A+
Stock's Price Stability	90
Price Growth Persistence	45
Earnings Predictability	100

Reprinted with permission.

Argus Research Corp.
42 Broadway
New York City, NY 10004
(212) 425-7500

Weekly Staff Report
Investment Advisory Bulletin
Less than 25,000 subscribers

Description of the publication:
    WeeklyStaff Report is an eight page report consisting of four parts:
- a "Market Outlook" section, which discusses market trends and prospects while identifying those forces expected to influence future performance;
- an "Economics" section which examines an economic issue of topical importance;
- a summary section, which summarizes those Argus reports issued in the prior week; and,
- a "Company Update" section, which updates previous reports as new information becomes available and highlights a buy/sell position for each security.

Investment selections in the publication are determined:
    Using fundamental analysis.

The track record for the publication, as reported by the publication, is:
    Not available.

The publication has been published continuously since: 1950

The cost of a subscription is: $390

The number of issues per year is: 52

A HOTLINE telephone service is: Available
    Cost for this service: Negotiable with subscription.

The publication can be delivered: Via first class mail

It is also worth mentioning that:
    Argus Research Corp. also publishes several other investment publications designed for both individual investors and investment professionals covering a wide range of topics. These reports include the:

- Weekly Staff Report
- Weekly Economic Review
- Viewpoint
- Portfolio Selector
- Investment Portfolio Guide
- Investment Analysis
- Energy Update

- Special Analysis
- Special-Theme Report
- Electric Utility Ranking
- Electric Utility Spotlight
- Special Situations Report
- Master List

All of the above reports can be bought separately or purchased as a group for a combined discount price of $125 per month. Of special interest is a premium service available to brokers which allows for an unlimited amount of analyst contact, live conference calls, and research opinions written on the broker's own letterhead.

ARGUS RESEARCH CORPORATION 42 BROADWAY NEW YORK, N.Y. 10004 (212) 425 7500
INVESTMENT RESEARCH SINCE 1934

ARGUS
WEEKLY
STAFF
REPORT

October 20, 1986
Vol. 53, No. 42

Copyright 1986, Argus Research Corporation
Not to be reprinted without express permission

THE MARKET

In view of all the negative news it has had to absorb in recent weeks, the market has made excellent headway, with the Dow Jones Industrials Average decisively moving past the 1800 mark last week. The earnings travails of IBM and other widely held high-tech companies, the typical investor's nervousness as the quarterly reports start rolling in (and which again are mostly lackluster), the intense uncertainty surrounding the economy, and another bout of weakness in the bond market have not succeeded in pulling the rug out from under the market as a whole. In particular, the Dow Transportation Average seems to be going from strength to strength at present, led by the high-flying airline group.

(Continued on Page 6)

ECONOMICS

There's more than a little confusion nowadays about where interest rates are headed. We suspect, though, that confusion is as rife within the Federal Reserve as it is everywhere else. Although the art of interest-rate haruspication has never been easy, the signals recently coming out of the Fed have been more than usually obscure.

Of course, the fact that there's a divergence of opinion among the members of the Federal Reserve Board is neither new nor earth-shattering. Ever since the appointment of Preston Martin to the Board of Governors in 1982, the Fed has been a livelier place. By early next year, there will be five Reagan appointees on

(Continued on Page 5)

In This Issue

The Market
Defensive and disinflation equities still make sense from an investment perspective — even in the absence of a strong bond market. Moreover, as corporate earnings improve, there should be a further significant rally in equity prices, one that should push the stock market to new highs.

Economics
The Federal Reserve isn't likely to loosen the monetary reins much further at this time. In our view, long-term rates will not change very much during the next 6-12 months.

Summaries of Recent Reports
Corning Glass Works
General Motors
Piedmont Aviation

Company Updates
Boise Cascade
Chemical New York
Community Psychiatric
Matrix Corp.
Morgan (J.P.)
Motorola
Shelby Williams
System Integrators

Reprinted with permission.

Wiesenberger Financial Services

Division of Warren, Gorham & Lamont
1 Penn Plaza
New York City, NY 10119
(212) 971-5000

Wiesenberger Investment Companies Service

Statistical Service
Number of subscribers is not available

Description of the publication:

Wiesenberger Investment Companies Service covers a wide assortment of significant data on over 4,300 investment companies of all types, sizes, policies, and portfolios, including the vital statistics of over 900 mutual funds. The funds are arranged alphabetically, and each is analyzed in a terse, one page format. Each report includes:

- a brief history;
- a description of the investment objectives;
- a quick portfolio analysis;
- an explanation of any special services;
- a statistical chart;
- information on personnel, advisors, and distributors;
- information on sales charges; and,
- the results of a hypothetical investment of $10,000 charted for the past ten years.

Investment selections in the publication are determined:

By periodically reviewing all major mutual funds.

The track record for the publication, as reported by the publication, is:

Not applicable.

The publication has been published continuously since: 1940

The cost of a subscription is: $295

The number of issues per year is: 1

A HOTLINE telephone service is: Not Available

The publication can be delivered: Via first class mail

It is also worth mentioning that:

- The subscription price of $295 includes the annual publication as well as monthly updates and quarterly supplements.
- Wiesenberger Financial Services publishes several other investment publications covering mutual funds.

THE INVESTMENT COMPANY OF AMERICA

The Investment Company of America was incorporated in 1933 to acquire the assets of a leveraged closed-end company of the same name. It was converted from closed-end to open-end status in 1939. The fund is the largest of several under the investment management of Capital Research and Management Company.

Long-term growth of capital and income are the primary objectives of this fund, with current income a secondary consideration. While predominantly a widely diversified common stock fund, the company has held substantial sums in cash and short-term Government obligations at times.

At the end of 1985, the fund had 81.5% of its assets in common stocks, of which a substantial proportion was in five industry groups: data processing & reproduction (8.1% of assets), chemicals (7.1%), banking (6.7%), telecommunications and health & personal care (5.9% each). The five largest individual common stock investments were IBM (5% of assets), Philip Morris (3.6%), Deutsche Bank AG (3.3%), Digital Equipment (2.9%) and Pacific Telesis (2.2%). The rate of portfolio turnover in the latest fiscal year was 17.5% of average assets.

Unrealized appreciation in the portfolio at the calendar year-end was 37.5% of total net assets.

Special Services: An open account system serves for accumulation plan and for automatic dividend reinvestment; requires an initial investment of $250; subsequent investments of $50 or more may be made at any time. Dividends and capital gains distributions accepted in cash may also be reinvested at net asset value within 15 days after payment date. A pre-authorized check plan is available to make regular monthly investments automatically (minimum, $25). Minimum requirement for a monthly withdrawal plan is $10,000; $5,000 is sufficient for quarterly payments. The minimum withdrawal for either is $50. Shares of the fund may be exchanged at net asset value for those of other funds in the American Funds group. Redeeming shareholders may reinvest redemption proceeds at net asset value in this or any other fund in the group within 30 days after redemption. Available are Business Retirement Plans, master or prototype corporate retirement plans, Individual Retirement Accounts, 403(b) Accounts, and Simplified Employee Pension plans.

Statistical History

						— % of Assets in —								
Year	Total Net Assets ($)	Number of Share-holders	Net Asset Value Per Share ($)	Offer-ing Price ($)	Yield (%)	Cash & Equiv-alent	Bonds & Pre-ferreds	Com-mon Stocks	Income Div-idends ($)	Capital Gains Distribu-tion ($)	Expense Ratio (%)	Offering Price ($) High	Low
1985	3,073,022,303	137,262	13.51	14.77	2.9	17	1	82	0.44	0.49	0.43	14.77	11.27
1984	2,402,434,488	132,884	11.00	12.02	3.5	6	1**	93	0.44	0.51	0.47	12.56	10.39
1983	2,359,908,594	128,983	11.26	12.31	3.4	13	1	86	0.44	0.45	0.44	12.72	10.45
1982	2,007,880,310	116,074	10.19	11.14	4.1	19#	—	81	0.48	0.55	0.46	11.36	8.12
1981	1,592,387,534	113,776	8.64	9.44	4.3	21#	1	78	0.43	0.66	0.45	10.37	8.98
1980	1,670,104,552	114,140	9.65	10.55	3.5	17	—	83	0.38	0.20	0.46	10.96	8.01
1979	1,438,137,226	116,059	8.50	9.29	3.3	3	—	97	0.31	0.09	0.47	9.55	7.94
1978	1,329,753,461	122,500	7.49	8.19	3.2	6	—	94	0.26	—*	0.49	9.39	6.87
1977	1,281,446,490	125,576	6.77	7.39	3.3	9	1	90	0.245	0.14	0.49	8.00	7.07
1976	1,458,499,808	132,142	7.35	8.03	2.9	3	—	97	0.24	0.115	0.46	8.06	6.56
1975	1,234,138,668	131,928	5.96	6.51	4.1	11#	—	89	0.27	0.035	0.48	7.06	5.18

* Payment schedule changed; 1978 capital gains distributed in 1979.
** Includes a substantial proportion of convertible issues.
Note: Figures adjusted for 2-for-1 split, effective 3/29/79.
Includes long-term U.S. Government issues.

Directors: Jon B. Lovelace, Jr., Chmn.; William J. Newton, Pres.; Charles H. Black; Robert L. Cody; John G. McDonald; R.J. Munzer; Clair L. Peck; Allen E. Puckett; James J. Shelton; Hugh J. Shumaker. There is an nine-member Advisory Board.

Investment Adviser: Capital Research and Management Company. Compensation to the Adviser is at an annual rate of 0.36% of the first $300 million of monthly net assets and 0.324% on assets in excess of $300 million.

Custodian: The Chase Manhattan Bank N.A., New York, NY.

Transfer Agent: American Funds Service Company, P.O. Box 60829, Terminal Annex, Los Angeles, CA 90060.

Distributor: American Funds Distributors, Inc., 333 South Hope St., Los Angeles, CA 90071.

Sales Charge: Maximum is 8½% of offering price, scaled down to 1% at $2 million, with further reductions on any excess over $3 million. Reduced charges begin at $15,000 and are applicable to subsequent combined purchases of any of the funds in the American Funds group on a permanent basis.

Distribution Plan: (12b-1) None.

Dividends: Income dividends are paid quarterly in the months of March, June, September and December. Capital gains, if any, are paid optionally in shares or cash in January.

Shareholder Reports: Issued quarterly. Fiscal year ends December 31. The current prospectus was effective in May.

Qualified for Sale: In all states and DC.

Address: 333 South Hope St., Los Angeles, CA 90071.

Telephone: (213) 486-9200.

An assumed investment of $10,000 in this fund, with capital gains accepted in shares and income dividends reinvested, is illustrated below. The explanation in the introduction to this section must be read in conjunction with this illustration.

THE INVESTMENT COMPANY OF AMERICA

Cost of Investment January 1, 1976 $10,000

(Initial Net Asset Value $9,150)

December 31, 1985

*Includes Value of Shares Accepted as Capital Gains $10,946; Reinvested Income Dividends $12,459.

$44,158 Total Value of Investment

$20,753 Value of Original Shares

— — — Total Return
——— Value of Original Shares

	1976	1977	1978	1979	1980	1981	1982	1983	1984	1985
Value of Shares Initially Acquired Through Investment of $10,000	$11,283	$10,392	$11,505	$13,057	$14,823	$13,272	$15,653	$17,296	$16,897	$20,753
Value of Shares Resulting From Reinvestment of Capital Gains and Income Dividends (Cumulative)	572	1,158	1,742	2,729	4,315	6,034	10,173	13,738	16,208	23,405*
Total Return	11,855	11,550	13,247	15,786	19,138	19,306	25,826	31,034	33,105	44,158

Dollar amounts of distributions reinvested:

	Capital Gains	Income Dividends
1976	$ 181	$ 374
1977	232	402
1978	—	449
1979	159	562
1980	371	734
1981	1,309	932
1982	1,229	1,175
1983	1,141	1,183
1984	1,406	1,290
1985	1,475	1,406
Total	$7,503	$8,507

Results Taking Capital Gains in SHARES and Income Dividends in CASH

Initial Investment At Offering Price, January 1, 1976	$10,000
Value as of 12/31/85 of Shares Initially Acquired	$20,753
Value of Shares Accepted as Capital Gains Distributions	$ 8,559#
Total Value, December 31, 1985	$29,312
Total Dividends PAID From Investment Income	$ 6,703

Dollar Amount of these distributions at the time shares were acquired: $5,801

Results Taking All Dividends and Distributions in CASH

Initial Investment At Offering Price, January 1, 1976	$10,000
Total Value, December 31, 1985	$20,753
Distributions From Capital Gains	$ 4,923
Dividends From Investment Income	$ 5,634

Reprinted with permission.

Zweig Securities Advisory Service, Inc.   **The Zweig Forecast**
900 Third Avenue   Investment Advisory Bulletin
New York City, NY 10022   Less than 25,000 subscribers
(212) 753-7710

Description of the publication:
> The Zweig Forecast regularly reviews stock market, monetary, momentum, and sentiment indicators, and recommends appropriate portfolio strategies and investments based on the results of these reviews.

Investment selections in the publication are determined:
> Using fundamental analysis for selection, technical analysis for timing.

The track record for the publication, as reported by the publication, is:
> 281% gain over a 6-year period.

The publication has been published continuously since: 1971

The cost of a subscription is: $245

The number of issues per year is: 18

A HOTLINE telephone service is: Available
> Cost for this service: Free with subscription.

The publication can be delivered: Via first class mail

It is also worth mentioning that:
> Zweig Securities Advisory Service, Inc. and Davis/Zweig Futures, Inc., a related organization, publish several other newsletters covering a variety of topics.

Vol. 16
Number 17
Nov. 14, 1986

THE ZWEIG FORECAST

OUTLOOK AND STRATEGY	<u>Sentiment</u> figures are decent but they have eased off from their best levels (our Composite is 117 vs. 130). Among the better indicators is <u>Mutual Funds Cash</u>. <u>Monetary</u> numbers are still good but <u>Tape</u> action could certainly be better. Investors are <u>40% Long</u> in Stocks/60% Cash, plus two Stock Index Futures positions equivalent to another 30% long.

ELECTION AFTERMATH

Zweig
Unweighted
Price Indices
Nov. 12, 1986
NYSE: 279.96
AMEX: 148.84
Dow: 1894

******
WALL $TREET
WEEK WITH
LOUIS
RUKEYSER:
I'll be a
panelist on
Dec. 5. The
guest is
Maryann
Keller.
******

INTERMEDIATE
INDEX of 36
technical
indicators is
moderately
bullish at
122. The
MONETARY MODEL
of 13 interest
rate and Fed
indicators is
"extremely
bullish."

The election has come and gone but despite a lot of Wall Street worry about the influence of a Democratic Senate victory, so far the market has been behaving "normally" under the circumstances. What Wall Street feared was the Republican loss of the Senate in a race close enough so that it could not be completely discounted before the fact. There have been three roughly similar cases in the post-war period and they help throw light on the current one.

In 1954, at the midpoint of Ike's first term, the Republicans lost control of the Senate, though as now, they still held the White House. The Dow actually shot ahead 2.1% the day after the returns were in and by year-end was 14.1% higher. A year after that at the close of 1955, the Industrials were 37.8% higher. In 1960 in a very close race the Republicans lost the White House when Kennedy edged Nixon. The day after the Dow gained .8% and it was 3.1% higher by the end of the year. By the end of 1961 the Dow had gained 22.2%. Finally, in 1976 the Republicans again lost the White House in a close battle when Carter squeaked past Ford. This time the Dow fell .9% the first day but by year-end it was up 4.0%. The next year was one of great divergence. By the end of 1977, the Dow Industrials had declined by 14.0% from Election Day, but the broader market, as measured by the Zweig Unweighted Price Index, had actually climbed by 15.1%.

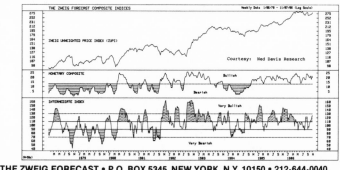

THE ZWEIG FORECAST • P.O. BOX 5345, NEW YORK, N.Y. 10150 • 212-644-0040

Published every 3 weeks plus special bulletins when conditions warrant. Includes hotline phone service.
Subscriptions: 6 months $145; 1 year $245; 2 years $415. (unlisted number sent to you separately).

Reprinted with permission.

Zweig Securities Advisory Service, Inc.   **Zweig Performance Ratings Report**
P.O. Box 5345   Investment Advisory Bulletin
New York City, NY 10150   Less than 25,000 subscribers
(212) 753-7710

Description of the publication:
    Zweig Performance Ratings Report is an investment advisory bulletin which uses computer-generated estimates of expected stock performance to identify which stocks will have the best relative performance over the coming six to twelve month period. Based on the results of this analysis, the report maintains a buy/sell list for subscribers to follow.

Investment selections in the publication are determined:
    Using fundamental analysis for selection, technical analysis for timing.

The track record for the publication, as reported by the publication, is:
    1279% gain for stocks rated number one for the period beginning May, 1976, and ending November, 1986.

The publication has been published continuously since: 1972

The cost of a subscription is: $150

The number of issues per year is: 24

A HOTLINE telephone service is: Not Available

The publication can be delivered: Via first class mail

It is also worth mentioning that:
    Zweig Securities Advisory Service, Inc. and Davis/Zweig Futures, Inc., a related organization, publish several other newsletters covering a variety of topics.

PUBLISHED TWICE A MONTH BY ZWEIG SECURITIES ADVISORY SERVICE, INC., P.O. BOX 5345, NEW YORK, N.Y. 10150

NYSE EDITION

Zweig Performance Ratings Report

$150 Annually   November 1986

Zweig's Performance Ratings are computer-generated estimates of how stocks are expected to perform over the next 6 to 12 months relative to each other. The scale runs from 1, the best 5%, down to 9, the worst 5%. As seen in the performance table, there are more stocks in the middle ratings—fewer at the extremes. The Performance Ratings are derived from numerous technical and fundamental variables — each weighted by our proprietary formula. The most significant factors are *Insider Trading, Earnings Trends, Price/Earnings Ratios* and *Rate of Return on Assets*. Other factors include Institutional Trading Activity, Short Interest, Money Flows (using price and volume data), Relative P/Es, "Unexpected" Earnings Changes, Debt/Equity, Book Value and Dividends.

The table shows the results that could have been earned since May 1976, by following the ratings published monthly in our companion service, THE ZWEIG SECURITY SCREEN. These results assume that one switched portfolios each month so as al-

PERFORMANCE RATING RESULTS

Perfor- mance Ratings	% of Stocks In Groups	Return 125 Months Since 5/76	Return For Oct.
1	5%	+1278.8%	+5.1%
2	8%	+1080.9%	+4.2%
3	12%	+ 685.0%	+2.7%
4	15%	+ 523.8%	+3.1%
5	20%	+ 360.2%	+3.7%
6	15%	+ 281.1%	+2.7%
7	12%	+ 208.5%	+3.6%
8	8%	+ 168.3%	+3.1%
9	5%	+ 123.7%	+3.3%
All Stocks:		+ 397.0%	+3.4%

ways to remain in the Number 1 stocks (or Number 2, etc.). The SCREEN publishes the above variables and many more such as Relative Strength, Beta and Industry Rating. In addition, the SCREEN runs numerous "Screens" each month including the Number 1 Performance Ratings; the Number 9's; all stocks with Insider "Buy" and "Sell" signals; best Relative Strength; Dividend Payers Selling Below Book Value; Low Price Stocks; Consistent Growth Stocks and more. Send $15 for a 2-issue trial or $125 for one year.

Also seen in the report you are holding are Insider Trades. They are the sum of all different corporate Insiders who bought or sold in the *last 6 months*. Studies over two decades have shown that stocks with multiple Insider buying tend to beat the market; stocks with multiple selling tend to lag. Data generally ignore transactions of less than 500 shares unless several Insiders make small trades. Insider data are courtesy of Vickers Stock Research, P.O. Box 59, Brookside, N.J. 07926.

STOCKS OF INTEREST

<u>INTERNATIONAL PAPER (IP - $74.13)</u> - The company has an above average "4" rating. International Paper is the world's largest producer of paper. The company's products include packaging and packaging materials (48% of sales), pulp and paper (34%), wood products (14%) and various others (4%).

Stronger than expected net income was reported for the third quarter ended September. Per share earnings were $1.66, an increase of more than five times last year's third quarter. Excluding the previous year's third quarter charge to earnings of $23 million, profit still more than doubled. Extensive capital expenditures, cost-cutting, unit sales increases and generally higher prices are beginning to be reflected in higher profits. The devaluation of the dollar has helped the company's exports in the pulp and container board area as well. The seasonally weak third quarter earnings were well above consensus estimates. Earnings growth in the fourth quarter should continue. Productivity is improving and, in addition, a capital gain of $0.25 a share will result from the sale of the company's headquarters building. For the

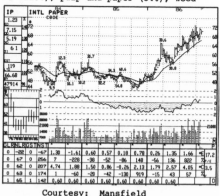

Courtesy: Mansfield

full fiscal year, earnings are expected to increase over 100% to the $3.90 a share area. This strong earnings momentum achieved by IP signifies a probable turnaround and shares of its stock should be considered for purchase. Stop at $60.13.

Reprinted with permission.

REFERENCE BOOKS

INTRODUCTION

Though lacking the immediacy inherent to other sources of investment information, investment books still represent one of the most signifient sources of investment information in use today. Investment books are being bought in record numbers, as both investment professionals and individual investors scramble to learn more about the newfangled investment vehicles that have come to fruition over the last several years.

Topics range from investment basics to technical analysis; from reading financial statements to predicting what the Federal Reserve policy will be; from how securities are processed to investing using a personal computer. On one hand, many of the books are being written by the "old masters" and carry with them decades of experience. On the other hand, many of them are written by the "future generation" and focus on the "cutting edge" of technology as it applies to Wall Street.

My reasons for devoting a chapter to recently released or revised investment books is simple: to provide a source for my readers to obtain additional information on subjects of interest. Though I have made every effort to include sufficient background within this text to support the terminology and constructs of the data that I have presented, certainly many readers will have interest in learning more about some specific topic than I have provided. It is for the benefit of these readers, then, that this chapter has been included.

The methodology used to select books for inclusion in this list was also quite simple: the books must have been published relatively recently, must still be of topical importance today, and must deal with material that is discussed in one form or other in this book. The books also have to be of *reference quality*—that is, designed to thoroughly address a topical area without significant editorial bias or prejudice.

Once again a standard format of presentation has been adopted. The title, author, publication date, and publisher are presented in the upper left-hand corner, and the number of pages and suggested retail price is included in the upper right-hand corner of each entry. Following that is a description of the intended audience of the book, the main subject of the book, and a very brief synopsis of the content. The entries themselves are organized alphabetically by title.

AFTER THE TRADE IS MADE: PROCESSING   **464 Pages**
SECURITIES TRANSACTIONS   **$24.95**
    Author: David M. Weiss
    Published: 1986
    Publisher: New York Institute of Finance

WRITTEN FOR:
Individual investors, investment professionals, and operations personnel.

SUBJECT:
The mechanics of securities processing.

BRIEF SYNOPSIS:
After the Trade is Made is a comprehensive book explaining the network of activites that follow the trading of a security. Across a backdrop of an operations flowchart, the book describes, step-by-step, the mechanics of securities processing. The book also describes each relevant department and its function, plus the rules and regulations that define accountability.

ANALYSIS OF FINANCIAL STATEMENTS   **350 Pages**
    Author: Leopold A. Bernstein   **$25.00**
    Published: Revised 1984
    Publisher: Dow Jones-Irwin

WRITTEN FOR:
Individual investors, investment and business professionals.

SUBJECT:
Analyzing financial statements.

BRIEF SYNOPSIS:
Analysis of Financial Statements reviews the tools and techniques for analyzing financial statements. It includes discussions on: the analysis of short-term liquidity; funds flow; capital structure; return on investments; and return on operations. The book focuses on both understanding the data which are analyzed as well as the methods by which they are analyzed and interpreted.

THE BASICS OF INVESTING (3rd Ed)

544 Pages
$31.95

Author: Benton E. Gup
Published: 1986
Publisher: Wiley Publishing Co.

WRITTEN FOR:
Individual investors.

SUBJECT:
Investment management and securities processing.

BRIEF SYNOPSIS:
Basics of Investing explains the basic processes of personal investing, blending descriptive, analytical, and theoretical material into an introductory "course" on investment management. Subjects covered include the various types of securities available; stock exchange trading practices; analyzing stocks; and managing a portfolio. The book also discusses speculative techniques of investing, and overviews many of the latest financial trends such as mergers, full service brokerage, and options on financial indices.

BEYOND THE INVESTOR'S QUOTIENT: THE INNER WORLD OF INVESTING

214 Pages
$19.95

Author: Jacob Bernstein
Published: 1986
Publisher: Wiley Publishing Co.

WRITTEN FOR:
Individual investors.

SUBJECT:
Identifying and understanding the psychology and emotional factors affecting stock market trading.

BRIEF SYNOPSIS:
Beyond The Investor's Quotient is a guide to understanding and managing the psychological and emotional factors which influence investor decision making and effectiveness. The book identifies common psychological hang-ups and highlights situations where investors often make mistakes. The book also attempts to identify personality types who may not be living up to their investment potential and offers specific plans to help those individuals "shape up."

COMMON STOCKS FOR COMMON SENSE INVESTORS

241 Pages
$19.95

Author: William E. Mitchell and Thomas R. Ireland
Published: 1986
Publisher: Wiley Publishing Co.

WRITTEN FOR:
Individual investors.

SUBJECT:
Establishing and maintaining profitable investments.

BRIEF SYNOPSIS:
Common Stocks for Common Sense Investors is a practical guide to establishing and maintaining a profitable investment program in common stocks. The book presents a scientific case against the "beat the market" investment strategy, and provides an alternative method developed by the authors. The book also demonstrates how to select a list of stocks that meets personal risk preferences; presents the criteria for good, cost-effective portfolio management; explains how to obtain a diversified portfolio, adjust risk levels and diversify internationally. Also included are: step-by-step instructions and worksheets to achieve financial goals; basic information on industry categories, special stockholder services for over 800 corporations; and a "shoppers guide" to discount brokers.

CONTRARY INVESTING: AN INSIDER'S GUIDE TO BUYING LOW AND SELLING HIGH

256 Pages
$16.95

Author: Richard Band
Published: 1985
Publisher: McGraw-Hill

WRITTEN FOR:
Individual investors.

SUBJECT:
Contrarian investment methods.

BRIEF SYNOPSIS:
Contrary Investing is a guide to contrarian investment methods. It is designed to help both small investors and sophisticated portfolio planners make money during any market condition. This book applies the contrarian approach to stocks, bonds, precious metals, commodities, futures, foreign currencies, real estate, and collectibles.

THE 1986 DOW JONES INVESTOR'S HANDBOOK

155 Pages
$9.95

Author: Phyllis Pierce, Editor
Published: 1986
Publisher: Dow Jones-Irwin

WRITTEN FOR:
Individual investors, investment professionals, and statisticians.

SUBJECT:
Dow Jones averages and stock records for 1985.

BRIEF SYNOPSIS:
The 1986 Dow Jones Investor's Handbook is a convenient reference book containing the complete record of the Dow Jones averages for 1985, along with earnings, dividend yields, and price-earnings ratios. The book also includes information on common and preferred stocks and bonds listed on the New York and American Stock Exchanges such as yearly high and low prices, net change, volume, and dividend rates as well as the year's most active issues. In addition, quotations are also included for more than 2,000 Over-the-Counter issues.

THE DOW JONES-IRWIN GUIDE TO USING THE WALL STREET JOURNAL

227 Pages
$19.95

Author: Michael B. Lehmann
Published: 1984
Publisher: Dow Jones-Irwin

WRITTEN FOR:
Individual investors and businessmen.

SUBJECT:
Using *The Wall Street Journal* to understand business, economic, and investment issues.

BRIEF SYNOPSIS:
Using The Wall Street Journal is an informative guide on using and understanding the complex economic and business data provided daily in *The Wall Street Journal*. Using the context of the business cycle, the book brings together such diverse pieces of data as GNP, the consumer price index, money supply, housing starts, and a host of other items, to produce a coherent picture of today's business economy and its future trends. In so doing, the book makes extensive use of charts, graphs, and actual articles taken from the *Journal* to demonstrate how these principal economic indicators all interrelate.

FED WATCHING AND INTEREST RATE PROJECTIONS: A PRACTICAL GUIDE

220 Pages
$29.95

Author: David M. Jones
Published: 1986
Publisher: New York Institute of Finance

WRITTEN FOR:
Individual investors, investment professionals, and economists.

SUBJECT:
Understanding the implications of the Federal Reserve's policies.

BRIEF SYNOPSIS:
Fed Watching offers practical guidelines for projecting interest-rate changes by anticipating policy shifts of the Federal Reserve. Specifically, the book discusses how to assess the influence of major Federal Reserve leaders and evaluate the impact of significant events. The book also documents and explains the Federal Reserve's effect on economic factors in general and interest rates in particular.

FINANCIAL PLANNING HANDBOOK: A PORTFOLIO OF STRATEGIES AND APPLICATIONS

443 Pages
$35.00

Author: Harold W. Gourgues, Jr.
Published: 1983
Publisher: New York Institute of Finance

WRITTEN FOR:
Sophisticated investors, investment professionals, and financial planners.

SUBJECT:
Financial planning.

BRIEF SYNOPSIS:
Financial Planning Handbook is a practical, step-by-step handbook on professional financial planning techniques. It presents the process of analyzing current financial position and developing specific strategies and tactics to achieve financial goals. A portfolio of model financial plans is also included, intended as a guide for readers to follow.

FUNDAMENTALS OF THE SECURITIES INDUSTRY:
AN INSIDE VIEW FROM WALL STREET

394 Pages
$32.95

Author: Allan H. Pessin
Published: Revised 1985
Publisher: New York Institute of Finance

WRITTEN FOR:

Individual investors and new investment professionals.

SUBJECT:

Investment products, securities trading, and transaction processing.

BRIEF SYNOPSIS:

Fundamentals of the Securities Industry is a resource tool presenting detailed information about the securities industry. The book covers a host of topics, including: investment products; security issuance and trading; transactions processing; technical and fundamental analysis; and industry practice, rules, and regulations.

GUIDE TO COMPUTER-ASSISTED INVESTMENT ANALYSIS

350 Pages
$24.95

Author: William B. Riley & Austin Montgomery
Published: 1982
Publisher: McGraw-Hill

WRITTEN FOR:

Computerized investors.

SUBJECT:

Computer-assisted investment analysis.

BRIEF SYNOPSIS:

Guide to Computer-Assisted Investment Analysis overviews investment analysis techniques available to computer oriented investors. Subjects covered by the book include: risk and return; transaction costs and margin; stock valuation; bond analysis; convertible securities and warrants; listed stock options; advanced option strategies; and portfolio analysis.

THE HANDBOOK OF FIXED INCOME SECURITIES
     Author: Frank J. Fabozzi & Irving M. Pollack, Editors
     Published: 1985
     Publisher: Dow Jones-Irwin

1101 Pages
$47.50

WRITTEN FOR:
Individual investors and investment professionals.

SUBJECT:
Fixed income investing.

BRIEF SYNOPSIS:
The Handbook of Fixed Income Securities provides comprehensive coverage of the many instruments in the fixed income securities market including recent innovations and investment strategies. Subjects covered include: government, agency, corporate, municipal, mortgage, pass-through, money market, and international instruments; bonds with warrants and put options; and zero and mini-coupon bonds. Complete coverage of investment strategies is also provided, along with a discussion of the determinants of interest rates and interest rate forecasting.

HANDBOOK OF INVESTMENT PRODUCTS
AND SERVICES (2nd Ed)
     Author: Victor L. Harper
     Published: 1986
     Publisher: New York Institute of Finance

510 Pages
$35.00

WRITTEN FOR:
Individual investors and investment professionals.

SUBJECT:
Various investment products.

BRIEF SYNOPSIS:
Handbook of Investment Products presents resource material on the full spectrum of investment topics. Along with evaluating the familiar forms of securities, the book also provides a detailed examination of several new types of retirement plans and trusts, option and commodity packages, a variety of mortgage-backed securities, pass-throughs, zero coupon bonds, and a host of other instruments. Additionally, the book discusses common traps in life insurance, tax deductions versus tax credits, and vesting and lump sum distributins.

THE HANDBOOK OF THE BOND AND MONEY MARKETS

320 Pages
$48.95

Author: David Darst
Published: 1981
Publisher: McGraw-Hill

WRITTEN FOR:
Individual investors.

SUBJECT:
Fixed income investing.

BRIEF SYNOPSIS:
The Handbook of Bond and Money Markets extensively reviews the products which make up the fixed income security markets; the forces that affect investments in these markets; the participants in these markets and the behavioral traits they commonly exhibit; and the methodology used to analyze these markets. Also included are discussions on the history and mechanics of price level changes, the causes and effects of inflation and deflation, and the effects of financial intermediation in the credit and capital markets.

INTRODUCTION TO BROKERAGE OPERATIONS DEPARTMENT PROCEDURES

175 Pages
$11.95

Author: New York Institute of Finance Staff
Published: 1979
Publisher: New York Institute of Finance

WRITTEN FOR:
Individual investors and new investment professionals.

SUBJECT:
Job functions within brokerage firms.

BRIEF SYNOPSIS:
Introduction to Brokerage Operations Department Procedures is a complete handbook on the operations flow within a brokerage firm. Readers will learn who does what, when, why, and how when an order is placed, as well as the terminology used when security transactions are processed. The book also explains the basic types of debt and equity securities along with how they are issued and traded. Additionally, the book includes flow charts and a glossary.

INVESTMENT MANAGER'S HANDBOOK

1037 Pages
$50.00

Author: Sumner N. Levine, Editor
Published: 1984
Publisher: Dow Jones-Irwin

WRITTEN FOR:
Individual investors and investment professionals.

SUBJECT:
Fundamentals of investment management.

BRIEF SYNOPSIS:
Investment Manager's Handbook provides a complete and comprehensive guide to developing portfolios for today's market. Subjects covered include: fundamentals of investment management; investment strategies, as they apply to a wide array of investment products; measuring and monitoring portfolio performance; legal and regulatory matters; portfolio types and purposes; money market portfolio management techniques; computer services; and market indices.

INVESTMENT STRATEGY

544 Pages
$34.95

Author: Robert Coates
Published: 1978
Publisher: McGraw-Hill

WRITTEN FOR:
Individual investors.

SUBJECT:
Investment costs, products, and strategies.

BRIEF SYNOPSIS:
Investment Strategy is an overview book which looks at a variety of topics ranging from the investment environment for stocks, fixed income securities, options, and futures, to the efficient market concept. The book also contains information on portfolio risk; inflation; rates of return; income taxes; tax sheltered retirement plans; investment companies; life insurance; social security; and the costs of investing.

THE INVESTOR'S DESKTOP PORTFOLIO PLANNER

220 Pages
$24.50

Author: Geoffrey Hirt, Stanley Block, and Fred Jury
Published: 1986
Publisher: Probus Publishing

WRITTEN FOR:

Individual investors, investment professionals, financial planners, insurance agents, and business students.

SUBJECT:

Portfolio planning.

BRIEF SYNOPSIS:

Investor's Desktop Portfolio Planner profiles all major investment instruments in terms of: its characteristics; historical risk and return patterns; liquidity; general and specific uses; strengths and weaknesses; and performance in various economic conditions. Each profile is constructed using standardized criteria to measure levels of performance, liquidity, and risk, and is presented in an easy-to-use, decision-making matrix format to facilitate accurate comparison between investment alternatives.

THE INVESTOR'S DICTIONARY

464 Pages
$16.95

Author: Jerry M. Rosenberg
Published: 1986
Publisher: Wiley Publishing Co.

WRITTEN FOR:

Individual investors.

SUBJECT:

Dictionary of investment terms.

BRIEF SYNOPSIS:

The Investor's Dictionary is a complete, up-to-date guide to investment terms and phrases. The book features over 8,000 entries, including terminology used in more than twenty five areas of investment endeavor. All terms are presented in investment language, and sometimes several meanings for the same word are presented. Both general and specialized entries are also included.

THE INVESTOR'S EQUATION: CREATING WEALTH   **225 Pages**
THROUGH UNDERVALUED STOCKS   **$27.50**
    Author: William M. Bowen IV & Frank P. Ganucheau III
    Published: 1984
    Publisher: Probus Publishing

WRITTEN FOR:
Individual investors, investment professionals, and financial planners.

SUBJECT:
Accumulating wealth by investing in undervalued stocks.

BRIEF SYNOPSIS:
The Investor's Equation explains how to accumulate wealth by using a long-term investment strategy of investing in quality companies with low price earnings (P/E) ratios. Included are discussions on what the P/E ratio approach is, why it works, and how to make it work for investors; how to analyze prospective companies; and how to understand a company's financial and management performance from the investor's point-of-view. The book also compares the power of the low P/E ratio approach to investing in gold, treasury securities, and bonds. The book's last chapter then provides all of the information necessary for investors to develop and manage their own portfolios of undervalued stocks, enabling them to compound wealth at above average rates.

LEVERAGE: THE KEY TO MULTIPLYING MONEY   **224 Pages**
    Author: Gerald Krefetz   **$17.95**
    Published: 1986
    Publisher: Wiley Publishing Co.

WRITTEN FOR:
Individual investors.

SUBJECT:
The proper use of leveraged investments.

BRIEF SYNOPSIS:
Leverage is an incisive guide which presents the rules and risks for the proper use of leveraged investments. It explains the treatment of basic leveraging principles, and illustrates how investors can use leveraged based investments, such as stock options, commodity futures, index options, options on futures, and financial futures, to maximize the potential of their own investment portfolios while minimizing downside risk. Additionally, the book explains both the advantages and disadvantages of each type of leveraged-based investment.

THE MONEY MARKET

728 Pages
$35.00

Author: Marcia Stigum
Published: Revised 1983
Publisher: Dow Jones-Irwin

WRITTEN FOR:

Individual investors, investment professionals, and corporate cash managers.

SUBJECT:

The U.S. money market.

BRIEF SYNOPSIS:

The Money Market covers in detail the major components of the money market, including:
commercial paper; municipal notes; certificates of deposit; Euromarkets; bankers acceptances;
treasury bills, notes, and bonds; government securities; federal funds market; and repurchase
agreements. The book also devotes a lengthy chapter to reviewing the main participants in
the market — the banks, dealers, investors, treasury and federal agencies, and the Federal
Reserve.

THE NEW MUTUAL FUND INVESTMENT ADVISOR

225 Pages
$22.50

Author: Richard C. Dorf
Published: 1986
Publisher: Probus Publishing

WRITTEN FOR:

Individual investors.

SUBJECT:

Mutual fund investing.

BRIEF SYNOPSIS:

The New Mutual Fund Investment Advisor is a guide to mutual fund investing. The book
teaches investors how to reap higher rewards by using a variety of well-defined market timing
strategies, when to buy and sell funds based on their current and historical net asset values,
and when to shift from one type of fund to another to profit from changes in the economy.
Other subjects covered include: evaluating fund performance; portfolio building; fund classifi-
cation; tax treatment; use of funds in retirement plans; and managing a fund portfolio using
advisory newsletters.

OPTIONS AS A STRATEGIC INVESTMENT (2nd Ed)

672 Pages
$35.00

Author: Lawrence G. McMillan
Published: 1985
Publisher: New York Institute of Finance

WRITTEN FOR:
Individual investors and investment professionals.

SUBJECT:
Option investing.

BRIEF SYNOPSIS:
Options as a Strategic Investment presents detailed information about options and option-related investment strategies. The book covers a host of topics including: option principles and basics; put and call option strategies; option combinations; non-equity options; arbitrage; and computers. Additionally, the book examines options as a security substitute and reviews the mathematical aspects of option investing.

THE SECURITIES INDUSTRY GLOSSARY

203 Pages
$14.95

Author: New York Institute of Finance Staff
Published: 1985
Publisher: New York Institute of Finance

WRITTEN FOR:
Individual investors, new investment professionals, and financial advisors.

SUBJECT:
Wall Street trading language.

BRIEF SYNOPSIS:
The Securities Industry Glossary is a specialized vocabulary resource tool covering the "jargon" of Wall Street trading. Over 2,000 entires are included, originating from all segments of Wall Street and its regulatory agencies.

STOCK INDEX OPTIONS: POWERFUL NEW TOOLS FOR INVESTING, HEDGING AND SPECULATING

220 Pages
$25.00

Author: Donald T. Mesler
Published: 1986
Publisher: Probus Publishing

WRITTEN FOR:
Sophisticated investors.

SUBJECT:
Stock index options.

BRIEF SYNOPSIS:
Stock Index Options explains the benefits of using stock index options to protect against and profit from changing market conditions without facing the risks associated with picking individual stocks. In addition, the book reveals all the "ins and outs" of using these investment vehicles, giving special consideration to using stock index options as the basis for a wide variety of investment strategies.

THE STOCK MARKET (4th Ed)

474 Pages
$24.95

Author: Richard J. Teweles & Edward S. Bradley
Published: 1982
Publisher: Wiley Publishing Co.

WRITTEN FOR:
Individual investors, investment and banking professionals.

SUBJECT:
Fundamentals, operation, and regulation of the stock market.

BRIEF SYNOPSIS:
The Stock Market provides a thorough overview of the stock market, discussing in considerable detail the topics of: fundamental information; operation of the stock exchanges; work of the securities houses; investing practices; and special investment instruments.

STOCK SELECTION: BUYING AND SELLING STOCKS   **241 Pages**
USING THE IBM PC   **$17.95**

> Author: Jeremy C. Jenks and Robert W. Jenks
> Published: 1984
> Publisher: Wiley Publishing Co.

WRITTEN FOR:
Computerized investors.

SUBJECT:
Using the IBM PC for stock market trading and analysis.

BRIEF SYNOPSIS:
Stock Selection is an instructional book on investing using the IBM PC. The book explains many time-tested methods used by professionals to select stocks using the computer. The book also explains how to use "valuation models" for identifying good investment opportunities, how to know when to buy aggressively, how to recognize the early warning signs of trouble, and how to choose an investment strategy appropriate for each specific type of investment personality.

TECHNICAL ANALYSIS EXPLAINED: THE SUCCESSFUL   **410 Pages**
INVESTOR'S GUIDE TO SPOTTING INVESTMENT TRENDS   **$39.95**
AND TURNING POINTS (2nd Ed)

> Author: Martin J. Pring
> Published: 1985
> Publisher: McGraw-Hill

WRITTEN FOR:
Market technicians.

SUBJECT:
Technical analysis.

BRIEF SYNOPSIS:
Technical Analysis Explained is a comprehensive guide to understanding and applying technical analysis to the stock, commodity, and gold markets. Subjects covered include: charting and chart patterns; trend analysis; cyclical analysis; market action and structure; price, timing, and volume factors; interest rates; and sentiment indicators.

THE THINKING INVESTOR'S GUIDE
TO THE STOCK MARKET

236 Pages
$9.95

Author: Kiril Sokoloff
Published: 1986
Publisher: McGraw-Hill

WRITTEN FOR:
Indivdiual investors.

SUBJECT:
Stock market investing.

BRIEF SYNOPSIS:
The Thinking Investor's Guide to the Stock Market discusses the motivations of the stock market, investor psychology, crowd emotions, technical indicators, and investment tactics. The book approaches the market from a timing perspective, teaching readers to identify what phase the market is currently in with respect to trends and cycles.

TIMING THE MARKET: HOW TO PROFIT IN
BULL AND BEAR MARKETS WITH TECHNICAL ANALYSIS

250 Pages
$25.00

Author: Weiss Research
Published: 1986
Publisher: Probus Publishing

WRITTEN FOR:
Individual investors and technicians.

SUBJECT:
Technical analysis.

BRIEF SYNOPSIS:
Timing the Market thoroughly overviews the topic of technical analysis. Subjects covered include: charting and chart patterns; trend analysis; cyclical analysis; Dow Theory; market action and structure; price, timing, and volume factors; and sentiment indicators. The book is filled with tables, graphs, and charts, and also includes step-by-step instructions on applying the techniques of technical analysis to specific markets.

WINNING: THE PSYCHOLOGY OF SUCCESSFUL INVESTING   **245 Pages**
     Author: Srully Blotnick   **$32.95**
     Published: 1978
     Publisher: McGraw-Hill

WRITTEN FOR:
Individual investors.

SUBJECT:
Interaction between investors and the market.

BRIEF SYNOPSIS:
Winning is the culmination of more than ten years of research and 1,000 case analyses, making it the first large-scale, real-world look at how individual investors and the market interact. Written in simple, straightforward language, the author describes the activities and impact of investors of various age groups in relation to various market conditions. Also included are discussions on sales techniques used by brokers and the reactions of investors as they relate to various stages of the market cycle. The practical significance of the survey findings are presented in a series of questions and answers.

GLOSSARY AND APPENDICES

GLOSSARY

Agency trade is a security transaction involving a customer and a broker who is transacting business on behalf of the customer and charging a commission for the service.

Agent is one who acts on behalf of others, not incurring any risk in the process.

American Stock Exchange (AMEX or ASE) is the second largest securities exchange in the United States.

AMEX (American Stock Exchange or ASE) is the second largest securities exchange in the United States.

ASE (American Stock Exchange or AMEX) is the second largest securities exchange in the United States.

Ask (offer) is the lowest price anyone has offered to accept for a security at any given time.

Assets are items of value owned by a company.

Back office is the transaction processing department of a brokerage firm.

Bear market is a market trend in which security prices are generally falling.

Bearer bond is a bond that is not registered in anyone's name and is payable to the holder.

Bid is the highest price anyone has offered to pay for a security at a given time.

Big Board (New York Stock Exchange or NYSE) is another name for the New York Stock Exchange, the largest securities exchange in the United States, founded in 1792.

Blue chip is the stock of a company that has earned a reputation for quality products and services and for its consistent ability to make money for shareholders.

Bond is an IOU or promissory note of a company, typically issued in $1000 increments, carrying a specified interest rate and maturing on a specified date.

Bondholder is the owner of a bond, that is, a party who has loaned money to a bond issuer.

Book value is the net worth of a company as determined by an accounting calculation.

Break-out is a distinct price movement made by a security after trading for a period of time in a consolidation pattern.

Broker (Brokerage firm) is an organization, licensed by the Securities and Exchange Commission, that acts as an agent to negotiate the purchase and sale of securities for others, charging commissions for this service.

Broker loan rate (Call money rate) is the interest rate charged on loans to brokers on stock exchange collateral.

Brokerage firm (Broker) is an organization, licensed by the Securities and Exchange Commission, that acts as an agent to negotiate the purchase and sale of securities for others, charging commissions for this service.

Bull market is a market trend in which security prices are generally rising.

Call money rate (Broker loan rate) is the interest rate charged on loans to brokers on stock exchange collateral.

Call option is the right to buy a stock at a specified price by a specified date.

Callable security is a security which, at the option of the issuer and as determined by a specified set of conditions, can be redeemed in whole or in part.

Capital gain is the profit generated when a security is sold for more than its purchase price.

Capital loss is the loss generated when a security is sold for less than its purchase price.

Cash sale (Same day) is a transaction that settles the same day as the trade occurs.

Clearing is the process of comparing a security transaction and freeing it and its associated payment from obligation.

Clearing corporation is an organization that specializes in clearing the security transactions of its members.

Clearing member is a brokerage concern that holds a membership in, and is therefore entitled to use the services of, one of the nation's clearing corporations.

Collateral is property pledged by a borrower to secure a loan.

Common stock is a security that represents a share of the common ownership in a corporation and has no preferential claims to income or assets.

Contrabroker is the brokerage firm on the other side of a security transaction.

Corporation account is a brokerage account opened by a corporation.

Correspondent is a brokerage firm that performs services for another brokerage firm.

Cost of goods sold is the cost of the inventory sold.

Current asset is an asset owned by a company that can be converted into cash in a relatively short period of time.

Current liability is money owed by a company that must be paid within one year.

Current yield is the cash return a security pays divided by the price of the security.

Custodian account is a brokerage account opened by a person of legal age for the benefit of someone who is not of legal age.

Day order is an order to buy or sell a security that expires at the end of the same trading day if it has not been executed.

Dealer is an organization, licensed by the Securities and Exchange Commission, who, acting in a principal capacity, buys securities, marks them up, and then resells them.

Debenture is a promissory note backed by the general credit of a company, rather than by any specific collateral.

Debt is an obligation of a company.

Depository Trust Company (DTC) is a central securities certificate depository that members of a clearing corporation use to hold their securities, thus facilitating the use of the clearing corporation's computerized bookkeeping system. This system is a faster, more economical way to process securities transactions than the physical process.

Discretionary account is an account in which someone other than the account holder has the right and responsibility to make purchase and sale decisions.

Dividend is a payment made to the stockholders of a company.

DTC (Depository Trust Company) is a central securities certificate depository that members of a clearing corporation use to hold their securities, thus facilitating the use of the clearing corporation's computerized bookkeeping system. This system is a faster, more economical way to process securities transactions than the physical process.

Earnings Before Interest and Taxes (EBIT or Income Before Interest and Taxes) is the income generated by a company from all sources, less all the expenses associated with generating this income, with the exception of interest charges, taxes, and extraordinary items.

Earnings statement (Income statement) is a statement issued by a company showing its earnings or losses over a given period.

EBIT (Earnings Before Interest and Taxes or Income Before Interest and Taxes) is the income generated by a company from all sources, less all the expenses associated with generating this income, with the exception of interest charges, taxes, and extraordinary items.

Ex-dividend is a security without rights to an upcoming dividend distribution.

Ex-dividend date is the day on which a security begins trading in the open market on an ex-dividend basis, normally the fourth business day prior to the record date.

Execution is the transaction of an order to buy or sell a security.

Ex-rights is without rights—shares that are trading ex-rights are shares trading without the right to subscribe to a new issue of stock that is offered to existing shareholders of a company.

Fiduciary account is a brokerage account opened by an executor, administrator, trustee, guardian, conservator, or committee that has been duly appointed to represent those parties concerned with the assets held in an account.

Fixed assets are physical assets used by a company in its operations.

Flag is a consolidation pattern that indicates a trend will continue, formed after a dynamic, nearly straight move in a market.

Floor broker (Two dollar broker) is a member of a stock exchange who executes buy or sell orders on the floor of the exchange.

Gap is a "hole" occurring in the orderly trading of a stock, when the highest price on one day is lower than the lowest price the next day or when the lowest price one day is higher than the highest price the next day.

Good Until Canceled order (GTC order or Open order) is an order to buy or sell a security that remains in effect until it is either executed or canceled.

Growth stock is the stock of a company whose earnings have grown or are expected to grow rapidly.

GTC order (Good Until Canceled order or Open order) is an order to buy or sell a security that remains in effect until it is either executed or canceled.

Income Before Interest and Taxes (Earnings Before Interest and Taxes or EBIT) the income generated by a company from all sources, less all the expenses associated with generating this income, with the exception of interest charges, taxes, and extraordinary items.

Income statement (Earnings statement) is a statement issued by a company showing its earnings or losses over a given period.

Individual account is a brokerage account opened by an individual.

Intangible asset is an asset whose actual value is difficult or impossible to determine.

Interest is the charge paid by a borrower to a lender for the use of money.

Investment club is a group of individuals who pool their funds for the purpose of investing.

Investment club account is a brokerage account opened by an investment club.

Joint account is a brokerage account opened by two or more individuals.

Joint tenants account is a joint account wherein, on the death of one tenant, the property in the account passes to the surviving tenant.

Liability is a claim against a company.

Limit order is an order to buy or sell a stated amount of a security at a specified price that can only fill at that price or a more advantageous one.

Liquid market is the ability of a market to absorb a reasonable amount of buying or selling without the market price being inflated or depressed excessively.

Liquidity is the ability to be quickly and easily converted into cash.

Long is a term signifying ownership of securities.

Margin account is a brokerage account that includes a line of credit that can be used for anything, as regulated by the Federal Reserve's Regulation T.

Margin call is a demand on a margin customer to add money or securities to a margin account so that the line of credit remains properly secured with respect to federal regulations (Regulation T).

Market order is an order to buy or sell a security at the best price obtainable on the market immediately upon the order reaching the floor of the exchange.

Market price (Price quote, Quotation, or Quote) is the current price at which a security is trading, determined by the forces of supply and demand.

Member is an individual who owns a seat on a stock exchange.

Member firm is an organization that has an officer, partner, or principal who is a member of a stock exchange.

Midwest Stock Exchange (MSE) is one of the largest securities exchanges in the United States.

MSE (Midwest Stock Exchange) is one of the largest securities exchanges in the United States.

Multiple (Price-Earnings ratio or P/E ratio) is the market price of a stock divided by its annual earnings per share.

Municipal bond is a bond issued by a state or municipal government that pays interest that is generally free from Federal income tax.

NASD (National Association of Securities Dealers) is the self- regulating association of the broker/dealer industry that sets and enforces rules of fair practice for the securities industry and whose primary purpose is to protect investors who deal in the over-the-counter market.

National Association of Securities Dealers (NASD) is the self- regulating association of the broker/dealer industry that sets and enforces rules of fair practice for the securities industry and whose primary purpose is to protect investors who deal in the over-the-counter market.

National Market Exchange (NME) is an electronic link that ties together some of the largest over-the-counter dealers in the United States, thereby creating a kind of pseudo-exchange for the transaction of over-the-counter securities.

New York Stock Exchange (Big Board or NYSE) is the largest securities exchange in the United States, founded in 1792.

Next day is a transaction which settles on the first business day following the trade date.

NME (National Market Exchange) is an electronic link that ties together some of the largest over-the-counter dealers in the United States, thereby creating a kind of pseudo-exchange for the transaction of over-the-counter securities.

Nonclearing member is a brokerage firm that is not a member of any clearing corporation and therefore must clear security transactions by physically moving certificates and money.

NYSE (Big Board or New York Stock Exchange) is the largest securities exchange in the United States, founded in 1792.

Odd lot is an amount of stock that is less than a round lot; that is, less than 100 shares for actively traded stocks and less than 10 shares for inactively traded ones.

Offer (Ask) is the lowest price anyone has offered to accept for a security at any given time.

Open order (Good Until Canceled or GTC order) is an order to buy or sell a security that remains in effect until it is either executed or canceled.

Option is a contract that gives the holder the right to buy or sell a stated amount of a stock (usually 100 shares) at a specified price within a specified time.

OTC security (Over-the-Counter security) is a security that is not listed or traded on an organized securities exchange.

Overbought market is a condition in which the market has moved up so quickly that it has used up much of the buying volume normally overhanging the market and is due for a pullback.

Oversold market is a condition in which the market has moved down so quickly that it has used up much of the selling volume normally overhanging the market and is due for a rally.

Over-the-Counter Security (OTC security) is a security that is not listed or traded on an organized securities exchange.

Pacific Stock Exchange (PSE) is one of the largest securities exchanges in the United States.

Partnership account is a brokerage account opened by a partnership, requiring the signatures of all of the general partners, and also requiring a copy of the partnership agreement.

Payment date is the date on which a corporation actually makes the distribution to the list of individuals that are entitled to receive it as per the record date.

P/E ratio (Multiple or Price-Earnings ratio) is the market price of a stock divided by its annual earnings per share.

Pennant is a consolidation pattern that indicates a trend will continue, formed after a dynamic, nearly straight move in a market.

Portfolio is the complete investment holdings of an individual or institution.

Preferred stock is a security that represents a share of preferred ownership in a corporation, having preferential claims to income or assets over those claims held by common stock.

Price-Earnings ratio (P/E ratio or Multiple) is the market price of a stock divided by its annual earnings per share.

Price quote (Market price, Quote, or Quotation) is the current price at which a security is trading, determined by the forces of supply and demand.

Principal trade is a security transaction involving a customer and a dealer who is working from inventory, wherein no commissions are charged but a mark-up is earned on the inventory position.

Profit taking is the act of realizing a profit by closing out a security position.

PSE (Pacific Stock Exchange) is one of the largest securities exchanges in the United States.

Pullback is a brief decline in prices occurring after a major move up.

Put option is the right to sell a stock at a specified price by a specified date.

Quotation (Market price, Price quote, or Quote) is the current price at which a security is trading, determined by the forces of supply and demand.

Quote (Market price, Price quote, or Quotation) is the current price at which a security is trading, determined by the forces of supply and demand.

Rally is a brief rise in prices occurring after a major market decline.

Record date is the date on which a corporation closes its list of security holders to determine who is entitled to receive a distribution or proxy solicitation.

Rectangle is a consolidation pattern formed as a result of a battle between two groups overhanging the market at different fixed prices.

Registered representative is an individual who works for a brokerage firm who is properly licensed to serve the investing public.

Regulation T is a Federal Reserve regulation that governs the amount of credit brokers can advance to customers who are buying securities on margin.

Regulation U is a Federal Reserve regulation that governs the amount of credit banks can advance to customers buying securities on margin.

Resistance level is a price level that temporarily halts an upward movement in price.

Reverse split is the division of the outstanding shares of a stock into a smaller number of shares.

Round lot is the most common unit in which securities are traded, typically 100 shares for actively traded stocks and 10 shares for inactively traded ones.

Safekeeping is a security held in the name of the customer but physically kept in the possession of the brokerage firm as opposed to being kept in the customer's possession.

Same day (Cash sale) is a transaction that settles the same day as the trade occurs.

Seat is a membership on a securities exchange.

Securities exchange (Stock exchange or Stock market) is an organized market for buying and selling securities.

Securities Investor Protection Corporation (SIPC) is a government-sponsored private corporation that insures brokerage customer accounts.

Security is an investment instrument such as a stock, bond, option, or warrant.

Settlement date is the day on which a security transaction is actually settled (securities and money are exchanged).

Short position is the ownership position of a security after a short sale has been made but before the position has been covered.

Short selling is the act of selling a security that is not currently owned, with the intention of buying it back at a cheaper price at some future point in time.

SIPC (Securities Investor Protection Corporation) is a government-sponsored private corporation that insures brokerage customer accounts.

Specialist is a member of a stock exchange, appointed by the exchange and charged with the responsibility of maintaining an orderly succession of prices for a specific security trading on the exchange.

Split is the division of the outstanding shares of a stock into a larger number of shares.

Stock is a security that represents a share of ownership in a corporation.

Stock dividend is a divident paid in additional shares of stock instead of in cash.

Stock exchange (Stock market or Securities exchange) is an organized market for buying and selling securities.

Stock market (Securities exchange or Stock exchange) is an organized market for buying and selling securities.

Stock symbol (Ticker symbol) is the unique symbol used by brokers to represent a security.

Stockholder is the owner of at least one share of stock in a corporation.

Stockholder of record is a stockholder whose name is registered on the books of the issuing corporation.

Stop limit order is an order to buy securities at a price above, or sell at a price below, the current market price, which becomes a limit order only when the security trades at or through that price.

Stop order is an order to buy securities at a price above, or sell at a price below, the current market price, which becomes a market order only when the security trades at or through that price.

Street name is a security held in the name of the brokerage firm instead of the name of the customer.

Support level is a price level that temporarily halts a downward movement in price.

Ticker symbol (Stock symbol) is the unique symbol used by brokers to represent a security.

Trade date is the day on which a security transaction is executed.

Triangle is a consolidation pattern formed resulting from an indecision on the part of buyers and sellers.

Two dollar broker (Floor broker) is a member of a stock exchange who executes buy or sell orders on the floor of the exchange.

Warrant is a security that gives the holder the right to buy another security at a stipulated price for a specified or perpetual period of time.

When, as, and if issued (When issued) is a conditional transaction in an authorized, but not as yet issued, security.

When issued (When, as, and if issued) is a conditional transaction in an authorized, but not as yet issued, security.

Yield is the cash return a security pays divided by the market price of the security.

Yield to maturity is the total return a bond will pay, including the yield and any gain or loss that will be realized upon maturity, computed so as to represent an annualized percentage.

APPENDIX A

Commonly Used Stock Market Acronyms

AMEX	American Stock Exchange
ASE	American Stock Exchange
Boston	Boston Stock Exchange
BSE	Boston Stock Exchange
CBOE	Chicago Board Options Exchange
CBT	Chicago Board of Trade
CD	Certificate of Deposit
CEC	Commodity Exchange Center
CFTC	Commodity Futures Trading Commission
Cincinnati	Cincinnati Stock Exchange
CME	Chicago Mercantile Exchange
DTC	Depository Trust Company
DVP	Deliver versus payment
GTC	Good until canceled
IMM	International Monetary Market
IRA	Independent Retirement Account
KCBT	Kansas City Board of Trade
MCC	Midwest Clearing Corporation
MidAm	Mid American Commodity Exchange
MnGE	Minneapolis Grain Exchange
MSE	Midwest Stock Exchange
MSRB	Municipal Securities Rulemaking Board
MSTC	Midwest Securities Settlement Corporation
NASD	National Association of Securities Dealers
NFA	National Futures Association
NME	National Market Exchange
NSCC	National Securities Clearing Corporation

NYFE . . . . New York Futures Exchange
NYSE . . . . New York Stock Exchange
OCC . . . . Options Clearing Corporation
OTC . . . . Over-the-Counter
PCC . . . . Pacific Clearing Corporation
PSDTC . . . . Pacific Securities Depository Trust Company
PhSE . . . . Philadelphia Stock Exchange
PSE . . . . Pacific Stock Exchange
SEC . . . . Securities and Exchange Commission
SIPC . . . . Securities Investor Protection Corporation

APPENDIX B

Office locations for Quick & Reilly, Inc.

Albany, NY	(518) 458-2395, (800) 342-3563(NY)
Atlanta, GA	(404) 261-6636, (800) 241-7577(N), (800) 282-0400(GA)
Baltimore, MD	(301) 685-6210, (800) 492-1629(MD)
Beverly Hills/Los Angeles, CA	(213) 859-9898, (800) 336-8940(N), (800) 521-1923(CA)
Boston, MA	(617) 451-5255, (800) 225-2318(N), (800) 882-1136(MA)
Buffalo, NY	(716) 856-7950, (800) 462-7170(NY)
Charlotte, NC	(704) 525-8730, (800) 438-6303(N), (800) 532-0478(NC)
Cherry Hill, NJ	(609) 667-4444, (800) 624-0754(NJ)
Chicago, IL	(312) 726-0010, (800) 621-9229(N), (800) 572-9050(IL)
Cincinnati, OH	(513) 241-3805, (800) 543-7252(N), (800) 582-1801(OH)
Clearwater, FL	(813) 799-6844, (800) 237-5611(FL)
Cleveland, OH	(216) 566-0026, (800) 362-0564(OH)
Columbus, OH	(614) 464-1222, (800) 282-9369(OH)
Denver, CO	(303) 572-9192, (800) 543-8971(N), (800) 543-2402(CO)
Detroit, MI	(313) 961-1600, (800) 482-8769(MI)
Ft. Lauderdale, FL	(305) 566-5990, (800) 432-8892(FL)
Greensboro, NC	(919) 854-0100, (800) 422-4555(NC)
Hartford, CT	(203) 727-0400, (800) 243-2693(N), (800) 842-0032(CT)
Huntington/Melville, NY	(516) 753-0180, (800) 323-3442(NY)
Kansas City, MO	(Opening soon)
Louisville, KY	(502) 583-9741, (800) 626-6124(N), (800) 752-6666(KY)
McLean, VA	(703) 893-7870, (800) 468-7301(N), (800) 572-0475(VA)
Miami, FL	(305) 454-9854, (800) 323-3204(N), (800) 432-4956(FL)
Milwaukee, WI	(414) 272-2207, (800) 242-1502(WI)
Morristown, NJ	(201) 539-0440, (800) 223-0352(NJ)
Nashville, TN	(Opening soon)
Newport Beach, CA	(714) 955-0971, (800) 421-5973(CA)
New York, NY	(212) 943-8686, (800) 221-5220(N), (800) 522-8712(NY)
Norfolk, VA	(804) 625-8211, (800) 582-8126(VA)
Northbrook, IL	(312) 498-6380, (800) 851-9875(IL)

Orlando, FL	(305) 422-7800, (800) 541-5050(N), (800) 432-2701(FL)
Palm Beach, FL	(305) 655-8000, (800) 327-7199(N), (800) 432-4400(FL)
Philadelphia, PA	(215) 568-6770, (800) 523-1412(N), (800) 462-2887(PA)
Phoenix, AZ	(602) 957-0266, (800) 543-7057(N), (800) 543-4798(AZ)
Pittsburgh, PA	(412) 261-0225, (800) 472-1564(PA)
Portland, OR	(Opening soon)
Providence, RI	(401) 273-5501, (800) 556-7510(N), (800) 662-5029(RI)
Raleigh, NC	(Opening soon)
Richmond, VA	(Opening soon)
Rochester, NY	(716) 454-4900, (800) 462-6425(N)
Sacramento, CA	(916) 925-9202, (800) 421-9823(N), (800) 421-9835(CA)
St. Louis, MO	(314) 231-8581, (800) 325-2629(N), (800) 392-2609(MO)
St. Petersburg, FL	(813) 327-5600, (800) 237-2780(N), (800) 282-8929(FL)
San Diego, CA	(619) 231-4444, (800) 424-2242(N), (800) 848-8844(CA)
San Francisco, CA	(415) 982-3210, (800) 543-1197(N), (800) 543-3114(CA)
San Jose, CA	(408) 298-6262, (800) 523-3653(N), (800) 523-3651(CA)
Seattle, WA	(206) 623-9889, (800) 637-3711(N), (800) 654-5515(WA)
Springfield, MA	(Opening soon)
Stamford, CT	(203) 356-9977, (800) 243-2661(N), (800) 942-7527(CT)
Tampa, FL	(813) 875-5522, (800) 282-6312(FL)
Washington, DC	(202) 872-8686, (800) 424-9790(N)
Wilmington, DE	(302) 654-1880, (800) 441-9797(N), (800) 282-1551(DE)

APPENDIX C

Office locations for Charles Schwab & Co., Inc.

Albany, NY	(518) 465-3411
Albuquerque, NM	(505) 881-7500
Atlanta, GA	(404) 231-1114
Austin, TX	(512) 480-8262
Bakersfield, CA	(805) 322-9800
Baltimore, MD	(301) 528-0900
Bellevue, WA	(206) 462-7900
Beverly Hills, CA	(213) 859-7200
Boston, MA	(617) 482-9500
Burlington, MA	(617) 229-2992
Carmel, CA	(408) 625-6622
Century City, CA	(213) 553-5400
Chevy Chase, MD	(301) 951-9155
Chicago, IL	(312) 853-3030
Cincinnati, OH	(513) 621-1234
Cleveland, OH	(216) 566-0909
Dallas, TX	(214) 979-0222, (214) 385-1561
Denver, CO	(303) 298-8200
Detroit, MI	(313) 567-3400
Fresno, CA	(209) 266-5300
Ft Lauderdale, FL	(305) 524-5700
Ft Worth, TX	(817) 870-9800
Great Neck, NY	(516) 829-3170
Hartford, CT	(203) 524-0900
Hong Kong	5-2676955
Honolulu, HI	(808) 523-5151
Houston, TX	(713) 759-1000, (713) 960-9775
Indianapolis, IN	(317) 236-9700
Irvine, CA	(714) 752-0070
Kansas City, MO	(816) 421-0700
Laguna Hills, CA	(714) 837-6333

LaJolla, CA	(619) 459-3313
Los Angeles, CA	(213) 617-0900
Memphis, TN	(901) 761-1790
Menlo Park, CA	(415) 325-2333
Miami, FL	(305) 371-5311
Midland, TX	(915) 686-9814
Millburn, NJ	(201) 379-7640
Minneapolis, MN	(612) 375-1300
Modesto, CA	(209) 575-0600
Nashville, TN	(615) 242-6551
New Orleans, LA	(504) 568-0200
New York, NY	(212) 370-1177, (212) 765-8900, (212) 938-0404
Newport Beach, CA	(714) 759-9200
Northbrook, IL	(312) 291-0300
Oakbrook Terrace, IL	(312) 953-9222
Oklahoma City, OK	(405) 235-7500
Omaha, NE	(402) 344-2050
Orlando, FL	(305) 425-3343
Palm Beach, FL	(305) 655-8900
Palm Springs, CA	(619) 322-2000
Paramus, NJ	(201) 368-0888
Philadelphia, PA	(215) 567-7700
Phoenix, AZ	(602) 263-5070
Pittsburg, PA	(412) 261-0100
Portland, OR	(503) 228-0900
Princeton, NJ	(609) 683-4343
Providence, RI	(401) 521-1400
Red Bank, NJ	(201) 530-1990
Riverside, CA	(714) 788-4600
Rochester, NY	(716) 423-9310
Sacramento, CA	(916) 920-3500
Salt Lake City, UT	(801) 355-9400
San Antonio, TX	(512) 227-8737
San Diego, CA	(619) 231-8300
San Francisco, CA	(415) 398-1000
San Rafael, CA	(415) 459-7444
Santa Barbara, CA	(805) 564-4491
Seattle, WA	(206) 624-2000
Spokane, WA	(509) 455-4595
St. Petersberg, FL	(813) 384-4700
St. Louis, MO	(314) 726-6100
St. Paul, MN	(612) 222-8600
Stamford, CT	(203) 359-8600
Stockton, CA	(209) 473-0700
Sun City/Youngtown, AZ	(602) 979-1440
Sunnyvale, CA	(408) 735-0100
Tucson, AZ	(602) 790-1988
Tulsa, OK	(918) 585-3122
Valley Forge, PA	(215) 265-7600
Virginia Beach, VA	(804) 490-9600
Walnut Creek, CA	(415) 947-5900
Washington, DC	(202) 638-2500
Westwood, CA	(213) 824-1400

More offices opening soon.

INDEX

Dear Customer:

Probus is thoroughly committed to publishing the highest quality materials for sophisticated investors in the stock, bond, real estate and futures and options markets.

As such, we would like to keep you (and your firm) abreast of forthcoming publications in these fast moving areas. In order to do this we ask that you supply us with your name, firm and address.

Thank you; we look forward to serving you.

Name _____

Firm _____

Address _____

City _____ State _____ Zip _____

BUSINESS REPLY MAIL
FIRST CLASS   PERMIT NO. 15424   CHICAGO, IL U.S.A.

POSTAGE WILL BE PAID BY ADDRESSEE

PROBUS PUBLISHING COMPANY
118 NORTH CLINTON STREET
CHICAGO, ILLINOIS   60606

NO POSTAGE
NECESSARY
IF MAILED
IN THE
UNITED STATES